Augustus the Strong

Augustus the Strong

Ruler of Poland & Saxony

A Study in Artistic Greatness and Political Fiasco

TIM BLANNING

ALLEN LANE
an imprint of
PENGUIN BOOKS

ALLEN LANE

UK | USA | Canada | Ireland | Australia
India | New Zealand | South Africa

Penguin Books is part of the Penguin Random House group of companies
whose addresses can be found at global.penguinrandomhouse.com.

First published in Great Britain by Allen Lane 2024

001

Set in 12/14.75pt Dante MT Std
Typeset by Jouve (UK), Milton Keynes
Printed and bound in Great Britain by Clays Ltd, Elcograf S.p.A.

The authorized representative in the EEA is Penguin Random House Ireland,
Morrison Chambers, 32 Nassau Street, Dublin D02 YH68

A CIP catalogue record for this book is available from the British Library

ISBN: 978–0–241–70514–8

Dedicated to the memory of three of the best of historians and the best of friends: Derek Beales, Peter Dickson, Hamish Scott

Contents

Contents

Contents

List of Illustrations

Photographic acknowledgements in italics

1. *King Augustus II of Poland*, portrait by Louis de Silvestre (1718). Gemäldegalerie Alte Meister, Dresden. *SKD/Bridgeman Images.*
2. *The Electoral Palace in Dresden*, engr. Georg Jakob Schneider (1679). Kupferstich-Kabinett, Dresden. *SKD/Bridgeman Images.*
3. The silver fire-screen in the audience-chamber of the Dresden Palace created by Albrecht and Lorenz II Biller of Augsburg (1708–10). Kunstgwerbemuseum, Dresden. *SKD/Bridgeman Images.*
4. *The election of Augustus at Wola outside Warsaw in June 1697*, painting by Johann Gottfried Krügner (1697–1704). Muzeum Narodowe, Warsaw. *Fine Art Images/Heritage Images/akg-images.*
5. *Cardinal Michał Stefan Radziejowski*, portrait by François de la Croix (1702). Rüstkammer, Dresden. *SKD/Bridgeman Images.*
6. Augustus with a 'Polish coiffure', engr. Johann Jakob Thourneijser after Anton Schoonians (pub. Vienna, 1697). *Biblioteka Narodowa, Warsaw.*
7. Broken horseshoe and accompanying note (1711). Rüstkammer, Dresden. *SKD/Bridgeman Images.*
8. *Johann Melchior Dinglinger*, portrait by Antoine Pesne, (1721). State Hermitage Museum, St Petersburg. *Fine Art Images/Heritage Images/akg-images.*
9. *The Court at Delhi of the Grand Mogul Aureng Zeb of Hindustan*, by Johann Melchior Dinglinger (1701–1708). Grünes Gewölbe, Dresden. *SKD/Bridgeman Images.*
10. Parade of the ladies led by Constantia von Cosel before the running at the ring at Dresden on 6 June 1709 (1710), by C. H. Fritzsche. Kupferstich-Kabinett, Dresden. *SKD/Bridgeman Images.*

Introduction[1]

Augustus of Saxony could have been a happy man. The accident of conception made him a member of the oldest and richest of all the princely families of the Holy Roman Empire of the German Nation, placing in his mouth a spoon of unalloyed silver.[2] Not even the apparent handicap of younger-son status delayed him for long, cholera removing his father in 1691, and smallpox despatching his elder brother three years later. At the age of twenty-four Augustus was the monarch of all he surveyed, looking forward with relish to a life of power and pleasure. Alas, when he died in Warsaw thirty-eight years later, on 1 February 1733, there was little of either remaining. As his gangrenous body sank towards oblivion, he lamented that the Polish throne that had cost him so much effort and money had been 'a crown of thorns'. Although never conspicuously pious, he summoned enough energy to croak out as his last words the confession: 'God forgive me, my entire life was one sin.'[3]

Few European rulers could record a longer list of military failures; even fewer have been forced to abdicate; hardly any have regained their throne courtesy of another power. It was somehow fitting that the only victory won under his aegis (Kalisz in 1706) was more an embarrassment than a triumph.[4] Yet there had been good times as well as bad times, with the occasional spark of achievement to lift his spirits and keep hope alive. Moreover, against political and military failure has to be set a cultural legacy which included making his Saxon capital, Dresden, one of the most beautiful cities in Europe and qualifying him to be classed as a great artist. His times had certainly been exciting. Augustus had played a significant role in one of those periods of European history when the pace of change accelerates and events occur with profound and long-lasting consequences. It was his bad luck to have to contend with two contemporaries of exceptional ability and demonic energy – Tsar Peter of Russia (b. 1672) and King Charles XII of Sweden (b. 1682). Trapped in the world-historical clash between these last two titans in the Great Northern War (1700–1721), hapless Augustus was ground into insignificance.

What started as a quadrilateral struggle, pitting Sweden against Denmark, Russia and Saxony,[5] quickly reduced to trilateral, as Denmark was knocked out in the first year. That was how it stayed until 1706, when Augustus's involuntary departure from the conflict shortened it to a duel between Russia and Sweden. Even when he returned to the fray in 1709, his subordinate status as a satellite of Russia became increasingly apparent. Revealingly, neither Saxony nor Poland were parties to the Peace of Nystad which brought the war to a close in 1721. Such a simple summary is more than a little misleading, as several other players were active at times, including Prussians, Hanoverians, Turks, Cossacks and Tatars, not to mention the numerous combatants engaged in the overlapping War of the Spanish Succession (1701–14), notably the Habsburg Monarchy, the Holy Roman Empire, Britain, the Dutch Republic, Savoy, Portugal and Spain. In this turbulent maelstrom embracing almost all of Europe, Augustus bobbed about helplessly like a plastic duck, often submerged but never quite sunk. It will be argued in what follows that an examination of his (mis)fortunes is justified not only by the importance of his own role, active or passive, but also by its contribution to an understanding of what made for success and failure in the Europe of this, or indeed any other, period.

It will also support one of Karl Marx's most penetrating observations, conveyed in the second paragraph of *The Eighteenth Brumaire of Louis Napoleon* (1852):

Men make their own history, but they do not make it just as they please; they do not make it under circumstances chosen by themselves, but under circumstances directly encountered, given and transmitted from the past. The tradition of all the dead generations weighs like a nightmare on the brain of the living.[6]

In the case of Augustus, the nightmare was concealed behind the glittering façade of the representational court culture that reached its apogee at Louis XIV's Versailles during his lifetime. It was 'representational' because its *raison d'être* was the re-presentation (in the sense of 'making present') of the power, glory, wealth and legitimacy of the patron, and it was 'court' because the ruler's court was at its centre.[7] Thanks to his education, travels and family tradition, not to mention personal inclination, this inheritance was for Augustus not a nightmare but a beautiful if evanescent dream, one which he never ceased trying to turn into reality. As the 'Sun King' of France was to be the model for Augustus (and for many other European sovereigns great and small), an introduction to the main features of his project is necessary.

The sharp end of the princely glory this culture advertised was martial prowess. For every male ruler not disqualified by physical incapacity, leading an army into battle was the ultimate justification of majesty. Among the many features that make Louis XIV's Palace of Versailles the *non plus ultra* of representational culture is its triumphalist proclamation of its creator's military feats. Every visitor was expected to be impressed by the plethora of images of Louis XIV as the hands-on hero – 'Louis XIV at the siege of Lille', 'Louis XIV at the siege of Cambrai', 'Louis XIV at the siege of Douai', 'Louis XIV crossing the Rhine', 'Louis XIV arriving at the camp at Maastricht' and so on, in what ultimately becomes an enervating sequence of boasting. The climax is reached in the Salon of War, dominated by Antoine Coysevox's mighty bas-relief depicting 'Louis XIV trampling on his enemies'. Particularly offensive to German visitors was the painting above, depicting 'Germania' and the imperial eagle cowering in terror before the might of Louis' France. In the Hall of Mirrors which then follows, seventeen of the twenty-seven paintings showed the smiting of foreign foes, nine of them celebrating victories in the war against the Dutch, concluded in 1678. At one end of the Hall, the Dutch folly of conspiring with France's enemies is depicted, at the other their humiliating submission, in a visual progress from provocation to retribution.[8] So awe-inspiring and intimidating could this triumphalist sequence of images prove that a Turkish envoy is said to have lost control of his bodily functions as he made his way past them, necessitating a change of clothes before he could complete his journey to the audience chamber. If that anecdote is authentic, it is perhaps the ultimate tribute to the success of Versailles and its representational culture.[9]

Louis XIV was not the first sovereign to take personal command of his army, of course. When he commissioned four huge tapestries depicting the victories of Alexander the Great, for example, or had Coysevox present him in the costume of a Roman emperor, he was following a well-trodden path linking antique to contemporary heroism. Modern armour was also acceptable, and arguably more relevant. Palaces were crowded with portraits and sculptures suggesting that their owners are on the battlefield. Whether it was Titian portraying Emperor Charles V on horseback, in full armour, spear at the ready, smiting the Protestant heretics hip and thigh at the Battle of Mühlberg, or Jan Wyck showing William III scattering the Catholics at the Battle of the Boyne, the fearless royal warrior was a trope of early modern iconography. They were not photographs – flattering liberties were certainly taken – but there were enough actual examples of rulers risking life and limb to sustain the desired image. In the lifetime of Augustus, apart from Louis XIV and his nemesis, William III, other rulers to go to war in person included Georges I and II of England, Charles XI and XII of Sweden, Frederick William the Great Elector and Frederick William I of Brandenburg–Prussia, Margrave Ludwig Wilhelm of Baden-Baden, John III Sobieski of Poland and Victor Amadeus of Sardinia, not to mention Augustus's father, the Elector Johann Georg III, whose martial enthusiasm was legendary.

Not even Louis XIV could always be on campaign. During the 1690s his personal involvement tailed off, the last siege he supervised in person being at Namur in 1692.[10] By then he was fifty-three, elderly by the standards of the day. Moreover, military success was proving increasingly elusive. If the War of Devolution (1667–8) against Spain was an unequivocal triumph, and the war against the Dutch (1672–8) could be talked up as a victory, the Nine Years War (1688–97) was a failure, and the War of the Spanish Succession (1701– 14) a defeat. Fortunately, *la gloire militaire* was only part of the representation project, necessary but not sufficient. More durable was the soft power deployed by cultural instruments. Building on the firm foundations laid during the previous reign by Cardinal Richelieu, Louis and his ministers, with Jean-Baptiste Colbert to the fore, raised France to be the undisputed cultural arbiter of Europe. All the arts were enlisted, financed and controlled, to propagate the image of Louis as the Sun King and his nation just as supreme in the service of Apollo as of Mars.

To these indoor pursuits must be added hunting, not just a form of recreation but *the* central royal and aristocratic peacetime activity. Anyone who has looked back from the inner courtyard of Versailles and marvelled at the size and splendour of the royal stables and kennels on either side of the Avenue de Paris, which can easily be mistaken for additional palaces, will know that this is no exaggeration. As the most scholarly study of French hunting put it, 'ever since Merovingian times, hunting had been inseparable from royal life. Pursuit of the stag is the royal activity *par excellence*'.[11] Even towards the end of his reign, Louis XIV was hunting 110 to 140 days a year.[12] Enormous areas were required to accommodate the very large amount of game of various kinds waiting to be slaughtered. The hunting reserve at Versailles was increased to 30,000 acres, 57,000 more were added with the purchase of the Rambouillet estate, tens of thousands more were available at Fontainebleau, to which the court moved every autumn, and in the forest of Compiègne, through which Louis had fifty-four new hunting roads cut and fifty-one bridges built.[13]

The clearest indication of the success of all these cultural initiatives was linguistic hegemony. When Louis came to the throne in 1643, French was only one of several competing languages. Either Spanish or Italian could have made as good a claim for ubiquity, while Latin still dominated academic discourse. But halfway through the reign it could be asserted by the Jesuit Dominique Bouhours that the French had outstripped even the Roman Empire, for whereas Latin arrived only in the wake of military occupation, the French language preceded conquest. Indeed, he suggested that even the common people of Europe were now adopting French, as if they sensed it was their manifest destiny to be annexed by their greater neighbour.[14] As Louis XIV's power began to wane, his admirers responded by turning up the volume. In 1694 the *Mercure Galant* gloried in the continuing linguistic conquests, which had spilled out over the frontiers to make French the lingua franca of all Europe, if not the world.[15] This nationalist hyperbole had a core of truth: in 1714, the year before Louis' death, the Holy Roman Emperor Charles VI deigned to sign an international treaty (Rastatt) drafted in the French language rather than Latin.[16]

As we shall see, as a young man Augustus drank deep at the cultural well of Louis XIV and his Versailles project. He also had a lot of fun. This might seem self-evident, but it needs to be emphasized, if only because so many serious-minded treatments of court culture give the impression that it was essentially functional, aimed at the maximization of power through the imposition of social distancing and social control.[17] But people also went to court because it was enjoyable, offering the best balls, banquets, gambling, music, theatre, opera, drinking, hunting and, last but not least, sex. It was also a gigantic patronage pump (not least for ecclesiastical preferment) and marriage market (the Duc de Saint-Simon recorded by name more than 1,000 persons whose marriages had been arranged at Versailles).[18] On the other hand, court life had its dreary side. Only the pious can have welcomed the innumerable religious services (Mass every day at Versailles) and not everyone can have relished the straitjacket imposed by the rigid hierarchy and strict etiquette. When Louis XIV turned bigot in his later years, the mood darkened. Directed by his deeply pious morganatic wife, Madame de Maintenon, whom he married secretly in 1683, he put a brake on lavish court festivities.[19] Versailles became *boring*. Although the grandees still attended on high days and holidays, increasingly they preferred their *hôtels* in Paris where the lights were brighter and the parties more fun.[20]

For pure unrestrained pleasure the place to be was Venice, the playground of the European elites. Adapting to the westward shift of Europe's economic axis, the Venetians found compensation for their loss of markets by turning to tourism. By the late seventeenth century, although their 'argosies with portly sail'[21] were still bringing home the spices of the East for re-export, the cloth and silk manufacturers were still sending their luxury items north of the Alps, and the furnaces of the Murano glass-makers were still blazing, they had fallen behind their Portuguese, Dutch, English and Bohemian competitors. But they still had a priceless asset passed down by their ancestors, in the shape of the most beautiful city in Europe, set in a cerulean sea and enjoying a climate especially attractive to anyone living north of the Alps. Giving nature a helping hand, they made the carnival season, from St Stephen's Day (26 December) to midnight on Shrove Tuesday, *the* great event in any socialite's calendar. Although it had been celebrated by the locals for centuries, it was only in the later seventeenth century that it really got into its stride as an international festival. Not the least of its attractions was the use of masks, which allowed all kinds of impropriety to be indulged with impunity.

If Venice was the headquarters of hedonism, there were plenty of other alluring destinations in Italy for northern visitors – Rome and Bologna for clerical enthusiasts; Florence for art lovers; Naples for operagoers; Sicily for vulcanologists; just to mention a few. By the time Augustus travelled south, it was axiomatic among European elites that a 'Grand Tour' (the term first appeared in print in 1676)[22] concentrating on travel around Italy was a *sine qua non* of a gentleman's education. As Dr Johnson put it: 'Sir, a man who has not been in Italy is always conscious of an inferiority, from his not having seen what it is expected a man should see. The grand object of travelling is to see the shores of the Mediterranean. On those shores were the four great empires of the world; the Assyrian, the Persian, the Grecian, and the Roman.—All our religion, almost all our law, almost all our arts, almost all that sets us above savages, has come to us from the shores of the Mediterranean.'[23] If the English were the most ubiquitous grand tourists, thanks to their greater wealth, there were plenty of other nations represented.[24] Among the German princes to stand out for enthusiastic patronage of the Venetian carnival was Augustus's father, the hard-living Elector Johann Georg III, who rented a large palace on the Grand Canal for a season of intensive self-indulgence. As we shall see, in this and many other respects his son was a chip off the old block.

To outline the culture into which Augustus was born, and in which he was brought up, is essential but potentially misleading, if allowed to stand without qualification. In the event, Augustus did prove to be an enthusiastic military monarch, the epitome of representational culture and one of the most self-indulgent hedonists ever to sit on a European throne, but this florid combination was not pre-programmed. He was indeed profoundly influenced by Karl Marx's 'tradition of all the dead generations' but there remained for him, as for every human being, an irreducible core of individuality. To employ one of Goethe's favourite classical aphorisms, '*individuum est ineffabile*' (the individual is inexpressible), to which he added his own version: 'every human being is wonderfully caught in his or her individuality'.[25] Trying to unravel the secrets of Augustus's psyche is difficult, because he was not given to introspection and his surviving correspondence is depressingly mundane, but an attempt has to be made. Not until his topsy-turvy career has been charted and analysed will that be done, although the reader may well be forming an opinion as the story unfolds. A premature rush to judgement should be resisted, for a final section will argue that, once the appropriate methodology is employed and a full range of evidence deployed, Augustus can be hailed as one of the most important creative artists of his era.

I.

The Gilded Cage

Brotherly enmity

At some point in April 1694, Augustus received news that his brother, the Elector Johann Georg IV, had contracted smallpox and was dying. His reaction is not known. It can be conjectured, however, with some confidence, that grief was not his dominant emotion. Not only had he never liked his brother, he had gone out of his way to record the fact in a draft for a novel he had written four years earlier, when recovering from his own mild attack of the illness (which had given him immunity).[1] 'These two brothers', he wrote, 'were constantly at war with each other', the older being jealous because nature had been so much more generous in bestowing gifts on the younger, and the younger being resentful because the accident of birth had made his unworthy sibling the heir to the Electorate. Augustus characterized himself as 'a lively fellow, carefree, showing from a young age that he was blessed with a strong body, a robust constitution, an amiable, generous disposition, equipped with everything that makes up an honourable man, more devoted to physical exercise than book-learning and a born soldier'. Johann Georg, on the other hand, was depicted as a depressive, irascible, feeble bookworm.[2]

What Augustus did not reveal was what the two of them had in common, namely a powerful libido. In 1688 the twenty-year old Johann Georg had fallen head over heels in love with the thirteen-year-old Magdalena Sibylla von Neitschütz, the daughter of a colonel in the Saxon army. Although she was undoubtedly of noble birth – her mother was a von Haugwitz – she was equally

9

clearly not a fit marriage partner for a member of the Wettin dynasty, the oldest and therefore the grandest in the Holy Roman Empire. His appalled parents (his mother was a Danish princess) sent Johann Georg off on a grand tour and then on campaign, in the hope that his passion would cool. As the equally libidinous but less monogamous father was conducting affairs simultaneously with the Italian singer Margarita Salicola and the Austrian Countess Margarethe Susanne von Zinzendorff (whom he called 'Suschen'), it is not difficult to imagine the vehemence of the three-way family rows that erupted.[3]

Absence only made the heart grow fonder. Once he succeeded his father as elector in 1691, Johann Georg at once recognized the beautiful Magdalena as his *maîtresse en titre*. He also promoted her father from colonel to lieutenant-general.[4] Rather strangely, he also got married to the unappealing Eleonore Erdmuthe, widow of the Markgraf of Brandenburg-Bayreuth, probably at the behest of his chief minister, Hans Adam von Schöning, who was seeking a rapprochement with Brandenburg. It was not a happy marriage. In the course of a heated argument about a gift to Magdalena, Johann Georg drew his sword, prevented from striking his wife only by the timely intervention of Augustus, who sustained a deep cut to his hand for his pains.[5]

The presence of a wife did not prevent the mistress from taking the lioness's share of the spoils. Showered with gifts, including a town palace in Dresden and a huge country estate at Pillnitz, just outside the city, Magdalena was also raised to the status of Countess of the Holy Roman Empire (*Reichsgräfin*) as 'Countess von Rochlitz' by Leopold I. The price was paid by the 12,000 Saxon soldiers sent off to the Rhine to fight and die for their emperor against the French.[6] They were led by the elector himself, accompanied of course by his mistress, who gave birth to a daughter in Frankfurt am Main. This idyll did not last long. On 4 April 1694 Magdalena died of smallpox. For her funeral procession, Johann Georg ordered the entire population of Dresden to turn out, on pain of punishment, to line the streets along which the cortege passed on its way to St

Sophia's Church (Sophienkirche), where her body was buried with all possible ceremony behind the altar.[7] He himself was prostrate with grief. The English envoy George Stepney reported: 'He is really to be pitied, for never prince had so violent passions, and any man who sees the agonies he suffers, cannot but be touched and suffer with him.'[8] As a lover, he had saved his best for last, selflessly nursing his beloved throughout her final illness, with the predictable result that he himself succumbed to the same disease twenty days later.[9]

Given their mutual dislike, Augustus would probably have disapproved of any woman his brother chose. In the event, he had showed his distaste by absenting himself from the court at Dresden and spending most of his time in Vienna and Berlin.[10] Unknown to him, it had been even worse than it looked, for Magdalena and her mother had rapaciously turned their control of the elector into hard cash. Among other things, they had extorted protection money from a group of Leipzig merchants by threatening to have their commercial privileges revoked.[11] The foreign diplomats were also paying large bribes to get Johann Georg's foreign policy influenced.[12] On her death Magdalena left 'six tons of gold',[13] estates at Pillnitz, Gorbitz and Pennrich, vineyards at Kostbaude, a pleasure garden at Plauen and a town house in Dresden later known as the 'Fürstenberg Palace', linked to the Electoral Palace by a secret passage.[14]

Once both mistress and elector were dead, Augustus could take revenge on the mother. She was promptly arrested, her possessions confiscated, along with those of her late daughter, and put on trial. The two Neitschütz ladies had been extremely unpopular with the plain people of Dresden, so this initiative got the new reign off to a good start. It is not clear whether it was Augustus himself or the judicial authorities who decided to charge her, not with corruption, of which she was undoubtedly guilty, but with witchcraft, of which she was (probably) innocent.[15] The assumption that the intensity of Johann Georg's passion could only be explained by supernatural forces is an interesting indication of the mores of late-seventeenth-century Dresden. Also striking was the application of torture during

Frau von Neitschütz's interrogation. What her prosecutors hoped to gain is not obvious; perhaps the location of her ill-gotten gains. If only 'the first degree' of pain was inflicted in the shape of thumb-screws, it was enough to prompt her to wear gloves thereafter, to avoid displaying the damage to her hands. More might have followed if Augustus had not intervened to put a stop to any further barbarity. He also ordered her release from prison sixteen months later, allowing her to return to her estate at Gausig, where she died in 1713.[16] He took responsibility for Johann Georg and Magdalena's daughter, paying for her upbringing and later arranging an advantageous match with a rich Polish noble, Count Piotr Dunin, the castellan of Radom, with whom she had five children.[17] Augustus also took swift action against the Saxon officials complicit in the Neitschütz depredations, the main target being the President of the Treasury, Ludwig Gebhard Freiherr von Hoym. He was packed off to prison and only released, in 1696, because Augustus urgently needed the huge sum (200,000 talers) the prisoner was prepared to spend on the purchase of a pardon.[18]

Chips off the old block

Augustus may have thought that he was very different from his brother, but they shared more than carnal enthusiasm. Also to the fore was their common conviction that the first duty of a true German prince was to lead his army into battle against the enemies of the Empire. Here, too, they were following a trail blazed by their father. Not for nothing was Johann Georg III known as 'the Saxon Mars'.[19] When he inherited the Electorate in 1680 he cut back sharply on court expenditure, redirecting resources to building up the army. While still crown prince he had signalled his martial interest by leading a small Saxon auxiliary force to campaign on the Rhine against the French in the 1670s. Once on the throne he proved to be one of the most effective allies of the Habsburg Emperor Leopold I, against both the French in the west and the Turks in the east. His finest hour came in 1683, when he led a substantial force of over 10,000[20] to assist the relief of Vienna from the greatest (and last) Turkish siege. During the battle on 12 September he was in command of the left wing, leading from the front until an anxious bodyguard extricated him from the hand-to-hand fighting.[21] By then he was so covered in blood as to be barely recognizable.[22] His army has been acclaimed for having 'performed some of the most gallant of all the action before Vienna' and credited with a significant contribution to the victory.[23] Saxon dragoons were the first allied troops to plant their standard in the Turkish camp.[24]

Conspicuously absent from the battle was Leopold I. When the Turks had broken into Austria in July he had fled to Passau, over 200 kilometres to the west, together with his family and court, a move which may have been prudent but also looked very much like cowardice. That was certainly how it seemed to his subjects, who tried to stop him leaving the Imperial Palace (*Hofburg*) and demonstrated their anger with curses and abuse as he made his way along the Danube.[25] When he reached Passau, however, he did make his own and possibly invaluable contribution to victory by praying every day before a famous image of 'Mary help us!' (*Maria hilf!*) in the eponymous pilgrimage church on the steep hill above the River Inn.[26] It is not recorded whether he followed the example of the most devout pilgrims by mounting the 321 steps on his knees each time he went. He did however fervently believe that it was the intervention of the Virgin which had scattered the infidel hosts, for it was with the cry 'Maria hilf!' that the Christian army began the assault on the Turkish besiegers. At his request, Pope Innocent XI declared the day of the battle a holy day in Mary's name throughout Catholic Europe.[27] The triumph confirmed Leopold's earlier avowal that 'in time of war I want the Blessed Virgin Mary as my general and in the peace-negotiations I want her as my ambassador'.[28]

Although he was undoubtedly an Empire loyalist, Johann Georg III was also a Lutheran and was unimpressed by Leopold's Marian devotion. Having rushed back to his battered but liberated capital, the emperor then succeeded in alienating his allies by treating them with indifference if not disdain, a poor return for their sacrifices of men and money, not to mention risking their own lives and limbs in his service. For the Protestants among them, a further source of friction was the persecution of their co-religionists being vigorously enforced by Leopold's officials in Hungary. Outraged by a dismissive reply to his remonstrance on the subject, Johann Georg III ordered his contingent to march straight home.[29] Leopold's neglect of basic courtesy also extended to his Catholic supporters. Annoyed that the commander of the allied army, the King of Poland, John III Sobieski, had not waited to allow him to be the first sovereign to enter Vienna, Leopold let his displeasure be known by frigid body language, including snubbing his son.[30] Quite apart from his irritation at being upstaged by Sobieski's premature victory parade, he was also alarmed by the possibility that the Hungarian rebels would offer their crown to Sobieski's son.

The summer of 1683 marked the high-water mark of Ottoman expansion in Europe and the beginning of a secular decline. Although this decaying process was drawn out over the next two centuries, the immediate world-historical importance of the Christian victory did not escape contemporaries. Sobieski sent an envoy to the Pope with the message 'We came, we saw, and God conquered' (*Venimus, vidimus et Deus vicit*), together with a banner mistakenly thought to be the holy banner of the Prophet. Across the continent, the feats that were done that day were celebrated in every conceivable medium. Overnight Sobieski became the most famous and venerated Pole of all time.[31] Alas, this was also the high-water mark of Polish success in Europe and the beginning of a downward path to mirror that of the Ottomans. The subsequent campaign petered out in the autumn, the Austrians went into winter quarters and the Poles went home.[32] They did not go empty-handed. With some relish, German observers recorded that during the night after the battle of 12 September, while the German contingents held their positions in case the Ottomans counter-attacked, their undisciplined Polish allies were busily looting the Ottoman camp and baggage trains. There was so much on offer, however, that the

Saxons did find a few things to take back to Dresden as trophies – five Ottoman tents, eleven cannon, several copies of the Koran, an elephant (which did not survive the journey) and a number of camels (although the attempt to establish a stud with them failed).[33] The most interesting booty was human, in the attractive shape of a young Turkish girl called Fatima, who found her way into the hands of the Polish Crown Treasurer Count Jan Jerzy Przebendowski and was eventually passed to Augustus, for whom she bore two children.[34]

Johann Georg III's two sons were too young to accompany their father to Vienna, being fourteen and thirteen respectively, but they certainly heard a great deal about it and were present at the victory celebrations when the conquering heroes returned to Dresden. They would also have been aware that several other princes of the Holy Roman Empire had been on the battlefield – indeed the attendance list reads like a supplement to the *Almanach de Gotha*: the Electors of Bavaria and Saxony; the Dukes of Lorraine, Saxony-Eisenach, Lauenburg, Holstein, Württemberg, Brunswick-Lüneburg and Palatinate-Neuburg; the Margraves of Baden and Brandenburg-Bayreuth; the Landgrave of Hessen-Kassel; the Princes of Hohenzollern-Sigmaringen, Anhalt-Dessau and Salm; and the Count of Waldeck.[35] In other words, Catholics, Calvinists and Lutherans had all combined in a joint imperial action against the Crescent.

The brilliant – and well-publicized – success at Vienna in 1683 confirmed the primacy of the warrior-king as a *beau idéal*. Every prince, great or small, now wanted to be depicted in armour, usually clasping a field marshal's baton and staring imperiously and imperturbably at the viewer as a battle rages behind him. Hyacinthe Rigaud's portrait of Louis XIV wearing French cavalry armour, now in the Prado, is just the most outstanding of innumerable examples.[36] Even the unfortunate Charles II of Spain (1661–1700), who throughout his childhood had to be carried as if he were a babe in arms, and even as an adult was usually incapable of walking or speaking, had to be painted in full armour (by Juan

Carreño de Miranda). As old as monarchy itself, the axiom that a ruler must fight as well as govern had been reinforced by the examples set by three successive French kings – Henry IV, Louis XIII and Louis XIV.[37] In short, a prince of Saxony, whether reigning elector or younger son, was marked out from birth to be a soldier. As soon as Johann Georg III's boys were old enough he took them off with him on campaign, to the Rhineland in the spring of 1689 to besiege Mainz, captured by the French the previous autumn.[38] That was something else the two boys had in common – enthusiasm for the military life. Gainsaying his brother's depiction of him as a weakling, when the elder succeeded as Johann Georg IV, he too went off to war on the Rhine at the head of his troops in 1693, and was preparing another campaign there for the following year when he died.[39]

Fun and games

Part and parcel of a masculinist attitude to conflict resolution was extramarital sexual activity. Breaking the seventh commandment ('Thou shalt not commit adultery' – Exodus 20:14) was almost de rigueur for early modern European sovereigns, most of the exceptions being those to whom heterosexual intercourse did not appeal (Charles XII of Sweden and Frederick the Great of Prussia, for example). The Wettins of Saxony were very much the norm. The most entertaining episode was provided by Johann Georg III in 1685, or rather by the 'Count von Hoyerswerda', the alias he used when visiting the fleshpots of Venice during the carnival season. Visiting the Teatro San Giovanni Grisostomo one evening to hear a *dramma per musica* with the singularly inappropriate title *Penelope the Chaste*, Johann Georg was overwhelmed with enthusiasm for the aforementioned prima donna, Margarita Salicola. There has been some debate as to whether he was attracted more by her voice or her beauty – both of which, by all accounts, were exceptional. There was the added spice of novelty, as this was the first female singer he had seen on stage, for back home all the female roles were sung by male *castrati*.[40]

La Salicola was attracted both by the elector's attention and by the very generous terms he offered for a move to Dresden. Unfortunately, there were a number of obstacles to be overcome, the easiest being release from her existing engagement (an entrepreneurial palm was greased) and the most intractable being the relationship she already enjoyed with the possessive Ferdinando Carlo Gonzaga, Duke of Mantua. To cover the back of the theatre's impresario against ducal retribution, it was pretended that she had been abducted by Johann Georg, although in reality they had just fled north. Pursued by a Mantuan posse, they reached the safety of Habsburg dominions in the Tyrol with only a couple of hours to spare. The story did not end there. The duke now resorted to angry correspondence supported by threats, including an order to his envoy to challenge Johann Georg to a duel if Margarita was not given up. Rumours of planned assassinations and poisonings abounded. With France supporting the duke and the emperor supporting the elector, even international conflict began to seem a possibility. To cut a long story short, eventually mediation by the Elector of Bavaria brought a peaceful resolution – Margarita Salicola stayed in Dresden and the Duke of Mantua's face was saved by a conciliatory letter from Johann Georg. Any amusement derived from this farce might be tempered by the thought that the cost of Johann Georg's Venetian adventure was met by the soldiers he had hired out to the Republic of Venice to fight against the Turks in the Peloponnese in return for 120,000 talers. Of the 3,000 who went, only 761 ever saw their homes again.[41]

Margarita remained in Dresden after the death of her patron, moving to Vienna in 1693. Two years later she was back in Italy, now known as 'Margarita di Sassonia'.[42] What is still not clear is whether or not she was the mother of an illegitimate child sired by Johann Georg in 1686 and legitimized with the name Johann Georg Maximilian von Fürstenhoff.[43] Supported after his father's death by his half-brother Augustus, he trained as an architect, entered Saxon service and enjoyed a successful career until his death in 1753.[44] In the meantime, his two half-brothers had been keeping up the family tradition of extramarital liaisons. Johann Georg IV's passion for Magdalena Sibyll von Neitschütz has already been noted. As for Augustus himself, his stable of mistresses became legendary, both in the sense of being prolific (354 is the number often bandied around, even by historians who ought to know better) and also in the sense of being grotesquely exaggerated, for the actual score was just eight.[45]

With the fashion for promiscuity set from the top by Louis XIV, the European trend-setter par excellence, staying on the straight and narrow path of monogamy was a special challenge during this period for those with the means and the power to indulge their carnal appetites. For young princes past puberty, temptation abounded. If adult supervision could sometimes be exercised within the confines of the court, once the young bloods set out on the essential rite of passage that was the grand tour, the traces could be kicked over as soon as the parental home faded into the distance. What should have been the restraining hand of the escorting tutor or chaplain was rarely applied firmly or consistently. Both of Johann Georg III's sons went on extensive grand tours and doubtless enjoyed themselves. Augustus did not need to wait, having started rather early, aged only sixteen, with a lady of the court, Countess Marie Elisabeth von Brockdorff.[46] When the affair was discovered, the lady was sent away from court and Augustus was sent off to Denmark to visit his grandparents, although when he came back his indulgent father allowed the countess to return also.[47]

Aware of the dangers which lay ahead for his two sons on their grand tours, although his own father had preferred to keep him at home and put him to work in the administration,[48] Johann Georg III made sure that the instructions for those in charge of their moral welfare made daily religious observance (and a sermon on Sundays) the top priority. He himself may have been a libertine, but he was a *pious* libertine, a combination which is an oxymoron, not a contradiction in terms.[49] On the other hand, when travelling through

Catholic areas, especially those recently annexed to France, there was to be absolutely no public discussion of religious issues. As his elder son set out in November 1685, at a time when Louis XIV was busily expelling tens of thousands of French Protestants after revoking the Edict of Nantes a month earlier, this was a prudent precaution.[50] In the event, Johann Georg junior's tour was rather short, lasting only just over a year. The itinerary was confined to northern Europe, the main destination being Paris and Versailles, of course, where he was presented to the Sun King; Windsor, where he was received by James II, still apparently secure on the throne from which he would be chased two years later; the Low Countries, including Brussels and Amsterdam; and various German courts. The detailed journal kept by the tutor reveals that this was a major undertaking, the party also comprising a chaplain, physician, tour director (*Stallmeister*) and numerous servants, making a total of twenty-one.[51] The omission of the south, which every German is supposed to yearn for, was made good in 1690 when he went to Venice, Bologna, Florence and Rome.

The original intention was to send the younger brother away for three years, perhaps because he was thought to need an extra layer of polish. His father stressed that the tour's purpose was to 'raise to a higher level of perfection all the virtues appertaining to a prince'.[52] The itinerary was to include all of Europe north, south and west of Saxony, including England and Scandinavia. In the event, the Glorious Revolution in England conspired with Louis XIV's simultaneous resumption of war with the emperor to force curtailment. Even so, by the time Augustus returned to Dresden in April 1689 he had been away for just one month short of two years.[53] Unfortunately, the dull daily journal kept by his tutor, Christian August Haxthausen, is singularly unhelpful in revealing his pupil's development. Only occasionally does a glimmer of light penetrate the pall of pedantic tedium. Taken at face value, it suggests that Augustus's main concern was religious, with every day said to have begun with a service of prayers and / or a sermon. This was obviously for the father's benefit, although he probably knew his son well enough to know that he was not spending so much time on his knees.

The highlight in every sense was the long sojourn in Paris/Versailles (June–September 1687 and May–November 1688), which Augustus reached shortly after his seventeenth birthday. Even those (or perhaps *especially* those) familiar with the overcrowded queue-ridden theme park that is Versailles today need to make an imaginative effort to recreate the palace as it was in all the glory of its first flush of youth, for it had only been the principal royal residence since 1682.[54] Like his brother before him, Augustus was travelling incognito, in his case using the pseudonym 'Count of Leisnig'. This was a common device to bypass the complications arising from disputes over precedence and etiquette. It did not prevent Augustus being presented to the king or consorting with princes of the blood royal and the high aristocracy, notably the Duke and Duchess of Orléans, whom he visited several times at Saint-Cloud.[55] The duchess had been born Elisabeth Charlotte of the Palatinate, although she was better known to posterity by her nickname 'Liselotte'. An indefatigable letter-writer (she wrote about 60,000, two-thirds in German, the rest in French), she sent the following assessment of Augustus to her aunt Sophie, wife of Elector Ernst August of Hanover and thus mother of George I of England: 'I cannot yet express a proper opinion of the prince: his features are not handsome, but he is well-built and has a pleasant expression, and he also seems to be more lively than his brother [Johann Georg] and is not so gloomy; but he doesn't say much and so one can't know what lies behind the exterior.'[56]

Normally loquacious at home, Augustus was probably more reticent at Versailles because his command of the French language was far from perfect. Nor was it improving much. Throughout his tour, he was supposed to be studying, especially languages, dancing and horsemanship. As the long-suffering Haxthausen complained, he was enthusiastic about the last of those, but negligent about the other two. It can be inferred that eventually the tutor was driven to despair, because he abandoned his usual discretion and reported candidly to the elector that, while he believed Augustus could derive some benefit from his tour, he would have to improve his attitude and wake up to what was needed.[57] Writing much later, the Duchess of Orléans recalled Haxthausen telling her at the time that the Paris experience had damaged Augustus terribly (*abscheulich geschadt*) and that his behaviour had been so dissolute that he could do nothing with him. Her own comment was that once young people succumbed to debauchery, there was no vice to which they would not resort, and that they thus became 'bestial'.[58] Alas, Augustus proved to be incorrigible. What he did take back to Saxony with him from France was an enthusiasm for grand court spectacles which bordered on addiction. Its most intellectual form was a taste for French opera and French drama. He was there at the right time, for this was the golden age about which Voltaire was to rhapsodize in *The Age of Louis XIV* (1751), lauding it as one of the four great creative periods of world history, the others being ancient Greece, classical Rome and the Italian Renaissance. Augustus demonstrated his own enthusiasm by being an avid visitor of the Académie Royale de Musique, as the Paris opera was officially known, brought to a peak of perfection by the recently deceased Jean-Baptiste Lully. Both at Versailles and Paris he was also a keen theatregoer, seeing thirteen plays by Corneille, eighteen by Molière and nine by Racine.[59]

In the autumn of 1687 the Saxon party moved south, with the less lively court at Madrid as their destination. At Bayonne, however, a prolonged halt had to be called, for Augustus fell seriously ill. Both the symptoms – a high temperature, hallucinations, extreme lethargy, loss of appetite – and the treatment – quinine – suggest that this may have been a case of malaria.[60] It was not until mid-December that he was well enough to leave, although then the journey proceeded smoothly enough and the party reached Madrid on the penultimate day of the year. There is little of value to be extracted from Haxthausen's journal entries about this episode. At a stretch, it might be worth mentioning the problem raised by the notoriously demanding Spanish etiquette over whether Augustus might keep his hat on when being received by King Charles II (in the end, both men held their hats under their arms).

Marginally more important was the bullfight that never was. Augustus informed his father on his arrival in Madrid that an '*ocsenfest*' (bullfight) had been arranged in his honour. Although it did not happen, that did not stop the notorious gossip Baron Pöllnitz from promoting one of the many myths about Augustus which were to earn him the sobriquet 'The Strong'. By this account, Augustus started the fight as a spectator but soon leaped into the arena to become an active participant: 'he was soon as skilful at it as any that were in the Career . . . and there shewed his surprising Dexterity and Strength. He struck the hinder-path of the Neck of one of those furious Animals with his Hanger [sword] that he had almost deprived it of its Head, and caused its final Fall. The Spaniards could not sufficiently admire him, nor could they be persuaded that a Man, not a Spaniard born, was master of such Strength and Dexterity.'[61] This account is completely fictitious, but worth mentioning if only to discredit the source of many of the spurious anecdotes relating to Augustus, especially about his fabled strength and priapism.

The most recent Polish biographer of Augustus, the late Jacek Staszewski, ingeniously suggested that the odd nugget of accuracy in Pöllnitz's scurrilous exposé might have derived from two pages written by Augustus in 1690, shortly after his recovery from a mild attack of smallpox, in which he sketched out what reads like an outline of an autobiography. It was known that Prussian agents had infiltrated the Saxon archives and so Staszewski, imaginatively if unconvincingly, speculated that one of them might have provided Pöllnitz with a copy.[62] What that document certainly did show was, firstly, that Augustus's mastery of written German was defective to the point of incomprehensibility and, secondly, that he was proud of his sexual conquests – which he called 'intrigues' or 'adventures' – with high-ranking aristocratic ladies, his most prestigious partner being a 'Conty' (Conti).[63]

After a month-long excursion to Portugal, which prompted

Augustus to boast that he had won the heart of a Portuguese prin-cess,[64] the party moved back to Paris, arriving in May 1688. What was intended to be a prolonged sojourn, followed by a visit to Eng-land and the Low Countries, was cut short by ever-strengthening rumours of war. Haxthausen may have failed to educate Augustus, or to keep him on the straight and narrow, but he was certainly alert to international developments, sending back to Dresden reports on French troop movements and military preparations. Very sensibly, as it turned out, in October it was decided that the time had come to leave France. With the Low Countries and Rhine-land likely to be combat zones, the safest way out of the country lay to the south-east. By mid-November the party had reached Lyon and soon afterwards crossed the frontier into the Duchy of Savoy. They were only just in time, for they had been pursued by an order from Louis XIV that Augustus be apprehended and interned. They had only been allowed to leave Paris because it was still hoped that the Elector of Saxony could be induced to stay neu-tral.[65] The Duke of Savoy refused a French demand that the refugees be extradited, earning Augustus's gratitude, friendship and – much later – a large consignment of Meissen porcelain (he received several valuable tapestries in return).[66]

Now the fun could begin again, in warmer climes and a less cen-sorious society. From the Savoyard capital Turin Augustus moved to Milan, accompanied by two Hanoverian princes, one of them being Georg Ludwig, the future King of England.[67] The destin-ation they were all looking forward to, however, was Venice, especially as the carnival season was already under way. Relations between Venice and Saxony were excellent, the latter being a source of mercenaries for the former, and the former being a source of funds for the latter. So the new arrival was sent two Ven-etian noblemen – Micheli and Molini – to show him all those delights that made the city an El Dorado for a man of Augustus's worldly tastes. Despite the rigours of the journey, transported on the last stretch from Padua by a gondola, on the first night Augus-tus went straight off to an opera at the Teatro San Angelo.[68] After the long journey from Paris, the teenaged Augustus was ready to party. Balls, banquets, brothels, gambling dens, theatres, opera houses were all available, and his two Venetian escorts made sure Augustus went to the best. He even got to see a bullfight, in St Mark's Square, albeit as a spectator not an actor.[69] More edifying, perhaps, was a separate visit to the basilica to witness the precious relics it housed, including several thorns from the Crown of Thorns and one of the nails used to impale Jesus on the Cross.[70]

Augustus no doubt enjoyed the Venetian fleshpots, but what he wanted even more was to go to war. Louis XIV's invasion of the Rhineland at the end of September 1688 presaged a major conflict, although no one knew at the time that it would last until 1697. With the war between the Austrian Habsburgs and the Ottoman Turks still rumbling along and with William III's invasion of England in November 1688 and campaigns in Ireland in 1688–91, Europe was aflame from the Atlantic to the Danube, an inviting prospect for a young would-be warrior keen to make a name for himself. Augustus had asked his father for permission to join the Saxon army when he was still in Paris and he now repeated the request from Venice.[71] It was granted in January 1689, when Johann Georg III told Haxthausen to take Augustus to Bologna and Florence, but to skip Rome and be back home by Easter, taking in Vienna en route.[72]

Court culture

With Augustus about to go off to war for the first time, a brief reflection on what he had experienced during his grand tour is in order. At every court he visited he found familiar objects, familiar rituals, familiar values – in short, a familiar culture. Although courts were as old as monarchies, they had been evolving at an accelerating pace in the early modern period.[73] In particular, there had been a tendency to settle in a permanent location rather than progress from one part of the country to another, although there might still be seasonal migrations, usually for hunting.[74] Peripatetic at the start of his reign, Louis XIV increasingly settled at Versailles before formally making it his main residence in 1682. One result of this trend was an increase in personnel and a concomitant increase in cost.[75] It also encouraged greater regularity of ritual and routine, or what John Adamson has termed 'a standardisation of expectations', including magnificent architecture, opulent interior decoration, big gardens, elaborate ritual, a clear hierarchy of rank, strict etiquette and, last but not least, demonstrative piety.[76]

There was also an international standardization of court pursuits. A crisp summary of what daily life at Versailles involved was supplied by the Duchess of Orléans in a letter to her aunt, the Electress of Hanover, in December 1676: 'I do beg your pardon for not writing for such an eternity. First of all I have been at Versailles, where I was kept busy the whole day long. We hunted all morning, got back at 3 o'clock in the afternoon, changed, went up to gamble until 7 o'clock, then to the play, which never ended before 10.30, then on to supper, and afterwards to the ball until 3 o'clock in the morning, and then we went to bed.'[77] The major omission from this schedule was a visit to the royal chapel, about which she was not particularly enthusiastic: 'it may be a great honour to sit next to the King in church, but I would gladly relinquish it because His Majesty won't let me sleep. As soon as I doze off, he nudges me with his elbow and wakes me up again, so that I am neither wholly asleep nor wholly awake. It gives me a headache.'[78]

This quotidian fare was punctuated by grand set pieces for grand occasions, such as the birth of an heir, the marriage of a daughter or the visit of a foreign sovereign. Then the boat could be pushed out far into an ocean of excess and expense. A clutch of celebrations across Europe in the 1660s announced the coming of age of the genre. If the first, chronologically speaking, was an equestrian ballet to mark the marriage of Duke Cosimo III Medici in Florence, the most spectacular was a week-long, multi-media extravaganza at Versailles with the sultry title *The Pleasures of the Enchanted Island*.[79] Officially, it was staged in honour of the king's mother, the dowager Queen Anne (of Austria), and his wife, Queen

Marie-Thérèse (of Spain), but the person he was really trying to impress was his young mistress Louise de la Vallière.[80] A good idea of what was on offer was provided by the title of the commemorative brochure published subsequently: *The pleasures of the enchanted island, with tilting at the ring; dramas combined with dance and music; the ballet of Alcina's palace; fireworks; and other refined and magnificent festivals, arranged by the King at Versailles on 7 May 1664 and continued for several days thereafter.*[81] Over eight days the 600 guests were treated to the very best that the richest and most powerful king in Europe could offer, including banquets, pageants, equestrian displays, tournaments, ballets (music by Lully), plays (by Molière, among them the premiere of *Tartuffe*), *comèdies-ballets* (music by Lully, text by Molière), illuminations, fireworks, and so on. The central theme was taken from Ariosto's *Orlando Furioso*, with Louis himself cast as the hero Roger, who overcomes the wicked sorceress Alcina and liberates the knights she is holding captive on her enchanted island. It might be thought that Mlle de la Vallière was not encouraged by the storyline.

Louis XIV may not have invented this form of court festival, but his enthusiastic adoption and assiduous propagation by well-publicized word and image certainly made it a *sine qua non* for his fellow sovereigns.[82] One dynasty that needed no prompting was the House of Wettin, for court festivals had been introduced to Saxony by the Elector Augustus I (r. 1553–86) in the late sixteenth century. One feature, which became popular from the middle of the next and was shared with other German princes, was a taste for celebrations in what was thought to be a plebeian style. Known as a 'Kingdom' (*Königreich*), 'Tavern' (*Wirtschaft*) or a 'Peasant Wedding' (*Bauernhochzeit*), this involved courtiers stepping out of their class for a day to dress up as a servant, artisan or farmhand. It need hardly be added that this play-acting did not stretch to wearing authentically plebeian clothes or consuming authentically plebeian food and drink.[83] The Saxon festivals also differed from the Versailles spectaculars because of their urban setting. One advantage of building Versailles on what was virtually a greenfield site was that Louis' creation faced no competition from aristocratic or ecclesiastical palaces in downtown Paris. The visual impact of the stand-alone palace as the visitor emerged from the forest was designed to be overwhelming. Back in Dresden, a familiar feature of festivals under Johann Georg II were the processions of richly costumed courtiers and gorgeously decorated floats, accompanied by bands of musicians, through the streets.[84] Some idea of the scale of the festivities organized by Johann Georg II is provided by Gabriel Tzschimmer's account, comprising 316 folio pages and thirty huge fold-out plates which recorded all the tournaments, hunts, processions, ballets, operas and plays of his reign.[85]

In other words, as Augustus travelled through Europe on his grand tour in 1687–9 he found himself in a familiar environment. There were some exceptions: while the baiting of animals was as popular in Dresden as anywhere else, the Saxons did not rise to the kind of ritual slaughter offered by a Spanish or Italian bullfight. Yet there was a difference. It was not so much that familiarity bred contempt, rather the reverse – it was the awareness that foreigners did those familiar things, but did them on so much grander a scale that left Augustus with something of an inferiority complex. The Electoral Palace in Dresden had something to be said for it: it was big; it contained a few impressive rooms (the 'Hall of Giants', for example); it had a picturesque location close to the River Elbe; but it paled by comparison with some of the palaces Augustus visited. The decorative scheme of the main state rooms, when completed (belatedly) in 1650, was 'rather provincial'.[86] By the reign of Johann Georg II it was even outpaced by the smaller but more modern palaces erected at Weissenfels and Zeitz by the two junior branches of the Albertine Wettins.[87] The response of the elector was not a major rebuild in the new baroque style, rather a refurbishment in a deliberately conservationist 'old German' (*altdeutsch*) style, which left the palace exterior still with steep roofs, irregular ground plan, asymmetric skyline and *sgraffito* façades.[88] It was charming, picturesque, but also old-fashioned, although there had been significant modernization inside.[89] A crucial shortcoming in the eyes of contemporary taste was the lack of a proper approach. When he first saw Versailles, Augustus would have seen a logical progression, from a broad *avant-cour*, more like an open square, narrowing to a square court, followed by a second and smaller court and finally a three-sided marble court focused on the holy of holies – the royal bedroom.[90] There was nothing comparable in Dresden, where the palace could be entered by several gates.

It is not clear what impressed Augustus most on his tour. The buildings? The paintings? The drama? The operas? The hunting? The banquets? The balls? The masquerades? The ladies of the court? The ladies of the brothels? Perhaps surprisingly, a good case could be made for the jewels. As we shall see later, Augustus devoted a great deal of time to and lavished enormous sums of money on jewellery of various kinds.[91] This was a family tradition: his grand-father, Johann Georg II, had been a fashion-setter in Germany in the 1670s with his French-style *justaucorps*, a knee-length coat lav-ishly decorated with precious stones.[92] Augustus's own taste can only have been intensified by his acquaintance with Louis XIV, about whom his most recent biographer has written:

> He loved jewels. In 1674 he wrote to Colbert of his need to have a case of jewels for himself and Madame de Montespan [his current mistress], so that they always had enough to suit the colour of their clothes . . . On great occasions, he was covered with jewels like the images of the Madonna carried in procession through the streets of Paris. He would wear them on his coat, hat, sword hilt and cross of the Order of the Holy Spirit. Once his coat of gold brocade was so covered in diamonds that he seemed to the Cheva-lier d'Arvieux to be surrounded by light.[93]

Jewels had obvious advantages: the admiration they excited was specific to the wearer; they announced wealth; they were easily portable; they could be turned into ready money in an emergency; and, because their settings could be modified to suit the current taste, they never went out of fashion. Although often overlooked by historians, a casket of jewels could be prized as much as a stable of horses or a collection of paintings.

The gilded cage

When he succeeded his brother in 1694, Augustus claimed that he was completely unprepared.[94] In one important sense he was right. His father had taken both his sons off to war, but had not made them serve an apprenticeship in the Electorate's civil administration. That lacuna was not filled when Johann Georg IV succeeded in 1690, as Augustus took himself off to Vienna, alienated by his brother's infatuation with his teenage mistress. On the other hand, he had never been more than a heartbeat away from power. At a time when smallpox, bubonic plague and other infectious diseases were rife, no incumbent could be secure on his throne – and no younger son could be without hope of ascending it. It cannot have been much of a surprise when Augustus found himself stepping into a dead man's shoes, and probably not much of a shock either, in view of the siblings' strained relationship. Given that Augustus immediately went to work, expelling Frau von Neitschütz and prosecuting her accomplices, the early days were not marked by any hesitation.[95]

In a more important respect, Augustus was certainly prepared for power, at least by his own lights. As this chapter has shown, by the late seventeenth century a princely culture had developed which was militaristic, sensual, hedonistic and representational. Everything Augustus had done since he escaped from the nursery had prepared him to emerge as its paradigm (or 'ideal type' in Weberian parlance). Not given to introspection, it never seems to have occurred to him that there were other models of kingship, other lifestyles, other world views (*Weltanschauungen*) available. He was in a cage – the bars were gilded but it was still a cage – and there was no room in which to turn round. Not that he ever wanted to. This was a culture that did not just allow or encourage, it positively privileged exhibitionism, narcissism, self-indulgence and sensualism. Brimming with energy, self-confidence and testosterone, the young Augustus took to it like a duck to water. For three years – 1694–7 – he could splash around happily, but then he went east and found himself in a very different kind of pond.

2.

The Polish Election

Augustus goes to war

When Augustus succeeded as Elector of Saxony in April 1694, he was already a combat veteran. He had seen action in five campaigns: on the Rhine for three consecutive years from 1689 to 1691; in the Netherlands in 1692; and on the Rhine and the Neckar in 1693.[1] These were the traditional battlefields of Europe, familiar to every European soldier. So it was a new departure for him when he signed an agreement with Emperor Leopold I in April 1695 to recruit, arm and supply a force of 8,000 Saxons to fight the Ottomans in Hungary. Knowing how pressured the Austrians were, Augustus had driven a hard bargain. The financial cost was to be met by the Maritime Powers (England and the Dutch Republic) and he himself was to be made commander-in-chief of all allied forces on the eastern front.[2] For the first time, he was off to war at the head of a multinational army, not as a subordinate member of his father's Saxon contingent. Showing that campaigning could be fun, on the march south from Dresden Augustus was accompanied by a throng of non-combatant courtiers, of both sexes it need hardly be added. At Karlsbad (Karlovy Vary) the company paused for rest and recreation, transforming the famous spa town into a carnival.[3]

Leaving his army to march east, Augustus went to Vienna, to confer with the emperor and his military advisers. To his dismay, he discovered that his title as commander-in-chief was to be honoured more in the breach than the observance. There was to be no major operation without imperial approval; he could act on his own initiative only in an emergency; and any decision he took would have to be approved by a council of war comprising Field Marshal Count Enea Silvio Caprara and three other general officers.[4] Doing justice to the events of 1695 and 1696 is hampered by a lack of detailed and reliable accounts.[5] Even the sketchy outline available, however, reveals that both campaigns were dismal failures, although Augustus's undeniable limitations as a commander were only partly to blame.

The campaign of 1695 got off to a slow start. The imperial army, numbering about 50,000, did not arrive at its assembly point at Ilok, on the Danube, forty kilometres west of Peterwardein (Novi Sad) until July. They were joined by their commander-in-chief at the end of the month, by which time they had moved further east to Futtak (Futog, now a suburb of Novi Sad). The strategic objective of this and the subsequent campaign was the capture of Temesvár (Timişoara), the fortified town which controlled the eponymous Ottoman province (*eyalet*), a roughly square bloc of territory stretching from the Danube in the south to the River Maros (also known as Mureş) in the north and from the River Tisza in the west to the Carpathian Mountains in the east. As it annoyingly projected north into what was otherwise Habsburg territory, posing a constant threat to Transylvania, its conquest was a top priority.[6] It was here, in the 'Banat of Temesvár', that all the manoeuvring and the modest amount of actual fighting took place. But before an advance from the Danube towards Temesvár could get under way, reports were received that the Ottoman Sultan Mustapha II had arrived in person at Belgrade with the intention of advancing north-west up the Danube to attack Titel and then Peterwardein. So the imperial council of war decided to stay put. Not for the last time, their intelligence proved to be inadequate. The sultan and his army were indeed on the move, but not in the direction expected. They crossed the Danube further east, at Pancsova (Pančevo) and then headed north to Temesvár.

A disaster followed. In what was intended to be a joint operation, Augustus had ordered General Friedrich von Veterani, in command of the imperial troops in Transylvania, to come south to join him at Arad, north of Temesvár on the Mureş. The conjunction was frustrated by the superior speed and aggression of the Ottomans, who on 7 September captured Lippa (Lipova), thirty kilometres to the east of Arad, seizing the large imperial depot of supplies, gunpowder and heavy artillery assembled in preparation for the siege of Temesvár. With the imperial army unable or unwilling to advance to meet him, Veterani was left to face the main Ottoman army alone at Lugos (Lugoj) on the River Timis, fifty kilometres east of Temesvár.[7] According to one authoritative account, Veterani's little army of 7,300 faced 28,000 Janissaries, 27,000 Spahis and 30,000 Tatars.[8] Predictably, the encounter was a massacre, only a handful of cavalrymen escaping the slaughter. Already dying from multiple wounds after heroic resistance, Veterani was decapitated and his head despatched to the sultan (who ordered that his remains be given a field marshal's burial).[9] What made this episode all the more harrowing was Veterani's deserved reputation as one of the most courageous, enterprising and successful of all the Austrian generals.[10] A further advance by Augustus and the main army up the Mureş as far as Deva, 150 kilometres east of Temesvár, was punching thin air, for the sultan and his own forces had gone home to celebrate their victorious campaign. At the beginning of October Augustus returned to Vienna, leaving his army to go into winter quarters.

The campaign of 1696 began earlier. Temesvár was again the main target. By the middle of June, Augustus had reached Csanád (Cenad) on the Mureş, forty-five kilometres east of Szeged, where the imperial army had assembled. Then nothing happened for two months, the council of war having decided not to take any action until the current deficiencies in supplies, money, siege artillery and gunpowder had been made good. By August they felt confident enough to launch a reconnaissance in force as far as Temesvár. Augustus then wished to begin a siege but was either overruled or was talked out of it by his colleagues on the council of war (accounts vary).[11] Once again, it was the Ottomans who proved the more proactive, crossing the Danube at Semlin (Zemun, now part of the Belgrade conurbation) and advancing north. The two armies met near the River Bečva (Bega) south-west of Temesvár and there fought a battle known by many different names, the most popular being 'Olasch', a place which appropriately no longer exists.[12] At the end of two days of fighting, both sides suffered heavy casualties and both claimed victory, which – as is usual in such cases – meant that neither could reasonably do so.[13] But the tactical draw was a strategic win for the Ottomans, who had achieved their main objective – to retain the key fortress at Temesvár. At the beginning of September Augustus again returned to Vienna, leaving what was left of his army to go into winter quarters.

To observers back in the capital, who could remember the glory days of 1683 when the Christians smote the infidel 'hip and thigh with great slaughter' (Judges 15:8) or of 1686 when Budapest fell to the warriors of the True Faith after an epic siege, or of 1691 when Margrave Ludwig of Baden defeated the Ottomans at Slankamen, the dismal news from the front in 1695 and 1696 was greeted with dismay and anger – together with a search for someone to blame. Not unreasonably, the first to be arraigned was the commander-in-chief, an especially inviting target because he was neither Austrian nor a Catholic. It was a charge repeated by nationalist Austrian historians subsequently, and for the same reasons.[14] There was plenty of substance in the indictment. Augustus arrived late and left early, clearly preferring the delights of Vienna to the rigours of life in camp. His attitude and conduct allow the inference that his motivation was personal self-aggrandisement rather than the objectives of the self-proclaimed 'Holy Alliance', under whose aegis the war against Islam was being fought. Although a veteran of several campaigns in the west, he had no first-hand knowledge of the very different conditions prevailing in Hungary, and his experience of command was confined to regimental level. Personally brave – several horses were shot under him during the Battle of Olasch, for example – he lacked the necessary charisma to inspire his rank-and-file.[15] Count Ernst Rüdiger von Starhemberg, the legendary defender of Vienna in 1683 and president of the war council (*Hofkriegsrat*), recorded that Augustus's abrasive behaviour towards his colleagues and overbearing arrogance (*rudesse im Commando und große Präsumption*) had caused serious discontent among his officers.[16]

34

Emperor Leopold was under no illusions as to his commander-in-chief's military ability. After the failure of 1695 he had wanted to replace him for the next year's campaign with Margrave Ludwig of Baden, but he had declined to transfer from the western front. Augustus had an unanswerable answer to his critics at the Austrian court, namely the ability to contribute more troops than anyone else. For the campaign of 1696 he raised his contribution by 50 per cent, from 8,000 to 12,000.[17] The same level of contribution to the Austrian war effort would have guaranteed him command in Hungary in the following year too. In the event, as we shall soon see, the sudden appearance of a much more attractive opportunity kept him away from the front. Emperor Leopold was in dire straits. He had been at war with the Ottomans since 1683, and with Louis XIV's France since 1688. His enormous but sclerotic empire just did not have the resources or the organization to sustain a two-front war for so long without outside help. That such an intensely devout Catholic could bring himself to employ as his commander-in-chief a heretic Saxon prince, whose Electorate was the home of the Lutheran Reformation, was an indication of the constricting toils in which he laboured.

There was less excuse for the continued employment of Caprara, a fine illustration of the fabled Habsburg habit of promoting rather than cashiering incompetents. He was old, ailing, reluctant to face the rigours of campaigning and understandably eager to get back to his estates in sunny Croatia.[18] Before he eventually left, he performed one last disservice for his employer by causing trouble, not just with Augustus but also with the other senior commanders. On 26 May 1696, Lord Lexington, the British minister at Vienna, reported to London:

The Elector of Saxony went away last Tuesday to Buda, where the whole army already is, and the siege of Temeswar is actually resolved. I wish them good success, but I own I very much fear, the preparations for such an enterprise being but slenderly made, the Generals all at disunion, and I believe some of them so inveterate, that they would rather the whole business should miscarry than that Caprara, who commands again, should succeed.[19]

The luxuriantly named Swiss soldier of fortune and diplomat François-Louis de Pesme de Saint-Saphorin recorded in his diary that Capraras's own secretary had told him that over the years his employer had fallen out with all the princes he had served, including Max Emmanuel of Bavaria, Johann Georg III of Saxony and Prince Eugene, on account of his 'cantankerous mood-swings' (*humeure assez défiante*).[20] Even more damaging was the information conveyed by Prince Starhemberg to Emperor Leopold in March 1697 that Caprara's orders had been derided and ignored by his subordinates.[21] Caprara's own predecessor, the Duc de Croÿ, had also been found wanting (and was to be found wanting again in 1700).[22]

All the generals, indeed all ranks, had reason to complain about the inadequate support given to the army by the authorities in Vienna. There were serious shortages of almost everything, at the top of the list being actual soldiers, supplies and pay. On the other hand, a commander with a strong personality and military ability could overcome problems of men and matériel, as Margrave Ludwig of Baden had demonstrated before his transfer to the western theatre of operations in 1692. Even more spectacular proof of the importance of the personal factor was provided by the radical change in the fortunes of war in 1697. Augustus had not attended the meetings of the war council in Vienna, under way since January to plan the upcoming campaign, only appearing in May. At the end of the month he went off to take the waters at the nearby spa at Baden. His therapy there did not preclude a grand ball for his officers, including his new second-in-command, Prince Eugene of Savoy, recently arrived from a successful campaign in Italy. On 12 June Augustus departed for Dresden, but was expected to travel back within two weeks, either to Vienna or direct to the front in Hungary. In the event, it was not he who appeared but one of his pages, bearing the arresting news that he had been elected King of Poland and would not be returning to the war.[23]

'With unusual speed', as the historian Max Braubach laconically observed[24] – and probably heaving a mighty sigh of relief – Emperor Leopold promoted Prince Eugene to be commander-in-chief. It quickly transpired that Prince Eugene brought to campaigning in Hungary everything that Augustus had lacked. He knew the terrain intimately, having campaigned there from 1683 to 1689; he had built up a formidable reputation as the most enterprising and successful of the imperial commanders; he knew how to win the respect of all ranks while maintaining strict discipline; he turned a Nelsonian blind eye to commands from Vienna to be more cautious; and, perhaps most important of all, he had the prestige and the contacts to extract from the Viennese authorities the wherewithal to prosecute the war effectively.[25] In dealing with the latest Ottoman advance on the Danube he delivered a masterclass in how to outmanoeuvre and then trap a numerically superior enemy. The result was the Battle of Zenta on the River Tisza on 11 September, justly hailed by Derek McKay as 'one of the most decisive battles ever to be fought in the Balkans'.[26] Between 25,000 and 30,000 Ottoman soldiers died, many of them drowned as they tried in vain to escape from a battlefield that had become a killing field, whereas imperial losses would be deemed unbelievable if they were not so well attested – twenty-eight officers and 401 rank-and-file.[27] No quarter had been granted to the Ottoman soldiers, even if a high ransom were offered by the captive.[28] The amount of booty seized was staggering, including several thousand cartloads of supplies, eighty-seven artillery pieces, herds of oxen, camels and horses, a war chest containing three million piasters, and the Great Seal that had hung round the Grand Vizir's neck as a symbol of his authority, this being the first time in the history of the Ottoman Empire that it had fallen into enemy hands.[29]

These were exciting times, one of those hurry-up periods of European history when the pace suddenly accelerated and events with far-reaching consequences occurred. In 1683 the last great Ottoman advance into the heart of Europe had been checked and the Christian Reconquista had begun. The annihilation of the Ottoman army at Zenta ensured that the shift in power would be irreversible.[30] It led to the Treaty of Karlowitz in January 1699 and Ottoman recognition of Habsburg rule in greater Hungary, including Croatia and Transylvania. Zenta was achieved by a force comprising Austrians, Hungarians, Serbian militia and contingents from several principalities of the Holy Roman Empire, its multi-national character personified by Prince Eugene who famously signed his name using three different languages – 'Eugenio von Savoie'.[31] Among them were between 7,250 and 10,000 Saxons (estimates varied).[32] After Zenta their presence in Hungary was no longer essential, but they were badly needed in the new kingdom of their now-royal master, who ordered them to march to Poland forthwith.[33]

The Polish election

On 17 June 1696, just as Augustus was getting ready to start his campaign against the Ottomans, John III Sobieski, King of Poland, died of a stroke while sitting in the garden of the Wilanów Palace south of Warsaw. Sixty-five years old, he had reigned since 1674. He remains the most famous and the most venerated of all Polish kings, in the words of Paweł Jaskanis, the director of the Wilanów Palace museum, 'a timeless icon of military success'.[34] But his victory at Vienna proved to be only the beginning of the end, or perhaps even the end of the beginning, to paraphrase Winston Churchill. Fourteen more years of fighting would be needed to force the Ottomans to accept defeat. They had not been glorious, especially not for Poland. Repeated attempts to advance south from Poland into the 'Danubian Principalities' (Moldavia and Wallachia) all ended in failure. In retrospect, the crucial year was 1686, when the Ottomans were still struggling to recover from the debacle at Vienna. In July Sobieski went south with a large army, 36,000-strong and supported by ninety artillery pieces. At first he appeared to make good progress, advancing deep into Moldavia, heading for the Danube. But he was not the first, and certainly would not be the last, to discover just how intractable the terrain could be. The governors (*hospodars*) of the two principalities declined to help; Austrian forces in the region had been withdrawn to assist the siege of Belgrade; the Tatar allies of the Ottomans harassed and destroyed what little forage there was to be found; and the Ottomans themselves evaded a major battle. Although the Poles got as far south as Fălciu on the River Prut, only just over 100 kilometres from the Danube, losses had to be cut. On 2 September Sobieski ordered the retreat. In the authoritative view of Józef Gierowski, this was a 'watershed moment' (*przełomowy moment*) in Polish history. A mighty effort had been made to raise money, men and matériel, and it had come to naught: 'in the three years since the triumph of Vienna, Poland had been reduced to a second-rate power'.[35] In September 1691, another abortive invasion ended in an even greater disaster, as the retreating army fell apart in terrible weather.[36]

This summary of John Sobieski's initiatives in the Danubian Principalities is relevant, because there was more to it than a continuation of the age-old war against the Ottomans. As the Polish throne was elective, the fortunes of the Sobieski family faced a precipitate decline when John died. A king of Poland had little power but much largesse to distribute in the form of land, offices and benefices. The ideal for any magnate therefore was to ensure that a member of his family was either elected during his lifetime (*vivente rege*) or was made certain to be elected after his death. Given the Polish nobility's richly deserved reputation for venality, simple bribery was one obvious method, but there was another: if the king could conquer a neighbouring principality and establish his family as the reigning dynasty, there was a good chance that the heir would be chosen as king of Poland to retain the territory's link to the Polish state. Modern Polish historians are agreed that it was this dynastic ambition which motivated Sobieski's ill-fated drive to the south.[37] No more successful was his attempt to marry his eldest son Jakub to the fabulously wealthy Ludovica Carolina Radziwiłł, sole heiress of the Birże line of the Radziwiłł clan.[38] Alas, despite being formally engaged, the lady jilted Jakub in favour of a son of the Elector of Brandenburg (Frederick William the Great Elector) and then, after that husband's early demise, Charles Philip of Neuburg, who eventually became Elector of the Palatinate.[39] Jakub had to make do with the latter's sister Hedwig Elisabeth, although she was certainly well connected as her sister Eleonora Magdalena was married to Emperor Leopold. Looks did not count for much in royal matches, but Jakub does not appear to have had much to offer: 'this Prince is black, has a thin and meagre look, and is of a low stature, more like a Frenchman or a Spaniard than a Pole . . . a weak and sickly person'.[40] As we shall see, Augustus was to copy John Sobieski very closely, both in his search for a principality to conquer and in his search for a high-born bride for his son.

King John was no more successful in his domestic policy, although he did greatly increase his family's landholding and wealth. As the military success which had brought his election faltered and then fell away, so did his authority inside Poland decline. The attempt to secure the election of his son *vivente rege* led to the formation of an alliance of three powerful magnate clans (Lubomirski, Sapieha and Grzymultowski) to exclude from the next election any 'Piast', i.e. any native-born Polish or Lithuanian candidate (especially if his name was 'Sobieski', although that was not spelled out).[41] Ailing and disillusioned, the king increasingly retired to his estates, leaving his formidable wife to fill the power vacuum. This was Marie Casimire Louise née de La Grange d'Arquien, better known as 'Marysieńka', the pet name used by Sobieski in their intimate correspondence and, for the sake of concision, here too. French-born, she had been in Poland since the age of five, arriving in 1646 in the retinue of Marie Louise Gonzaga, wife of two successive kings of Poland, having married first Władysław IV Vasa and then his brother and successor John II Casimir Vasa, unions which provided an indication of papal flexibility when granting dispensations to kings (at least Herodias had only been married to Herod's *half*-brother).[42] Marysieńka was also a widow when she married Sobieski in 1665, having been married first to the magnate Jan Zamoyski, although her widowhood had lasted only three months. It was at her insistence that her second husband successfully campaigned to be king in 1674.[43]

As this suggests, she was nothing if not ambitious. One of her missions was to promote the interests of the land of her birth at the expense of Poland's traditional alliance with Austria. Her task was made easier by the emperor's tactless treatment of the Poles after the siege of Vienna and the continuing exploitation of their war effort in pursuit of purely Habsburg objectives. The campaigns in the Danubian Principalities may have brought little or nothing to Poland, but they did divert enough Ottoman and Tatar forces to facilitate Austrian victories in Hungary. As her husband became increasingly disengaged from government in the early 1690s, Marysieńka arrogated more and more power, seeing herself as the regent. Her pro-French project was aided and abetted by two of the leading lights of the state – Michał Radziejowski, Archbishop of Gniezno and Primate of the Polish Church, and Stanisław Jabłonowski, the Crown Grand Hetman (the senior military rank in Poland). In 1692 a treaty was negotiated with the French ambassador, the Marquis de Béthune, Marysieńka's brother-in-law, to establish a close diplomatic and commercial relationship, to promise mutual support in case of aggression by a third party, to end the war with the Ottomans, to provide French support for Marysieńka's son Alexander at the next royal election, and to make her father a *duc et pair* of France. This package turned out to be a step too far. In a last assertion of royal will, King John refused his approval.[44]

If it be wondered why it was her second son that was to be promoted when the vacancy occurred, the answer is that Marysieńka was at daggers drawn with her eldest son Jakub. The rational explanation for their venomous estrangement is that Jakub had married into the extended Habsburg family (his wife was a sister of the empress).[45] Although speculative, it is more likely, however, that they had simply fallen prey to the intense generational conflicts that seem to be such a feature of royal families (and not just in Poland). Symptom rather than cause were the scandalous events which followed the death of the old king. With his father's body still warm, Jakub mounted his horse and rode into Warsaw, where he demanded entry to the castle. Luckily for him, the officer commanding the guard was an old friend, who duly obliged. Jakub promptly took possession of his father's treasure, plus the seals of the two main offices of state.

On the following day, the widowed queen and her two younger sons arrived, but Jakub refused them admission. Understandably, this caused a tremendous sensation. Elżbieta Sieniawska, for example, one of the wealthiest, most cultured and influential grandes dames of the age, wrote to her husband describing the unedifying spectacle of Jakub Sobieski standing in the street outside the castle and telling his mother to go away.⁴⁶ Eventually Jakub was induced to relent, not least because the body of his father was due to arrive at any moment from Wilanów. The scandal only grew when Jakub explained that he had excluded his mother to stop her stealing his father's possessions. Things could only get worse, and they did. When the body was laid out in state, those who thronged to pay their respects were surprised to find that the late king was not wearing a crown. Marysieńka explained that she had moved it to a place of safety because she was afraid that Jakub would steal it. That was too much even for her supporter Archbishop Radziejowski, who was now head of the state as 'Interrex' (acting sovereign) by virtue of being Primate. He insisted that the crown be restored to the royal head forthwith.⁴⁷ That was not the end of the affair. In Warsaw Marysieńka told anyone and everyone that, although not Polish by birth, she was entirely Polish 'emotionally' and that if they wished to do well by their country, the last person they should elect king was her son Jakub. The latter responded by announcing to all and sundry that his mother had burned the title deeds to two Sobieski estates which King John had assigned to his daughter-in-law.⁴⁸

This distasteful imbroglio did nothing to advance Jakub Sobieski's bid to succeed his father. It also handed Marysieńka's many enemies a propaganda weapon they immediately exploited to the hilt, launching a brutal pamphlet war against her.⁴⁹ This was no storm in a teacup. The fallout from the family feud included a radical shift in the policy of France, always a major player in any Polish election and never more so than in 1696. To understand why the French attached so much importance to the outcome, a little background is needed. Over the past two centuries, the central axiom of French foreign policy had been resistance to both the Spanish and

Austrian branches of the House of Habsburg. One of the main diplomatic weapons deployed had been the construction of an 'Eastern
Barrier' (*barrière de l'est*), an alliance with states to the east of the
Habsburg Monarchy, the most important being Sweden, Poland
and the Ottoman Empire. On occasions this had worked very well,
the most spectacular example being the intervention by Gustavus
Adolphus in Germany in 1630 to put a stop to the Habsburg Emperor
Ferdinand II's triumphal march to the Baltic. Very annoying, on the
other hand, had been John Sobieski's rescue of the Austrian Habsburgs at Vienna in 1683. By 1696 it was clear that the moribund last
Spanish Habsburg, Charles II, could not live much longer, and, as
he had no heir, a contest over his inheritance was certain. Poland in
the hands of a French ally would be an invaluable asset in the inevitable showdown between the two hereditary enemies.

   Although the Franco-Polish treaty of 1692 referred to earlier
had not been ratified, thanks to King John's refusal, the devotion
to France of the queen was not in doubt. Consequently, the French
starting point when the interregnum began was to support which-
ever of her sons – Alexander or Constantine – she preferred. Jakub
had obviously ruled himself out by marrying into the Austrian
camp. But then the French ambassador to Poland, Abbé Melchior
de Polignac, intervened. Ever since his arrival in the country in
1693 he had worked closely with the queen, but now he had to
inform his court that Marysieńka was so intensely unpopular
among the Polish nobility that no one handicapped by her support
could possibly succeed.[50] As any Polish magnate proposed would
immediately attract the jealous opposition of all the other magnates, he argued, the only way forward was to support a French
prince of the blood, the best candidate being François Louis de
Bourbon, Prince de Conti. His election would turn 'a Poland that
was German into a Poland that was French'.[51] Louis XIV agreed,
although specifying that the election campaign must not cost
more than one million *livres*.[52] That occurred in the autumn of
1696. Confusingly, at about the same time Marysieńka was recon-
ciled with her son Jakub, for reasons that no one has been able to

explain. As events were to prove, however, the maternal embrace may well have been the kiss of death.

For the time being, Jakub Sobieski was still in the running, not least because he had won the support of Sweden and Brandenburg by promising that Poland under his rule would not attempt to regain territories lost to them in the past. He then alienated Brandenburg by promising to cede Royal (West) Prussia to Sweden.[53] There was plenty of time for this sort of horse-trading. The first stage in a royal election was the 'Convocation Sejm', summoned under the presidency of the Primate, as Interrex, to provide for continuity in the administration of law and collection of revenue, to represent the country with foreign powers and to make arrangements for the election. The pace was leisurely. King John had died on 17 June, the Sejm did not meet until 29 August. It was an exceptionally rancorous affair, getting off to a bad start when the service held in St John's Cathedral in Warsaw to inaugurate the proceedings was disrupted by a stormy protest at the presence of a baldachin in front of the main altar, to which the Interrex was not entitled. The mood did not improve when the deputies got down to business, with the ejection of Marysieńka from the city at the top of the agenda. So heated did it all become that at one point the Bishop of Poznań led a procession of priests into the chamber in procession, bearing candles and sprinkling holy water to calm everyone down. Alas, this intervention only served to raise the temperature even higher.[54] Against a background of mutinies in the army and burgeoning civil strife in Lithuania, the necessary unanimity could not be achieved and so the Sejm was broken up. A confederation then had to be formed to fix the date of the election (15 May 1697).[55] Also agreed was a ban on the election of another Piast (not that Jakub Sobieski paid any attention to that).[56]

It might well be asked what Augustus had been up to in the meantime, having rather faded from our view. As we have seen, when Sobieski died he was campaigning in the Banat of Temesvár and did not return to Vienna until the beginning of September. He would have learned of the vacancy shortly after it occurred, of course, not least because it had implications for the conduct of the war. Although nothing can be proved, it is likely that his decision to compete for the Polish throne was immediate. It has even been suggested that it was a wish to enhance his martial credentials that prompted him to take the fight to the Ottomans in August, resulting in the Battle of Olasch.[57] Saxon ambitions with regard to Poland were of long standing. In July 1691 Augustus's father had secured an undertaking from Ernst August of Hanover to support a Saxon candidate at the next election in Poland (in return for Saxon support for the title of Elector for Hanover).[58] There is some dispute as to how firm that commitment was, but it is certain that the Saxons had their eye on Poland at least from 1691.[59] So did other princes, of course. During the winter of 1696–7 a number of candidates were canvassed, as well as Jakub Sobieski and the Prince de Conti – Margrave Ludwig of Baden, Elector Max Emmanuel of Bavaria (Marysieńka's son-in-law), Charles of Neuburg, Duke Leopold of Lorraine and the Polish magnate Stanisław Jabłonowski.[60] Even the deposed King of England, James Stuart, was considered at one point by Louis XIV as a way of getting him off his hands.[61] The most charming was Livio Odescalchi, Pope Innocent XI's nephew, who was hoping that his distinguished service at Vienna in 1683 and the offer of his substantial collection of classical sculptures would make up for his penury.[62] They all fell by the wayside, disqualified by loss of interest or lack of funds.

Augustus had plenty of both. Once the Dresden Carnival ended on 26 February 1697, he launched his campaign. The first step was to send an envoy, Colonel Erich Theodor von Rosen, to Rome to seek the support of the Pope and – even more importantly – of the French through Louis XIV's envoy to the Holy See, Cardinal Toussaint Forbin Janson. Rosen was authorized to convey Augustus's intention to convert to Catholicism, a *sine qua non* for any aspiring candidate in Poland. The response was disappointing. The Pope was sceptical about Augustus's sincerity, unsurprisingly, and did not accept the conversion as genuine until well after the election.[63] As for the French, the signal from Versailles was unequivocal support for Conti.[64] Nothing daunted, and showing what was to become his trademark ability to switch horses, Augustus now sought help from Vienna. With Conti's prospects looking increasingly good, and Jakub Sobieski's fading rapidly, Augustus had to become the Austrian candidate *faute de mieux*, a transition that was complete by the end of May 1697. His election would be doubly welcome in Vienna: not only would he keep Poland out of the French camp, his conversion would mean that the confessional balance among the electors of the Holy Roman Empire would be tilted decisively towards the Catholics.[65]

Augustus's agent in the election campaign was the thirty-year-old Pomeranian noble Jakob Heinrich von Flemming, in Saxon service since 1694. He was to become Augustus's closest and most loyal minister until his death in 1728.[66] He was well travelled, well educated, intelligent, cultured and a good linguist. He also had good Polish connections, partly from his Pomeranian upbringing and partly because his cousin was married to Jan Jerzy Przebendowski, the castellan of Chełmno.[67] Not the least of his assets was his command of the Polish language.[68] When the interregnum began, Przebendowski supported Jakub Sobieski, although he was also said to be acting as an agent for the French ambassador Polignac.[69] In February he had been to Dresden to encourage a Saxon intervention, arguing that the competition offered by Conti was blunted by the fact that he was resident in France and the inadequate funds made available to Polignac to bribe the avaricious Polish nobility.[70] On 2 May, with the Election Sejm only two weeks away, Flemming and Przebendowski arrived in Warsaw to launch the campaign. They issued a manifesto in which Augustus was hailed as a descendant of the Saxon Emperor Otto III who had placed a crown on the head of Bolesław the Brave (in the year 1000); as a man with a heroic military record against the Ottomans, despite his youth; as a warrior who would win back the lost territories; as a visionary who would revive the Polish economy; and so on.[71]

One crucial commitment offered by Augustus's agents was that he would abandon his Lutheran heresy in favour of the True

Faith. Everyone agreed that this was absolutely essential. Apostasy does not seem to have caused Augustus any qualms at all. Paraphrasing Henry IV of France, he may well have thought that the Polish–Lithuanian Commonwealth was worth a Mass. He does not appear to have been an ardent Lutheran in the first place. In his contemporary character sketch, Johann Michael von Loen commented: 'It is said that he changed his religion. I would concede that to be true, if I thought that he had any religion to change. It is well known that from his youth he has been a freethinker . . . He had no religion when he converted to Rome, so it can't be said that he changed his religion, rather that he adopted one.' He added that the depth of Augustus's piety was revealed after his conversion when he responded to being chided by his confessor for lax attendance at Mass by placing the proffered rosary around the neck of his pet dog.[72] In the same vein, the Duchess of Orléans expressed amazement that Augustus had converted because he had always been so reluctant to go to church, but now he would find that the Catholic priests would make sure he was regular attender.[73] For public consumption, his ostentatious Catholic piety was often on display. Indeed, it has been conjectured that Polish pride in the conversion of such a glittering prize as the Elector of Saxony, the home of heresy, made an important contribution to his success.[74]

One member of his entourage who did have serious reservations was none other than Flemming, who insisted that Augustus sign a declaration that he was converting in a personal capacity only; that no attempt would be made to force his new religion on his subjects; and that nothing would change in the ecclesiastical and religious structure of Saxony.[75] The ceremony initiating Augustus into the Catholic Church was conducted by his kinsman Christian August of Saxony-Zeitz, Bishop of Raab, who himself was a convert, in the Chapel of the Virgin of Loreto in the Imperial Palace at Baden near Vienna on 2 June.[76] In the course of the service, the bishop intoned: 'in accepting the Catholic religion, may Your Electoral Highness be led not by any earthly consideration but solely by the yearning for the salvation of your soul!' In reply, Augustus duly affirmed that 'profane motives' were wholly absent and that his only concern was his spiritual welfare.[77] Less redolent of high principle was the careful manner in which the certificate of conversion was drafted, with the date being omitted and no explicit renunciation of Protestantism mentioned. With good reason, it has been argued that this was to allow him to renege if the election did not go according to plan. It did not stop Flemming broadcasting to the Poles the cynical fiction that Augustus had been converted 'by the Holy Spirit' two years earlier.[78]

During the run-up to the election a lot of money had changed hands – or rather, in many cases, *promises* of money. Forced to be prudent by the ruinous state of his finances after so many years of war, Louis XIV had insisted that no money be disbursed until the election was over and the right result achieved. Credit notes sent from Versailles were accordingly post-dated.[79] He was also sceptical about Polignac's assurances that Conti's success was certain, sending a second envoy – François de Castagnères, Abbé de Châteauneuf – to check. In the event, the latter confirmed Polignac's assessment and combined with him to urge both the despatch of more money and the personal appearance of their candidate.[80] This good advice was not heeded. Neither the money nor Conti arrived. Having spent what money they did have on the provincial assemblies (*sejmiki*), they had nothing left when the Election Sejm began.[81] Things were very different in the Saxon camp, where Augustus proved to be nothing if not a competitor. He set about raising money in every way he knew. He pawned, he borrowed, he mortgaged, he sold. The Saxon crown jewels were pawned to the Jesuits of Vienna, who were told to authorize their colleagues in Warsaw to lend up to a million gulden.[82] He mortgaged the Saxon administrative district (*Amt*) of Borna to the Ernestine branch of the Wettins of Saxony-Gotha for twenty-four years for 300,000 talers.[83] He sold his feudal rights to the Abbey of Quedlinburg to Brandenburg, also for 300,000 talers.[84] He sold the Duchy of Lauenburg to Brunswick-Lüneburg for 1,100,000 gulden.[85] It would be wearisome to list all the assets that Augustus liquidated in pursuit of the Polish throne. Suffice it to say that he had no compunction about permanently diminishing his inheritance.[86] 'Whatever it takes' was his motto.

All this used up time, of course. Flemming, in effect Augustus's campaign director, had enough experience of Poland to know that both magnates and rank-and-file *szlachta* (nobility) wanted cash in hand, not paper promises. So a crucial role in winning their support was Augustus's good relations with a number of Jewish financiers. In this crucial respect, Augustus had made his own good fortune. In February 1696, or in other words before the Polish opportunity arose, he had informed the town council of Leipzig that he had appointed Berend Lehmann of Halberstadt to be his 'court Jew' (*Hoffude*) and that during the three annual fairs he must be allowed to trade in the city without being obliged to pay extra dues. Included in the concession were the Hanover court Jew Löffmann Berentz and his two sons. Predictably, the anti-Semitic councillors were outraged, informing Augustus that Jews were 'even more vexatious than Turks and Moslems, being public and declared enemies of Our Saviour and all Christians'.[87] Augustus not only insisted, in 1698 he added that, when attending the fairs, Jews should be allowed to conduct their religious services.[88] Lehmann was very well connected across Europe, enjoying the priceless ability to raise large sums of hard cash quickly. As we shall soon see, that enabled him to make a decisive intervention in the Polish election.

From the middle of May 1697 the szlachta began to arrive at the village of Wola just to the west of Warsaw, since 1573 the traditional site for royal elections. As every adult Polish nobleman was entitled to attend, thousands and then tens of thousands eventually gathered.[89] Fortunately there is a fine painting of the scene by Martino Altomonte, the late king's court painter (and available online in high resolution).[90] It shows an extensive meadow, with the towers and spires of Warsaw in the background. In the foreground there is a wooden pavilion (the 'Szopa'), which served as the assembly room of the senators present, and an open space on which the elite are seated, separated from the rest of the crowd by a deep ditch. In the background can be seen many groups of szlachta, for whom the proceedings at the centre would have been completely inaudible. According to one report, there was also much raucous music to be heard from bugles, trumpets, fifes and drums, and no doubt there were many booths selling food and drink.[91]

It was a long time before the assembled company got down to the real business of the Sejm. More than a month passed in rancorous debate about the causes of the disorders in the army; equality between Poland and Lithuania; the disgraceful conduct of the emperor in omitting the salutation 'Serenissima' from his communication (the Commonwealth gloried in the title of *'Serenissima Respublica'*); and other such matters of moment. It was not until 15 June that a Marshal of the Sejm could be agreed on. As the successful candidate, Kazimierz Bieliński, was known to be a member of the French party, the position of Conti began to seem impregnable.[92] In reality, it was much less secure than it looked – Polignac's money had never been enough and had now run out, Conti himself was still in France, and – most fatally – those willing to vote for him were moved to do so not because of who he was but because of who he was not. By that was meant: he was not Jakub Sobieski, whose star had waxed and waned since his father's death but still gave off enough light to illuminate the way to Conti as the lesser of two evils.

This flaw in the Conti camp opened the way for Augustus, who came to the party very late. It was on the last day of May that Polignac reported to Versailles that 'un certain chevalier Flemming', sent in secret by the Elector of Saxony, had informed him that his master would wish to be a candidate if Conti's election was unlikely. Polignac had replied that the religious difference was an insuperable problem and that anyway it was much too late, to which Flemming rejoindered that Augustus had converted and was confident he could succeed.[93] It was even later, following another brief visit to Vienna, that Flemming and the rest of his team began their campaign in earnest. Crucially, the Austrian representative, the Bishop of Passau, managed to persuade a reluctant papal nuncio, Gianantonio Davia, to confirm that Augustus's conversion certificate was

genuine.[94] They were only just in time. On 26 June, Cardinal Radziejowski, in his capacity as Interrex, began the voting, the electors
being grouped by 'banners'. By this time all the other candidates
had fallen away, including Jakub Sobieski. On 24 June his remaining
supporters had agreed to switch their support to Augustus, given
that Sobieski's financial exhaustion made his election impossible.
Their passage was lubricated by the application of money, Jakub
Sobieski alone receiving 200,000 talers.[95] Even so, at the end of the
first day of voting Conti was well in the lead, by 210 banners to forty.
Radziejowski would have done well to proclaim his candidate king
there and then, but he postponed a final count until the following
day. This was probably a response to the angry protests from the
opposition, and possibly also a wish for the unanimity that was such
a feature of Polish political culture. Jacek Staszewski, however,
believed that it was religion that was responsible: the cardinal was
needed in Warsaw to keep an appointment to consecrate a new
delivery of relics for an altar in the Church of the Holy Cross.
Although barely credible, it appears that no one knew the identity
of the saint to whom the bones belonged, so Radziejowski simply
announced that it was St Felicissima, a conveniently obscure third-
century Umbrian martyr, and made her the patron for all future
elections into the bargain.[96]

Radziejowski then returned to Wola and spent the night in his
carriage, looking forward to proclaiming Conti as king the next
day. He had not reckoned with the enterprise of Augustus's agents.
During the night, the 100-odd pupils of the Jesuit College in Warsaw
were kept hard at work copying out Augustus's list of promises to
the Polish nation (most of which he failed to keep).[97] The papal
nuncio's endorsement of Augustus's conversion certificate was
also broadcast, reinforced by more secular encouragement.[98] Early
in the night Berend Lehmann arrived with a cartload of barrels
containing 40,000 talers in coins, which Flemming promptly had
distributed to the szlachta, along with liberal supplies of food and
drink.[99]. The same simple pecuniary technique had been used
already to recruit a number of magnates and their clans, fuelled by

the very large sum released by the Warsaw Jesuits.[100] Also during the night, the anti-Conti representatives of Bavaria, Brandenburg, Neuburg, Lorraine and Venice met to pool their individual funds and add them to the Saxon hoard (albeit as loans rather than gifts).[101] So, with all this hard cash swilling around on the Wola field, it was no surprise that voting on the next day, 27 June, took quite a different turn. By early evening it was reported that the balance had been almost exactly reversed – 63 banners for Conti, 185 for Augustus. That was clear enough, but Radziejowski took the previous day's vote to be definitive, proclaimed Conti king and hurried off to Warsaw to hold a *Te Deum* in St John's Cathedral. Once again the Augustus team had an answer, in the shape of Stanislaw Dąmbski, Bishop of Cujavia, second in the Church hierarchy and therefore authorized to act 'in the absence of the Primate'. Well, the Primate was indeed absent, so Dąmbski now proceeded to proclaim Augustus as king and went off in turn to St John's Cathedral to hold a rival *Te Deum* (whether the same choir was employed is not revealed). Dąmbski had started as a supporter of Jakub Sobieski, changing over to Augustus when the writing on the wall became too obvious to miss. Benefiting from his timely move to what proved to be the winning side, the Dąmbski family then embarked on a steep upward trajectory to become the dominant landowning family in Cujavia.[102]

Both sides now sought to make good their claim of victory. Radziejowski sent a courier off to Versailles to urge Conti to travel to Poland just as fast as he could. It was good advice but was not followed. For the past six months, Polignac had been telling Versailles that Conti should get ready to leave at a moment's notice, equipped with the necessary men and money to enforce his claim. In the event, he did not leave Paris until 3 September, did not board his ship at Dunkirk until the 7th and did not arrive off Danzig until the 30th, more than three months after the election.[103] His reception was not encouraging. Not only was he refused permission to disembark, insult was added to injury when the citizens held a ceremony of thanksgiving for the election of

Augustus, firing salutes and singing a *Te Deum*, in full view of the rival king waiting offshore.[104] As the Huguenot refugee Parthenay observed, 'They were almost all of them Protestants, and consequently more inclined to a Roman Catholick of a few Days standing, than to a Prince of the Blood of Louis the Fourteenth, who had taken Pains to extirpate the Protestant Religion in his Dominions.'[105] The French party then moved down the coast to Oliva, where they were able to go ashore. Meanwhile, Flemming, Przebendowski and the rest of the Augustan team had moved smartly to consolidate their position. On 28 June Flemming had agreed, in Augustus's name, to accept the *pacta conventa* (articles of agreement), the conditions which formed the contract between king and nation. First introduced in 1573 for the first royal election, following the end of the hereditary Jagiellon line, they amounted to a written constitution.[106] Varying from election to election, they resembled a ratchet – always clicking upwards at the cost of royal authority. As we shall see, the *pacta conventa* of 1697 were no exception.

Augustus takes control

After the disputed election Radziejowski wrote to Augustus, informing him that Conti had been elected and lamenting that a 'small number' of malcontents had claimed to have elected Augustus instead. He urged him to have nothing to do with this illegal action.[107] Unsurprisingly, his request went unanswered. On the contrary, Augustus showed again that, when he wanted something, he did not hold back. He had arrived back in Dresden from Vienna in the middle of June. Three days later he went to Görlitz, ninety kilometres east of Dresden, close to the Silesian frontier, where he had assembled 4,100 cavalry and 3,000 infantry.[108] On receipt of the good news from Warsaw he moved east to Breslau, with the cooperation of the Austrian authorities, establishing his base at Tarnowitz (Tarnowskie Góry), where he was received by a group of Polish supporters more than 1,000-strong, including – crucially – the Crown Grand Hetman Jan Stanisław Jabłonowski. In a demonstration of mutual confidence, Augustus entrusted the latter with command of the troops and Jabłonowski signalled his subordinate status by kissing Augustus's hands. This exchange symbolized that the new king had taken control of the state ('that agency in society which has a monopoly of legitimate force', as Max Weber memorably put it.) Augustus also seized the opportunity to impress his new subjects with his gorgeous apparel, appearing 'in a costly blue coat, covered in gold embroidery, festooned with diamond-encrusted button-holes and diamond buttons, and wearing sword, hat, garters and shoe-buckles all covered in diamonds of exceptional size, a most magnificent ensemble valued at a million talers'.[109] The party then moved on to the Marian shrine at Piekary Śąskie, where Augustus attended his first public Mass. In the course of the service he signed a confession of the Catholic faith, together with the *pacta conventa* signed on his behalf at Warsaw by Flemming.[110]

The next all-important step was the coronation at Kraków.[111] Three apparently intractable ceremonial problems had to be overcome. Tradition demanded that the body of the late king be buried before his successor was crowned, but Sobieski's remains were still in Warsaw. That was overcome by the simple expedient of burying an empty coffin. Also easily resolved was the absence of Archbishop Radziejowski, as the pliable Dąmbski was enlisted 'in the absence of the Primate'. More problematic was the requirement that the crown jewels be used, for they were inaccessible, the eight guardians having taken an oath not to hand over the keys to a man they considered a usurper. In a solution worthy to be ranked with Alexander's severing of the Gordian knot, a hole was knocked in the wall allowing extraction of the regalia while bypassing the locked door. Another local difficulty was the reluctance of the governor (*starosta*) of Kraków, Count Wielopolski, to admit a king not elected by 'the whole nobility', but it was overcome by a diamond bracelet for his wife and a gold box for himself. Where there was an Augustan will, a way could be found.[112]

One aspect of the ceremonies in Kraków that needs to be stressed is regalia.[113] On his entry to Kraków on 2 September, Augustus rode on a white horse wearing a cloak of gold braid edged with ermine, blue silk waistcoat and breeches, secured with diamond and ruby buttons, and all the numerous accessories of man and horse festooned with diamonds and rubies.[114] He rode under a purple silk baldachin, signifying his royal status, carried by six municipal councillors, and accompanied by a huge procession, including a large contingent of Saxon soldiers sporting newly manufactured white uniforms. And so it continued, each day a different outfit more gorgeous than the previous. No wonder that he called for more funds from Berend Lehmann, who sent 250,000 talers from Hanover.[115] For the actual coronation ceremony he surpassed himself, his personal design combining antique German, Roman and Polish elements – a cuirass over a Roman tunic and sandals, a blue silk cloak edged with ermine and embroidered with golden flowers, a hat surmounted with white feathers, and everything sparkling with diamonds thought to be worth a million talers. Unfortunately, it all proved too much for a hot day in July. As the Bishop of Cujavia was reading the profession of faith during the High Mass Augustus fainted and had to be revived with a draught of wine. The cuirass, which he had been wearing for four hours by that stage, was removed.[116] The service continued, but his opponents of course made the most of what could be interpreted as an omen or derided as weakness – was this crumpled figure the self-styled 'Hercules Saxonicus'? they asked.[117] It is easy to sneer at Augustus's penchant for dressing up and showing off, but judgement should be reserved until the whole panoply of his cultural endeavours has been reviewed and when a more qualified verdict may seem in order.

With the coronation over, Augustus was now King of Poland. He might well have quoted King Richard II's lines from Shakespeare's eponymous play:

> Not all the water in the rough rude sea
> Can wash the balm from an anointed king.[118]

But just as Richard's nemesis, Bolingbroke, was approaching when those lines were spoken, so was there another aspiring king in the offing in 1697. On the day that Augustus was crowned (15 September), the Prince de Conti's squadron, commanded by the famous privateer Jean Bart, was passing through the rough rude sea of the Sound into the Baltic.[119] There the similarity ends. While poor Richard was clearly heading for disaster, Augustus was taking resolute action to ensure that he did not go the same way. The Saxon troops who had helped Prince Eugene to win the Battle of Zenta on 11 September were ordered to come north to Poland by forced marches.[120] As Conti had only brought 300 soldiers with him, he had to rely on local supporters flocking to his colours. Some did, but most flocked away again when they found he had not brought enough money to pay them. On 8 November the force of 3,000 cavalry sent by Augustus from Kraków reached Oliva. Meeting no resistance, they took the opportunity to loot everything the French had left behind when they hurriedly re-embarked. On the following day, Conti cut his losses and sailed home to France.[121] He took with him Polignac, who was made the scapegoat for the whole inglorious episode and banished to his abbey in Normandy.[122] His parting shot was: 'The French party has right on its side, but does not have a king, but the Elector of Saxony has money and an army and stands at the gates of the Republic.'[123]

More serious for Augustus was the opposition being organized inside Poland by Radziejowski as a formal insurrection (*rokosz*), although it proved to be short-lived. Once Conti had fled, some of his supporters prudently made peace with the new king, notably Hieronim and Stanisław Lubomirski and Bishop Załuski. Needless to say, their defection was encouraged by money; in the case of Hieronim Lubomirski it was the 40,000 talers given to his wife Constance.[124] It was also a case of *cherchez la femme* when, late in 1697, Radziejowski started to signal his wish for a rapprochement. In this case the conduit was his mistress, Konstancja Towiańska, whom – in the time-honoured fashion of Catholic priests – he called his 'housekeeper' but everyone else called 'La Cardinale'.[125] She had already taken money from Polignac and later was to add the Elector of Brandenburg to the list of her benefactors.[126] Further defections from the opposition camp were encouraged when Pope Innocent XII at last overcame his doubts, in November congratulating Augustus on his conversion and proclaiming proudly to the world at the beginning of 1698 that the leader of the German heretics had been reclaimed for the Church.[127] There was still some way to go before Augustus could relax. An attempted 'Pacification Sejm' in April 1698 proved abortive, although it was followed by a deal with Radziejowski the following month which brought his insurrection to an end. This was the Treaty of Łowicz, named after Radziejowski's estate where it was signed, by which Augustus renewed his commitment to Catholicism, agreed to withdraw his Saxon troops, and promised to reimburse Radziejowski for the sums he had advanced to Polignac during the election campaign. The papal nuncio had played a decisive role in the mediation.[128] A second attempt at a Pacification Sejm in June 1699 was surprisingly successful, formally recognizing Augustus as the lawful King of Poland.[129]

Why Augustus won

Two years after his election, Augustus could afford to relax a little. Lithuania was still unsettled, although even there the endemic infighting between the dominant Sapieha clan and the rest had died down for the time being. This is a good moment to reflect on his achievement, not least because it reveals a lot about what made for success and failure in Europe at the time. Of the several explanations available, pride of place in the negative category must go to the failure of French policy. Louis XIV simply would not commit enough money, nor could he provide the impetus that was sadly lacking in his chosen candidate. Understandably perhaps, Conti had been reluctant to leave the comforts of Versailles and Paris for the relative austerity of eastern Europe. So he delayed his departure from France until it was too late, and abandoned Poland as soon as the first Saxon cavalryman hove into view. Louis would have done much better to have accepted Augustus's offer of an alliance, made on at least three separate occasions, twice through Baron Rosen, in Rome early in 1697 and Copenhagen in April, and again through Flemming in Warsaw just before the actual election.[130] Just a glance at a map should have shown that the opportunity to take Silesia as a land bridge between the now-united realms of Saxony and Poland made Augustus a natural enemy of its Habsburg rulers.[131]

Another negative contribution was the role played by Russia. Tsar Peter had no preference for any particular individual unless the candidate in question was supported by the French, in which case he was adamantly opposed. It is easy to see why. In 1696–7 he was still engaged in a war with the Ottomans as part of the Holy Alliance, of which Poland was also a member. A French-sponsored king in Warsaw would certainly withdraw from both the alliance and the war, thus allowing the Ottomans to divert both their own forces and their Tatar allies currently fighting the Poles to the Russian theatre of operations. A Franco-Polish alliance might well also lead to war and the cancellation of the Treaty of Perpetual Peace of 1686, which had confirmed Russian possession of left-bank Ukraine.[132] An inexpensive way of influencing the Polish election was to rattle the sabre periodically. Six months before the actual election, for example, with Conti riding high in the polls, the Russian minister in Warsaw, Aleksei Vasilevich Nikitin, was heard to say that if Conti became king, 100,000 Russian soldiers would immediately invade. A declaration issued to the 'Primate, Senate and the whole Republic' on the very eve of the election was more measured in tone but also warned that success for Conti would be a threat to the 'perpetual peace' between Poland and Russia. It pointed out that the King of France was already the friend and ally of the Turkish sultan, so if the King of Poland was added to that alliance, the unity of Christendom would be shattered. On receipt, Nikitin took it round to the Primate's palace, where a banquet attended by 300 szlachta was underway. Radziejowski refused to accept it on the grounds that Nikitin had arrived unannounced. Undaunted, the envoy went outside and read out a Polish translation to anyone who cared to listen. A second, similar note, received after the election on 29 June, was printed and distributed far and wide.[133]

All this is well authenticated; what is less easy to determine is the effect it had on the Polish szlachta. Were they intimidated by the prospect of the notoriously destructive Russian hordes coming west? Or were they so outraged by Russian interference in their cherished freedom of election that the démarche proved counter-productive? Lucjan Lewitter's verdict, based on an intimate knowledge of a wide range of sources, commands respect: 'No one who has carefully and dispassionately considered the available evidence could possibly deny that the double election was to some extent due to Russian interference.' On the other hand, he also points out that Nikitin was told that, if the election of Conti proved to be unanimous, that second minatory note was not to be presented.[134] It was the skill and determination brought to bear by Augustus and his team which ensured a split election and thus the Russian intervention.

And that identifies the decisive positive explanation. Between them, Augustus, Flemming, Przebendowski and Berend Lehmann commanded more energy, more enterprise, more physical force and more money than the competition.[135] Whether it was his cynically mendacious conversion, or the shameless plundering of Saxon assets, or the rapid transfer of Saxon veterans from the Balkans, or the showering of money on all and sundry, Augustus showed a ruthlessness and speed of action which suggested he had been reading *Julius Caesar* as well as *Richard II*. It was he who took the 'tide in the affairs of men' at the flood, leaving Radziejowski, Jakub Sobieski and Conti 'bound in shallows and in miseries'.[136] He was fortunate that the political culture that had developed in Poland, at least since the monarchy became elective in 1573, was so venal. Reviewing the progress of this latest interregnum, the conclusion is inescapable that everyone involved, from the greatest magnate to the most impoverished szlachta, had no compunction about selling their votes to the highest bidder. Although simple prejudice such as hostility to the French or the Russians or even 'the Germans' (as supporters of any Austrian candidate were termed) certainly played a part, it is hard to find evidence of decisions ever being taken in the public interest, however defined. As Józef Gierowski commented, it was both the longest and the most corrupt interregnum in Polish history (so far).[137] In this environment it was the deepest pocket that determined the outcome. All of Augustus's opponents – Jakub Sobieski, Marysieńka, Polignac – sprayed around what money they had, but their stocks were soon exhausted. To paraphrase Cicero: 'The sinews of a Polish election are infinite money.'[138]

Yet this was not simply an auction, with the kingship being sold to the highest bidder. The place to look for a political programme is the *pacta conventa*, the set of conditions to which every king had to swear before being crowned and which were adjusted at each election to meet current circumstances.[139] Of the thirty-seven articles required in 1697, some refer to abuses of the previous reign, as in 'The Queen shall not meddle in any affairs of state'; some are aimed at Augustus's foreign nationality, as in 'The King's court and guard shall be composed of natives of the Kingdom'; some are designed to reinforce the privileges of the szlachta, as in 'Every nobleman shall be exempted the duty upon salt, and have free possession of mines'; some set out an ambitious foreign policy, as in 'The King shall endeavour to recover the Ukraine, and to conclude a perpetual peace with Muscovy'; many are very specific, as in 'In the trials called *Post Curialia*, the laws called *Pacta Henricea* shall be observed'. Overall there is a strong conservative flavour: 'the method or order usually followed . . . no new economy . . . according to ancient custom . . . the ancient liberties . . . shall be re-established'.

Only the first three could be said to represent an ideological position, and the third of them – 'Liberty of conscience shall continue inviolable' – had been increasingly at odds with practice during the previous century. However, the other two did go to the heart of the Polish constitution. The first asserted the right to a free election and the rejection of hereditary monarchy. This was the szlachta's central political axiom and will be discussed a little later. The second stated: 'No King shall be elected who is not a member of the Roman Catholic Church and does not swear to continue in the same communion.' By 1697 the high waters of the Counter-Reformation had washed away what had once been the most multi-confessional landscape in Europe: in 1572 Protestants had been in a majority in the Polish lower house, while in the Senate Protestants and Catholics were evenly balanced.[140] A century later Catholics had achieved a virtual monopoly, the last Protestant member of the Sejm dying in 1718.[141] Moreover, this was militant Baroque Catholicism with a capital 'B', untainted by any mere Jansenist reform impulses.[142] No doubt briefed by Flemming and Przebendowski, Augustus was happy to play the conversion card for all it was worth. At his coronation he issued a declaration proclaiming:

> Who can recite the mighty deeds of the Lord who by a special miracle of his divine grace has plucked Us from darkest heresy to the all-holy Roman Catholic Faith. We will not prophesy what Almighty God, who does nothing without a reason, intends by granting Us the Holy Faith and putting Us on the throne of this bulwark of Christianity, other than to spread the gospel in lands where the Muslim temples of idolatry have shamefully stood for so long, for Our heart burns with ardour against the enemies of the Cross, and to devote to the struggle the resources of Our lands.[143]

The iron cage

Of all the roles played by Augustus, 'Roman Catholic Crusader' must rank among the least convincing and it may be doubted whether even the more devout Polish szlachta believed him. Turning back the tide of Islam never did engage his energies. These were prodigious but were soon absorbed and then exhausted by the intractable problems he was about to encounter. As he struggled to turn his royal status into royal power, did he perhaps have an inkling that he had just made a terrible mistake? One acute observer was in no doubt. The Duchess of Orléans, better known as Liselotte of the Palatinate,[144] wrote to Sophie, Electress of Hanover on 1 August 1697 the following shrewd assessment:

> That the Elector of Saxony could not be satisfied with being an Elector only goes to show what I have long observed, that no one can be really happy in this world and everyone foolishly sets about throwing away his happiness, for this Elector would have been a thousand times happier if he had gone on enjoying a quiet and peaceful life as Elector of Saxony instead of becoming King of such a factious and volatile nation, of which he will never be the absolute lord and master but will only ever be king in name only and not in reality.[145]

3.

The Iron Cage

A weak state

By making the most of a favourable international situation; by spending huge sums of money; by pretending he shared traditional Polish values (wearing national costume after his coronation, for example); and by showing superior initiative, Augustus had won. Reviewing the next thirty-five years (he died on 1 February 1733), it has to be concluded that his decision to seek election was a terrible mistake. All his life he was a keen but inept risk-taker, a gambler who always called *va banque!* and always raised when he should have folded, but this was one wager that brought him nothing but stress, privation, disappointment and misery. The one political achievement that might have made him think it had all been worthwhile – the eventual election of his son as his successor – was not secured until after his death. Yet, for all his apparent failures, Augustus did qualify to be ranked among the great European rulers, not by the successful application of hard power, but by his transformation of Dresden and its region into one of the finest cultural complexes in Europe. It was a feat handicapped, not facilitated, by the Polish throne. How much greater would have been the return if the millions of talers, and tens of thousands of lives, squandered in the fruitless pursuit of dynastic and territorial gain, had been freed for investment in Saxony.

Augustus can only have had a superficial knowledge of what he was getting himself into. All his interest and experience had been in western and southern Europe. He had never travelled in Poland, did not speak the language and never bothered to learn it.[1] Since he had spent the interregnum in Hungary, Vienna or Dresden, he arrived in Poland unencumbered by prior knowledge. It is unlikely that either Flemming or Przebendowski had alerted him to the intractability of the problems awaiting him, since both had a vested interest in his success. Happily, none of them carried the teleological burden. Knowing that Poland disappeared from the map of Europe for more than a century, following the three partitions of 1772–95, has created the temptation to turn its previous history into an endless investigation of the causes of this catastrophe. So every scholar should bear in mind Leopold von Ranke's dictum: 'every epoch stands in a direct relationship to God, and its value in no way depends on what came after it, it has its own identity'.[2] Nevertheless, many of the problems besetting Poland were of long standing and need to be discussed, however briefly, to indicate that Augustus was confronted by a very weak state.

The political inheritance

The problems were of three kinds, although they all interacted, the first being constitutional/political. The place to start is the closing years of the reign of Sigismund II. Knowing that he would be the last of the Jagiellons, in 1569 he organized an amalgamation of the Kingdom of Poland with the Grand Duchy of Lithuania, hitherto ruled in a personal union only, to form the Polish–Lithuanian Commonwealth. Although it was not unusual for royal dynasties to die out, in most cases a cadet branch could be found – the Bourbons to replace the Valois, the Stuarts to replace the Tudors, the Austrian Habsburgs and the Bourbons to replace the Spanish Habsburgs, the Hanoverians to replace the Stuarts, and so on. In the Polish case this was not possible. So, if a successor could neither be procreated nor discovered, he would have to be elected. So far, so obvious, but what made the Polish case special were the arrangements laid down for the election after the death of Sigismund in 1572. Directed by Jan Zamoyski, it was decided that the franchise should embrace all adult male szlachta, who would be summoned to the great meadow at Wola near Warsaw to vote in person (*viritim*).[3] Zamoyski's status as one of the most powerful of the Polish magnates did not prevent him creating an inclusive image of noble equality, with a vote of the least of the landless szlachta counting for as much as his own. By eschewing the more obvious solution of election by the Sejm, Zamoyski had invented a tradition which was to have a profound influence on the course of Polish politics.[4]

The new regime did not get off to a good start. The first successful candidate was Henri de Valois, brother of Charles IX, King of France. Henri did not like Poland, and Poland did not like Henri. He did not arrive until January 1574, eight months after his election, and left again in June the same year, when the death of Charles elevated him to the French throne as Henri III. Despite its brevity, his sojourn did immortalize his memory by giving his name to the 'Henrician Articles'. It must have been through gritted teeth that the new king agreed to restrictions on royal power so much at odds with the autocratic concept of monarchy prevailing in his native France. He and his successors were required to convene a Sejm every two years; to accept a senatorial council whose consent was required for all policies in the intervals between Sejms; to seek senatorial approval for marriage; and to respect the privileges of the nobility, especially religious freedom. Crucially, any new taxes were conditional on Sejm approval. Perhaps most ominous of all the articles was that which legitimated resistance on the part of the szlachta if the king acted against the country's 'laws, liberties, privileges or customs'.[5] Well might the new king exclaim: 'on my faith, these Poles have only made me *a judge*!'.[6] Probably bisexual, the twenty-two-year-old Henri may also have been repelled by the further condition that he marry the late king's fifty-year-old sister Anna.[7] Looking back on the events of 1573–5, Konstanty Szaniawski, Bishop of Cujavia, lamented in 1717: 'the greater part of the Commonwealth's liberties date from the times of King Henri and since then they have degenerated into a veritable anarchy.'[8]

That was a minority view and moreover one that owed a lot to the special circumstances of 1717, the year of the 'Silent Sejm'.[9] For most of the szlachta, it was the threat of despotism that caused anxiety. Writing early in Augustus's reign, Stanisław Dunin Karwicki advanced a long list of royal prerogatives, foremost among them the control of huge amounts of patronage (both lay and ecclesiastical) and land.[10] He had a point, for in the king's gift were about 25,000 offices and around 15 per cent of the total land surface of the Commonwealth.[11] Yet every apparent despotic tool was flawed: the fortunate office-holders were irremovable, could only be dismissed for felony and had no reason to display gratitude once the ink was dry on their deed of appointment.[12] The same applied to the distribution of royal estates, which had to be leased again within six weeks of any vacancy and were then held for life.[13] Yet *any* power exercised by the king was suspicious to the szlachta, whose concern for their 'golden liberty' bordered on paranoia. This has been well put by Anna Grześkowiak-Krwawicz:

> he must not have power over the army, as he might use it against the nation; he must not control the treasury, as access to funds would enable him, not only to corrupt the nation's representatives but also to raise troops and pursue autonomous policies; he especially must not have the right to impose taxes, as this would enable him to oppress his citizens; he must not have any influence over foreign policy, as he might drag the country into war or make unfavourable alliances; the system of justice must remain outside his realm of influence; under no circumstances should he have any influence over legislation, despite the fact he was the only individual with legislative initiative.[14]

The mismatch between szlachta fears and the powers the king actually exercised was too obvious to miss. A popular simile making the rounds was 'the king is like a Queen Bee – head of the hive, but with no sting'.[15] It is a verdict repeated by many historians, as in 'Poland was a confederation of 200,000 hereditary sovereigns' (Frans Gunnar Bengtsson); 'a conglomerate of 60,000 noble dominions' (Thomas Wünsch); 'The Polish king was a *princeps*, a "leading dignitary" not a *dominus*, a "lord" ' (Jerzy Lukowski); 'The king, for all practical purposes, had been deprived of effective power. He was regarded by the magnates as a pawn' (Catherine S. Leach).[16]

If the king was weak, so were the central organs of government. By the Henrician Articles, the Sejm could meet for only six weeks and even then often spent most of the time arguing about factional issues. Unlike any other European legislative assembly, the Polish Sejm insisted on unanimity. A fundamental law was the *Nihil Novi* of 1505 which decreed 'nothing new without common consent' (*Nihil novi nisi commune consensu*).[17] In its original form, the principle only envisaged the need for groups of protestors to be accommodated by negotiation and compromise, so the full negative effects were long delayed.[18] It was a new and alarming departure when it was deemed to apply to a single dissenting individual, as was the case in 1652 when an agent of the Radziwiłł interest announced his opposition to the prolongation of the Sejm. This was the notorious *liberum veto*. When invoked, it necessitated the termination of the Sejm and the invalidation of all measures agreed before that point. The Sejm did not pass individual laws but all of them together at the end of their deliberations as 'Sejm constitutions' so if one failed, all did.[19] Just to make matters worse, the *liberum veto* could be deployed at the *sejmiki* too.[20] In Robert Frost's authoritative view, the *liberum veto* 'sounded the death knell for the Sejm's chances of developing into an effective parliamentary body'.[21] Józef Gierowski apostrophized it as 'a serious disease'.[22] Of forty-four Sejms convened in the second half of the seventeenth century, fifteen were broken and two more ended without enacting a single piece of legislation.[23] Taking a longer view, of the fifty-three Sejms held between 1582 and 1762, 60 per cent ended without result: the *liberum veto* had become a *liberum rumpo*.[24]

In the long intervals between Sejms, policy-making devolved to the king and the Senate council, the latter seen, in true Polish style, 'both as an organ of the central government and a check upon it'.[25] There were no ministries, no centrally organized judicial system and no diplomatic service.[26] Nor was there a bureaucracy, prompting a foreign visitor early in the eighteenth century to remark that there were fewer civil servants in vast Poland than in the tiny Italian principality of Lucca.[27] Consequently, implementation of decisions made at the centre by king or Sejm depended on the *sejmiki* in the provinces. In the course of the seventeenth century, their responsibilities grew to embrace most areas of public life, including finance and military matters. Constitutionally, it was only the king who was authorized to convene a *sejmik*, a requirement that was easily evaded by the simple expedient of repeated adjournments, so that by the last quarter of the century they were meeting on average once a month.[28] For the szlachta, the *sejmiki* represented grass-roots democracy, more direct and therefore more legitimate than the central Sejm.[29] Unfortunately, they were also just as prone to rupture. As Richard Butterwick has pointed out, this meant that the untimely death of a district judge could paralyse the courts for months, if not years, as no successor could be chosen by a *sejmik* that was repeatedly broken.[30]

Given that the 'golden liberty' was confined to the 6–8 per cent of the population enjoying noble status,[31] this was not a regime that could be described as a democracy. Nor could that noun be used even when preceded by the qualifier 'szlachta', for increasingly it was the magnates who predominated. This was a development which progressed inexorably during the seventeenth century for socio-economic reasons to be discussed shortly. Lip service continued to be paid to the myth of equality between richest and poorest nobles, as in the popular saying 'a nobleman in his manor is equal to a palatine',[32] but it was the magnates who came to dominate. By the time Augustus arrived in Poland, it had become 'a magnate oligarchy' or 'a federation of magnate-ruled statelets'.[33]

The 'Deluge' and its aftermath

A powerful boost to this and other baleful developments had been delivered during the disastrous period beginning in 1648 and bearing the graphic sobriquet the 'Deluge' (*Potop*). The insurrection in

1648 by Cossacks and Ukrainian peasants led by Bohdan Khmelnyt-skyi was followed by war with Russia, Sweden and Prussia. The shock was all the greater because Poland had escaped the worst of the strife that had wracked Europe for the previous century. There had been no Polish equivalent of the French Religious Wars, the Revolt of the Netherlands or the English Civil War. In 1630, just as the Thirty Years War was devastating the Holy Roman Empire next door, the magnate and poet Krzysztof Opaliński boasted that Poles could view the carnage 'like a safe spectator on the shores of the sea [who] gazes calmly upon the tempest raging before it'.[34] This was partly due to the confessional pluralism enshrined in the Henrician Articles and partly to political energy. As Robert Frost has written, 'Poland–Lithuania was the most dynamic state in northern and eastern Europe between 1450 and 1617.' As the German crusading states on the southern Baltic decomposed, Poland had taken the lion's share of the carcase.[35]

Alas, these happy times turned out to be the calm before the storm, which struck belatedly but ferociously. The horde that followed Khmelnytskyi may have numbered as many as 300,000, driven by hatred of nobles, townspeople and Jews and a lust for loot.[36] By the time the *Potop* wars finally ended in 1667, the population of Poland had declined by between a quarter and a third, in some areas even by as much as half. Many towns, including Kraków, Warsaw and Wilno (the capital of Lithuania), were reduced to ashes.[37] Between 100,000 and 125,000 Jews perished in repeated pogroms.[38] In the view of a recent director of the Royal Palace in Warsaw, the *Potop* was more devastating than the Second World War.[39] One long-term detrimental result was a further weakening of an already anaemic urban culture. Another was paradoxical: because the Commonwealth had somehow managed to survive this ultimate challenge, conservatives could argue that the old ways were still the best ways. In particular, the heroic defence of the Pauline monastery Jasna Góra at Częstochowa, which housed the fabled image of the Black Madonna, against attacks by the Swedish heretics confirmed that God was still protecting His chosen people.[40]

So the reform programmes of the 1650s and 1660s could be consigned to the archive as lost opportunities.[41] This was the time when the *liberum veto* came to be seen as essential for the preservation of the szlachta's 'golden liberty' and a bulwark against monarchical absolutism. The appetite came with the eating – it was used twice between 1652 and 1662, but five times more between 1664 and 1668. [42] By the Sejm of 1688, polarization had reached the point at which not even a marshal could be chosen and so no business could be initiated. The damage inflicted by this immobility was highlighted by news of a Tatar incursion in the south, resulting in the abduction of thousands of inhabitants, many of whom perished from cold and hunger as they were transported to the Crimean slave markets. Another victim was the failed attempt to reconquer the southern fortress of Kamieniec Podolski.[43] Antony Polonsky's bleak verdict on the *Potop* was: 'the Commonwealth never fully recovered from this debacle'.[44]

The military and financial inheritance

As these last two episodes suggested, the Commonwealth was failing in its fundamental task of protecting its members. The Polish army was no longer the force that had crushed the Swedes at Kircholm in 1605 or the Ottomans at Khotyn in 1621.[45] The glorious charge of the cavalry at Vienna in 1683 proved to be a last hurrah. The decline had been both absolute and relative. While the neighbouring states had been adapting, the Polish–Lithuanian forces had been regressing. Whether the changes in the conduct of war in Europe in the sixteenth and seventeenth centuries can be called a 'military revolution' has been a much-debated issue. That they occurred is not in doubt. Geoffrey Hosking has helpfully summarized them under four headings: 1. the deployment of large masses of well-disciplined infantry equipped with firearms; 2. the use of highly mobile light cavalry able to fight when necessary as infantry (dragoons); 3. an increase in the size and penetrative power of artillery; 4. a strengthening of fortifications designed to withstand this artillery.[46] Only the second of those characterized the Polish way of war, but all could increasingly be found among their Swedish, Prussian and Russian competitors.

This was partly due to a gradual loss of ambition and enterprise in the course of the seventeenth century. The energy which had fuelled the capture of Stockholm in 1598 or Moscow in 1610 had ebbed away as the szlachta came to insist on a pacific foreign policy: they would defend their country but not seek to expand it.[47] Even the great expedition to Vienna in 1683 had been opposed by many. In her general history of the period, Urszula Augustyniak has argued that the army came to be seen more as a threat to liberty than a means of protection. This encouraged a fatalist attitude which left the defence of the Commonwealth to God and viewed defeat in war as His punishment for Poland's toleration of heretics. The upshot was that, at a time when other European countries were increasing the size of their armies, the Poles were engaged in demilitarization.[48] She was supported by Mirosław Nagielski, who identified as the most intractable problem 'a simple lack of fighting spirit (ducha bojowego)'.[49] If these assessments lack precision, they are supported by statistics relating to the military participation ratio, for whereas Prussia maintained three to four soldiers per 100 inhabitants, Poland–Lithuania could only muster one per 500–600.[50] The aversion to a standing army was of course shared by the British, who also viewed it as a threat to civil liberties, the difference being that Great Britain is an island and moreover one that was protected by a large navy. For a continental power surrounded by potential predators, this was one libertarian prejudice the Poles could not afford.[51]

On the other hand, nor could they afford to have a standing army of any strength from a financial point of view. To quote Cicero once more, this time in his own persona, 'the sinews of war are infinite money'. Even delivering a finite sum of modest proportions was beyond the Polish fiscal system as it developed in the early modern period. The levy on the vast royal domains of a quarter (kwarta) was supposed to cover defence, justice and administration, as well as the personal costs of the king and his court. In practice it was wholly inadequate, sufficient to finance only 1,500–2,000 soldiers.[52] One way forward, popular elsewhere in Europe, was an indirect tax on consumption in the form of an excise. That was tried in 1657, 1659 and 1673, but never became a permanent imposition, thanks to opposition from the szlachta. Customs dues and the Jewish poll tax helped, but did not go very far. The same could be said for income derived from the mining of salt, lead and silver and profits generated by minting coin.[53]

In the second half of the seventeenth century, any attempt at reform faded away, as responsibility for maintaining individual units of the army was passed on to the *sejmiki*, whose chief concern, not unnaturally, was to limit their liability. The upshot was that the regular income required to underpin a viable system of public credit never materialized. Although the Sejm had the knowledge and the legislative control to do what was necessary to modernize the country's fiscal system, it was inhibited by its ideological attachment to a weak state. Despite being the second-largest country in Europe, Poland's annual budget was 1/36th of France's and 1/18th of the Ottoman Empire's. Even Denmark's was twice as large.[54] In the judgement of Anna Filipczak-Kocur, 'it was the nobility's pursuit of political "freedom" – virtually at any cost in the later seventeenth century – which prevented the Commonwealth of the two nations from becoming a modern fiscal state'.[55]

Lack of money meant lack of numbers. When Augustus arrived in the country in 1697, the regular (*komputowe*) Crown army was nominally 18,250-strong, to which must be added the 6,000 on the Lithuanian establishment.[56] Numerical deficiency was just one of the fourteen causes of military weakness identified by Mirosław Nagielski, which also included organizational confusion; inappropriate tactics (what worked when fighting the Tatars or Cossacks was ineffective against western European armies); the mediocre quality of leaders appointed for political reasons; inferior weaponry (slow to adopt flintlock muskets); low level of training; and a lack of *esprit de corps*.[57] Somewhat more positive was Marek Wagner, who pointed to the significant improvement of the artillery achieved by Marcin Kątski, but even he concluded that the overall verdict on the state of the army in 1697 had to be 'unequivocally negative', for it had fallen behind in financing, organization, equipment, training and tactics.[58] To that can be added indiscipline resulting from pay that was always irregular and often wholly absent. Just as the Convocation Sejm was getting under way at the end of August 1696, news arrived of the formation of a confederation of the Crown army at Wiśniowiec (Vyshnivets), east of Lwów, led by Piotr Bogusław Baranowski. Although the stated grievance was pay, it was also a faction-fight between two magnate clans, Lubomirski (supporting Conti in the upcoming elections) and Jabłonowski (supporting Jakub Sobieski).[59] To make matters worse, the long-simmering struggle in Lithuania between the dominant Sapiehas and the rest of the nobility was now coming to the boil with the formation of another confederation, this one led by Grzegorz Ogiński.[60] In any other country these would have been called mutinies, but in the Commonwealth they were legitimized by a long tradition of quasi-legal insurrection. It was not until the following spring that a settlement of the Baranowski *rokosz* was negotiated. In the meantime, the unpaid soldiers busily helped themselves to whatever they could find. A state in which the armed forces are out of control of the government and legislature, but wreak havoc on their own people, is a weak state indeed.

One final military problem needs to be mentioned, for it was to have a detrimental effect on Augustus's attempts to govern Poland. This was the role of the hetmans, or military commanders. There were four of them – two Grand Hetmans (one each for 'Crown' i.e. Poland and Lithuania) and two Field Hetmans as their deputies. As they served for life, they were more like independent warlords than royal servants. Not even the Habsburgs, who were famously prone to reward failure by promotion, could boast such an invidious arrangement. In theory they could be removed for treason, although that did not stop the Lithuanian Grand Hetman Janusz Radziwiłł switching to the Swedish side in 1655 or his next-but-one successor Michał Kazimierz Pac accepting 100,000 zlotys to place his army at the disposal of Emperor Leopold rather than King John Sobieski.[61] Nor did Dymitr Jerzy Wiśniowiecki feel inhibited about conspiring with the Austrians to depose King John despite his appointment as Grand Hetman of the Crown.[62] The *rokosz* launched by the Crown Grand Hetman Jerzy Lubomirski in 1665–6 ended in the withdrawal of King John Casimir's reform programme and his abdication in 1668.[63] And so on. In theory the king was commander-in-chief, in practice he was supplanted by the hetmans, who progressively expanded their authority to include organization, military justice and even diplomacy.[64] The Commonwealth itself had no permanent diplomatic service, but the hetmans had the right to maintain their own representatives in Transylvania, Moldavia, Wallachia, Crimea and at Constantinople.[65]

Sarmatism

Underpinning the szlachta's concern with defending their 'golden liberty' against monarchical absolutism was a unique political culture that came to be known as 'Sarmatism'. As with so many ideologies, the '-ism' was invented (in 1765) only as the phenomenon itself was fading, and was intended to be derogatory.[66] Another familiar paradox was its relatively recent development, despite purporting to refer to events of great antiquity. Indeed, there could be no older ancestral claim, for when God addressed Adam and Eve in the Garden of Eden, the language he used was Polish, or so the szlachta Franciscan friar Wojciech Dębołęcki maintained.[67] Only slightly less fanciful was the belief that the Polish nation originated with Japheth, son of Noah.[68] From his seed there grew a mighty people, who during the early centuries of the Christian era migrated north. These were the Sarmatians, God's chosen people. Inventive medieval chroniclers traced their further progress by recounting a geographical division in the sixth or seventh century when three brothers went off on hunting expeditions in different directions: Čech to the west, Ruś to the east and Lech to the north. By the six-teenth century, Lech had been promoted from a mythical to a historical figure, hailed as the founder of the Polish nation.[69]

As they progressed from Mesopotamia (the putative home of Noah) to central Europe, the Sarmatians had demonstrated their martial prowess by defying Alexander the Great and defeating Julius Caesar. So impressed had been the former that he assigned them dominion of all the lands between the North Sea and the Adriatic.[70] This sort of imaginative scenario was not peculiar to the Poles, of course, for most European ethnicities looked back through the mists of myth to find heroic ancestors. However, the Sarmatian ver-sion, as it developed in the seventeenth century, took on a number of special characteristics. There is general agreement that a water-shed was reached with Mikołaj Zebrzydowski's *rokosz* of 1606–7. Although eventually pacified, the insurrection did paralyse royal attempts at reform, inspire a flood of publications extolling the Sar-matian world view, and ensure that the future belonged to the nobility, especially the magnates. Indeed, Piotr S. Wandycz has argued that it killed off any hope that szlachta democracy might have developed into parliamentary government, leaving instead only in its wake 'an unruly oligarchy'.[71]

At the heart of the Sarmatian ideology was the cult of szlachta liberty. To western political theorists, this looked more like licence. Montesquieu was not alone in thinking that 'the independence of each individual is the purpose of the laws of Poland, and what results from this is the oppression of all'.[72] There was certainly a devil-take-the-hindmost attitude among some Poles when express-ing their attachment to unrestrained liberty, as in the defiant cry of the Jesuit Walenty Pęski (1632–81): 'the purgatory of freedom is better than the hell of despotism. Thanks to the protection of Provi-dence we keep falling and yet we shine, we keep perishing and yet we live. We do not disapprove of the institutions of foreign coun-tries. They are good for them, but not for us. With this anarchy of ours we succeed just as well as any other nation with the best of governments.'[73] More classical was Rafał Leszczyński's dictum, borrowed from Sallust: 'better to have dangerous liberty than pacific servitude' (*malo periculosam libertatem quam quietam servitum*).[74] As Poland–Lithuania was bordered by Russia, the Ottoman Empire, the Habsburg Monarchy and Brandenburg–Prussia, the feeling that the country was an island of liberty in an ocean of despotism was certainly understandable.[75] Moreover, as the seventeenth century progressed, the increasingly absolutist regimes in the latter group seemed ever more likely to swamp the sole surviving land of liberty in east-central Europe, a fear that fuelled a potent combination of pride and paranoia.

In the same way that slave-owning Thomas Jefferson was vulnerable to a charge of hypocrisy when he repeated the Sallust quotation just cited, so was Rafał Leszczyński, who controlled – even if technically he did not 'own' – a large number of serfs. That was just one of the contradictions inherent in the Sarmatian liberty cult. The Polish nobles' ingenious chroniclers knew their Bible well enough to be able to deal with that problem. The solution was found in 'dual origin': the Polish szlachta descended from Japheth, the most virtuous of Noah's sons. The mass of the population, on the other hand, were the descendants of Ham, the most degenerate of Noah's sons, who 'saw' his father's nakedness and was punished by a curse laid on his own son: 'a servant of servants shall he be unto his brethren'.[76] So, it was concluded, the exclusion of non-nobles from the golden liberty of their masters was authorized by Holy Scripture.

Also beyond the pale were non-Catholics. This was a more contentious issue, because religious toleration had been written into the constitutional settlement of 1573 and was formally renewed by each new monarch on his election. It was a pluralism that was very unusual in late-sixteenth-century Europe and in Poland too it became progressively more unusual as the Counter-Reformation gathered momentum. Sarmatism was never a fixed programme, it evolved with the changing aspirations of the bulk of the szlachta. By the 1650s at the latest, a militant form of Catholicism was becoming central to their self-image. During the *Potop* wars against Russia and Sweden in the 1650s, when the loyalty of both the Orthodox and the Lutheran nobility was called into question, Catholicism became established as 'a defining mark of the Sarmatian identity'.[77] The nobles saw themselves as God's chosen instrument, protecting Europe of the True Faith against both heretics and infidels.[78]

The association was confirmed by the wave of Catholic enthusiasm unleashed by the victory over the Swedes at Jasna Góra in 1655 and King John Casimir's subsequent proclamation of the Virgin Mary as 'Queen of Poland' in Lwów Cathedral on 1 April the following year.[79] The old faith also took on a national-cum-social distinction, as Protestantism was seen as an urban Bohemian (Hussite) or German (Lutheran) import favoured by non-Sarmatian merchants and artisans. So 'a fanatical Counter-Reformation Catholicism became a component of Sarmatian patriotism' (Neal Ascherson).[80] The Sarmatian God was the szlachta's ally, keeping a close watch on their inviolable liberties. He could rely on the help of the Queen of Heaven (also Queen of Poland after 1656), presented as a staunch defender of the 'noble liberties of the Sarmatians' by Dionizy Chełstowski in his poem *The Splendour of the Crown of Twelve Stars* (1711). Heaven was an idealized version of the Polish–Lithuanian Commonwealth, albeit one with a perfectly functioning Sejm, subjects who never rebelled, no external enemies and a king who would never dream of imposing an *absolutum dominium*.[81]

As so often, religious hostility was intensified by politics. All Sarmatians were Slavs, but not all Slavs were Sarmatians. Once again, the chroniclers came to their aid, declaring that the Russians were not Sarmatians at all but Scythians, a people of a much lower order.[82] All the other Slav nations would be welcome in the capacious Sarmatian tent – so long as they recognized that 'Poland is the capital and queen of all Sarmatia' (*Polonia caput ac regina totius Sarmatiae*).[83] Russia was an odious place of tyranny, dismissed by the popular epithet 'coercion is a Russian thing' (*musi to na Rusi*).[84] As Klaus Zernack has shown, the negative image of Russia was well established by 1600 and went on intensifying during the following century.[85] Xenophobia was not only directed against their eastern neighbours, however. All Polish historians writing about Sarmatism have drawn attention to this as a prevalent feature. Stanisław Cynarski, for example, portrayed the typical Sarmatian as demonizing all foreigners, especially Germans and Italians, and apostrophizing the French as reckless, the English as hypocritical, the Dutch as dim, the Spaniards as proud, and so on, in a parade of familiar stereotypes.[86] The devil was often depicted wearing German dress.[87] The obverse was a fierce pride in what were claimed to be uniquely Polish characteristics, neatly summed up by the celebrated poet Maciej Kazimierz Sarbiewski: 'You won't find another nation that is not inferior to the Poles in some way, and you won't find any to which the Poles are not superior in some way.'[88]

This was a sense of distinctiveness that came to be expressed in a Sarmatian form of dress and appearance, an idiosyncratic adaptation of Turkish and Tatar models. Its basic element was a *żupan* (a long button-through kaftan), over which was worn a *kontusz* (a waistcoat with long sleeves cut open below the elbow) or a *delia* (a robe cut close at the top but loose below the waist), secured by a long ornate sash bound round the waist. Wide breeches could be added underneath. For winter wear, a *bekiesz* (a long sheepskin coat decorated with braid and fastened with loops) or a *ferezja* (a heavy cloak lined with fur) was added. Boots were made of soft leather, caps of fur. Accessories usually included a sword and/or a pole-axe.[89] The vestiary ensemble was completed by a partly shaven head resembling a monk's tonsure, counterbalanced by luxuriant moustaches.[90] Following his election, Augustus had himself depicted with the former, his long hair braided in a chaplet, but remained clean-shaven.[91] Needless to say, rank and fortune were reflected in the nature of the fabric and the amount of gold thread and precious stones used in its decoration, the *kontusz* sash being the main medium for ostentatious display. A Polish noble in full fig would certainly have stood out from the crowd at a western court, but no record has survived of anyone bold enough to wear it there.

The appeal of Sarmatian culture to the Polish szlachta was a symptom of narrowing horizons. The palmy days of the mid-sixteenth century, when the country was a pluralist haven and the ark of the refugees, darkened when the pressures exerted by a vigorous Counter-Reformation intensified. This was spearheaded by the Jesuits, who dominated all aspects of the movement.[92] By 1552, four years before the death of their founder, Ignatius Loyola, there was already a college in Vienna to which Polish ordinands soon flocked.[93] The first Jesuit house in the Commonwealth was founded at Braniewo in 1564, followed by Vilnius in 1569, Poznań in 1571, Polotsk in 1580, Danzig in 1585, Toruń in 1593, Lwów in 1585, and so on.[94] There were twenty-five Jesuit colleges by 1600, by which time they had attracted several thousand students, Catholics and non-Catholics, by offering an excellent education.[95] A dramatic illustration of Jesuit success was the election of John Casimir Vasa as king in 1648, for he was both a Jesuit and a cardinal and had to seek papal dispensation to revoke his vows before ascending the throne. After his abdication twenty years later he returned to the Order, finding an agreeable retirement home as Abbot of the Benedictine monastery of Saint-Germain-des-Prés in Paris.

A country which voluntarily chooses a Jesuit as its sovereign is not a country in which non-Catholics can feel comfortable. The discomfort had begun with the election of Stephen Báthory as king back in 1576. Although anxious to maintain religious peace, he was also an enthusiastic promoter of the Jesuits, founding several colleges and elevating their academy in Wilno to university status. He also made full use of his most important prerogative, by favouring Catholics when appointing to high office or leasing royal estates. It was a policy continued by his long-reigning successor Sigismund III (r. 1587–1632). Any magnate seeking to further the interests of himself and his family had a strong material motive for remaining loyal to the old faith, or embracing it, or returning to it. An early indication of the force of this consideration was provided by the fortunes of the Nieśwież branch of the Radziwiłłs. Following the death of Prince Mikołaj 'The Black', who had been the leading supporter of Calvinism in Lithuania, his eldest son – also Nicholas – not only converted but induced his numerous siblings to do likewise. He himself became Grand Marshal of Lithuania, while his brother Jerzy became Bishop of Vilnius and then Bishop of Kraków (the richest see in the country) and a cardinal.[96] Of course this is not to exclude the possibility that the Holy Spirit was also at work, guiding the Radziwiłłs back to the path of righteousness. Other high-profile converts were Jan Zamoyski (1542–1605), who became Grand Chancellor of the Crown and Crown Grand Hetman, and Lew Sapieha (1557–1633), who became Grand Chancellor of Lithuania and Grand Lithuanian Hetman.[97] In Counter-Reformatory Poland there were earthly as well as heavenly rewards for being a Catholic.

As this suggests, it was the failure of the non-Catholics to capture the monarchy which led to their eventual exclusion (as in France in the same period). They had failed to change the structure of the established Church. There was no dissolution of the monasteries, for example. With the bishops still in the Senate and leading magnates beginning to drift back, the balance of confessional power tilted steadily in favour of the old faith. When Sigismund III, who had been educated by Jesuits, came to the throne there were thirty-eight Protestant senators; when he died there were just two.[98] Moreover, this was not just the fate of the elites. The principle of *cuius regio ejus religio* (he who rules decides the religion) worked just as well in the Commonwealth as it did in the Holy Roman Empire. Every time a noble changed religion so were his subjects encouraged, or even required, to follow him. In the Poznań palatinate, for example, around two-thirds of Protestant churches were returned to Catholicism between 1592 and 1627.[99] After 1632 no new Protestant churches could be built in royal towns.[100] In the same year, the Election Sejm inserted a new clause requiring 'due observance of the rights of the Catholic Church' (*z zachowaniem praw Kościoła katolickiego*), which was to prove a powerful weapon in the campaign to marginalize non-Catholics.[101] It was not just a case of exclusion and coercion. The Jesuits conducted missionary activities aimed at all sections of society. They were supported by numerous other religious orders, old and new, which expanded rapidly in the seventeenth century. The number of monasteries increased from

227 with 3,600 inmates in 1600 and to almost 500 with 7,500 in 1650, to 674 in 1700 with 10,000.[102] The trend continued: between 1700 and the first partition in 1773, the number of male houses increased by 48 per cent and female houses by 40 per cent.[103] As these figures suggest, there was no equivalent in Poland of the Jansenist or 'Reform Catholic' movement which invigorated ecclesiastical and religious structures in the Habsburg Monarchy and many of the principalities of the Holy Roman Empire. In his penetrating analysis of the decline of the Ottoman Empire, William McNeill blamed the persecution of the Shi'a 'heresy' for cultural ossification and a 'studied indifference to any but the traditional patterning of the life of the mind [which] allowed Europe to outstrip the Ottoman world in one realm of thought and action after another'.[104] *Mutatis mutandis*, the same could be said of Poland.

Growth of Latin-rite monasteries 1600 to 1772–3[105]

Year	Number of orders	Number of provinces of regular clergy	Number of religious houses	Number of members
1600	15	15	227	3,600
1650	20	24	470	7,500
1700	27	34	674	10,000
1772–3	27	46	884	14,500

Sarmatian culture was made up of chivalrous ideals, pacifism, a deep attachment to a rural way of life, provincialism, generous hospitality, suspicion of 'foreign ways', ancestor worship, a cult of liberty, patriotism, piety, all the Christian virtues and a love of history that often merged into myth. Viewed on its own terms it was an attractive package, conjuring up an image of a pastoral idyll populated by patriarchal squires, benevolent parish priests and happy peasants. Polish historians have been less sympathetic, suggesting that this was an increasingly ossified culture without a future, as it turned more introverted, selfish and class-conscious. In Urszula Augustyniak's view, chivalry became martyrology, the cult of the homeland became xenophobia, and religious devotion became bigotry and superstition.[106] Stanisław Cynarski's withering verdict was: 'Sarmatism, born under the influence of historical legend, became synonymous with conservatism, devotion, backwardness and darkness.'[107] It was appropriate, he suggested, that its most original contribution to European culture was the funerary monument. Polish art historians agree that baroque art and architecture in Poland was mainly derivative, borrowing not only foreign models but foreign artists as well.[108]

From an English perspective, Sarmatian culture has much in common with the programme of the Tory Anglican squirearchy of the post-1660 Restoration. Many of the adjectives and epithets listed in the previous paragraph could be applied to the latter. The big difference lay in the relationship with the Crown. For the Tories the main enemy was the republican nonconformist, who had killed the king and then proved unfit to govern. For the szlachta the main enemy was the king and his fell plan to replace golden liberty with despotic absolutism. So long as that axiom held sway – and it was strengthening all the while – any chance of cooperation to reform the Commonwealth was a non-starter. More disabling still was the almost total absence in the Commonwealth of anything resembling the sort of opposition that in England developed into the Whigs, who demonstrated in and after 1688 that a state based on the sovereignty of the king in Parliament could be both free and strong. The comparison is obviously unfair, for England's socio-economic situation was so profoundly different, and it is to Poland's problems in this sector that I now turn. Even compared with William III, Augustus had a lot on his plate.[109]

Country and towns

This chapter has been concerned mainly with the elites of Poland–Lithuania for the good reason that this is not a history of Poland but a study of Augustus's life and times. It was the elites, especially the magnates, who determined what he could and could not do. However, their own freedom of action was constrained by the country's social and physical situation, which needs at least to be sketched. Fundamental was distance. Every European country was difficult to traverse in the age of the quadruped, but Poland was more difficult than most. Covering around a million square kilometres, it was the largest country in Europe, apart from Russia. It was also the most thinly populated (again, apart from Russia), with an average of only eleven people per square kilometre in 1650, compared with forty-three in Italy, thirty-five in France and nineteen in the Holy Roman Empire.[110] Moreover, the population of those other countries increased appreciably in the later seventeenth century, whereas that of Poland declined, thanks to plague and war, to reach only six million in 1715.[111] The average density (which at best can only be a rough guess) concealed huge regional discrepancies – between a relatively high figure in the north-west and virtually uninhabited tracts in the far south-east.[112] In the middle of the eighteenth century, 50 per cent of Lithuania consisted of forest and marsh, a figure which rose to 70 per cent in the borderlands with Russia.[113] Travelling from the Baltic coast to Vilnius, the diplomat Ghillebert de Lannoy journeyed through unbroken forest for two days without seeing a single habitation.[114]

As Fernand Braudel observed, 'distance is the enemy of empire'.[115] Poland–Lithuania was blessed with many navigable rivers, notably the Vistula (running south–north) and the Dnieper (running north–south). It was the former which allowed the fertile Polish plains to become the granary of western and southern Europe in the sixteenth century. That still left very large areas where wheeled transport was always difficult and often impossible, restricting markets to the range of a packhorse. David Landes's description of pre-industrial France – 'a mosaic of semi-autarkic cells' – applies *a fortiori* to the trackless forests and swamps of the east.[116] If it is 'city air that makes for freedom' (*Stadtluft macht frei*), a patriarchal regime flourishes best in the torpid atmosphere of the countryside. Every generalization about such a vast country invites endless qualifications about regions (and regions within regions) and exceptions (and exceptions to the exceptions). Even so, it can be stated that most inhabitants were peasants and most peasants were in a dependent relationship with a noble landowner. It was this which struck most foreign visitors as distinguishing Europe east of the River Elbe from the centre and the west of the continent. Their comments were invariably negative, for example: '[the peasants] are no better than Slaves to the Gentry, for they have no Benefit of the Laws, can Buy no Estates, nor Enjoy any Property no more than our Negroes in the West-Indies can' (Bernard O'Connor) and 'the peasants are serfs or slaves . . . who are transferred from one master to another like so many head of cattle' (Archdeacon Coxe).[117]

Just how wretched was the lot of the peasants is still much debated. So fragmentary is the evidence, and so various are the circumstances, that consensus will never be reached. The current historiographical trend is to introduce a little more light to what traditionally has been a vista of unrelieved gloom. Polish peasants did have a legal existence; could own land and make contracts; and could not be sold 'off the land' like slaves, only as part of a whole estate.[118] It remains the case however that many of them were subject to heavy and increasing labour dues and were exploited by their landlords' various monopolies.[119] The periodic eruptions of what were often *extremely* violent peasant insurrections indicated that social conditions were often intolerable, although ethnic, racial and religious hatreds were also involved. For the purposes of understanding Augustus's problems, it is perhaps more important to appreciate that lords and peasants formed part of a single cultural community, sharing the same religion, the same beliefs in magic and witchcraft and the same ingrained prejudices. The lord was by his nature exploitative and often abusive too, but he also saw himself as the protector as well as the judge and owner of 'his' peasants.[120]

This was a conservative rural world into which agricultural innovation came late, if at all. The dominance of the three-field system ensured that yields stayed low. If anything, they fell, from 5–1 (i.e. one grain producing five) in the sixteenth century to 4–1 in the next and even lower during and after the devastations visited by the *Potop*, exacerbated by long-term climate change. The use of iron for the manufacture of agricultural tools was almost unknown: wooden ploughs were standard in Poland, while in Lithuania the even more primitive *socha* (a 'two-pronged fork' plough consisting of two short shares attached to a board, without wheels and penetrating the soil less than two inches) was in common use.[121] In Urszula Augustyniak's view, the expansion of serfdom and the great latifundia had led to a deterioration in the quality of agricultural implements.[122] In the face of stagnating or falling grain production, the successes posted by cattle- and horse-breeding, commercial fish-farming, bee-keeping and wax-manufacturing were of marginal importance.[123] The same could be said of such pockets of enterprise as that of 'the industrious, peaceable and personally free Mennonite farmers whose ancestors had originally been religious refugees from the Netherlands'.[124]

In this social structure, there was little chance that the great mass of the population would enter the system as either labourers or consumers. Often tied to the village in which they born, and with a horizon limited by the search for subsistence, they and their szlachta lords (many of whom were indistinguishable from peasants) were the lead weights that kept the Polish economy stationary. It has been estimated that 92 per cent of the lesser szlachta and 40 per cent of the middling could not write.[125] An inevitable knock-on effect of their plight was the backwardness of the urban sector. Even before the *Potop* struck, there were only eight towns with populations of over 10,000 and three of those (Danzig, Toruń,

Elbing) were in West ('Royal') Prussia, originally German creations and still having significant German-speaking Protestant populations. Warsaw, which had replaced Kraków as the principal royal residence in 1611, was reduced to a 'ruined shell' during the *Potop*, its population plummeting from 18,000 to 6,000.[126] Most of the other settlements classified as 'towns' were in reality agricultural communities, their inhabitants earning a living by cattle-breeding and brewing.[127] As the neighbouring szlachta benefited from their right to import goods tariff-free and promoted their own manufacturing enterprises manned by serfs, the artisans of these little towns were hopelessly uncompetitive.[128] In short, Augustus found an economy marked by *de*industrialization. Even after the expansion of the eighteenth century, the Commonwealth would still lag a long way behind western Europe. By 1790 the urban share of the total population in Britain was 40 per cent, in France 20–30 per cent, and in neighbouring Prussia 27 per cent. The most optimistic assessments for Poland are 10–15 per cent, with the more pessimistic going down to 6 per cent.[129]

More dynamism was shown by the large Jewish population. Sporadically present since the tenth century, it had increased rapidly from the late fifteenth, as refugees fled persecution in the Holy Roman Empire and the Habsburg Monarchy.[130] Further expansion was due to natural increase, thanks to a lower age of marriage, better hygiene and midwifery, communal support for the new-born, lower rates of alcoholism and exemption from military service. By the middle of the eighteenth century, numbers had reached around three-quarters of a million, by far the largest total of any country in Europe or indeed the world.[131] The English clergyman William Coxe recorded that the most striking feature of Lithuania was the ubiquity of Jews: 'if you ask for an interpreter, they bring you a Jew; if you come to an inn, the landlord is a Jew; if you want post-horses a Jew procures them; if you wish to purchase, a Jew is your agent'.[132] However, their numbers were subject to the sharp fluctuations inflicted by periodic pogroms, the worst occurring during the Khmelnytskyi rising after 1648, 'a calamity dwarfed only by the twentieth-century Nazi extermination' (Wiktor Weintraub).[133] Although estimates as to how many Jews perished during that decade of horror (1648–57) fluctuate wildly, there is no doubt that tens of thousands were put to death, often in horrific fashion.[134]

Religious and ethnic hatreds were joined by social violence. Because they served noble landowners as collectors of rents, taxes, tolls and debts, and as enforcers of labour dues, and were also lessees of szlachta milling, brewing and distilling monopolies, for the oppressed peasants Jews were demon figures, proxies for their own masters. The illiterate nobles needed the literate Jews.[135] Two popular sayings were: 'Every nobleman has his Jew' and 'Poland is heaven for Jews, paradise for the nobles and hell for the serfs.'[136] Particularly hated was the '*arenda*' system, by which the leaseholder (*arendarz*) was allowed to keep anything he could extract from the peasants on the land he rented above the fixed sum paid in advance. With leases only valid for two to three years, the incentive to squeeze out the last drop was inexorable.[137] As Jews were excluded by law from owning property, they had no incentive to invest in the long-term innovations currently driving massive increases in productivity in western Europe. Moreover, their frequent role as moneylenders made them especially vulnerable at times of upheaval when killing a creditor also expunged a debt.

Living as a self-governing – and highly taxed – state-within-a-state, divided from the Christian population by religion, language, dress and culture, Jews were the highly visible scapegoats when times that were always hard lurched into catastrophe.[138] This endemic hostility masked a missed opportunity. Despite their restrictions, Jews dominated long-distance trade and the financial sector in the Commonwealth. They dealt with England and the Dutch Republic through Danzig and with the Ottoman Empire and Hungary through Lwów and Kraków, and were active at the trade fairs of Frankfurt am Main, Leipzig, Breslau and Hamburg.[139] They owned the river boats which took grain to the Baltic ports and brought back wine, cloth and consumer goods which they sold in their shops. They owned enterprises dealing in clothing, soap, glazing, tanning, furs, etc.[140] As Jakub Goldberg put it, they represented a 'substitute bourgeoisie' (*Ersatzbürgertum*).[141] Yet the kind of productive interaction between Jewish and Gentile enterprise and capital which had such a beneficial effect on Amsterdam or London did not develop. The Jews continued to be 'rejected, condemned, cursed and excluded' along with 'pagans, heretics, schismatics and bad and disobedient Catholics', as Bishop Krzysztof of Szembek put it in *A Short Collection of Christian Teachings* in 1714.[142] As Józef Gierowski lamented, the Jews did make a major contribution to the economic revival following the Great Northern War, but it was not enough to overcome the lingering effects of the war and the continuing domination of the szlachta.[143]

An intractable state

No seventeenth-century European state was easy to govern. The Catalans, Portuguese, Dutch, French, Bohemians, Neapolitans, Hungarians, Muscovites, Scots, Irish and English all revolted against their respective sovereigns, the last-named killing one king and dethroning another. By the end of the century, however, central authority had been restored in most countries. If not exactly 'absolutist', regimes were certainly more stable. It was a paradigm shift that had not reached the Polish–Lithuanian Commonwealth. It never did. So firmly established were the constitutional arrangements that secured the szlachta's golden liberty, so deep were the roots of Sarmatian culture, that any incoming monarch with reformist ambitions would soon find himself caught in toils, especially if he were a German ex-Protestant coming from a principality thought to be the epitome of 'absolutism'. What Augustus needed was a prolonged period of peace, to give himself time to settle in gently and prove that he was not the aspiring despot depicted by his numerous enemies. Instead, he rushed headlong into foreign adventures that would bring only misery both to himself and his new subjects.

4.

The Great Northern War

Two wars end . . .

Three months after Augustus's election as King of Poland the Peace of Ryswick was signed, in September 1697, bringing to an end what now proved to be the Nine Years War, which had pitched Louis XIV's France against a European coalition. Although all the participants were suffering various degrees of financial exhaustion, no one supposed it would be anything more than a truce. That was because it left unsettled the burning issue of the day, namely the future of Spain and its huge empire. So sickly was the incumbent, Charles II, that his death had been expected almost from the moment of his accession in 1665. Against all the odds, he had lingered on from decade to decade, but it was now clear that the end was approaching. As he was the last of his line, the two main claimants to his inheritance were Habsburg Austria and Bourbon France, both of whose current rulers – Leopold I and Louis XIV – were grandsons of kings of Spain (Philip III and Philip IV respectively). Intense diplomacy to organize a peaceful partition, orchestrated by William III of England, was foiled by Spanish insistence that their possessions remained intact. It was to free their hands for what was likely to be a bitterly contested succession that the belligerents in the Nine Years War (France versus Spain, the Habsburg Monarchy, England, the Dutch Republic and the Holy Roman Empire) had agreed to peace at Ryswick.

For the same reason, the anti-French coalition was keen to bring to an end the long-running war in the east against the Ottoman Empire. Thanks to Prince Eugene's crushing victory at Zenta in

September 1697,[1] the defeated Ottomans were now ready to negotiate. The terms proposed by the English and Dutch mediators were
based on the principle of *uti possidentis* – i.e. the new boundary
would be drawn according to the current military situation. That
suited the Austrians, for their armies had reconquered Hungary and
beyond, and the Venetians did well too, gaining the Dalmatian coast
and the Peloponnese. However, it was unacceptable to their Polish
and Russian allies, who would have had little or no territorial gains
to show for their efforts. Knowing that peace could not be long
delayed, Augustus sought to strengthen his hand by trying to launch
an invasion of Moldavia in the summer of 1698. This did not go
well. Delays in assembling the army meant that the campaigning
season was judged to be over before operations could commence.
Meanwhile, a force of Tatars had devastated their way through
Poland as far west as Lwów before being defeated by a Polish army
led by Felix Potocki at Podhajce (today's Pidhaitsi) on 8–9 September.[2] This was to be the last engagement of the war. Before anything
further could be undertaken, peace had been signed at Karlowitz
(today's Sremski Karlovci) on 26 January 1699.

After sixteen years the 'Great Turkish War' was over. The Peace
of Karlowitz was more momentous than its better-known predecessor of Ryswick. It was the first international agreement between
the Ottoman Empire and a coalition of European powers and the
first time that the Ottomans had accepted mediation, recognized
defeat or even formally acknowledged the existence of non-Muslim
states.[3] On the other side, it proved 'a decisive turning point in Austrian history' (Michael Hochedlinger). For more than a century and
a half the Habsburgs had been fighting the Turks with their backs
to the wall, including two close-run sieges of their capital. Now
they were back on the offensive, brimming with self-confidence as
they embarked on what came to be known as their 'heroic age'
(*Heldenzeitalter*).[4] Augustus also had some reason for celebration.
Disregarding *uti possidentis*, Poland had gained substantially at
Karlowitz – the return of Podolia with its capital Kamieniec Podolski (albeit with its fortifications razed), plus the palatinate of

Bracław.[5] Secondary benefits were an end to Ottoman tribute payments and predatory Tatar raiding; an exchange of prisoners; free movement for merchants; and permission for Catholic priests to minister where there were existing churches.[6] Polish historians have been dismissive – 'a prestigious defeat' (*prestiżową klęską*) (Urszula Augustyniak), 'small compensation' (Norman Davies), and 'not in the interests of Poland' (W. D. Koroluk).[7] The fact remains that Augustus was the only King of Poland to add territory to the Commonwealth between 1632 and 1795 (when Poland disappeared from the map altogether). And he managed that thanks to the contribution to the Holy Alliance made by the Saxon armies during the Great Turkish War.

On the other hand, it is very likely that Augustus was disappointed by what he regarded as a premature end to the war in the south. If only he had been able to mount a successful campaign against the enfeebled Ottomans, so vulnerable after Zenta, he might have been able to wrest from them Moldavia, Wallachia and even Transylvania too, to form a hereditary principality. Once that was achieved, he anticipated, his own successors would be such an irresistible choice for the Polish electors that Poland–Lithuania would also become hereditary.[8] That was less fanciful than it looked in the world of fluid frontiers that was eastern Europe, no more so than – say – the progress of the Electors of Brandenburg to become Kings of Prussia (and eventually German emperors). Even more visionary was the prophecy Augustus seems to have believed it was his destiny to fulfil. At Torgau in Saxony in 1696 he had been impressed by a painting of tigers defending a man attacked by lions. It turned out to be the depiction of a dream recounted in a book of arcana, foretelling the triumph of Protestantism and the elimination of both Islam and Rome. This was *The Silken Thread of the World*, first composed in the sixteenth century and recently updated by a Lutheran pastor, Johann Wilhelm Petersen, for the good reason that the original dates had come and gone without anything happening. It was now foretold that a great hero would arise in the east, a half-Danish Saxon prince called Augustus, who would be elected King of Poland in 1696, then become Holy Roman Emperor, conquer Hungary, the Ottoman Empire and part of Asia and rule a great new empire from Constantinople. The climax of his dazzling career would be to usher in Christ's second coming and the Last Judgement.[9] Apart from the minor detail of being a year out over the election date, this phantasmagoria impressed Augustus greatly. He would not be the first (or last) religious sceptic to be deeply superstitious. He ordered his court historian Wilhelm Ernst Tentzel to write a refutation of those who believed it to be nonsense and in April 1697 (i.e. shortly before the Polish election) immersed himself in the writings of the famous sixteenth-century French seer Nostradamus. Once his actual election appeared to have confirmed the continuing accuracy of the prophecy, he set about collecting 'Cabbalistica and Geomantica' and other 'curious writings' from Saxon libraries.[10]

Also unhappy about the end of the war against the Ottomans was Tsar Peter of Russia, whose drive to the south was just then gathering momentum. A major victory had been the capture in July 1696 of the fortress of Azov, commanding the entry of the River Don to the Sea of Azov. So alienated was he from his erstwhile allies in the Holy Alliance that he refused to sign at Karlowitz, accepting only a two-year truce with the Ottomans. In March 1697 he set out on his 'Grand Embassy' to the west, with a view to learning the techniques and recruiting the personnel that would reinforce the next stage in his planned expansion. Returning the following summer, he was in Vienna when his plan to travel on to Venice to study their dockyards was rudely interrupted by news of an insurrection back in Moscow launched by the *streltsi*, units of the regular army. Hurrying home, he found time to stop off at Rawa, north of Lwów, on 10 August to meet the new King of Poland.

This was less a meeting of minds than a mutual indulgence of gross appetites. For three days and two nights the two men feasted and drank in an orgy of excess, pausing only to review each other's military escorts. They also talked politics. As they met in a separate room, with no one else present and nothing committed to paper, it will never be known for sure what was said. With Peter speaking in

Dutch and Augustus in German, eavesdroppers would have been hard put to make out what was being said. Their speech may well have become increasingly slurred, as it was recorded that they got through twelve kegs of Hungarian wine, in addition to unspecified amounts of champagne and 'other foreign beverages'.[11] Did they decide on a joint attack on Sweden? If so, was it Peter or Augustus who took the lead? The weight of what evidence is available suggests that it was Peter who made the running. During the Grand Embassy, Swedish envoys reported that Peter was making no secret of his determination to secure a port on the Swedish-dominated Baltic. That was confirmed when Louis XIV told the French ambassador in Stockholm to pass on similar intelligence to the Swedish ministers.[12] After Peter had returned to Moscow and suppressed the *streltsi* revolt with characteristic brutality, he went on to Voronezh to superintend naval construction. While there, he informed the Saxon envoy, Georg Karl von Carlowitz, that he wanted a war against Sweden in alliance with Saxony–Poland, to recover lost territory and to improve Russian trade. Indeed it was known that he was planning a commercial empire on a route stretching from China, India and Persia across the Caspian to the Russian river systems and the Baltic.[13] The Polish historian of Ukrainian origin W. D. Koroluk found in the Russian archives a draft treaty for a Russo-Saxon alliance, with a preamble stating that during their meeting at Rawa the tsar had raised the need to wrest back from Sweden the territory seized unlawfully from Russia in the early seventeenth century.[14] The Swedish historian with the best knowledge of the sources – Sven Svensson – stated unequivocally that Peter came to Rawa with a plan of attack on Sweden already formed, although he added that Augustus's support was also held to be important.[15]

Although not conclusive, that all seems clear enough. Significantly, scholars who maintain their agnosticism on the question of the instigator appear to be unfamiliar with Koroluk's book and hence with the draft treaty he discovered.[16] It seems reasonable to conclude that Peter was intending to go to war in the north, sooner or later, a decision hastened by the realization that the Austrians were determined to make peace with the Ottomans. This coincided with Augustus's simultaneous realization that his original plan to carve out a Wettin principality in the south would come to nothing. A secondary source of agreement was the need for mutual support in dealing with domestic opposition. Although the situation had improved recently, Poland was anything but settled and there was still a danger that Conti would return from France to try another fall.[17] For his part, Peter was still worried about a renewed attempt by supporters of his exiled half-sister Sophia to depose him in her favour.[18] Also persuasive is the argument that the main result of the Rawa meeting was the cordial relationship established by the two carousing birds of a feather. The Austrian diplomat Christoph Ignaz von Guarient reported to Emperor Leopold that the two men had got on so well that they exchanged swords and clothes, so Peter returned to Moscow wearing Augustus's coat and hat.[19]

. . . and another war begins

The Rawa meeting was in August 1698, yet the war in the north did not begin until February 1700. Slow-burning in its inception, the eventual conflagration came to involve so many conflicting interests that more than two decades of often desultory and always confusing warfare were needed to bring resolution.[20] As its sobriquet – 'The Great Northern War' – suggests, this was a truly momentous conflict, permanently altering the European states system. Essentially, it was a war launched by Denmark, Saxony and Russia to dismember the Baltic territories seized by Sweden during the first half of the seventeenth century.[21] The time seemed ripe. As the Swedes themselves appreciated, their empire resembled an inverted ziggurat – a large mass supported precariously by a much smaller base. Sweden proper had a population of barely 1,250,000 (rather less than Denmark–Norway), handicapped further by 'an underdeveloped economy with relatively low yield ratios, a short growing season and a government which raised a large proportion of its income in kind'.[22] Its success had been due mainly to the one-off brilliance of Gustavus Adolphus (r. 1611–32) and the problems of its neighbours, distracted by the 'Time of Troubles' in the case of Russia, the *Potop* in the case of Poland and the Thirty Years War in the case of everyone else. Sweden's long frontiers and limited resources made a defensive strategy in wartime very difficult, as its armies could only be sustained by being sent away to live at the expense of other states.[23] In the decade immediately preceding the Great Northern War, this structural problem was exacerbated by serious harvest failures and diminishing copper exports.[24]

Belief in the fragility of Sweden's power was strengthened by the poor performance of its armed forces in the 'Scanian War' of 1675–9. Although successful against the Danes on land, the naval war had been a disaster, as was the attempt to invade Brandenburg. That ended in defeat at the Battle of Fehrbellin on 28 June 1675 at the hands of Frederick William the Great Elector (r. 1640–88), usually seen as the first step on Brandenburg–Prussia's long road to hegemony in Germany. It was only thanks to the energetic diplomatic intervention of Louis XIV that the war ended without territorial loss.[25] In response to his desperate financial situation at the end of the war, Charles XI (r. 1660–97) launched an expropriation campaign in 1680 which became known as the 'Great Reduction'. This was nothing less than the repossession by the Crown of all land alienated in the past to nobles, both in Sweden and in the Baltic provinces. In the course of the next twenty years, landowners lost around half of their estates. Many were regranted to the original owners, but only in return for substantial payments. Particularly hard hit were the nobility of the Swedish provinces on the southern Baltic. In Estonia about half of their estates were affected and in Livonia five-sixths.[26]

An empire whose elites have been alienated is an empire ripe for raiding. Among those who spotted the opportunity, the most vocal was Johann Reinhold von Patkul, best known for his grisly end (of which more later), but also a key player in the origins of the war. His place of birth in 1660 was a Stockholm prison, where his father, a Livonian noble, was being held on suspicion of treason. In 1689 Patkul junior was back in Stockholm, this time as a member of a Livonian delegation sent to protest at both Charles XI's estate reductions and his encroachments on the province's self-government rights. Quick-tempered and outspoken, Patkul's tough talking annoyed Charles so much that he had him tried for *lèse-majesté*. Fearing quite rightly that he was to be sentenced to death, he fled to Germany with a price on his head, eventually finding refuge in Brandenburg. It was there, in May 1698, that he met Jakob Heinrich von Flemming, one of Augustus's senior advisers, and briefed him on the current situation in Livonia. Because Augustus's sights swivelled north during the course of the summer, following his meeting with Tsar Peter at Rawa, Livonia became very topical, so Patkul was summoned to Poland to give expert advice on the situation there. At his first of many meetings with Augustus, on New Year's Day 1699 at Grodno, he told his all-too-willing auditor that it would be easy to conquer the province.[27]

From that moment, Patkul was Augustus's main instrument, propelled to pole position by force of character, eloquence and, above all, by his gift for telling his master what he wanted to hear. His case sounded convincing: not only were the Livonian elites ready to rise in revolt against the Swedes, he argued, the urban population was just as alienated, thanks to the exploitative commercial regime.[28] This was more than fantasy, for in February 1699 a group of Livonian nobles went to Dresden to tell Patkul that a force of 24,000 could be mustered to assist their liberators.[29] Moreover, there were two other natural enemies of Sweden who could be enlisted – Tsar Peter with the promise of Ingria and Karelia, and Christian V of Denmark with the even more enticing prospect of Scania.[30] Indeed, it was the Danes who had taken the first step. In the spring of 1697, a diplomat, Paul Heins, was sent to Moscow to negotiate an agreement. Nothing then happened for over a year, for the good reason that Peter was away in western Europe on his 'Grand Embassy'. It was not until the end of October that Heins got to see him, and even then the pace was lethargic. An alliance between Russia and Denmark was not agreed until 21 April 1699 and not ratified by Peter until the following November.[31]

What became a Triple Alliance was gradually coming together. The pace was accelerated by the death of Christian V on 25 August 1699. Like too many eldest sons kept waiting for succession, his twenty-eight-year-old son and successor, Frederick IV, was keen to make a name for himself. He promptly dropped his older, more cautious advisers, appointing in their place young men sharing his forward policy.[32] It was bad news for the peace of northern Europe that so many other ambitious young men had come to the throne recently – Tsar Peter (b. 1672) became sole ruler in 1696, Augustus (b. 1670) was elected King of Poland in 1697, and Charles XII (b. 1682) succeeded as King of Sweden in 1697. The youth and inexperience of the last-named was a further argument employed by Patkul to show potential combatants that aggression could be risked with impunity. It was well known, he added, that the new king was only interested in hunting bears and generally causing the sort of mayhem that teenagers delight in.[33]

That was true. Charles's misbehaviour had been on a truly royal scale. Hunting bears was one thing, coursing hares in the Chamber of Deputies or riding into the Royal Palace on a reindeer quite another.[34] Things got worse when Frederick IV, Duke of Holstein-Gottorp arrived in Stockholm in the spring of 1698 to marry Charles's sister Hedvig Sophia. Yet another recently elevated young ruler (b. 1671), Frederick appears to have been only too pleased to lead his younger brother-in-law further astray. It was even rumoured that he had a cunning plan to debauch the king to death, so that his own wife could inherit the throne.[35] In the event, the two revellers went no further than smashing crockery, throwing furniture out of windows, bear-baiting, competing to sever the necks of calves and sheep with a single sword-stroke (which flooded the Royal Palace with blood) and nights spent breaking windows as they roistered their way through the streets of Stockholm. A favourite game involved contestants riding at a live goose suspended from the ceiling and decapitating it by grasping its greased neck. They were not deterred by the ecclesiastical authorities instructing three pastors to preach sermons on the text 'Woe to thee, O land, when thy king is a child' (Ecclesiastes 10:16).[36]

One pastime to which Frederick failed to introduce his otherwise willing pupil was sex, for Charles remained 'obstinately chaste'. So much so, in fact, that worried courtiers considered commissioning the distinguished chemist Urban Hjärne to concoct an aphrodisiac to be administered to the king without his knowledge.[37] As Charles was the last of his line, it was imperative to get him married and procreating as soon as possible. He declined to cooperate, turning down a contender from the House of Holstein with the comment 'she is as ugly as the devil and has a big mouth'.[38] He never changed, the entreaties of his mother and sister being met with silence, evasion or simple refusal.[39] He spent his entire adult life in the homosocial world of the army and was probably a repressed homosexual, although there is no conclusive evidence.[40] Diagnosis at a distance of three centuries is obviously problematic, but some Swedish psychiatrists have concluded that his behaviour was consistent with the symptoms of Asperger's syndrome, namely: difficulties in communicating with others; severely limited empathy and paucity of emotion; insensitivity to pain; fixation of main interests; pathological stubbornness; and problems with verbality (Charles was famous for his legendary taciturnity).[41] To those must be added a taste for severe punishment bordering on sadism. That unattractive trait was revealed early by his reaction to a letter received in 1698 from Jacob Boethius, the pastor of Mora, a small town 300 kilometres north-west of Stockholm. Quoting Isaiah 3:4, which warned against rule by children, the intrepid pastor told the king that the declaration of his maturity had been premature. Charles's immediate response was to have him sentenced to death. Later that was commuted to life imprisonment in the grim fortress of Nöteborg on the eastern periphery of the Baltic, where he spent twelve years, perhaps contemplating Proverbs 8:5 ('By me kings reign, and princes decree justice').[42]

Charles's relationship with his brother-in-law Frederick was not confined to carousing. High politics was also involved, thanks to the long-running 'Schleswig-Holstein Question'. This knottiest of dip-lomatic entanglements is best known for having occasioned the celebrated remark of Lord Palmerston: 'Only three people have ever really understood the Schleswig-Holstein business – the Prince Consort, who is dead – a German professor, who has gone mad – and I, who have forgotten all about it.'[43] In actual fact, the essential issue is not that difficult to grasp. The two duchies were ruled by different branches of the Oldenburg family, which in the early six-teenth century had divided into two branches: Glückstadt, which took Denmark, and Gottorp, which took most, but not all, of Schleswig-Holstein.[44] To complicate matters further, Holstein was a fief of the Holy Roman Empire but Schleswig was not. Predictably, this created a lawyer's paradise of endless litigation, as – also predictably – the two branches of the Oldenburgs were usually at loggerheads. At no time was this more so than in the late seven-teenth century as a result of King Charles X's marriage to Hedvig Eleonora of Holstein-Gottorp in 1654. More than ever before, the Swedes had a 'Trojan Horse' inside the Danish territories.[45] In May 1697 Christian V of Denmark took advantage of what was expected to be the prolonged minority of Charles XII by sending an army into Holstein to demolish fortresses built in Gottorp territory.[46] He was foiled by the decision of the Swedish regency council to declare Charles of age in November the same year.

Still only fifteen (he celebrated his sixteenth birthday on 17 June 1698), Charles positively welcomed the opportunity to show the world what he was made of. As we have seen, one of his first actions was to marry his sister Hedvig Sophia to his new best friend Fred-erick of Holstein-Gottorp. He also got ready to rattle the sabre, encouraged by support from the international consortium which guaranteed the status quo in Schleswig-Holstein by the Treaty of Altona of 1689. When Frederick went home in August 1698 he did so as commander-in-chief of Swedish forces in Germany, an appointment which was tantamount to putting them at his disposal in the dispute with Denmark. He was also accompanied by the Swedish quartermaster-general Magnus Stuart, who then carried out a survey of the Holstein fortifications and drew up a project for their reconstruction. Charles was clearly getting ready for war and an attempt by the Danes to open direct negotiations was rebuffed.[47] In the summer of 1699 he raised the temperature still higher by agreeing to send reinforcements across the Baltic, so that by the autumn 7,000 were available.[48] With the advantage of hindsight, it can be said that Charles's intervention on behalf of his brother-in-law made war in the Baltic inevitable: 'it was the tumbling pebble that began the avalanche'.[49]

Charles XII's most recent (and best) biographer, Bengt Liljegren, believes that Charles expected the Danes to back down. Christian V might well have done so, but his son and successor (after 25 August 1699) Frederick IV proved to be the mirror image of his Swedish rival and, moreover, he knew he was not alone.[50] Charles did not suspect that it was not just Frederick he was taking on, but Augustus of Poland and Peter of Russia too. So poor was Swedish intelligence that the negotiations for a Triple Alliance continued undetected for more than two years. As they neared completion in the course of 1699, Augustus put up a smokescreen by sending off a minister to Stockholm with assurances of goodwill. In Moscow, an elaborate subterfuge was mounted to convince a visiting Swedish delegation that all was well, including a written assurance that all existing treaties would be observed 'faithfully, strictly and completely'.[51] Among those fooled was the Swedish minister in Warsaw, Mauritz von Vellingk, who was on the receiving end of a charm offensive launched by Augustus and his chief adviser, Flemming. Their blandishments included the prospect of a close alliance between Poland and Sweden and, for Vellingk himself, a strong hint that he might be appointed chief minister in Saxony.[52] They succeeded beyond their wildest dreams, for Vellingk was still confirming Augustus's pacific intentions *even after the war had begun*. Not unreasonably, perhaps, Charles believed his envoy, commenting: 'we treasure King Augustus's good faith and have received so many right-minded assurances from him that we cannot doubt it'.[53]

With Charles seeking war with Frederick, and deluded into

thinking the conflict could be isolated, and with Frederick, Augustus and Peter seeking war with Charles, the actual outbreak could not be long delayed. They all thought the time was ripe. It is worth repeating what ought to be obvious: when a potential enemy's capability is underestimated and when one's own assets are overrated, war comes near. When that potential enemy has made a similar miscalculation, war is certain.[54] While Charles and Frederick had been squaring up in the western Baltic, the other two protagonists had been getting things organized in the east. To free his hands in the south, Peter sent instructions to his negotiators at Karlowitz to accelerate peace with the Ottomans, if necessary by making concessions.[55]

Meanwhile, Augustus had been busy strengthening his position in Poland. In May 1698 he reached agreement with the Prince de Conti's former supporters, by which they accepted his election; in June 1699, a 'Pacification Sejm' consolidated his position; in September, consent for military action was secured from the Primate, Cardinal-Archbishop Michał Radziejowski, by a massive bribe of 100,000 talers (actually paid to the prelate's mistress, Konstancja Towiańska); in December 1699 the civil war in Lithuania between the Sapieha clan and their numerous enemies was settled (for the time being).[56] Augustus had also advanced his plans for Livonia. On 24 August 1699 he signed an agreement with Patkul, representing the Livonian nobility, to launch a joint attack to put an end to Swedish rule. In return, the Livonians were to recognize Augustus as hereditary ruler, although the country would remain a Polish fief.[57] That, he reasoned, would also mean that the Poles would go on electing Saxon rulers as their king, to continue to benefit from Saxon control of Livonia's commercial prosperity and strategic importance.[58] Assembling the necessary forces on the frontier also allowed Augustus to satisfy the requirement of the Pacification Sejm that all Saxon troops (apart from a small bodyguard) leave Poland. Of course he did not announce the true purpose of their march to the north. For public consumption, that was justified by reference to two pressing needs: for labour to develop facilities at the port of Połąga (today Palanga) in Samogitia (north-west Lithuania), and the restoration of order in Lithuania.[59]

With their offensive alliances concluded in the autumn of 1699, Frederick IV and Augustus were ready for action. Tsar Peter was committed to joining them as soon as the Turkish war was brought to an end. Believing that the Swedes suspected nothing, the plan was to launch a surprise attack on Riga. Once that was in Augustus's hands and the Livonian nobles had risen in revolt, it was believed, the whole province would fall. It was also expected that the suitably impressed Poles would then hurry to take their share of the spoils of the collapsing Swedish empire. Alas, it all went horribly wrong. The Saxon envoy von Carlowitz had obtained permission from the Swedish governor of the city, Erik Dahlbergh, to pass through en route to Moscow. When it transpired that he would be accompanied by no fewer than thirty waggons carrying his 'luggage', escorted by a hundred dragoons, alarm bells began to sound. So Dahlbergh had the convoy intercepted and inspected at some distance from the city. Removing the covers on the waggons revealed a force of Saxon infantry, packed together 'like herrings in a barrel' (*jak śledzie w beczce*), along with the equipment needed for seizing the ramparts.[60] Dahlbergh swiftly went to work, sending women and children out of the city, razing the suburbs, taking all the other precautions necessary to resist a siege and rounding up all the disaffected locals.[61]

More disappointment followed. With Riga still firmly in Swedish hands, the restive Livonian nobles began to have second thoughts about joining the invasion. Unheroically but sensibly, they decided to wait and see how the campaign progressed. Consequently, the great rising promised by Patkul never transpired, violence being confined to sporadic attacks by peasants on their lords.[62] The whole operation had taken too long. The original date for the *coup de main* at Riga had been 16 November 1699, but it was not until the beginning of February the next year that it was actually attempted. It had taken longer than expected to assemble the troops; negotiations with Brandenburg to obstruct the Swedes sending reinforcements had proved difficult; the weather deteriorated at the wrong time – plus all the other forms of friction that habitually impede military planning. Although barely credible, some accounts maintain that Augustus's commander, Flemming, took time off at a critical moment to get married.[63] Although that is doubtful,[64] it was the case that Augustus did not allow the outbreak of war to disrupt his staying at home for the carnival festivities in Dresden. The Russian ambassador's highly coloured reports on the jollifications provoked vehement criticism from Tsar Peter, especially when news of the Riga fiasco reached him.[65]

There were so few Swedish troops in Livonia when the invasion began that a few deceptively easy successes could be scored. Two forts were captured, Kobron opposite Riga and, more importantly, Dünamünde at the mouth of the River Düna, which fell on 14 March after a short siege.[66] Grandiloquently renaming the latter conquest 'Augustusburg' could not conceal the fact that the whole operation was going badly. Augustus was in charge and it was he who was to blame for the inadequate preparation. The 126 pieces of artillery ordered from the Dresden armoury in October[67] proved to be too little too late. The siege was fundamentally misconceived from the start, for there was no navy to cut Riga off from the sea and ammunition of the wrong calibre had been sent for the siege guns.[68]

Meanwhile, at the other end of the Baltic, an even greater disaster was unfolding. In March 1700 a Danish army of around 20,000 marched into Schleswig-Holstein, driving the heavily outnumbered Swedish and Holstein-Gottorp troops back to the fortress of Tönning, which they then besieged. Charles XII's advisers wanted him to send a holding force to Holstein while concentrating on Livonia. They were overruled by their seventeen-year-old master, outraged by the attack on his beloved brother-in-law. Showing what was to become his trademark decisiveness, Charles ordered the recruitment of seven additional regiments – about 20,000 men – and the mobilization of the fleet lying at the new port of Karlskrona created by his late father. In June, an Anglo-Dutch fleet, twenty-five ships strong, arrived from the north at the entrance to the Sound, intent on upholding the terms of the Altona agreement against the Danes. To the south, the Swedish navy was confronted by a strong Danish naval force, blocking the Drogden Channel west of Saltholm Island off Copenhagen. The eastern channel – the Flint – was wider, but considered too shallow for battleships. Charles simply ordered his admirals to sail through it regardless. Thirteen of the largest vessels had to be left behind and five went aground and had to be towed free, but the bulk of the fleet got through and linked up with the Anglo-Dutch navy. It was the first time such a feat had been accomplished. The Danes, who fancied themselves as the master mariners of the Baltic and derided the Swedes as 'just farm boys dipped in sea water' (*endast bonddränger doppade i saltvatten*), were so out-gunned by the combined fleets that they withdrew hurriedly to Copenhagen.[69]

That was daring enough. It was followed by another stunning coup, as Charles used his naval superiority to ferry his army across the Sound from Scania to Danish Själland. Two weeks later, despite bad weather, he had amassed a force 10,000-strong and prepared to march on Copenhagen, where he intended to destroy the Danish fleet from the land side. The completely outwitted and outmanoeuvred Frederick IV panicked. The terms of the Peace of Travendal, signed on 18 August, represented capitulation: unilateral withdrawal from the Triple Alliance, an undertaking not to aid Sweden's enemies in future, and for Holstein-Gottorp the restoration of all rights plus a substantial financial indemnity.[70] An important incidental benefit for Charles was that the suitably intimidated Prussians abandoned any idea of joining the Triple Alliance.[71]

Yet Charles was deeply disappointed – and so he should have been. These were not his terms but those of the Maritime Powers. They did not want to see Denmark eliminated, they wanted to preserve it, to maintain their beloved balance of power in the Baltic, and so they stopped Charles before he could get to Copenhagen and destroy – or capture – the Danish fleet in its entirety.[72] At least, that is the rational explanation for his anger, and he did tell his senior admiral, Count Hans Wachtmeister, that his war aim was the destruction of the Danish fleet.[73] In view of his subsequent conduct, it can also be speculated that another motive was a visceral desire to exact revenge on the treacherous Frederick for the insult and injury inflicted on his brother-in-law. Along with this psychological flaw, it should be noted for future reference that he had not learned all the right lessons from his dazzling success. He rightly saw the advantages of speed of decision and aggression, but he failed to appreciate the potential of combined operations. If his army had been the sharp end pointed at Frederick IV's heart, it was the navy which had put it there. More generally, the episode had shown that Charles was never likely to anticipate the maxim of Clausewitz that war should be an instrument of politics, not an end in itself.

The Danes dealt with, Charles could turn to the traitors in the east, now exposed as double-dealing villains, professing friendship while preparing to stab him in the back. His first thought was to go straight for Augustus in Saxony, but that was ruled out by the refusal of Frederick of Brandenburg to allow Swedish troops to cross his territories and also by the determined opposition of the Maritime Powers.[74] So it had to be Livonia. Augustus had not been idle during the spring and early summer. Despite the failure of the initial strike at Riga, he had brought in significant reinforcements from Saxony. By the middle of July a force of 17,000 had been assembled and a formal siege was begun.[75] It did not go well. General Otto Arnold von Paykull reported that the rank-and-file's lack of pay and poor conditions were encouraging desertion and even threats of mutiny. A successful engagement was fought against a Swedish force on 29 July, with Augustus opening the assault in person at the head of his dragoons, but no progress was made with the main objective. That was because the first ships bringing the siege artillery did not arrive until 13 August, having taken a barely credible *six months* to travel from the arsenal in Dresden. Poor-quality gunpowder, incompatible ordnance and a general lack of expertise meant that the bombardment made no impact on Riga's stout defences. On the first day, 19 August, no shots reached their target and only two on the following day.[76] No attempt was made to take the city by storm, despite the huge numerical advantage enjoyed by the Saxons.

Then came news of the Peace of Travendal. Reinforced from Finland, the Swedish commander increased the Riga garrison to 6,000 and withdrew with his remaining forces to the north to await the arrival of Charles.[77] Suitably impressed by the Swedish triumph in the west, Augustus decided to cut his losses. Now anxious about a possible strike against Saxony, he sought French mediation for a peace, abandoned the siege of Riga on 18 September and sent his army into winter quarters.[78] He was not deterred by the knowledge that Peter had now declared war on Sweden and was taking an army to besiege Narva, the heavily fortified port that was the strategic key to Estonia and Ingria, 350 kilometres to the north-east of Riga. The Russians arrived outside the city on 22 September and began a bombardment on 18 October.[79] Cooperation between Augustus and Peter was obviously leaving a great deal to be desired. Indeed it has been suggested by some Russian historians that Augustus saw Peter more as a potential enemy than an ally. It was certainly the case that Patkul had expressed alarm that the conquest of Narva would have allowed Peter to move on to take control of Livonia.[80] On the other hand, it was believed by many diplomats at the time that, if Peter had known about the Danish collapse, he would not have declared war on Sweden.[81] This was the first indication that the usual weakness of coalitions – a diversity of aims – would become a recurring feature of the Great Northern War.

Augustus's prudence was soon proved to be justified, at least in the short term. On 1 October 1700 the Swedish fleet, numbering around 200 vessels, set sail from Karlshamn. On the second day it ran into a snowstorm driven by gale-force winds, an ordeal which forced several to return to port or seek shelter off Ösel Island, killed hundreds of horses thrown about in the holds and made Charles – and everyone else – extremely seasick for the duration of the five-day voyage. Together with the stress and strain of the Danish operation, this revelation of the unpredictability of maritime operations put him off sea travel for good. As we shall see, it was also to be a branch of warfare he now neglected, very much to his disadvantage.[82] No doubt heaving a sigh of relief, what was left of the expedition made landfall at Pernau (today Pärnu in Estonia) on 6 October. The first choice to be made was whether to go west to attack Augustus or east to deal with Peter. By the time the army was ready to move off in the middle of November, it was clear that the former had gone into winter quarters, so east it had to be. It says a great deal for the discipline of the Swedes that they withstood the horrors of the seven-day march that followed: persistent rain during the few hours of daylight, frosts by night, no supplies because the waggons could not keep up on the glutinous 'roads' and sleeping in the open, not to mention the prospect of facing a numerically superior enemy when they arrived.[83]

Charles was deterred neither by the privation nor the odds, replying to all warnings with the vow that he would strike at the Russians no matter how numerous for God marched with him: 'in war victory is decided by God and he can just as easily give it to the few as to the many.'[84] This was another early sign of a distinctively Carolingian brand of warfare – reliance on Providence. It had an immediate impact. When they arrived at Narva, without hesitation, Charles sent his 10,500 Swedes to attack 35,000 Russians.[85] On the side of his enemies, all was not well. At 3 a.m. on the morning of the battle (30 November) Tsar Peter took himself off, hurriedly appointing a very reluctant Duc de Croÿ as commander. The latter's protests that he knew no Russian, knew nothing about the Russian army and its methods, was not used to command and that the Russian army was notorious for its hatred of foreigners were to no avail.[86] The Swedes went into battle crying 'With God's help!' (*Med Guds hjälp!*). As they advanced, a providential snowstorm blew out of the west, blinding the defenders, most of whom turned and fled, crying the Russian equivalent of '*sauve qui peut*' (*беги, если твоя жизнь тебе дорога*). Their misery was completed by the collapse of the bridge across the Narva, into whose icy waters untold numbers fell. By the time darkness put an end to the massacre the Swedes had suffered around 2,000 casualties, their enemies between four and five times more.[87] In as much as any tactical skill had been needed on the side of the victors, it had been supplied by General Carl Gustaf

Rehnskiöld, but Charles had certainly distinguished himself by his personal example, leading both cavalry and infantry attacks with exceptional courage.[88] Convinced that the battle had proved that God was on his side, his first action on the following day was to go into Narva to attend a service of thanksgiving. He had also enjoyed the battle enormously, the best bit being, as he told his good friend Colonel Axel Sparre, watching the bridge collapse and the Russians struggling in the water being shot from the bank 'like sitting ducks'. More dangerous in the longer term was his conviction that the Russians were useless as soldiers because they would not stand and fight. So he let go the thousands of prisoners captured, although his inability to feed them may have been as important a consideration as contempt.[89]

King Charles had every reason to be pleased with himself. Not only had he inflicted a humiliating defeat, he had captured a huge amount of booty – 149 cannon, thirty-two mortars, huge quantities of arms and ammunition, 146 flags and banners and a war chest of 262,000 talers.[90] Moreover, the tsar had run away in a spectacular act of cowardice.[91] Russia was undeniably vast in girth, but the Narva fiasco seemed to prove that its head was a poltroon and its members were made of clay. For the foreseeable future, Charles concluded, Russia no longer counted. When the year of glory 1700 began, he had been confronted by three treacherous sovereigns. Two he had dealt with in no uncertain fashion. It was now high time to administer the same medicine to the one he regarded as the most treacherous of the lot – King Augustus.

Nemesis: Charles XII in Poland 1701–1706

Invasion

The war begun by Augustus with such high hopes had quickly turned sour. The surprise attack on Riga had failed; the siege had been abandoned; his Russian ally had been humiliated. He knew that a victorious and vengeful Charles would be coming for him next. So frantic attempts were made during the course of the winter to secure mediation – from the French, from the Austrians, from the Prussians, from the Maritime Powers, it didn't matter who, so long as they got him out of the war.[1] They were all keen to help, eager to recruit his army for their own imminent war over the Spanish succession. But Charles would not listen. He never listened to anybody. He would tolerate no diplomats in his camp, and all written approaches were referred to the Chancellery in Stockholm, which in effect meant delaying them *sine die*.[2]

For the time being it was all quiet on the eastern front, for all combatants had gone into winter quarters at the end of 1700. The Swedes had moved south to Lais (to the west of Lake Peipus, today Laiusevälja), the Saxons north-west into the Duchy of Courland (part of present-day Latvia). Charles stayed with his soldiers, sharing their privations; Augustus returned to the relative comforts of Warsaw. It was not until the following June that things began to move again. Handicapped by a broken arm sustained in a riding accident, Augustus stayed at home, putting General Adam Heinrich von Steinau in charge. His army had been strengthened by the accession of a strong Russian force, whose despatch had been agreed by Tsar Peter at a meeting at Birże (today Biržai in

Lithuania) in February 1701. So keen was Peter to keep his ally in the war that he offered both 200,000 talers and 20,000 men, sent off in April under Prince Nikolai Repnin to join the Saxon camp.[3] On arrival at Riga, Steinau formed a defensive line on the left (west) bank of the River Düna opposite Riga.

In June 1701 Charles was also on the move, having waited for reinforcements to arrive from Sweden. He had not been idle. Back in the winter, the resourceful governor of Riga, Erik Dahlbergh, had been told to assemble in secret a flotilla of various craft suitable for use as floating batteries and for transporting a large force across the Düna. The prolonged preparatory work paid off. During the night of 18–19 July, 195 boats ferried across 535 cavalry and 6,600 infantry, covered by a smokescreen and supported by an intense artillery bombardment. Although taken initially by surprise, the Saxons put up stiff resistance, launching several counter-attacks. After a fierce battle lasting five hours, Steinau decided there was no prospect of pushing the Swedes back over the Düna, so ordered a withdrawal. This was undoubtedly a Swedish victory. Once again, Charles had shown impressive qualities as a commander, combining careful preparation with swift decisive action both before action commenced and on the battlefield itself. He had also set a personal example, leading his troops off the boats and on to the shore under heavy fire.[4] The discipline and elan of his army had once again proved superior. But the result was not what Charles had sought. The plan had been to cross the river and then deliver a blow so heavy that Augustus would never recover.[5] Such a defeat, it was hoped, would also precipitate a *coup d'état* inside Poland. In the event, strengthening winds prevented the prompt construction of the pontoon bridge needed to get the main force of cavalry across in time to carry out a full-scale pursuit. By the time it was built, the Saxons were long gone. So the defeat could not be turned into a rout.[6] Conspicuously absent from the fray were the Russian auxiliary troops, who arrived late to join the Saxon army, played no part, and then left for home.[7] The Saxons too were ordered to pack up and return to Saxony. Not only was there was nothing to be achieved in Livonia for the time being, the Poles had been clamouring for their removal with mounting insistence.

With the advantage of hindsight, we can see that the critical moment of the whole Great Northern War had arrived, even though hostilities had barely begun. Charles had now confronted all three of his enemies: Frederick IV he had forced out of the war with humiliating ease; Peter he had sent packing in equally shameful retreat; Augustus he had sent home with a bloody nose and his tail between his legs. With the Danes disabled for the foreseeable future, which of the other two should he pursue to destruction? It can be surmised that, if Charles had delivered the knock-out blow planned at the Düna crossing, he would have turned back against the Russians, confident that his western flank was now secure. While it is true that the eastern plan was not finally abandoned until September 1701, it is more likely that he had long intended to go west and deliver the *coup de grâce* to Augustus, for three related reasons.

Firstly, it was now clear that Charles was nursing a hatred of Augustus bordering on the pathological and possibly related to their close affinity, a paradox common to many families, not all of them royal. Rarely mentioned is the fact that they were first cousins, their mothers being daughters of King Frederick III of Denmark. Apart from their genes, the two sons were very different. Charles had grown up in the shadow of his cousin Augustus, who was twelve years older, much more worldly (Charles never went on a grand tour), much more charismatic, much more extrovert, better-looking, more successful with women, less pious. Secondly, Charles had reacted with extreme vehemence to being gulled by Augustus. It will be recalled that Charles had 'treasure[d] King Augustus's good faith' in what turned out to be the prelude to the invasion of Livonia, and was understandably enraged when exposed as a naïve dupe.[8] Dismissing Louis XIV's attempt at mediation, Charles described Augustus's behaviour as so disgraceful and contemptible as to deserve divine retribution and the contempt of all right-thinking people. Thirdly, he made up his mind at an early stage that nothing less than Augustus's ejection from the Polish throne was the only fitting punishment for such treacherous duplicity. It was an obsession which became 'the dominant aim of his life'.[9] That minimum demand was voiced as early as May 1701.[10] He should have recalled the warning issued by Aeschylus in his *Agamemnon*:

> Shameless self-willed infatuation
> Emboldens men to dare damnation,
> And starts the wheels of doom which roll
> Relentless to their grievous goal.

More prosaically, as dethronement would require direct intervention in the domestic affairs of Poland, Charles was always going to go west first.

He was also drawn into Polish affairs by his entanglement in the Lithuanian Civil War. After rumbling along throughout the late 1690s, in December 1699 it had been damped down by Augustus's intervention.[11] In the autumn of the following year it flared up again with a vengeance. In a full-scale battle at Olkieniki on 18 November 1700, with thousands involved on both sides, the Sapieha clan had been crushed by an army led by a rival magnate, Hrehory Ogiński. In a bloody aftermath, Michał Sapieha, son of the Lithuanian Grand Hetman Kazimierz Jan Sapieha, was hacked to death in cold blood.[12] The enormous Sapieha estates were then devastated and expropriated by the victors. As Augustus had lent his support – rather tentatively, it must be said – to the Ogiński party, the Sapiehas looked to the Swedish king for support, their approach mediated by the ever-slippery Jakub Sobieski. Although based mainly in Lithuania, the Sapiehas had estates and connections right across the Commonwealth, so they had considerable potential as a fifth column.[13] As Charles got ready to intervene in Poland, he seized the opportunity, sending off a small force of cavalry to Samogitia to protect Sapieha property against the depredations of the Ogiński forces.[14]

That was in the autumn of 1701. On 15 September he received

reassurance about the situation in the east with news of a victory won by a small army led by General Wolmar Anton von Schlippenbach against a numerically superior force of Russians under Count Boris Sheremetev at Rauge (Rõuge in Estonia), eighty kilometres west of Pskov.[15] At the end of the year, by which time the Swedes had gone into winter quarters in Courland, Charles took a direct interest in events in neighbouring Lithuania, goaded by raiding of parties led by Oginski. In one of those mercurial if irresponsible gestures which kept his subordinates on their toes, he set off in secret one night, accompanied by only a small escort, travelling on sledges. No one knew where he had gone. In fact he had got as far south as Kowno (today Kaunas in Lithuania, about 100 kilometres north-west of Vilnius), reconnoitring as he went and leaving a small force behind.[16] When he got back, towards the end of December 1701, he was greeted by two bits of urgent news, one good and one bad. The good news was the capitulation of the fortress at Dünamünde north of Riga, after a long and heroic siege during which the original Saxon garrison of over 1,000 was reduced to sixteen officers and fifty-three rank-and-file.[17] It was the last remnant of Augustus's invasion of Livonia. The bad news was the defeat of Schlippenbach in a rematch with Sheremetev at Erastfer (today Erastvere in Estonia), forty kilometres west of Lake Peipus. As the first Russian victory of the war, it was celebrated by Tsar Peter with corresponding splendour. It gave him personally, and his army more generally, a massive boost of confidence after so many setbacks. The shame of Narva had been laid to rest.[18] The Russians promptly moved into Livonia, from which they were only to be dislodged in the twentieth century.

Charles XII goes to Warsaw

The little expedition of December had taken Charles over the border into Poland–Lithuania for the first time, although his detachments had been operating there in defence of the Sapieha estates.

Technically, he had been on the Commonwealth's soil since September, for the Duchy of Courland was its fief, and the Poles had been quick to protest at the encroachment. Nor had they appreciated the manifesto he issued when arriving, offering a stark choice between dethroning Augustus and suffering all the consequences of war.[19] Not unreasonably, they protested that Augustus had never consulted them about attacking Swedish territory; that he was involved only in his capacity as Elector of Saxony; and that their country was not a party to the war. So they asked him to stay away. He was not going to. He took his army across the Lithuanian frontier in January 1702 as a man with a mission, a mission which eventually destroyed him. As Frans Gunnar Bengtsson put it: 'there is no doubt that his decision to depose Augustus is the great lunacy of Charles XII's life, corresponding to Napoleon's Spanish hallucination. It condemned him to a Sisyphean struggle whose scope he could hardly have imagined.'[20] When the news finally filtered back to Russia, Peter was understandably delighted. His hands were now free, at least for as long as Charles was stuck in the Polish morass. Had he the gift of prophecy he might well have anticipated the words recorded by Winston Churchill when he learned of the Japanese attack on Pearl Harbour: 'I went to bed and slept the sleep of the saved.'[21]

A very different emotion prevailed among Charles's advisers, who believed he should stay out of Poland and turn east. From Stockholm came letter after letter imploring him to make peace with Augustus, including one from his mother.[22] The aged former chancellor Count Bengt Oxenstierna issued advice based on decades of first-hand experience of dealing with the region: Poland was a country that could not be conquered; it had no 'fixed points', so that the Poles could only be chased around and never nailed down; they were more dangerous running away than when offering resistance; they were 'slippery and inconstant' (*slippriga och obeständiga*) and only out for personal gain; and, crucially, they would never accept dethronement, especially not when it was dictated by a foreign Protestant sovereign and the target had converted to Catholicism.[23] Barring the disparaging comment on the Polish national character, he was to be proved right on every count, but Charles was not listening. As the French diplomat Comte d'Avaux observed: 'it is enough just to suggest something to him to make him do the opposite, especially when there are people he thinks want to control him'.[24] That was true generally, and doubly so when his decision about the fate of Augustus was challenged. That was what the Sapieha brothers, for example, discovered in March 1702 when they had a long meeting with Charles, conducted in Latin. He promised to guarantee the return of all their estates and offices but demanded in return their declaration of support for dethronement. Their warning that this would be extremely difficult brought the curt rejoinder: '*Ego semel dic et fac!*' (That is what I say, get on with it!).[25]

For Charles, 'my will' was synonymous with 'God's will'. General Magnus Stenbock, who probably knew him better than anyone, lamented to Oxenstierna in December 1700 that Charles was impervious to reason because he believed it was God who was telling him what to do.[26] So Oxenstierna should not have been surprised when the recommendations referred to in the previous paragraph were simply ignored. Moreover, Charles's God was very much the avenging deity of the Old Testament, a text he knew intimately from his intensive biblical education.[27] His sense of being on a mission to punish all those contravening the ninth of the Ten Commandments (Thou shalt not bear false witness) was plain to contemporaries: 'he sees himself as God's public prosecutor, sent to punish all infidelity' (d'Avaux), and 'he sees himself as God's enforcer on earth'(General Jakob Spens).[28] Even in an age when strict religious observance was the norm, Charles stood out for his personal piety and literal adherence to the Word. Among the victims of his uncompromising faith was Guardsman Johan Schröder, a married man found guilty of sleeping with another married man's wife. Despite the argument offered by the court's presiding officer that this 'double adultery' was not a capital crime in any other European country, and that even in Sweden it had not been enforced since time out of mind, Charles was adamant. It was Mosaic Law (Leviticus 20:10) and so both lovers were put to death by royal fiat.[29] In the face of this moral austerity, a sinner such as Augustus could expect no mercy, given that he was not only a serial adulterer but also a suspected non-believer, and – worse still – a cynical apostate, a deserter from the pure teaching of Luther (to whose tomb at Wittenberg Charles later made a pilgrimage)[30] for the false doctrines of the papal Antichrist. There was certainly a strong religious element in Charles's aversion to Augustus. Among other things, he was outraged by the rumour that Augustus was about to obey a papal command to have his son and heir converted to Catholicism and that the infant would then be married to a Habsburg princess.[31] As we shall see later, promotion of Protestantism was a top priority for Charles.[32]

In January 1702 Augustus made two desperate attempts to persuade Charles to negotiate a peace. The first was mediated by Countess Aurora von Königsmarck, his first *maîtresse en titre* and still a friend although her brief reign in the royal bedchamber had ended more than four years before. The ostensible purpose of her mission to the Swedish camp in Courland was to secure a pardon for her brother-in-law Carl Gustav von Lewenhaupt, a Swedish subject but in Saxon service, and to secure restitution of the family's estates expropriated by Charles XI's reductions. That was genuine enough, but she was also commissioned by Augustus to deliver documents containing peace proposals. The stratagem was a fiasco. Charles refused to see her and rode away when she ambushed him.[33] Indeed, this clumsy initiative only served to provoke derision among the diplomatic community. The Marquis de Bonnac expressed surprise that Augustus should have sent the beautiful Aurora to a man well known to have 'as much aversion to women as to peace' (*autant d'éloignement pour les femmes que pour la paix*).[34] A second mission, by the Saxon minister Friedrich Vitzthum von Eckstädt, was even less productive. Not only was the hapless envoy arrested and locked up for not having a proper pass, his papers were seized. Alas, among them was a document in which Augustus made some extremely unflattering comments about his Polish subjects, and which Charles was to publicize later to cause maximum embarrassment.[35] Even more damaging was the revelation that Augustus might offer to cede Polish territory to Sweden in return for a peace treaty.[36] Another attempt to secure peace negotiations, this time launched by the Polish Sejm, also got nowhere.[37]

As Charles made plain, he would not negotiate with a king he was determined to dethrone. While still in winter quarters at Lais the previous year, he had said that it would be an eternal blot on his glory if he were to enter into even the most trivial negotiation with a man 'who had prostituted himself in such a mendacious manner' (*som sig så malhonett prostituerat*).[38] That was bad news for Augustus, now anxious to get out of the war at almost any cost. Equally worrying for everyone else in the region, including the Swedes, was the growing fear that Charles was enjoying himself too much to want to stop. In the view of d'Avaux, Charles's approach to warfare was not rational: he seemed to be afraid that if he made peace with Augustus, he would have to stop fighting.[39] He himself lent support to that alarming verdict when telling Olof Hermelin, a senior member of his staff: 'we shall make war against the Poles for another ten years and then twenty years against the Russians'.[40] After only two campaigns, Charles was emerging as the antithesis of Clausewitz's central message: 'war is nothing but the continuation of politics by other means' (which is, of course, a normative not a descriptive statement). The great theorist devoted only a few words to Charles, but they hit the bullseye: 'he is not thought of as a great genius, for he could never subordinate his military gifts to superior insights and wisdom, and could never achieve a great goal with them'.[41] In a revealing answer to a question from one of his generals, Axel Gyllenkrook, about his plans, he said: 'I have no plan' (*Jag har ingen dessein*).[42] Charles went to war in 1700 before his eighteenth birthday and was still at war when he died eighteen years later. If he had not been killed by a stray bullet when besieging Fredriksten in Norway on 11 December 1718, he doubtless would have gone on fighting as long as he could draw breath.

As winter drew to a close in Courland, it was time for Charles to move in for the kill. In February 1702 the Swedish army crossed into

Lithuania, taking Vilnius at the end of March and reaching Grodno the following month. Whenever resistance was offered, it was crushed.[43] On 15 May Charles reached Praga on the Vistula opposite Warsaw. On entering the city, Charles went to the Castle Square to hold a church parade. Lutheran hymns were sung and the king, his officers and his soldiers all took the knee to thank God for delivering the city to them.[44] Oxenstierna's predictions now started to come true. Unfortunately for Charles, he soon discovered that the Almighty could not deliver up the state along with the city. It had simply disappeared: king, Senate, Sejm, the Primate – they had all gone away. The most important opposition figure – Cardinal-Archbishop Michał Radziejowski, Primate of the Church in Poland – was ensconced in the primatial palace at Łowicz, eighty kilometres west of the capital. Only the threat of physical retrieval by Swedish cavalry induced him to return, together with another leading magnate, Rafał Leszczyński. They found that 'negotiating' with Charles meant listening to non-negotiable demands, of which three stood out: dethronement of Augustus, convocation of the Sejm, and a fresh election. They told him that dethronement would be unacceptable to the Polish nobility, the most they could offer being the erosion of royal powers to the point that Augustus would be king in name only.[45] Charles's dismissive response was 'in which case they are stupid'.[46] It mattered not one jot that their opposition to dethronement was shared by Charles's own advisers. Josias Cederhielm, for example, attacked his master's insistence on it as 'disreputable, pernicious, indeed doomed' (*lumpna samt fördärveliga, ja förbannade*).[47] As we shall see, Charles did eventually achieve his objective – but it was Augustus who had the last laugh.

Opposition in Poland

Not the least of Augustus's many problems was his split regnal personality. He had gone to war as Elector of Saxony, but it was being waged in Poland and about Poland. He claimed, of course, that he was acting in the interests of his Polish subjects, indeed he pointed out that the *pacta conventa* they had imposed on him actually required him to regain territories lost in the past to other powers. The obvious rejoinder was that the Sejm had not been consulted before the war was started, even though the constitution required its prior approval for any action taken by the king in foreign affairs.[48] Moreover, the Polish ministers condemned Augustus's war as 'unjust and impolitic'.[49] So when Augustus sought retrospective approval, and future support, at a Sejm convened in May 1701, he was met with a demand that he secure an immediate peace with Sweden and withdraw his Saxon troops from the Commonwealth.[50] It got worse. In July, the Senate sent a letter to Charles XII, actually *congratulating* him on his victory at the crossing of the Düna, asking him to withdraw his army from Courland, offering mediation between him and Augustus and stressing their own state's neutrality.[51] On the other hand, as Charles's Swedish critics had predicted, his insistence that Augustus be deposed did not go down well with the Polish political class, hypersensitive to anything smacking of foreign interference in their domestic affairs. The certain reaction in Augustus's favour which resulted did not however move them to support his war. When the Sejm reconvened in December 1701, all it was prepared to do was to protest against the Swedish occupation of Courland and offer mediation if it was withdrawn.[52] It was only when Charles arrived in Warsaw in May 1702 with the non-negotiable demand that Augustus be dethroned that the Senate steeled itself to order the army to resist the invasion and authorized Augustus to bring back his Saxon troops.[53]

Why were the Poles so reluctant to resist the Swedes? Part of the reason was a desire for a period of rest and recuperation following the long Turkish war.[54] It was encouraged by folk memories of the wars against the Swedes of the mid-seventeenth century, when Poland had been devastated from one end to the other. The better-informed also knew just how ill-prepared was Poland, financially and militarily, to go to war against a state which had just overwhelmed the Danes and the Russians. Another reason was a disagreement about the direction of hostilities. Many, if not most of the szlachta believed that the real enemy was not Sweden but Russia, so the target for Polish expansion should be not the Baltic but Ukraine, and that Kiev was a much more desirable prize than Riga.[55] Augustus was being disingenuous when he claimed he was just following the requirements of the *pacta conventa*, because the 'lost territories' whose recovery was demanded were first and foremost the huge areas ceded to Russia by the Truce of Andrusovo (1667) and the Treaty of Perpetual Peace (1686), not Livonia.[56] So his war against Sweden was doubly offensive to most Poles because it also involved an alliance with the detested Russians – 'an alliance between the sheep and the wolves', as one pamphlet put it.[57] So outraged were the Crown Grand Hetman Jabłonowski and his son-in-law Rafał Leszczyński by the deal struck at Birże by Augustus and Peter that they leaked the terms to Charles. Radziejowski did likewise.[58] Things had come to a pretty pass when the most senior military and ecclesiastical dignitaries of the country were both prepared to pass secrets to their ruler's enemy.

In their defence, it could be claimed that they were acting to defend the Commonwealth's constitution and, in particular, the 'golden liberties' of the nobility. It was axiomatic for both magnates and szlachta that Augustus was aiming to establish an absolute monarchy. The untrammelled exercise of royal power did seem to be all the rage in Europe during the second half of the seventeenth century. Wherever the Poles looked, the fell forces of authoritarian government were on the march – in Bohemia after 1620, in Denmark in 1660, in France in 1661, in Brandenburg in the 1660s, in Sweden in 1680 and in Hungary after 1683.[59] The counter-examples of the English execution of Charles I in 1649 and the ejection of his son in 1688 counted for little. One of Charles XII's most seductive propaganda ploys was the repeated accusation that everything Augustus had done since his election had been aimed at 'the destruction of Polish liberties'.[60]

Yet if the szlachta's sensitivity was understandable, it was exaggerated, being based on a misunderstanding of what Augustus intended. Like any self-respecting ruler, he certainly intended to maximize his prerogatives by retrieving those usurped in the past and by making the most of those that had survived. On the other hand, he neither planned nor executed anything approaching the brutal rigour shown by Louis XIV with his *'Jours d'Auvergne'*, the emasculation of the *parlements*, or his military operation against Marseilles.[61] His Polish opponents were also missing the point: Augustus's priorities were not political but dynastic. To promote the interests of the House of Wettin, he was seeking not an absolute but a hereditary monarchy. In addition, as I shall argue later,[62] he was always more interested in – and enthusiastic about – the representational aspects of kingship than about power politics. Also misguided was the szlachta's belief that Augustus was an absolutist ruler in Saxony. As we have seen, and shall see again later, his powers as elector were extensive but limited and his attempts to enhance them at the expense of the Estates mostly failed.[63]

The dominant figure in the campaign to reduce Augustus's powers in Poland was Cardinal Michał Radziejowski. His formal ascendancy came from his position as Archbishop of Gniezno, making him second only to the king in the Polish political hierarchy, for he was *ex officio* Primate of the Church and Interrex during royal vacancies. He also had the personal attributes to make the most of his dignities, for he was every inch the over-mighty prelate: high-born (King John Sobieski was his uncle), rich, intelligent, ambitious, eloquent, devious, unscrupulous, bold and enterprising.[64] He even looked the part: a tall, physically intimidating figure, said to have been handsome in his youth, although by 1700, when he was fifty-five, prelatical high living had given him the corpulent dimensions and scarlet complexion often associated with his calling.[65] He was also treacherous and corrupt, consistently loyal only to his mistress Konstancja Towiańska and her son (reputedly his son too).[66] As recorded earlier, both had done very well financially from selling their influence during the political turmoil of the early part of the reign.[67]

Troubling the waters in which the Radziejowskis could fish so profitably were the magnates and their clientage systems. No attempt will be made to trace their labyrinthine dealings and double-dealings, for therein lies the path of confusion if not madness. The Commonwealth's political culture was so imbued with factional warfare, and so starved of any sense of civic responsibility, that identifying ideological fault lines is difficult. Among the higher echelons, Augustus never succeeded in forming a party of supporters beyond the direct beneficiaries of his patronage, and even they could betray him with impunity as soon as they were appointed, thanks to their jobs-for-life tenure. It has been noted already that the greatest magnate clan in Lithuania – the Sapieha – were among the earliest to defect to the Swedish camp, where they were put on Charles's payroll and joined his invasion of the Commonwealth.[68] Less dramatic but ultimately more disturbing was the example set by Rafał Leszczyński, leader of the most powerful clan in Greater (north-west) Poland. In the spring of 1700 he headed a grand diplomatic mission to Constantinople, instructed by the Sejm to seek an agreement with the Ottomans against Russia.[69] This of course was clean contrary to the policy currently being pursued by his king. Although his embassy failed, it dramatized the dysfunctional nature of the Polish state at this time.

Also keen for a war against Russia was Crown Grand Hetman Stanisław Jabłonowski, whose secular status in the Commonwealth rivalled that of Radziejowski in ecclesiastical affairs. During the interregnum, he had even been canvassed as a possible successor to John Sobieski and a marriage to the latter's widow was mooted.[70] To foil any such plans, his arch-rival Hieronim Lubomirski had encouraged a 'military confederation' (a euphemism for 'mutiny') organized by soldiers protesting at arrears of pay.[71] It was not to be the last time that Lubomirski engaged in conduct that would have been deemed treason in most polities. He was also the unworthy recipient of Augustus's largesse when a rash of fatalities in 1702 put a number of high offices at the king's disposal. Hoping to make sure of the support of the leading clan in Lesser Poland, Augustus appointed Hieronim Lubomirski Crown Grand Hetman in succession to Stanisław Jabłonowski.[72]

The Battle of Kliszów

Lubomirski's first assignment was to organize the Crown army for action against the Swedes. When Charles advanced on Warsaw from the east in May 1702, Augustus withdrew south to the old capital at Kraków and set about mobilizing armed resistance to the pursuit he knew would be coming. On 5 June he issued a proclamation calling on the Polish nobility to fight for their Catholic faith, their king and their Fatherland.[73] He was helped by Charles's intransigence in the face of repeated peace initiatives. At least a rump of the Sejm now responded to Augustus's demands for assistance. A meeting of the council of the Senate at Kraków on 21 June agreed that the regular Polish army should combine with the Saxon forces.[74] Meanwhile, Charles had sent orders to Nils Gyllenstiern in Pomerania to the north and Carl Mörner in Podlasie to the east to hurry south to Kraków with their armies of around 10,000 and 4,000 respectively. He himself set off from Warsaw on 26 June with about 8,000. On 16 July Augustus and his army made camp at Kliszów, north of Kraków, where they were joined the following day by Lubomirski and a Polish force consisting mainly of cavalry but including an artillery regiment. It was believed from intelligence gathered from prisoners taken in a skirmish that Charles had not yet been joined by the Pomeranian and Podlasien contingents and had only 9,000 men at his disposal. In reality, Mörner had arrived on the 17th, although Gyllenstiern was still a long way off.[75]

Battle was joined on 19 July. By the standards of the war raging on the other side of Europe it was a small affair. Over 100,000 fought at Blenheim, probably less than a third of that number at Kliszów. The qualifying adverb 'probably' needs to be inserted because estimates vary so much, from 10,000 to 20,000 Swedes and from 16,000 to 24,000 Saxons and Poles. Yet it was fierce enough while it lasted. The decisive moment came early, after Charles had strengthened his left wing by moving infantry from the centre to join the cavalry. Spotting a gap opening up between the Swedish centre and left,

Augustus ordered Lubomirski to send his Polish cavalry to attack. This he did, leading the charge himself, but was checked by intensive Swedish musket fire. Expecting a delay while the Swedes reloaded, Lubomirski charged again but had not reckoned with the rapidity with which the new flintlocks could be made ready and again his cavalry were forced to retreat. His orders for such a contingency were quite clear, namely to redeploy his squadrons to a position behind the Saxon infantry, to act as a reserve. Instead, he took them off the battlefield altogether and never returned.[76] Their only achievement had been to kill Charles's brother-in-law, Frederick Duke of Holstein-Gottorp, with a lucky artillery shot. His replacement, Otto Vellingk, commented after the battle: 'the Polish cavalry held their position well enough against the first volley but after the second they turned and retreated as fast as we could advance and disappeared from view'.[77]

Left exposed by the departure of the Polish cavalry, the Saxon infantry on the right wing were now at the mercy of a pincer movement of combined Swedish forces. That in turn allowed pressure on the Saxon left wing to be increased with a series of assaults led by General Carl Gustav Rehnskiöld. All accounts agree that the Saxons resisted tenaciously. Flemming in particular distinguished himself by leading several counter-attacks until seriously wounded for a third time. Augustus too proved that, whatever his failings as a tactician, he did not lack personal courage, having been in the thick of the action at the head of his cuirassiers.[78] At the end of the day, however, it was the Saxons who retreated. Charles had won his fourth major battle in less than two years. He had proved once again that he was a superlative battlefield commander, flexible and decisive in adapting his tactics, and inspiring his soldiers with courage and charisma. His swiftly improvised flanking attack, which turned the battle, anticipated Frederick the Great at his best.[79] Once again too, the Swedish army – the infantry in particular – had shown iron discipline, courage and endurance. As so often with victorious armies, the Swedes suffered fewer casualties than their opponents. Once again, the figures vary wildly. The best guess seems to be that the

Saxons lost about 2,700 in dead, wounded and prisoners, the Swedes about half that. The unheroic Poles, unsurprisingly, escaped with minimal casualties of under 100. One detail worthy to be recorded is the fate of the 900 Saxon prisoners who were enlisted in the Swedish army and sent off to perform garrison duty in Pomerania. As their convoy neared the Silesian frontier, they overwhelmed their guards in a mass escape, some going back to Saxony, others returning to Augustus's colours.[80]

After the battle, the main talking point was the conduct of Lubomirski. In a classic demonstration of *qui s'excuse, s'accuse*, he rushed to explain himself. Among his excuses were: he had not expected to have to fight a battle, thinking he was only there for a review; there had been inadequate reconnaissance and coordination; he had no knowledge of Augustus's battle plan (in fact there had been a council of war on the eve of the battle); fighting had started before he had time to put his force in combat readiness; he was facing the best army in Europe without the necessary infantry and dragoons; the Saxon infantry had run away, exposing the Polish cavalry.[81] That last accusation was particularly outrageous, as the Swedes themselves confirmed in their accounts. Charles himself contemptuously remarked that the Poles should give up trying to make war and stick to what they were good at – ploughing.[82] On the other hand, accusations of cowardice levelled against Lubomirski and his men by some later historians were unjustified. They did not 'refuse to fight' (Władysław Konoczyński) and were not an 'undisciplined horde of horsemen' who ran away (Otto Haintz).[83] Nor is there any evidence that Lubomirski had been bribed by the Swedes.[84]

It was not a martial deficiency that prompted Lubomirski to leave the battlefield but political calculation. It was his head rather than his heart that went missing. During the run-up to the battle he was in regular correspondence with Benedykt Sapieha, who was serving in the Swedish army.[85] To find a commander exchanging letters with an enemy staff officer before a battle is certainly unusual in the annals of warfare, if not unique. Unsurprisingly, Cardinal Radziejowski was also busily doing his best to help his king's enemies. When Augustus sent out appeals to the *sejmiki* to rally to the defence of their country, Radziejowski sent to the same addresses a warning that Augustus was not to be trusted, was only pursuing his own interests and would flee back to Saxony, leaving them in the lurch if things went wrong.[86] After the battle, he spread the preposterous story that Lubomirski had withdrawn because he feared that Augustus was about to *combine* with the Swedes to annihilate the Polish contingent.[87] What is clear is that both Radziejowski and Lubomirski were agreed that Augustus must not be allowed to win the military victory that would strengthen his own position – and weaken theirs – inside the country.[88] Whatever the motivation, Jan Wimmer was surely justified in branding Lubomirski's actions as treason (*zdrada*).[89] Rather more contentious is the further accusation that Lubomirski was mainly responsible for the Saxon defeat, although it has been shared by other historians, and even by a Swedish combatant, who remarked after the battle that if Lubomirski had combined with the Saxons, the Swedish position would have been destroyed (*zniszczeni*).[90] Such was the superior combat prowess of the Swedes, however, they would probably have won anyway.

Just as at the Düna crossing, Charles was victorious but disappointed. He had intended to defeat Augustus so comprehensively that he would give up and go home, leaving the field free for a Swedish puppet to be elected in his place. In the event, Augustus and his Saxons had withdrawn in good order, had regrouped at Kraków and brought over reinforcements from Saxony. With an army 16,000–17,000-strong, he lived to fight another day.[91] For his part, Charles too had wounds to lick and gaps to fill. And the slow-moving Pomeranian army of Gyllenstiern had *still* not arrived. There was also a growing challenge from the Polish army, whose officers were proving much more bellicose than their reluctant commander Lubomirski. Anxious to expunge memories of the Kliszów humiliation, they were engaging in small-scale but effective raids on Swedish outposts and lines of supply.[92] Charles himself, not for the first or last time, was being oddly passive. Kliszów had been fought on 19 July, yet it was not until 11 August that he advanced on Kraków and, having entered the city, he stayed inactive for another two months.[93] He should have been pondering the wise words of Oxenstierna of the previous March, especially the prediction that Poland was a country that could not be conquered.[94]

Poland is a country that cannot be conquered

Far from eliminating Augustus and turning east to deal with Tsar Peter, Charles spent the next *four years* trying to impose his will on the Polish–Lithuanian Commonwealth. It proved to be as slippery as the magnates who dominated it. Every time he seemed to have a firm grasp, it squeezed out between his fingers. In Nils Herlitz's graphic image, Poland was a mirage which one could see but which faded from sight when one tried to grasp it.[95] Eventually Charles lost patience, left the country and bearded his enemy in his Saxon den, where he did get a decision (although it did not prove to be final). Detailing the inconclusive military ins and outs of 1702–6 would be a wearisome business, certain to enervate even the most determined reader. More enlightening, it is hoped, will be an investigation of why a Swedish victory proved so elusive. In lieu of a narrative, a list of the most important engagements or episodes in Poland (excluding the fighting in the Baltic theatre of operations) is provided below, as a chronological point of reference. The approximate distances from Warsaw are included to illustrate the multi-directional extent of Charles's frustrating odyssey:

19 July 1702: Charles defeats Saxons commanded by Augustus at Kliszów, 200 kilometres south of Warsaw

21 April 1703: Charles defeats Saxons commanded by Adam Heinrich von Steinau at Pułtusk, fifty kilometres north of Warsaw

14 October 1703: Charles captures Toruń (Thorn), 185 kilometres north-west of Warsaw

19 August 1704: Saxons commanded by Johann Mathias von der Schulenburg defeat Swedes commanded by Johan August Meijerfelt at Poznań, 280 kilometres north-west of Warsaw

25 August 1704: Charles captures Lwów (Lemberg, Lviv), 340 kilometres south-east of Warsaw

1 September 1704: Augustus captures Warsaw

6 November 1704: Saxons commanded by Schulenburg defeat the Swedes commanded by Charles at Poniec (Punitz), 300 kilometres west of Warsaw

21 July 1705: Swedes commanded by Carl von Nieroth defeat Saxons and Poles commanded by Otto Arnold von Paykull at Warsaw

January 1706: Charles advances to Grodno, 250 kilometres east of Warsaw, but fails to bring the Russians to battle

13 February 1706: Swedes commanded by Carl Gustav Rehnskiöld defeat Saxons and Russians commanded by Schulenburg at Fraustadt (Wschowa), 320 kilometres west of Warsaw

Late April 1706: at Lutsk, 340 kilometres south-east of Warsaw, Charles abandons his pursuit of the Russians

27 August 1706: Charles invades and occupies the Electorate of Saxony[96]

It did not have to be like that. At any time during those four years, Charles could have secured favourable peace terms. Moreover, as a bonus, he could probably have turned Augustus into an ally for a joint operation against Tsar Peter. In the aftermath of Kliszów, he was visited three times by a Polish deputation led by Stanisław Morsztyn, the Palatine of Mazovia, seeking to mediate a settlement, and each time he refused to meet them.[97] Both the council back in Stockholm and the ministers travelling with him urged him to make peace, now that he was in a position to dictate terms. Among other things, they pointed out that Peter was taking advantage of his enemy's prolonged sojourn in Poland to conquer one Swedish possession after another in the eastern Baltic. He was not to be moved. With God's help, he rejoindered, the lost territories could easily be regained.[98] To every Polish initiative he replied that he would not make peace until Augustus had been dethroned.[99]

He did not help himself by waging war in a curiously short-winded manner. Intense bursts of action (Narva, the Düna crossing, Kliszów, the Lwów expedition) were followed by long periods of inertia. After Düna he had tarried in Courland and Livonia, not arriving in Warsaw until May 1702, although he could have been there the previous autumn. Then he paused for several weeks, allowing Augustus to get himself organized (although in the event it did not matter much). In 1703 he was stationary at Jakubowice in Lesser Poland for six weeks and almost six months outside Toruń; during the winter of 1703–4 he was nearly six months at Heilsberg (Lidzbark Warmiński) in Warmia; in 1704–5 over eight months at Rawicz in the far west, near the Silesian border; and in 1705 five months at Błonie in Greater Poland. As we shall see, in 1706–7 he spent almost a year in Saxony.[100] Of course, some of the breaks were dictated by the need for rest and recuperation, the stubborn resistance of the Toruń defenders and inclement weather, but the pattern also fits well with a man who liked making war so much that he wanted to spin it out *ad infinitum*. In a penetrating analysis of 'Charles and his army', Gunnar Arteus concluded that he was driven to wage war 'to infinity' so that he would never have to leave the life in camp he loved so much.[101] A more transcendental explanation offered by Boris Akunin is that Charles was waiting for a message from the Almighty that it was time to move on again.[102]

Exemplifying Charles's idiosyncratic style of warfare was the expedition he launched in the late summer of 1704. Reinforced with 9,000 fresh troops from Sweden, in the middle of July he set off on a mission to crush Augustus once and for all. Heading south to the heartlands of Augustus's support in Lesser Poland, he rendezvoused with Rehnskiöld and his army at Sandomierz and advanced to Jarosław, by which time it was clear that his quarry had given him the slip. Nothing daunted, Charles pressed on to Lwów, probably attracted by being told that it had never been captured.[103] After token resistance it fell on 7 September, yielding 600 prisoners and a huge amount of booty extorted by levies and requisitions.[104] During the two weeks he spent in the town, he received two kinds of bad news. The first was of more Russian successes in the east, where Dorpat and Narva had fallen. The strategic and symbolic importance of the latter was colossal, a landmark if not a turning point in the struggle for the control of the Baltic. The second blow was more surprising – Augustus had captured Warsaw! Yet such was Charles's 'adamantine confidence' that he behaved as if nothing had happened.[105]

The election of anti-king Stanisław Leszczyński

Nothing of lasting value had been gained by this adventure, but much had been lost. In the verdict of one of Charles's more objective biographers, it had been 'a massive miscalculation'.[106] What made the loss of the Polish capital so damaging was the presence within its walls of Stanisław Leszczyński, the man chosen by Charles to be Augustus's successor as King of Poland. He had not been the first choice. When the campaign to dethrone Augustus started, the candidacy of the French Prince de Conti had been the preferred option. That was dropped when Louis XIV's attention became concentrated on the Spanish succession. Moreover, Conti himself had no wish to return to Poland following his brief and disheartening sojourn in the country in 1697.[107] Next on the list was another former candidate for the throne, Jakub Sobieski, who had long courted Charles. Despite his problems – Habsburg-connected wife, difficult mother, unprepossessing personality – some support among the szlachta was generated by lingering loyalty to his father. It was strongest in Greater Poland, always the centre of resistance to Augustus. Indeed, so strong was the hostility that the province's representatives were refused admission to the Sejm held at Lublin in June 1703. In revenge, on returning home they formed an anti-Augustan confederation, aided and abetted by the Swedish forces besieging Toruń.[108]

To the fore in promoting the confederation was Radziejowski, who had been allowed to attend the Lublin Sejm, although he probably wished he had been excluded by the time it was over. Knowing full well about his treasonable ducking and weaving, supporters of Augustus were determined to expose him as a traitor. He was denounced in plenary session for having brought a Swedish army into the country 'to its great detriment'; his attempts to defend himself were ruled out of order; and he was compelled to kneel before Augustus and swear an oath not to promote the Swedish cause but to serve loyally the interests of the Commonwealth.[109] Humiliated and enraged, Radziejowski slunk away, perhaps muttering, like Malvolio, 'I'll be revenged on the whole pack of you'. If so, he was certainly as good as his word. The anti-Augustan confederation soon spread from the palatinates of Kalisz and Poznań to embrace all Greater Poland. In January 1704 Radziejowski then took the next step by summoning the entire szlachta to Warsaw, where a general confederation – the 'Warsaw Confederation' – was founded. On 14 February Radziejowski also convened a council which declared Augustus to be dethroned and an interregnum to have begun, although procedural complications delayed publication until May.[110]

In the meantime, a sensational development had dashed the royal cup from Jakub Sobieski's lips just as he was about to raise it. Ever since Augustus's election, he had been living on the family estates in Silesia (part of the Habsburg Monarchy) together with his younger brothers Alexander and Constantine. On 27 February 1704, as he was travelling with Constantine to Breslau, he was ambushed by a posse of about twenty Saxon officers, carried off to Saxony and locked up in the Pleissenburg Castle at Leipzig.[111] And there the kidnapped Sobieski prince stayed. This audacious *coup de main* was certainly illegal. Equally certainly, it was highly effective. In the view of Ragnhild Hatton, it was probably 'the largest single cause' for the failure of the grand design she believed Charles entertained.[112] Charles now had to start again without his nominated puppet. His first thought was to substitute Alexander Sobieski for his brother, but he very sensibly declined the offer and hurried back to Silesia. Other possible replacements were mooted, only to fall by the wayside – Crown Grand Hetman Lubomirski? Too old, too slippery, too greedy. Grand treasurer of Lithuania Benedykt Sapieha? Too arrogant, too imperious, too brutal. Grand Chancellor of Lithuania Karol Stanisław Radziwiłł? Too unreliable, too unpopular.[113]

So it might be thought it was a case of *faute de mieux* when Stanisław Leszczyński emerged as Charles's choice. However, he also had positive assets: he owned enormous estates in Greater Poland, partly inherited from his father Rafał and partly from his wife Katarzyna née Opalińska; he was well educated, articulate, charming and sociable.[114] He also made a good impression on Charles when he travelled to the Swedish camp at Heilsberg in March 1704, as a member of the Warsaw Confederation's delegation seeking to negotiate a peace treaty. The two young men (Stanisław was twenty-seven, Charles twenty-two) clearly got on very well, engaging in 'long conversations'.[115] All who met Stanisław commented on his handsome appearance and winning ways – *'une physiognomie heureuse'* was the verdict of the Marquis de Bonnac.[116] In a memoir produced by the French Foreign Office for an envoy being sent to Charles XII in 1707, it was stated that Charles had picked Leszczyński 'by the inclination he conceived for this Palatine, who reciprocated by showing him a special attachment'.[117] Further meetings cemented the relationship. As we have already noted, when Charles made up his mind, nothing could change it. Objections from his advisers, both Polish and Swedish, that Stanisław was too young, too inexperienced, too weak and too little known made no impression. Not the least of Stanisław's attractions may have been his well-known devotion to the Swedish cause – 'he behaves like a Swedish minister' was the comment of Arvid Horn, who was well placed to judge, having been Charles's representative with the Warsaw Confederation since its inception.[118] It was a verdict that has been echoed by many historians: 'without a will of his own, he was the perfect puppet' (Nicolai Pavlenko) and 'when confronted by Charles, Stanisław melted like wax pressed with a hot iron' (Władyslaw Konopczyński).[119]

Choosing Stanisław required only an act of Charles's iron will. Getting his choice through the formal election process proved to be more challenging. Only the determined application of military force induced even a small number of szlachta to turn up to the Election Sejm on 9 June 1704. No Palatine, only one senior official (Benedict Sapieha) and only four senators were present when the vote was due to be taken on the Wola field outside Warsaw. Stanisław's supporters from Greater Poland were prepared to vote for him, but there was also noisy opposition, especially from the Podlasian deputation, shouting that the whole operation was illegal, invalid, an insult a gross violation of szlachta liberty, a foreign diktat, etc., etc.[120] An embarrassed Radziejowski had made himself scarce so the Bishop of Poznań, Mikołaj Święcicki, was brought in as a substitute, doing nothing to raise the tone of the proceedings by being obviously drunk (his usual condition). Losing patience, Horn rode into the middle of the assembled company and shouted to his escort: 'Exclude anyone who is opposed!'[121] It was also the Swedish soldiers who shouted 'Long live King Stanisław!' (in Latin) as his election was proclaimed.[122] 'Pale and trembling', as well he might have been, the new king made his way into his capital for a *Te Deum*.[123] So irregular had been the proceedings ('a travesty of Polish law', in Robert Frost's authoritative verdict) that not even the requirement to swear to *pacta conventa* had been observed.[124]

It can now be appreciated just how unwelcome was the news reaching Charles in Lwów in September 1704 that Augustus had arrived in Warsaw. The Swedish satrap's reign in his capital had lasted only two months. After taking refuge in the castle, the small Swedish garrison commanded by Horn surrendered after three days. Just in the nick of time, King Stanisław and his family escaped, one account stating that they fled in such a hurry that one of the infant princesses was left behind with her nanny in a crib in a stable.[125] Cardinal Radziejowski also managed to get away, to Danzig. Ironically, he chose a Lutheran city because the city fathers were sure to refuse any application for the execution of a warrant issued by Pope Clement XI for his extradition to Rome.[126] Less nimble was the bibulous Bishop Święcicki, who was packed off, first to Saxony and then to Italy, where he was locked up in a papal prison at Ancona.[127] Before he left he had to witness the systematic looting of his episcopal residence.[128] Much greater was the damage inflicted on the Primate's palace, where, among other things, a vast cellar full of Hungarian wine fell prey to the thirsty Saxon and Russian invaders.[129]

Augustus now showed his limitations as a military strategist by squandering the advantages his initiative had brought. Within a few weeks, Charles had returned and the chance to turn the fortunes of war had passed.[130] Nevertheless, even Augustus's many detractors have had to admire his audacious enterprise in launching the raid on Warsaw. Among other things, it exposed the anti-king's total dependence on his Swedish master. Stanisław himself had no access to public funds and virtually no army. Even his rolling acres in Greater Poland were out of reach and now fell prey to the devastation so expertly and enthusiastically meted out by roving bands of Saxons, Russians and Cossacks. Together with the patently coercive nature of the 'election', the move ensured that the new regime never acquired legitimacy. That was rubbed in once again when Charles set about trying to organize a coronation. In Polish political culture this was much more than a ceremony, being an integral part of kingship, and it had to be conducted in the traditional way, using the traditional insignia.[131] In 1704–5 that was not possible, because Kraków was deep in Augustan territory and Augustus had removed the insignia (crown, orb, sceptre, coronation sword, etc.) to Dresden. As Stanisław had no money, Charles had to purchase a new set.[132] With the Primate refusing to leave his Danzig refuge, the Archbishop of Lwów, Konstanty Zieliński, had to be enlisted. He was swiftly rewarded when King Stanisław appointed him to all

temporary, for Charles came back in 1705 to deal with that province too, including torching 140 villages of just one landowner, Atanazy Miączyński.[138] Crude it may have been, but it was a tactic that got results. When he reached Lwów, the Palatine of Kiev, Józef Potocki, fearful for his extensive Ukrainian estates, hurried to switch sides, taking the rest of the extensive Potocki clan with him.[139] Needless to say, Charles's enemies responded in kind. Augustus reacted to the formation of a confederation in the palatinates of Kalisz and Poznań by laying waste its supporters' properties.[140] The worst that could happen to a district was to be owned by a magnate who switched from one side to another, thus doubling the likelihood of reprisals. Such was the fate of the Lubomirski lands at Łańcut, visited in turn by Saxon and then Swedish marauders. Along with physical damage came the infectious diseases often carried by soldiers, cholera in the case of Łańcut.[141] As we shall see later, the Russians, and especially their Cossack irregulars, set new standards of horror when they arrived, but for the time being they were operating beyond the Polish–Lithuanian frontier.[142]

The example was set from the top. Charles was ruthless when it came to requisitions. Among the orders he issued were: we must get supplies in any way possible, and no account should be taken of the suffering of the local people; the preservation of the army is the only thing that matters; if any resist, string them up, even if there is only a modicum of proof (*halva bevis*); they must be terrorized into believing that even babes in arms will not be spared.[143] That last threat was not meant to be a bluff, as an explicit order to General Rehnskiöld in May 1703 not to spare babies revealed.[144] The other side of the coin was laying waste a district to deny its resources to the enemy. Arvid Horn was told to 'make the country across a wide region utterly desolate'. Charles himself seems to have positively relished terrorizing the civilian population, boasting to Rehnskiöld in August 1703 that recently he had 'burned down a whole town and hanged the citizens' (*bränt upp en hel stad och hängt borgarna*).[145] He also approved and recommended to others the technique employed by the notorious Magnus Stenbock to collect levies: in any town the soldiers started by burning down houses in the suburbs, and then moved street by street towards the centre, torching property as they went, until the money was produced.[146] Well might the French diplomat the Marquis de Bonnac remark: 'his harshness too often becomes cruelty, especially in the manner in which he has treated the Poles'.[147] Stenbock was also in business for himself, boasting in letters to his wife about all the loot he had seized: silver tableware, diamonds, sapphires, gold chains, clothes, furs, beds and wallpaper were all packed up and shipped home. Even sacred artefacts such as chalices were sent back.[148] This was not the best way to win friends and influence people on behalf of King Stanisław. On the other side, King Augustus's cause was not helped by the evil reputation quickly acquired by his Saxon soldiers, many of whom were not Saxon at all, but had been recruited from the semi-criminal flotsam and jetsam of all nations that provided the rank-and-file of most European armies.

Russians to the rescue?

For all the reasons identified in this chapter, despite five years of mostly successful fighting, Charles had failed to nail down Augustus and free his hands for a campaign in the east. Tsar Peter was well aware of the priceless respite this gave him and did all he could to postpone the day of reckoning. As he wrote to General Boris Sheremetev in August 1702, at all costs Charles had to be kept embroiled in Poland.[149] Two years later, Patkul – now in Russian service – reinforced the message when conveying an order to the Russian ambassador in Warsaw, Count Fedor Golovin: 'the basis of our policy must be to keep Charles in Poland, ruin him there and then impose peace with sword in hand'.[150] So every time Augustus began to look shaky and in the mood for a separate peace, Peter intervened with financial and military assistance to keep him going. The Birże agreement of February 1701 was the first major injection, the second was a promise of an auxiliary force and a large subsidy in October 1703, a third was the Treaty of Narva of 19 August 1704.

The last of those was the most important, coming directly after the election of Stanisław Leszczyński as anti-king, when it seemed that Charles was finally taking control of Poland.[151] This was a formal defensive/offensive alliance and, moreover, was signed by Augustus as King of Poland, for his supporters there had finally agreed to a formal declaration of war on Sweden. By its terms, Peter committed to sending west a well-equipped army 12,000-strong with appropriate artillery support and to paying an annual subsidy of 200,000 roubles. He also agreed that Livonia should go to Poland when peace was signed. For his part, Augustus was to raise a Polish army of 48,000 and give an undertaking not to make a separate peace.[152] This was obviously an unequal treaty reflecting an unequal relationship. As there was no prospect of Poland ever raising an army of that size, the promise of Livonia was illusory (and so it proved).[153] On the other hand, the Russians now had their foot in the Polish door, as their army had now been officially granted access. Dislodging it was going to prove very difficult. In the gloomy judgement of Józef Feldman, the Treaty of Narva was the first step along a road leading to the decomposition of the Commonwealth and ultimately to its partition.[154]

At least Augustus and his Polish subjects had the big battalions of Russia on their side. Just how much they were worth is a different matter. On the one hand, Peter had learned the lessons of his defeat at Narva in 1700. That 'provoked him to completely overhaul the army, taking to their logical conclusion reforms which his father had pursued more tentatively'.[155] In the place of semi-feudal levies he created a permanent standing army, recruited, trained and equipped by the state. Eventually, the *'rekrutchina'* system would lead to his army becoming the second-largest in Europe (after the French).[156] During the early stages of the Great Northern War, however, it left a great deal to be desired, both in quality and quantity. His reformed state was still very much work in progress, his resources limited, his distractions numerous. By 1705 he had reached 'the limit of his capability'.[157] The British envoy Sir Charles Whitworth reported to London: 'his [the tsar's] Dominions are exhausted of men to recruit to his armies, and drained of money to entertain them, and pay his subsidies to the King of Poland'.[158] That was shown when an auxiliary corps was sent west to reinforce Augustus just when the Treaty of Narva was being concluded. Numbering 15,000 when it left, by the time it reached Poland about a third had deserted. More generally, it has been concluded: 'the army of Peter the Great was ill-fed, poorly trained, often underequipped, and frequently undisciplined. Soldiers fled from it in droves and died in it like flies.'[159] That was Augustus's verdict too, as he complained repeatedly and bitterly about the non-arrival of Russian soldiers and the worthlessness of those who did turn up. What they were best at was looting, rape and general mayhem.[160]

Arriving at a judicious assessment of Peter's contribution during the years 1700–1706 is hampered by the knowledge that eventually he won the war and was rewarded with the sobriquet 'Peter the Great'. There is also a natural tendency, especially among Russian historians, to concentrate on the successes of the early period – the capture of Nöteborg in 1702, Nyenskans in 1703, Dorpat and Narva in 1704, and Mitau in 1705. Yet these were soft victories, achieved against weakly defended, isolated garrisons. After his humiliation at Narva in November 1700, for the next few years Peter studiously – and sensibly – avoided any confrontation with the main Swedish army in open battle.[161] It was not until the autumn of 1705 that he felt strong enough to take the initiative. Augustus too was in the mood for another roll of the dice. Following his audacious but short-lived raid on Warsaw in the autumn of 1704,[162] he had spent most of the following year back in Saxony, reinforcing his army.[163] Now the two allies devised an ambitious plan to catch Charles in a pincer movement, their main army advancing from the east and a second advancing from the west. In October the Russians occupied Grodno, 250 kilometres north-east of Warsaw, with the intention of beginning their invasion the following year.

It all went horribly wrong. Firstly, Peter had to leave the army in December to deal with a serious insurrection at Astrakhan on the lower Volga, so Augustus was in command. Next, Charles seized the initiative with one of his favoured winter campaigns, taking the fight to his enemies in January 1706 with a lightning march to Grodno, covering 385 kilometres in just twenty-one days. He left behind a force 13,000-strong under the command of Carl Gustaf Rehnskiöld to cover any incursion from the west. Following standing orders, the Russians at Grodno retreated behind fortified positions as the Swedes approached. Augustus, however, managed to escape with around 4,000 cavalry, leaving the Russian General George Ogilvie in charge. In the west, meanwhile, the Saxon General von der Schulenburg had crossed into Poland from Saxony via Silesia. The revised plan now called for him to combine with Augustus's cavalry coming from the east, by now reinforced to about 8,000.[164]

The result was the Battle of Fraustadt, arguably the most catastrophic military debacle in the whole Great Northern War. Augustus was largely to blame. Schulenburg had told him repeatedly that his 'army' was not fit for purpose, consisting of an ill-assorted mixture of raw Saxon recruits and French, Bavarian and Swiss mercenaries forcibly conscripted from the French army following its defeat at the Battle of Blenheim in 1704. The Saxon cavalry had been decimated at Pułtusk and most of the infantry had been taken prisoner at Toruń.[165] A direct order from Augustus obliged the reluctant commander to offer combat.[166] Nor did Schulenburg receive any help from Augustus, who unaccountably failed to combine the two forces. The issue was quickly decided when the dreaded Swedish infantry advanced. Afterwards there was much mutual recrimination between Saxons and Russians, with each blaming the other. The most detailed modern account makes it clear that it was the Saxon centre that was attacked first and collapsed first, setting an example that was swiftly followed by the Russians. On the other hand, some Saxon units did offer resistance, prolonging the agony for another couple of hours.

In any event, the rout was total.[167] Of Schulenburg's 18,000, 4,000 were killed, 7,500 were taken prisoner and only 6,500 escaped to run away another day.[168] Slaughter in hot blood was rounded off with slaughter in cold blood. In what one Swedish historian has branded 'one of the most shameful episodes in Swedish history', Russian prisoners were shot or bayoneted to death on the direct orders of General Rehnskiöld. As one eyewitness, the dragoon officer Joachim Mathiae Lyth, recorded in his journal: 'General Rehnskiöld formed a circle of dragoons, cavalry and infantry, in which all the remaining Russians had to assemble, about five hundred men in all. They were immediately shot and bayoneted to death without any mercy so that they fell down upon each other like slaughtered sheep.' Another dragoon, Alexander Dahlberg, remarked that it was 'a rather pathetic sight' (*ett rätt ynkligt spektakel*).[169] The massacre was also given explicit approval after the event by King Charles.[170]

That was the end of the great pincer movement plan. Tsar Peter ordered Ogilvie to make his escape from Grodno and withdraw south-east to Brześć Litewski. This he managed to do in an epic retreat, reaching safety at Kiev by the end of April. Luckily for him, his Swedish pursuers had been held up by the collapse of their bridge across the Neman, destroyed by the ice floes released by a sudden thaw.[171] Charles then elected to try to cut through the Pripet Marshes, the vast waterlogged terrain around the eponymous river and its numerous tributaries, to get ahead of his quarry. He failed, his progress impeded by Russian sappers destroying what bridges there were and felling trees to block the forest tracks. Starving and exhausted, the Swedes reached Pinsk, at the confluence of the Pina and the Pripet, on 24 April where they had to rest. This was a region so inaccessible that it had never before seen an army, let alone a king.[172] The whole operation had been a waste of time, although Charles tried to rescue something from the wreckage by devastating the estates of known opponents of King Stanisław.[173] Although the intimidated szlachta hastened to voice their support for the latter, it must have been obvious to Charles that as soon as he and his army moved on, they would go back to their bad old ways, even more alienated from the new regime than in the past.[174]

During the late spring and early summer of 1706, Charles had plenty of time for reflection as he rampaged through Volhynia.

A lot had gone right for him recently, but the mirage that was control of Poland still shimmered out of reach. Peter had been chased back whence he came, Augustus's latest army had been shattered at Fraustadt, yet like 'roly-polies', the lead-weighted dolls that always roll back upright every time they are knocked over, his enemies were still standing. Peter had gone home to regroup and reinforce. Augustus still had troops and was still moving around Poland, causing trouble for King Stanisław. No biographer has ever been able to decide exactly when Charles took the decision to cut the gordian knot, for he never committed his thoughts to paper and certainly not to his entourage. It is most likely that at some point in July 1706 he decided it was high time to march to Saxony and crush his tormentor in his lair. On 7 July he and his main army marched off from Jarosław, heading west. Until now he had been deterred by the opposition of Emperor Leopold and the Maritime Powers, preoccupied with the War of the Spanish Succession. However, Marlborough's crushing victory at Ramillies on 23 May had allayed their fears of the two wars intertwining.[175] Switching on the green light himself, Charles and his army crossed into Silesia at Rawicz on 22 August, reaching the Saxon frontier six days later. After six years of evading his fate, Augustus's day of reckoning had finally arrived.

6.

Augustus in Saxony

Invasion: the Swedes in Saxony

There was no resistance to the Swedish army when it marched into Saxony on 28 August 1706. The defences were virtually unmanned, any lucky survivors of the Fraustadt debacle having taken refuge in neighbouring Thuringia. Nor was there any popular resistance. That was largely due to fear of reprisals, inspired by the horror stories lodged in the folk memory of Swedish depredations during the Thirty Years War. Reinforced by richly embroidered tales of recent atrocities in Poland, this sent waves of refugees fleeing north to Brandenburg.[1] Well aware of his army's evil reputation, Charles imposed a strict disciplinary code, also making sure that a reassuring copy was sent to every Saxon household. Another selling point for the devoutly Lutheran population was the demonstrative religious observance of the Swedish soldiers, required to attend two church parades every day.[2] Indeed there is evidence that in some places Charles was greeted with the ringing of church bells, welcomed as the successor of the great Protestant hero Gustavus Adolphus, the hammer of the Habsburg Catholics. It was an association he fostered by going straight to the battlefield of Lützen to visit the memorial marking his ancestor's glorious end, and establishing his headquarters at Altranstädt Castle nearby.[3] As we shall see later, although the burden imposed on the Saxons by the Swedish military administration was heavy, it was regular and mostly unsullied by freelance looting and rapine.

Meanwhile, back in Poland, Augustus had been desperately trying to rescue something from the wreckage. As soon as it became clear that Charles was heading west, his top priority was preventing an invasion of Saxony. Two senior officials, Treasury President (*Kammerpräsident*) Anton Albrecht von Imhoff and Privy Councillor Georg Pfingsten were sent off to intercept Charles and seek a settlement. As their target had spent the previous six years adamantly refusing to have anything to do with Augustus, their chances of success were zero. And so it proved. By the time they caught up with him on 12 September he was already in Saxony, so the main point of their mission had failed before it had started. What then transpired gave rise to a prolonged controversy among both contemporaries and historians but need not delay us long. The main evidential problem relates to the instructions given to the two envoys by Augustus on 16 August which were lost (improbable) or destroyed (more likely). The most authoritative guess is that they authorized making peace on any terms, but *only* if Charles could be prevented from invading Saxony.[4]

Predictably, Imhoff and Pfingsten got nowhere in their dealings with Charles's representative, Count Carl Piper. They offered all kinds of concessions – slices of Polish territory; war with Russia; Lithuania for Stanisław now, plus Poland when Augustus died – but none of them made any impression whatsoever.[5] Piper simply replied to all blandishments: 'this is the will of the King, my lords, and he never changes a decision.'[6] So the treaty they had to sign was a perfect example of a victor-imposed diktat (and therefore valid only so long as the victor was victorious). Charles's main directives were: Augustus's immediate abdication and withdrawal from Poland; renunciation of all alliances directed against Sweden; liberation of the two Sobieski brothers; the handing-over of all Swedish deserters; and the Swedish army was to 'over-winter' in Saxony at Saxon expense.[7] It is not clear what happened when Pfingsten took the document back to Augustus, except for the all-important fact that on 10 October it was signed.[8]

The plot now thickens, coagulating into what might be called a comedy of errors were it not for the loss of human life the episode involved. Formally, Augustus had left the war, left Poland and left his Russian ally (in the lurch). Tsar Peter, however, was blissfully unaware of all that was going on. He was a long way away, besieging the Swedish fortress of Viborg in Finland. Deputizing for him in western Poland was General Alexander Menshikov, commanding a substantial army of Russians, Saxons and pro-Augustan Poles and Lithuanians, totalling 35,000. Also in the region was a much smaller force of Swedes under General Arvid Mardefelt, numbering 4,000, supported by 8,000 anti-Augustan Poles and Lithuanians.[9] When Pfingsten set out to bring the Altranstädt treaty to Augustus, Charles also charged him with informing Mardefelt of the ceasefire. Alas, Pfingsten delegated the task to a third party, who failed to carry it out.[10] Once the treaty was signed, Augustus also tried to tell Mardefelt that hostilities had ceased but was not believed. Not unreasonably perhaps, the Swedish general took the view that it was just a ruse. He had a direct order from Charles to stand his ground and that he intended to do.[11] On 28 October he did get confirmation from Charles that the fighting had stopped, but by then it was too late to withdraw, the enemy cavalry having cut off his line of retreat.[12] On the other side, Menshikov appears to have been determined to score a victory before the campaigning season was over. Augustus could not own up to him that he had made peace.[13]

On 29 October battle was joined. What was always going to be an unequal struggle was made impossibly lopsided by the flight of Mardefelt's Polish–Lithuanian contingent. Not even Swedish infantry could expect to defy odds of 8–1, especially as they included in their ranks unenthusiastic defectors from the Saxon army who had turned their coats after Fraustadt.[14] After much mutual slaughter, Mardefelt surrendered. The haul for the victors included ten artillery pieces, thirty standards, a huge waggon train and, among the prisoners of war, five generals, 100 officers and 2,000 other ranks.[15] Although Menshikov was the commanding general, Augustus had not only been present but had been in the thick of the action, displaying 'great courage' according to one usually unsympathetic Polish historian.[16] Any pride he may have taken in the deeds he did that day should have been tempered by acute shame at having

Louis de Silvestre, *King Augustus II of Poland* (1718)

2. Georg Jakob Schneider,
The Electoral Palace in Dresden (1679)

3. The silver fire-screen in the
audience-chamber of the Dresden
Palace created by Albrecht and
Lorenz II Biller of Augsburg,
(1708–10)

Johann Gottfried Krügner, *The Election of Augustus at Wola Outside Warsaw in June 1697*

5. François de la Croix, *Cardinal Michał Stefan Radziejowski* (1702)

6. Augustus with a 'Polish coiffure'.
Engraving by Johann Jakob Thourneijser
after Anton Schoonians (Vienna, 1697)

7. The accompanying note reads:
'The enclosed horseshoe was broken apart
by His Royal Majesty of Poland and Elector
of Saxony on 15 February 1711 in the 41st year
of his life and was passed to me by Chief
Superintendent von Ziegler to be preserved in
the Treasury. Done at Dresden on 16 February
1711 – Tobias Beutel, Art Custodian'

8. Antoine Pesne, *Johann Melchior Dinglinger* (1721). He is holding one of his masterpieces, *The Bath of Diana*

Johann Melchior Dinglinger, *The Court at Delhi of the Grand Mogul Aureng Zeb of Hindustan* (1701–8)

10. Parade of the ladies led by Constantia von Cosel before the running at the ring at Dresden on 6 June 1709

11. A selection of Augustus's mistresses (clockwise from top left Aurora von Königsmark, Princ Lubomirksa, Maria Magdalena von Dönhoff and Countess Cos

The Zwinger, designed by Matthäus Daniel Pöppelmann (1710–28) as it is today. The picture ˙llery on the right, designed by Gottfried Semper, was added in 1847–54

13. This statue of Hercules, by Balthasar Permoser, on the Wall Pavilion of the Zwinger was Augustus's favourite self-representation

14. Moritzburg, the palatial hunting-lodge transformed between 1723 and 1733

15. A 'managed hunt' at Moritzburg in 1718

allowed a completely pointless engagement which killed or wounded more than 2,000 combatants. Trying to make amends, he sent an abject apology to Charles and released all the Swedish prisoners of war.[17] That Augustus should regret – and have to apologize for – winning his only victory somehow encapsulated his inglorious military career.

Pointless the Battle of Kalisz may have been, but it was not without consequences. The most dire struck Johann Reinhold von Patkul. Although he had transferred to Russian service in 1701, he had remained at the centre of the action, as Tsar Peter's personal envoy to Augustus.[18] In reality he was the servant of neither, his only objective being the interests of his native Livonia. That fierce loyalty, wedded to his quarrelsome, passionate personality, led him to sail too close to the wind when promoting his personal agenda. Falling foul of both Augustus and his ministers, in December 1705 he was arrested and imprisoned in the Sonnenstein fortress in Saxony.[19] He was still in custody when Charles arrived in August the following year, although by that time he had been moved to Königstein (which, ironically, also housed the Sobieski brothers, whose kidnapping he had devised in 1704). He must have known what was coming, for in December 1701 he had been denounced on the orders of Charles as a rebel, a traitor and a perjurer who had disseminated 'pernicious lies, insults and libels'. The libellous pamphlet in question was ordered to be burned by the public executioner.[20]

That its author would follow it into the flames was certain. Clause eight of the Treaty of Altranstädt, calling for all 'deserters' to be surrendered, had been inserted expressly to ensure that Patkul would receive his just deserts.[21] Augustus was now lobbied hard not to hand him over by a group including Patkul's rich Saxon fiancée, the widow of Count Einsiedel, and the English diplomat John Robinson.[22] How little understanding of Charles did they show when offering to pay 60,000 talers for an act of clemency! Although not entirely certain, it is likely that the intention to allow Patkul to escape was foiled either by the unexpectedly early arrival of a Swedish posse sent to collect him or by Augustus losing his nerve.[23]

According to the Austrian envoy, Count Franz Ludwig von Zinsendorff, Augustus offered a 'substantial' sum in return for Patkul's pardon but was turned down.[24] As the Swedish army was eating Saxony out of house and home, and would go on doing so until all Charles's wishes had been met, he had to be obeyed.

This was an affair that left a nasty taste all round. Patkul may have been born a Swedish subject but he had severed all his links with Livonia and had sold all his property there long ago. As an accredited Russian diplomat, he should also have been granted immunity (not that it had been respected by Augustus when imprisoning him the previous year). None of that cut any ice with Charles, who both ordered a court martial and told its president, Rehnskiöld, to make the death penalty originally passed by Charles XI in 1689 *more severe*.[25] An appeal for clemency from his own beloved sister was firmly rejected.[26] Decapitation was not deemed to be sufficient, so Patkul was to be broken on the wheel first. What that meant in practice was revealed when Patkul was put to death at Kaźmierz (in Greater Poland near Poznań) on 10 October 1707 in accordance with the precise instructions written in Charles's own hand. A detailed account was recorded by an eyewitness, the Lutheran army chaplain Lorenz Hagen. This was actually requested by the victim, who wished his fiancée to know that he died thinking of his love for her.[27] Within a circle formed by 300 horsemen, Patkul was tied to the wheel. The executioner then began his gruesome task, using a sledgehammer. As it fell for the first time, Patkul screamed 'Jesus! Jesus! Have mercy on me!' Every bone in his body was then broken, including his spine. Hagen recorded that the clumsiness of the inexperienced executioner meant that the agony was prolonged. It only ended when Patkul pleaded 'Cut my head off! Cut my head off!' *(Kopf ab! Kopf ab)*. Perhaps sickened by what he was having to do, the executioner deviated from Charles's script and obliged, although it took four attempts before the head was severed.[28] A frustrated Charles promptly cashiered him.[29] What was left of the body was then hacked into four pieces and displayed, together with the severed head, at intervals along the road to Warsaw.[30]

Even in a Europe where inhuman punishment was commonplace, Patkul's fate horrified contemporaries.[31] Of all the humiliations heaped on Augustus by Charles, the requirement to hand over Patkul was seen as the most severe.[32] It has resonated ever since. So revolted was Kasimir von Jarochowski that, in his otherwise authoritative account of Patkul's end, he could not bring himself to go into the details of what was done.[33] However, facing up to Charles's sadism cannot be avoided when assessing Augustus's challenges. Having to handle the mercurial Tsar Peter was one thing; dealing with the seriously unbalanced Charles was quite another. One means of defence adopted by his admirers is simply to ignore, or hurry past, such unwelcome events. It is some measure of Ragnhild Hatton's determination always to present her hero in the best possible light that her only reference comes in a terse footnote: 'Patkul was executed in September 1707.'[34] That is not the way to present what became one of the most notorious quasi-judicial atrocities of the eighteenth century, rivalled only by the equally ghastly end of Louis XV's would-be assassin Robert-François Damiens in 1757.[35] Voltaire's verdict on Patkul's demise was 'there is not a civilian in all Europe, nay even the vilest slave, but must feel the whole horror of this barbarous injustice.'[36]

These were halcyon days for Charles. Seven years of arduous endeavour had been crowned with success in all departments: Augustus had been forced to abdicate; Stanisław Leszczyński had been crowned King of Poland; Poland itself had been reduced to a Swedish colony; and the presumptuous rebel Patkul had been tortured to death. Particularly striking was Charles's determination to elevate Stanisław and humiliate Augustus, who was obliged to write to his rival congratulating him on his election as King of Poland.[37] As the Austrian envoy Zinsendorff observed, 'he [Charles] is the personal friend of Stanisław and very sensitive about anything appertaining to the Polish royal dignity he had created for him'.[38] Last, but not least, the involuntary sacrifices of Saxony had allowed the Swedish army to be prepared for what was intended to be the final chapter, namely the destruction of Tsar Peter and his empire. This objective was spelled out by Count Piper in late February 1707 to Zinsendorff, who reported to Vienna that Charles was convinced that only total victory could end the Russian war. Not even the return of all conquered territory would be sufficient for 'Muscovite power' would have to be destroyed root and branch and for all time.[39] Indeed, rumours were circulating that Charles intended to depose Peter. So long as he was in a position to use western techniques to mobilize Russian resources, not only Sweden but all European countries would be at risk. The tsar would have to be dethroned and replaced by a submissive satrap – Alexander Sobieski was mentioned as a likely candidate.[40]

In the meantime, the Swedish invaders were living off the fat of the Saxon lands. There has been much dispute as to how many there were of them, not least because numbers fluctuated during their sojourn. The low estimate is 20,000, the high 45,000, the most authoritative 30,000.[41] As their daily ration included nearly two pounds of meat (at a time when the average *weekly* allowance was about that), half a pound of butter or bacon and seven litres of beer, plus bread and vegetables, the burden was undoubtedly heavy.[42] To that must be added more irregular supplies of clothing and firewood and all the others bits and pieces an army needs, including personal services, especially transport.[43] Nowhere does it seem to have been recorded how much the thousands of Swedish horses consumed, but it must have been colossal. The most popular estimate of the total bill was in the range 23,000,000– 35,000,000 talers. In Upper Lusatia alone, the figure given is the equivalent of 'eight tons of gold'.[44] To feed their guests' appetites the Estates of Saxony had to raise a huge loan in Amsterdam and Augustus borrowed 600,000 talers in Hanover, assigning to the elector his share of the county of Mansfeld as collateral.[45]

In short, every Saxon inhabitant paid a heavy price for their ruler's *folie de grandeur*. Yet it could have been much worse. There was no repetition of the wild days of the Thirty Years War when the population had fallen by 40 per cent.[46] Exploitation was heavy but organized. There were no exemptions for nobles or clergy.[47] For the most part, discipline was maintained, complaints were investigated and compensation paid.[48] Fortunately, the harvest of 1706 had been good and the winter of 1706–7 was mild.[49] Paradoxically, the huge sum raised by the financial levies may actually have given a boost to manufacturing in the Electorate, for much was spent on locally produced goods, especially uniforms. Once the Swedes withdrew, manufacturers switched their capacity to supplying Saxon, Polish and even Russian armies.[50] The Leipzig fairs continued and may even have benefited from the presence nearby of King Charles, who *malgré lui* became a major tourist attraction.[51] Also drawn to the Swedish camp (but not Charles personally) were flocks of prostitutes from all over Germany and Bohemia, responding to the military equivalent of the naval summons 'the fleet's in'. Predictably, the result was an epidemic of venereal disease.[52]

After almost a year of occupation, Charles had achieved his multiple objectives: to impose a favourable peace settlement, to humiliate Augustus personally, to advertise to the world that Saxony had deserted the anti-Swedish coalition, to allow his army an extended period of rest and recuperation, and to extract so much in the way of resources from Saxony that it would be incapable of hostile action for the foreseeable future.[53]

By most Saxons, however, whatever the circumstances, a mighty sigh of relief was heaved when the Swedes eventually left, in mid-August 1707. To all appearances the Swedish army was in peak condition – 24,500 cavalry and dragoons and 20,000 infantry, well fed, well clothed, well shod, reinforced by new drafts from Sweden and riding on fresh horses. Yet, with the advantage of hindsight, all was not well. They had been living in clover for too long to wish to return to the bleak conditions of the wintry east. Among the senior officers – and the rank-and-file too, probably – there was a feeling that it was high time to make peace and go home.[54] Of the generals, Arvid Horn, Magnus Stenbock, Carl Nieroth and Jacob Burensköld retired and went back to Sweden. The senior civilian minister accompanying the army, Count Piper, wanted to go with them, saying he would gladly sacrifice two-thirds of his estate if he could enjoy the remaining third in peace, but Charles refused to let him go.[55]

A year of rest and recreation had not been the ideal preparation for taking on a Russian army much more formidable than any the Swedes had faced in the past. At the risk of getting ahead of events, the Russian campaign, culminating in the great surrender at Perevolotjna in July 1709, was to show that Charles had been to the well once too often. He himself had not mellowed in the slightest. In the view of Ernst Carlson, the uninterrupted sequence of victories and the flattery of his entourage had convinced him of his invincibility. Resistant to any kind of criticism or objection, even the slightest disagreement excited an enraged response.[56] The Austrian envoy, Count Johann Wenzel von Wratislaw, complained to Vienna that he was having to negotiate with 'a wild man' who was not accessible to reason.[57]

It was this unique style of 'negotiating' which delayed Charles in Saxony longer than was good for him. The ostensible reason for keeping the army there was the clause of the Altranstädt treaty which allowed it to stay until all the terms had been met. Augustus had kept his side of the bargain, however belatedly and sulkily, by April 1707. It was a dispute with Vienna which then delayed matters, although it need not delay us for long.[58] The most intractable issue proved to be Charles's determination to extract from Emperor Joseph I a commitment to observe the terms of the Peace of Westphalia of 1648 relating to the rights of Protestants in Silesia. As Sweden had been a guarantor of that treaty, Charles was certainly entitled to intervene. Equally certainly, the Habsburgs had behaved illegally, by turning Protestant churches over to Catholics, closing Protestant schools, forcing Protestants to attend Catholic processions, and much else besides.[59] It has also been conjectured that Charles was keen to impose his will on the emperor to keep him quiet when the Russian campaign began.[60]

When the Swedes had crossed into Silesia in August 1706, waiting for them had been a large assembly of Protestants, complaining about persecution and imploring Charles to follow the liberating example set by his illustrious ancestor Gustavus Adolphus.[61] He was only too pleased to oblige, but inducing the Habsburg ruler of

Silesia to cooperate proved difficult. Having to submit to the command of a heretic vassal (Charles was an imperial liegeman thanks to his German territories) was a bitter pill for Joseph I to swallow. After gagging for several months, he had to force it down. With his armies committed to fighting the French in the west, he was in no position to resist a Swedish invasion of his hereditary lands. On 21 August 1707 his envoy Count Wratislaw signed the agreement by which over 100 churches and many schools were returned to Protestantism and consistories re-established.[62] Architectural expression of the new regime were the six large, new and beautiful Protestant 'Churches of Grace' (Gnadenkirchen) built at Hirschberg (Jelenia Góra), Landeshut (Kamienna Góra), Teschen (Cieszyn), Militsch (Milicz), Freystadt (Kożuchów) and Sagan (Żagań). Those at Hirschberg and Landeshut were modelled on St Catherine's Church in Stockholm as a gesture of gratitude to their Swedish saviour.[63]

Augustus in Saxony

It need hardly be added that Augustus did not meekly accept his fate. Although his emotions were not recorded, it is easy to imagine how deep was his sense of resentment at the treatment meted out by his young cousin. All he had managed to save from the wreckage was the abstract title of 'king', but he was the King of Nowhere, for the Altranstädt treaty expressly forbade him to call himself 'King of Poland'. But nothing could be done until the fortunes of war changed. In the meantime, Augustus deployed his martial energy in the west, hiring out a force of 9,000 Saxon soldiers to the Maritime Powers for 832,848 Dutch gulden. They were deployed to the Netherlands, where they contributed to the allied victories over the French at Oudenarde in July 1708 and Malplaquet in September 1709.[64] Augustus himself had joined them in 1707 and 1708, not as a combatant but rather as a 'battlefield tourist'. As he informed his ministers when he set out in July 1708, he was embarking on a 'journey of pure pleasure, to give me some light relief after all the troubles I have had to put up with'.[65] Although he did spend some time in Prince Eugene's camp, where he maintained a luxurious table, he spent more time enjoying himself in the fleshpots of Brussels.[66] A special attraction was a dancer at the Opera, Mademoiselle Duparc, who followed him back to Dresden when he returned, much to the annoyance of the current *maîtresse en titre* Countess Cosel (of whom more later).[67]

Back in Saxony, wounds were being licked in the aftermath of the Swedish occupation and, no doubt, curses being were being levelled at the man held responsible. Fortunately for the long-suffering Saxons, the natural buoyancy of their economy soon brought relief. Augustus was the lucky sovereign of the most prosperous principality in the Holy Roman Empire. Both cause and symptom was the allied fact that it was also the most densely populated, its rate being almost on a par with that of the Dutch Republic and twice that of Brandenburg–Prussia.[68] Nature had been kind to Saxony in three ways. Firstly, with the Rivers Elbe, Oder and Saale it supplied the excellent waterways that were so important in any pre-railway age.[69] Secondly, it had located Leipzig at a main European crossroads from which five trade routes extended – to Poland and Russia; the Habsburg Monarchy and the Balkans; the Rhineland; the Hanseatic cities; Bavaria and southern Europe.[70] Thirdly, it had stocked Saxony with a generous variety of natural resources – silver, iron, semi-precious stones, tin, copper, lead, zinc, bismuth, cobalt, coal, marble, kaolin, alum, vitriol, borax, peat, coal and saltpetre. In the well-named 'Ore Mountains' (*Erzgebirge*) in the south, a long-established mining sector was out-produced in Germany only by Habsburg-ruled Silesia and Styria. Moreover, the latter two extracted mainly iron ore, whereas in Saxony silver was still important – the average total for the period 1680–1730 was four and a half tons per annum. As all mineral rights belonged to the elector, these 'regalia' were an important source of income. Making good use of this natural bounty, merchants and entrepreneurs had developed a thriving manufacturing sector, including cotton in Chemnitz, linen in Upper Lusatia, woollens in Lower Lusatia, damask in Zittau, lace in the Vogtland (in the south-west), firearms in Olbernhau, mirrors in Dresden, silk and gold or silver thread in Leipzig, and so on.[71]

The Saxons were also in the vanguard of European proto-industrialization in terms of manufacturing organization.[72] An investigation of *Gewerbelandschaften* (defined as those parts of Germany with an above-average density of industrial employment, and selling a large percentage of their output outside the region) between the middle of the seventeenth century and the end of the eighteenth showed that fully three-quarters were to be found in Saxony-Thuringia.[73] By the second half of the seventeenth century, twenty 'factories' (i.e. places where all manufacturing processes were concentrated in one enterprise) had been established, a figure which doubled during the course of Augustus's reign.[74] Other indicators of a modernizing economy were inventions (dyes, mining machinery, lens-grinding and -polishing, colour-printing of fabrics, movable type for printing maps and music); the industrial processing of agricultural products (timber, silk, tobacco, luxury fruit items, potatoes); and patents.[75] In terms of occupation, Saxony was undoubtedly the most advanced principality in Germany, with a third of the population living in towns, 40 per cent engaged in rural manufacturing and only 25 per cent peasants actually tilling the soil.[76] Tedious these economic data may be, but they are needed to explain why Augustus saw his state as the gift which kept on giving when it came to raising money and men to fight his wars. As Frederick the Great (for whom Saxony performed the same involuntary service during the Seven Years War) observed, the Electorate was like a flour sack, for no matter how often one hit it, a puff always came out.[77]

The road to the dark satanic mills of industrialization was crooked and bumpy. Periodic outbreaks of labour unrest, especially among the miners, indicated that the benefits were not equally shared.[78] Leaving aside the periodic visitations of wars and epidemics, there were obstinate structural obstacles to be overcome. Chief among them was the territorial fragmentation of the Holy Roman Empire, the very antithesis of a free-trade zone. Shipping goods down the

Elbe to Hamburg, for example, was impeded by no fewer than forty-eight customs posts. On the Oder, a long-running dispute between Swedish-ruled Stettin (Szczecin) and Brandenburg-ruled Frankfurt an der Oder had wrecked what was once a flourishing riverine commerce, its prolonged cessation leading to a deterioration of the riverbed. Closely allied to this were trade wars, waged with special vehemence by the Prussians, exemplified by Frederick William I's proclaimed intention to wipe Leipzig off the face of the earth. Eventually reason prevailed and a trade treaty was signed in 1728. But that was the same year in which, at the other end of Saxony, the Austrians imposed a 20 per cent tariff on all Saxon linen crossing the Bohemian frontier.[79] A German customs union – *Zollverein* – was more than a century down the road.

Leipzig and the public sphere

As we shall see, Augustus was arguably the most flamboyant hedonist and most conspicuous consumer of his age,[80] so he might not have been expected to take a close interest in the material nuts and bolts of his state. But he did. Patent protection for innovations, state-sponsored trading companies, grants to manufacturers, coinage reform, a major input to the imperial guild regulation of 1731, improvements to roads and bridges – all indicated a close and sustained interest in promoting the economy. So did his regular visits to the Leipzig trade fairs, where he convened meetings of entrepreneurs to discuss matters of common interest. In 1703 a group of them was formed into a regular consultative commission.[81] Although fairs had been held at Leipzig since the twelfth century, it was only during the second half of the seventeenth century that they developed into 'the marketplace of Europe'.[82] By the time Augustus came to the throne, a Saxon tradition of business-friendly legislation had allowed the Leipzig fairs to overtake their rivals, most notably Frankfurt am Main.[83] The gap that opened up with the latter was especially noticeable in the book trade, in which

Leipzig achieved a dominant position. It was strengthened further by Augustus's tolerant attitude to confessional matters.[84] By the first decade of the eighteenth century, the city was producing four times as many titles as its erstwhile rival.[85]

The Leipzig fairs then went from strength to strength, despite the problems caused by the war. By 1715 – halfway through Augustus's reign – they were collectively three times the size of Frankfurt's, in terms of revenue generated.[86] Visual evidence of the city's wealth can still be seen in the magnificent town houses dating from the period. The 'Romanus House', which still stands on the corner of The Brühl and Catherine Street, was as grand as the aristocratic palaces in Dresden.[87] The ambition of the merchant-princes can also be seen in their portraits, for example Ismael Mengs's depiction of the silk-dealer Johann Burghard Raab as a baroque hero, albeit one whose chosen emblem is not a sceptre or a sword but a bolt of the cloth that made his fortune.[88] Travellers were also impressed. In a travelogue published in 1690, Johannes Limberg, who had spent the previous year in the city, wrote that the Leipzig merchants enjoyed a status and prosperity comparable with their colleagues at Amsterdam or Lyon. Especially impressive, he noted, was the fact that these merchant princes travelled to church on Sundays in their own carriages.[89] In a play staged at Hamburg in 1710 entitled *The Bon Vivant or the Leipzig Fair*, life in the city at fair-time is depicted as business liberally mixed with a riotous round of pleasure, with drinking, smoking, dancing and love-making supplemented by displays of wild animals (lions, tigers, panthers, elephants), a puppet theatre and acrobatic performances.[90]

Much of this success was due to the enterprise of the local burghers, rather than Augustus. It was their initiative which established a stock exchange in 1678 and a commercial court in 1682. The cultural life of the city, including its theatre and opera, was also in their hands.[91] This might suggest a fundamental contrast between the two main Saxon cities: Leipzig – commercial, citizen-run, Lutheran, with a middle-class culture, versus Dresden – residential, monarchical, with a Catholic ruler and an aristocratic court culture. In reality, the relationship was more complementary than adversarial. Augustus was so often in Leipzig – he visited the fairs at least thirty times – that the city regularly took on the air and appearance of a ruler's residential city (*Residenzstadt*). When in town, he stayed with the rich businessman Andreas Dietrich Apel, whose baroque residence on the Market Square was a palace fit for a king, although Apel did charge 2,000 talers a year for the privilege.[92]

For everyone engaged in trade, Augustus was a welcome visitor, for he spent freely at the fairs, one of his main sources of luxury goods. Moreover, he turned his sojourns into popular festivals in which the whole community joined. There were processions, firework displays and various entertainments, the most popular being 'fishermen jousting' (*Fischerstechen*), involving competitive aquatic games with much ducking and general merriment.[93] This should sound a warning against a common belief that old-regime culture was characterized by a growing 'distancing' of ruler and elites from the rest of the population.[94] It might work for Louis XIV's Versailles (whose meretricious glamour dazzled contemporaries and has misled historians), but not for Augustus.[95] As we shall see later, his representational 'display culture' included many popular elements.[96]

In Leipzig, he also made a powerful contribution to the further expansion of the fairs by adding the Polish connection. Although his ambition to make his two countries economic twins was not realized, access to the Polish market undoubtedly helped Leipzig, not least because it opened up trading routes further to the east and south.[97] A report on the fairs written in 1718 identified merchants from Austria, Transylvania, Moravia, Hungary and Russia, as well as Poland.[98] Despite the difficult conditions created by the Great Northern War, several thousand merchants from all over Europe visited.[99] Less to the taste of the strictly Lutheran Leipzig town council, although doubtless economically beneficial, was Augustus's arranging for Calvinists, Catholics and Orthodox to have places of worship during the fairs.[100] Even more contentious was his directive to the town council in 1698 that Jews must be allowed to conduct religious services while attending the fairs and to have access to the dealing arcades on the same terms as Christians.[101] To guard against their persecution by the municipal authorities, Jewish traders were issued with electoral safe conducts.[102]

The limited horizons of the city fathers made life difficult for anyone deviating from Orthodox Lutheranism but could not prevent the emergence of a flourishing public sphere. At its heart was the university, which on Augustus's accession could still reasonably claim to be the most prestigious and best-attended in the Holy Roman Empire. The operative word is 'still', for it was slowly falling behind the times, thanks to the inflexible Lutheran Orthodoxy of the ruling professoriate. It was this which had led Christian Thomasius, one of the most influential figures of the early German Enlightenment, to flee down the road to Brandenburg-ruled Halle in 1690, where he helped to found a new university four years later. In 1687 he had aroused the ire of his colleagues by delivering a lecture in the German language, reputedly the first scholar ever to do so. Adding insult to injury, he used it to attack the prevailing academic scene in Leipzig for its pedantry and outdated scholasticism and called for a radically revised curriculum.[103] In a striking illustration of both the volatility and vitality of German higher education, his new home at Halle was soon challenging its more venerable neighbour. Also involved in its promotion was another refugee from Leipzig, August Hermann Francke, although he was forced out, in 1691, because of his Pietism.[104] The appointment of another Leipzig graduate, Christian Wolff, in 1706 confirmed the transition. Until the emergence of another shooting star, in the shape of the Hanoverian university of Göttingen, founded in 1734, Halle enjoyed top ranking, drawing off both teaching talent and students from its rival. In 1711 an official visitation of Leipzig blamed falling enrolment on idle professors, undisciplined students, the problems caused by the war, the high cost of living, the reluctance of parents to send their children to a state ruled by a Catholic, and competition from Halle.[105]

Yet Leipzig flourished, albeit no longer in lonely eminence. Its professors continued to publish learned treatises, showing that attachment to conservative opinions did not exclude distinguished scholarship, and the stream of students from elsewhere in the Empire never ceased to flow. When the grandee Maximilian Ulrich von Kaunitz sent his son Wenzel Anton, the future Habsburg chancellor, off to be educated at a Protestant university in 1730, Leipzig was the first choice. The young man's tutor reported that it was definitely the place to be, thanks to its supremacy in the all-important fields of imperial law and history.[106] Thirty-five years later, Johann Caspar Goethe took the same view when he sent his son to the same destination. Johann Wolfgang would have preferred to go to Göttingen, but his three-year sojourn in the city changed his mind and provided the material for possibly the most celebrated of all depictions of student life in German literature – 'Auerbach's cellar' in Goethe's *Faust*, where Leipzig is lauded as 'a miniature Paris'.[107] More mature commentators also enthused about the 'Athens of Germany' (Pierre Bayle), 'a place where one can see the whole world in microcosm' (Lessing).[108] Luise Gottsched, who arrived in 1735, praised its beauty, the burghers' gardens being especially attractive; the modesty, good manners and sociability of the inhabitants; the cleanliness of the streets; and the solid construction of the houses. She added that the university was well attended, with the numerous foreign contingent bringing in plenty of money, and trade in general was flourishing.[109]

Luise's husband, Johann Christoph Gottsched, had fled to Leipzig in 1724 to avoid conscription into the Prussian army (his exceptional height made him a prime target for Frederick William I's 'regiment of giants'). He quickly became the leading light of the long-standing 'German Society', dating back to a student association founded in 1697 to promote literature written in the German language. Its members were also firmly committed to the Enlightenment ideas propagated by Thomasius, Leibniz and Wolff, demonstrating that there was more to Leipzig than Orthodox Lutheranism.[110] The society also had a pronounced nationalist flavour. In 1740, on the occasion of what he believed to be the ter-centenary of the invention of printing, Gottsched posed a rhetorical question: 'Of all the nations today, is there one that has more reason to inspire patriotic love and pride than Germany?' Among its achievements he listed the number of European sovereigns of German birth; the conquest of northern Europe by the German language; the invention of gunpowder; the Protestant Reformation; the discovery of heliocentric cosmology; natural law; differential calculus . . . Pausing for breath, he broke off to thank Providence for allowing him to be born a German. There was no need to go on, he added, for there was one invention which by itself singled out Germany as supreme – the printing press.[111] That Gottsched had struck a responsive chord among educated Germans was shown by the rapid spread of German Societies to other parts of the Empire, attracting a total membership of around 3,000.[112]

Voluntary associations such as the German Society were a constituent part of the rapidly expanding 'public sphere', a cultural sea change to be found all over Europe, albeit on a descending gradient from west to east. It can be defined as a cultural space situated between the private world of the family and the official world of the state, allowing previously isolated individuals to come together to exchange information, ideas and criticism.[113] The German Society added another important component when it formed its own library, although only for the use of its members.[114] More generally accessible in Leipzig were two public libraries – the large municipal library maintained by the town council and the even better-stocked library at the university.[115] Leipzig was also famous for its coffee houses, another medium for public debate, the first being established in 1694, to be joined by seven more by 1723.[116] Gottsched's friend Theodor Johann Quistorp gave a perhaps rather rose-tinted account of their role in forming public opinion:

A coffee-house is like a political stock exchange, where the most gallant and wittiest heads of every estate come together. They engage in wide-ranging and edifying talk, issue well-founded judgments on matters concerning the political and the scholarly world, converse sagaciously about the most secret news from all courts and states, and unveil the most hidden truths.[117]

Wider still was the rapidly expanding reading public created by increasing literacy rates. A virtuous circle was bringing a greater variety of publications to market at cheaper prices, thanks to economies of scale, as the book catalogues of the Leipzig fairs attested. More titles encouraged more readers, who in turn encouraged the production of more titles. The 'reading revolution' that was the most significant cultural development of the eighteenth century was well under way in Leipzig during Augustus's reign. It can be tracked by the growth of periodicals, a very recent European phenomenon usually dated to 1665 when the *Journal des Sçavans* was first published in Paris. An early imitation, indeed the first ever German-language scholarly journal, was *Acta Eruditorum*, edited by Otto Mencke, professor of moral philosophy at the University of Leipzig, which first appeared in 1682 and continued in publication for exactly a century. Directed more towards the general public that was now becoming a meaningful concept was *Monthly Conversations*, edited and mostly written by Christian Thomasius from 1688 to 1690, mixing entertainment with instruction.[118] Unsurprisingly, the indefatigable Gottsched was to the fore in founding, editing and writing periodicals – *The Rational Critics* (1725–6), *The Honest Man* (1727–8) and *Contributions to a Critical History of German Language, Literature and Rhetoric* (1732–45).[119]

Also precocious was the arrival of Freemasonry, 'the first secular, voluntary association ever to have existed on a pan-European scale'.[120] In its modern form, it can be traced only to London in 1717. Although the foundation of the first German lodge had to wait twenty years, Freemasonry was then given a substantial boost by the induction of Crown Prince Frederick of Prussia in 1738, followed by the creation of his own lodge at Berlin after his accession to the throne in 1740.[121] It was in the following year that Leipzig followed suit, when seven young men from the merchant community founded the lodge 'At the Three Eagles', attracting forty-six additional members by the end of its first year.[122] Another important voluntary association promoted music. Public concerts had begun in Leipzig in the 1680s, staged by a *Collegium Musicum*, an informal gathering of student musicians. When Georg Philipp Telemann came to the city in 1701 to study law at the university he founded another, which involved around sixty singers and instrumentalists. Surviving his departure in 1705, it was the centre of civic musical life. From 1729 until 1736 the director was Johann Sebastian Bach, the cantor of the Church and School of St Thomas. Twice-weekly performances in taverns and coffee houses were accessible to anyone with the price of admission.[123] By 1730 there were three such *Collegia* in operation, all providing regular concerts.[124]

Thanks to its fairs, book trade, libraries, periodicals, university, voluntary associations and concerts, Leipzig became the paradigmatic public sphere in German-speaking Europe. As such it played a crucial role in the development of the region's literary culture that would take it from neglect to respect. It is important to be aware of the 'cringe factor' afflicting German intellectuals *c.*1700. They were only too well aware of the low opinion in which they were held by their French neighbours, currently glorying in the golden age of the Sun King. In 1671 the Jesuit Dominique Bouhours claimed that the French had outstripped even the Roman Empire, for whereas Latin arrived only after military occupation, the French language had preceded it. He doubted whether any German was capable of becoming a *bel esprit*.[125] In his article 'Allemagne' in the supplement to Diderot and d'Alembert's *Encyclopédie*, Charles-Claude de Montigny acknowledged German candour, courage and love of liberty but also endorsed the familiar 'muscular but dim' stereotype. Germans were physically robust, well qualified for waging war and skilled in the mechanical sciences, he conceded, but they regarded the fine arts with disdain and so 'had abandoned culture to their neighbours'.[126] Adrien Baillet blamed the Germans' rough climate for their lack of 'refinement, subtlety, brilliance, liveliness, delicacy, and playfulness'. Their laborious attempt to compensate by hard work, he added, had only led to Germany being chosen by Minerva 'as the best place in which to stable her mules'.[127]

That was all going to change. In his penetrating analysis of the cultural environment from which Goethe and the other great literary figures emerged, Nicholas Boyle laid special emphasis on the 'decisive impulse' provided by Leipzig, especially by Gottsched, who 'is rightly regarded as initiating the modern epoch of German literature'.[128] This was not a world in which Augustus played a leading role, but neither was it a world separate from or hostile to him. What was most distinctive of the great surge of creativity in the German world of the eighteenth century was the symbiosis of the court and city. Leipzig was amphibious, primarily commercial but bearing important residential and representational characteristics too. It was the seat of the Electorate's highest court (*Oberhofgericht*), highest ecclesiastical authority (*Konsistorium*), central postal office and the main tax authority.[129] Although mainly self-governing, the university was an electoral creation and ultimately subject to the elector's direction. There was also a fortress with a garrison commanded by a governor appointed by the elector. In short, a significant proportion of the city's population was employed directly or indirectly by the state. As Boyle concludes, 'literature and philosophy will join theology, and the other, more obviously court-dependent arts in being produced by and for officials – the class of teachers, pastors, secular civil servants and university professors'.[130]

Opposition

In short, for all its dominant burgher ethos, Leipzig's political culture was not hostile to Dresden. The conflicts habitually found in any urban community were contested between groups of citizens, not between citizens and ruler. Given Augustus's imperious temperament and the pride of Leipzig's city fathers, however, occasional friction was inevitable. One clash which left Augustus looking foolish was over his imposition in 1701 of Franz Conrad

Romanus as one of the three mayors. The new appointment's first task was to arrange for the introduction of street lighting, duly inaugurated on Christmas Eve 1701 with 700 oil lamps.[131] More important for Augustus was Romanus's extraction from the town council of large loans to finance the war in the east.[132] Other services to the city included support for Telemann's *Collegium Musicum* and a new organization for poor relief. But Romanus, who was only thirty years old when taking office, then succumbed to hubris. To build his palatial residence he borrowed heavily, made some injudicious investments and then forged municipal bonds in a desperate attempt to stave off bankruptcy. Arrested in 1705, he remained in custody until his death forty-one years later without ever being properly tried and convicted in a court of law.[133]

In 1710 Augustus again placed one of his trusted followers on the Leipzig council. This time it went much better. Gottfried Lange was young, enlightened and dedicated to promoting his ruler's interest, but without the extravagant tastes that had destroyed Romanus. He became mayor in 1719, remaining in office until his death in 1748. Posterity has every reason to thank Augustus for securing his appointment, for it was Lange who led the group on the council which forced through the appointment of Johann Sebastian Bach as cantor at St Thomas's Church in 1723. This was the happy outcome of a struggle between the old guard, who wanted a cantor to be a schoolteacher first and director of music (*Kapellmeister*) second, and the Lange party who insisted it should be the other way round. Bach demonstrated his gratitude by naming his first-born son Gottfried and inviting Lange to be godfather.[134] All those involved came together at Leipzig on 27 May 1727 when Bach performed before Augustus to celebrate his fifty-seventh birthday. This was a special occasion, for Augustus had come straight from Poland, where earlier in the year his gangrenous big toe had been amputated. Although he did not know it then, it was an operation that was to give him another six years of life.[135]

A not wholly convincing case has been made for seeing the struggle over Bach's appointment as a microcosm of the wider confrontation between enlightened absolutism (represented by Augustus, Lange and Bach) and the political opposition centred on the Saxon Estates.[136] The latter were organized in three chambers: 'Counts and Lords' (including representatives from the universities and three religious foundations); the owners of noble landed estates (*Ritter*); and the towns. It was the second group which offered the most determined opposition to Augustus's plans to increase his powers. These country gentlemen were among the most conservative in the Holy Roman Empire, which is saying a good deal. They were determined to defend their exemption from direct taxation at all costs, instinctively averse to any form of innovation, and fiercely intolerant of any form of Christianity that was not Orthodox Lutheran.[137] Much better off than their equivalents in many other German principalities, notably Brandenburg–Prussia, they were less beholden to their ruler for employment in his administration or army.[138] As Augustus was always looking for more money – for the Balkan campaigns, for the Polish election, for the Great Northern War, for his famously extravagant court, etc. – relations were bound to be strained. There were some similarities with the conflict between the Stuart kings of England and their Parliaments, although the Saxon version did not end with decapitation or even dethroning.

Mercifully, there is no need to follow its history in any detail.[139] The pattern was, essentially, government initiative, Estates resistance, confrontation, compromise. Augustus set the pace from the start with demands for increased taxation, and the Estates responded with demands for reduced taxation.[140] So far, so conventional, but Augustus had a powerful shot in his locker. This was the 'Great Commission' he appointed in 1698 to conduct an audit of all government agencies and officials. Equipped with inquisitorial powers, it set about uncovering and punishing the corruption it unearthed in almost every authority in almost every district.[141] Understandably, those on the receiving end were outraged. So much so, in fact, that Augustus had to intervene to order less severity. By then it had served its purpose. The intimidated Estates were ready to do a deal.

In March 1700 they made a one-off payment of 1,000,000 talers in return for the abandonment of the commission.[142] They proved to be the real victors. For the short-term gain of money that soon disappeared into the bottomless pit that was the Great Northern War, Augustus had given up what could have been a priceless weapon in effecting a revolution in government.[143] Attention then switched to fiscal reform. Right at the start of his reign, Augustus had announced his intention of introducing indirect taxation in the form of an excise. As the nobles who dominated the Estates were exempt from direct taxation, they were vehemently opposed. For just that reason, the excise was welcomed by many towns.[144] After being introduced here and there, in 1707 it was imposed generally, administered not by the traditional fiscal administration run by the Estates but by the new General Excise College subject only to the elector. At the same time Augustus moved to establish a parallel political authority free from Estates control. This was the 'Privy Cabinet' (*Geheime Kabinett*), starting out as an informal group of close advisers before being given a formal title, status and structure in 1706, with departments for domestic, foreign and military affairs.[145] The old central body, the 'Privy Council' (*Geheime Rat*), dominated by the nobility and supportive of the Estates, was not abolished but bypassed.

These techniques were employed throughout Europe by rulers seeking to enhance their control. So was another of Augustus's methods, namely the employment of officials without local connections. Many of his most important associates were from out of state, the most important being Hans Adam von Schöning (Brandenburg), Anton Egon von Fürstenberg (Swabia), Jakob Heinrich von Flemming (Pomerania), August Christoph von Wackerbarth (Lauenburg), Johann Matthias von der Schulenburg (Magdeburg) and Ernst Christoph von Manteuffel (Pomerania). Needless to say, these appointments aroused the ire of the native Saxon nobility. Especially offensive was the appointment of the Catholic Prince Fürstenberg as governor (*Statthalter*) in 1697, to act as regent during Augustus's long absences in Poland, described by modern Saxon historians as 'a coup' and 'a terrible provocation'.[146]

Ironically, Fürstenberg took umbrage when the Revision Commission was abolished and gravitated towards the Estates.[147] Augustus explained his policy in two autograph documents which are undated but probably composed in 1705. In the first, headed 'Recommendations for posterity', he insisted that the native nobility must be tamed, turned into obedient state servants and favoured over commoners only if possessing superior talents. Resistance should be penalised by expropriation of their estates. A second and shorter document castigated the Saxon nobles for usurping the elector's power and called for their subordination.[148] He continued to marginalize the Estates until the end of his reign. In 1705–6, the parallel administration under his personal control was extended by the creation of a General Excise College and a General Military Tribunal. Three years later the Estates' standing committee, agreed as part of the 1699 compromise, was abolished.[149] In 1728 new regulations took a leaf out of Louis XIV's book by stating that the Estates could continue to remonstrate against any proposed piece of legislation but the elector could simply reply 'That is my will' (*Tel est notre Plaisir*).[150]

Presenting even an abbreviated account of Augustus's domestic policies in Saxony in an interesting way would challenge the most eloquent of writers. But it cannot be avoided. His aims were clear, his achievements less so. Patently, he did want to exclude the Estates totally and to make himself as absolute as any early modern ruler could be. Although he certainly made progress towards that end, the Estates were still in being when he died, still a nuisance and still in control of direct taxation.[151] His frequent absences in Poland and the need to divert resources there meant that his attention to Saxon affairs was sclerotic. The huge expenditure on warfare and conspicuous consumption strained even sturdy Saxon sinews. If only he had declined entrapment in the iron cage that was Poland, he might have created an equally powerful but more benign version of his grim Prussian neighbour. Given that Saxony was part of the Holy Roman Empire, he could not have avoided the War of the Spanish Succession but he could surely have stayed out of the Baltic wars. Yet the balance was not entirely negative. Thanks to its natural buoyancy, Saxony recovered quickly from the Swedish occupation of 1706–7, expanding rapidly in population and prosperity. Reporting from Dresden in 1727, the Prussian official von Viebahn commended Saxony's good government. Under the industrious and prudent first minister, Jakob Heinrich von Flemming, he recorded, the finances were in good order, debts had been paid off, audits were regular, credit was good with loans offered at 2–3 per cent and there was a cash surplus of 3,000,000 talers in the treasury.[152] Where Augustus had been an unequivocal failure was in war and diplomacy and it is high time to turn back to events on the international stage.

The Resurrection of King Augustus: the Return to Poland

The Swedish invasion of Russia

In the aftermath of the Altranstädt debacle and the Swedish occupation, retrenchment was the order of the day for Augustus. What remained of the army was sent off to fight in the Low Countries, subsidized by the Maritime Powers.[1] A less ambitious man might have cut his losses and settled for an easy life in Saxony, perhaps spiced by the occasional holiday in the fleshpots of Venice. But Augustus had not given up. Over the previous ten years he had come to know his former Polish kingdom all too well, better in fact than his Swedish rival. So he knew that the only certain thing about that wobbly colossus was its unpredictability. Charles had put King Stanisław on the throne, but could he keep him there? The ranks of the small minority of the Polish political nation that had supported his election did not grow much, even after Augustus's abdication. A few magnates crossed over, notably the Morsztyn clan in Lesser Poland, but the majority remained uncommitted or hostile, as did the majority of the szlachta.[2] Even the burghers of Danzig, who had more reason than most to resent Augustus, remained stubbornly loyal, refusing to recognize Stanisław as legitimate.[3]

Particularly ominous was the continuation of the Sandomierz Confederation, formed back in 1704 in support of Augustus.[4] Deserted by his abdication, they declared an interregnum, postponing a new election until victory over Charles and Stanisław had been achieved.[5] That uncertain event was not going to be soon enough for Tsar Peter, who set about looking for an alternative King of Poland immediately after Augustus had departed. He considered plenty – the Crown Grand Hetman Adam Mikołaj Sieniawski, the Hungarian insurgent Ferenc Rákóczi, the imperial Field Marshal Prince Eugene, a Prince of Nassau, Alexander Sobieski, his own son Alexei – all declined or were found wanting. Enraged by Augustus's unilateral peace, the Battle of Kalisz fiasco and, not least, by the surrender of Patkul to the tender mercies of King Charles, it was through clenched teeth that Peter eventually concluded that Augustus would have to be restored.[6]

As to when – or whether – that might happen, all depended on the outcome of the attack on Russia which Charles set in motion as soon as he and his army left Saxony in August 1707. Such was its impact on the subsequent history of Europe that the tag 'world-historical' is justified. This was no blitzkrieg. Such were the enormous distances involved that it all took a very long time. It was not until July 1708 that the Swedes reached the Dnieper and another year was to pass before the decisive battle was fought, at Poltava. The lethargic pace was determined by supply problems. Never was the old saw that 'an army marches on its stomach' better illustrated.[7] Knowing that the Russians would do their utmost to scorch the earth over which their enemy would march, Charles had instructed his commander in Livonia, General Adam Ludwig Lewenhaupt, to gather huge stocks of food and forage, load them all on to a waggon train of corresponding size, and then proceed south to link up with the main army. He was also to bring with him 12,000 reinforcements. Trying to gather supplies in a region devastated by war and decimated by plague took much longer than expected. By the time the convoy set out, it was several weeks behind schedule. Lewenhaupt did his best, but the string of around 4,000 waggons, stretched out over at least twenty kilometres, made painfully slow progress along roads turned into quagmires by unseasonably heavy rain.[8]

Meanwhile, Charles was wrestling with an increasingly intractable quandary. His original plan envisaged a direct march on Moscow to knock out Peter with a single punch. The expected total victory was to be followed by the dethronement of the tsar and his replacement by a puppet of the Stanisław Leszczyński variety or the division of Russia into a number of principalities.[9] He would not be the last invader to underestimate the distance to be travelled. When he launched his campaign, he was closer to the west coast of Ireland than to Moscow.[10] He won a minor tactical victory at Holowczyn on 4 July, but the strategic picture had not altered. As he looked east after crossing the Dnieper all he could see were clouds of smoke rising from fields and villages set ablaze by Peter's Cossacks and Kalmucks. And still there was no sign of Lewenhaupt; indeed Charles had no idea where the relief convoy was. For the first time, his iron will faltered. Early on in the march, when his quartermaster-general, Axel Gyllenkrok, had stressed the dangers of venturing so deep into enemy territory, Charles had rejoindered with the jaunty aphorism: 'We must take risks while fortune smiles on us!' (*Vi måste våga, så länge vi äro i lyckan*). It was a very different Charles who sought advice from Gyllenkrok some weeks later as to the best route to take. On being told that this depended on his plan of campaign, Charles replied that he had no plan (*Jag har ingen dessein*). Gyllenkrok thought he must be joking, but Charles assured him he was serious. At a council of war also attended by Piper and Rehnskiöld, the decision was taken to abandon a direct thrust at Moscow in favour of a move to the south, to left-bank Ukraine, where supplies were expected to be more plentiful. An obvious third option – to return the way they had come – was ruled out by Charles, never prepared to contemplate anything that looked like a retreat.[11] This uncertainty demonstrated that Charles was a peerless battlefield commander but hopeless strategist, in both respects the polar opposite of Tsar Peter.[12] The difference was that the latter was aware of his limitations and always relinquished command when action commenced to a general who knew what he was doing.

It was now the middle of September and the days were getting shorter. Although the hapless Swedes did not know it yet, their enemy was about to be joined by a powerful ally in the shape of 'General Winter'. The winter of 1708–9 was to prove not just 'the winter of the century' but 'the winter of the *millennium*',[13] and moreover for all of Europe (even the lagoon at Venice froze). Of course it was the same for both sides, but only in the sense that the temperature was the same. Playing at home, the Russians enjoyed the priceless advantage of 'interior lines', and could replace men and matériel from their limitless hinterland, whereas the Swedes were moving further away from their base with every step they took.[14] To make matters worse, at the beginning of October the Lewenhaupt convoy was intercepted by a Russian army commanded by Peter in person at Lesnaya (today Lyasnaya in Belarus) and destroyed.[15] It was the first time the Russians had defeated a Swedish army in open battle. All the supplies, cannon and horses were captured or destroyed. Although Lewenhaupt succeeded in extricating part of his force, less than half eventually reached Charles and the main army, bringing with them only what they could carry.[16]

As autumn turned into winter, the temperatures kept falling. By the time Hadiach (Гадяч, sometimes transliterated as Gadjatj) was reached on 23 December, it was simply too cold to allow any further progress. Corporal Erik Larsson Smepust wrote that he had seen birds fall dead from the sky.[17] Estimates of the number of soldiers who froze to death have varied from 'between three and four thousand' (Tarle), 'more than one thousand' (Fuller), 'many' (Liljegren) or 'some' (Hatton).[18] An attempt to capture the neighbouring fortress of Veprik ended in failure at a cost of 400 dead and 600 wounded. The stout resistance offered by the Russian garrison highlighted another of Charles's miscalculations, namely his continuing underestimate of his enemy's fighting capacity. This was noticed much earlier by Captain James Jefferyes, a British officer accompanying the Swedish army. In July he had reported to London: 'one observation I have made sinse [*sic*] the late action, viz that the Svedes are forc'd to own the Muscovites have learnt their lesson much better, and have made great improvements in military affairs sinse the battle of Narva, and if their soldiers had shew'd but half that courage their officers did (which for the most part are foraigners) they had probably been too hard for us in the late action'.[19] He was referring to the engagement at Holowczyn, where success had only served to confirm Charles in his belief that the Russians could always be beaten.[20]

Jefferyes also spotted an associated problem when he wrote later in the campaign: 'Though we speack but little of peace at present, yet there are but few among us who do not heartily wish for it, for the officers as well as the common soldiers begin to be tir'd of their continuall fatigues.'[21] With the advantage of hindsight, we can see that Swedish morale had been declining for some time, heralded by the return home of several senior officers following the occupation of Saxony in 1706.[22] In retrospect, the year the Swedes had spent there had been a golden age. The further east they went, the more depressing were the conditions and the bleaker the prospects. Shortly after the victory at Holowczyn, Colonel Magnus Posse wrote home that it never stopped raining, the roads were impassable, the villages deserted, there was nothing to buy to eat or drink and that only divine intervention could save them. Much worse was to come when they turned south towards Ukraine. On the first stretch, lasting a week, there was no food or forage of any kind, they had to bivouac in the open because there were no tents and the forest tracks were repeatedly blocked by trees felled by Russian irregulars. The dragoon Joachim Lyth recorded that the soldiers kept asking: what are we going to eat? What are we going to drink? How are we going to get through the winter? Even more alarming was the response of Lewenhaupt's survivors when ordered to march off after the debacle at Lesnaya. As darkness fell, discipline began to collapse as the soldiers plundered their own waggons, got drunk and deserted. A whole unit of around 1,500 just disappeared, eventually turning up at Riga some months later.[23]

Charles could be forgiven for not anticipating the full ferocity of General Winter, but his arrogant underestimate of his opponents was more culpable. Chief among those he despised was Tsar Peter himself. Remembering him only as the man who ran away rather than face him at Narva in 1700, Charles failed to appreciate just how determined, resourceful and ruthless Peter had become. Believing what he wanted to hear, Charles had been persuaded by reports that a Swedish invasion of Russia would set off an insurrection by both nobility and common people.[24] Peter was counting on just the reverse. At a council of war held at Żółkiew (now Zhokva, Ukraine) at the end of 1706, a plan devised by General Boris Sheremetev was adopted. An open confrontation was to be avoided by retreat, with the enemy weakened by scorched earth and constant harrying by irregular forces until the time was ripe for a counter-strike.[25] Making full use of Charles's prolonged sojourn in Saxony, the population of the Russian frontier region had been instructed to prepare hiding places for food and livestock.[26] In the event, the laying-waste of the march routes was so effective that one Swedish historian has concluded that Charles could not have supplied his army satisfactorily even if Lewenhaupt's convoy had survived.[27]

Tactical retreat as the Swedes advanced did not mean inactivity, as the devastating strike on Lewenhaupt had shown. The Russians knew the terrain, had better sources of intelligence and could draw on vastly greater human, equine and material reserves. When the Swedes lost a man, he could not be replaced. In November 1708, it was this advantage that had allowed the Russians to win the race to reach the Cossack capital of Baturin first and remove or destroy the artillery and large stocks of food and forage.[28] When Charles arrived a few days later, he found only a smouldering ruin. The disappointment was all the greater because it also marked the end of what once seemed like a promising alliance recently concluded with the anti-Russian Cossacks.

The key player in this subplot was the legendary Ivan Mazepa. His long and exciting life was to inspire verse epics by Byron, Pushkin and Victor Hugo, a tone-poem by Liszt and an opera by Tchaikovsky. All that concerns us, however, was his single-minded pursuit of independence for Ukraine. For most of his long life (he had been born in 1639) that meant supporting Russia, which he had visited frequently, establishing a good personal relationship with Tsar Peter. However, from the late 1690s he had grown increasingly discontented with what had come to seem an unbalanced relationship. In 1699 he wrote to Peter, pointing out that during his twelve years as hetman of the Cossacks he had conducted eleven campaigns on behalf of Russia against the Tatars and the Turks but the results had not been commensurate with the sacrifices. The treaties bringing the Turkish war to a close had given Russia and the Holy League plenty but the Ukrainian Cossacks nothing.[29]

That whine should have sounded a warning, but it was not heeded. Committing what Tarlé dubbed '*une erreur effroyable*', Peter continued to take Mazepa's support for granted.[30] Rightly fearing that Cossack Ukraine was to be absorbed into the Russian Empire, from 1705 Mazepa was making approaches to King Stanisław and his Swedish master, concluding a formal agreement at the end of October 1708.[31] Denunciations of Mazepa's 'treachery' had been blithely ignored in Moscow; indeed it was the accusers who were packed off to the accused, who promptly put them to death.[32] Great was Peter's fury when he found that he had been hoodwinked and terrible was his revenge when Menshikov razed Baturin to the ground and slaughtered all its inhabitants, men, women and children. Yet it had no impact on the outcome. Mazepa had promised Charles 20,000 Cossacks – in the event he had only just over 1,000 with him when he arrived in November 1708.[33] The great majority of Cossacks stayed away, deterred by a Russian propaganda campaign harping on the heresy of the Lutheran Swedes, by the fear of the tsar's wrath and by his offer of three roubles for every Swede they killed.[34] In March 1709 Mazepa did succeed in persuading the Zaporozhian Cossacks to join him, but it was too little too late and succeeded only in bringing a fearful punitive expedition to their capital at the Sich on the lower Dnieper.[35]

At least the Cossacks had made some contribution to the Swedish campaign. Nothing at all was forthcoming from another anticipated ally – the Crimean Tatars. Charles had been wooing them and their Turkish overlords for almost as long as he had been in Poland.[36] In the spring of 1708 he had sent an envoy to the Tatar capital Bakhchysarai in the Crimea and had received an encouraging response from Khan Devlet II Giray. Also promising in the same region was the anti-Russian insurrection of the Don Cossacks led by Kondraty Bulavin, which had been gathering momentum since the previous autumn. If their march west had succeeded in taking the key fortress of Azov, the Tatars and then the Turks might well have joined in too. In the event, swift counter-action ordered by Peter brought the Cossack advance to an abrupt halt in July 1708.[37] Continuing to hope, Charles was still counting on the arrival of 40,000 Tatars when the campaign reached its climax in the summer of 1709. Peter had been more astute, realizing that the decision about Tatar involvement would be taken at Constantinople, not at Bakhchysarai. It was there that he concentrated his diplomatic effort, assisted by copious bribes, while he himself showered gifts on the Turks he met at Azov in April 1709. The result was that a council held at Constantinople the following month voted for peace and the Tatars were told to stay at home. The destruction of the Zaporozhian Sich in May 1709 completed the pacification of the south.[38]

A last potential source of reinforcement was of course Poland itself. It was in this sector that Charles's failure was most glaring and most fateful. Well aware that support for his puppet king was only thin and patchy, he left behind 8,000–9,000 Swedes commanded by General Ernst Detlef von Krassow, to provide some backbone for Stanisław's Polish army of uncertain reliability. When the time was ripe, their combined forces were to march east to join Charles for a final assault on the Russians. This never happened, for the good reason that their way was barred by the army of the San-domierz Confederation, supported by Russian auxiliary units.[39] The crucial moment came at Koniecpol, about 100 kilometres north of Kraków, on 21 November 1708, when Stanisław's army of around 10,000, led by Józef Potocki, was routed by roughly the same number of Sandomierz and Lithuanian troops led by Jakub Zygmunt Rybiński.[40] A second half-hearted attempt, led by Stanisław, to break through to Ukraine in the spring of 1709 was abandoned when news came that a Russian force was approaching.[41] The last hurrah of the Leszczyński loyalists came on 24 May when they were defeated by Augustus's main supporter in Poland, the Crown Grand Hetman Adam Sieniawski, and the Russians of Heinrich von der Goltz.[42]

In all these ways, the Russian expedition undertaken by Charles fell apart. Temperamentally unable to cut his losses, he journeyed on to the disaster that was now inevitable. It was still his intention to resume his march to Moscow. A first attempt, in February 1709, was foiled by bad weather. Before a second could be launched it was necessary to capture Poltava, a fortress on the River Vorskla, a tributary of the Dnieper. Charles also hoped that the siege, which began on 2 May, would force the Russians to risk an open battle. It proceeded slowly, as the 4,000-strong garrison resisted stoutly. Charles was still nursing the forlorn hope that help would be coming from the Tatars and from King Stanisław.[43] Charles still believed that it was a sense of inferiority that kept Peter away, but that was no longer the case. Russian intelligence knew all about the losses their enemy had suffered. Recovering from a bout of illness that had kept him at Azov, in June, Peter and his main army moved against Poltava, to relieve the fortress and to crush Charles.[44]

The course of the battle on 8 July has been retold many times and need not delay us long.[45] In the nine years that had passed since the humiliation of Narva, Peter had transformed his army. The Russian command now displayed determination and resourcefulness, their rank-and-file courage and endurance. In particular, the enterprising use at Poltava of battlefield redoubts (fortified positions) to break the Swedish assault may have been decisive. The Russians also enjoyed a two-to-one advantage in numbers and a massive superiority in field artillery, the latter probably being crucial.[46] It also deserves mentioning that Peter himself had laid to rest the ghost of Narva by being in the thick of the action, as the colonel in command of an infantry battalion (Sheremetev being in overall command) and had his hat shot off while rallying his troops at a crucial moment.[47] On the other side, the course of the battle made clear that two years of incessant campaigning in often atrocious conditions had drained Swedish morale. It was not improved by the knowledge that Charles had been wounded by a stray bullet before the battle and had to be carried around on a litter. For the first time, the fabled Swedish infantry turned and ran when confronted by Russian charges. The casualty figures revealed the severity of the rout that ensued. In round figures, the Swedes lost 7,000 killed and 3,000 taken prisoner, the Russian figures being 1,300 killed and 3,200 wounded.[48] Swedish losses amounted to nearly 60 per cent.[49] The prisoners of war were sent off to the Russian interior to perform hard labour. Only a quarter ever got home after the peace in 1721.[50]

That was not the end of it. The remnants of the defeated army – around 16,000 – restored some sort of order in their ranks and retreated south along the River Vorskla. They were accompanied by Mazepa and his Cossacks, who had taken no part in the battle. But when they reached the confluence with the mighty Dnieper, which is almost two kilometres wide at that point, they found themselves trapped in a cul-de-sac. There was no bridge, no ford and only a few boats. Charles, Mazepa and the top brass were ferried across, while some of the others swam with or without their horses. Many drowned. On the following day, 11 July, Menshikov and the Russian advance guard arrived in pursuit. For Lewenhaupt, in command after Charles's flight, the choice was now between heroic last-ditch resistance ending in a massacre or a negotiated surrender. Around a third of his troops were ill or wounded.[51] After consulting all his officers of the rank of colonel and above, he chose the latter, so 1,161 officers and 13,138 other ranks became prisoners of war. To that total must be added 4,843 civilians, including 1,657 women and children.[52] The Cossacks were not parties to the agreement, being regarded by the Russians as traitors, not combatants. Some managed to escape, the rest were summarily put to death.[53] The capitulation at Perevolotjna deserves to be ranked with Poltava itself as a catastrophic Swedish defeat – indeed was more damaging in its consequences.[54]

Although he had escaped over the Dnieper, Charles was still not safe, for the Russians were hard on his heels. It was not until he reached the Turkish fortress of Ochakov on the Black Sea that he could breathe more easily. His reception was mixed. On the one hand, the sultan welcomed any ally in his epochal struggle with the Russians; on the other, Charles's mercurial reputation had preceded him and his military value had been compromised by defeat.

At the 'invitation' of his hosts he reluctantly moved to Bender, 250 kilometres to the west in what today is Moldova. He was still thinking in terms of an early return to Poland. In October he sent Axel Gyllenkrok and a small detachment of Swedes and Cossacks to reconnoitre the Polish frontier to see whether he might get across in force. Not only did they find that the Russians had everything strictly controlled, they themselves were taken prisoner.[55]

That was how it stayed – five long years of exile were to pass before Charles could begin the perilous journey back to his army in the north. His victor meanwhile organized a colossal victory parade in Moscow, with seven triumphal arches, giant visual depictions of Russian victories, all the city's churches ringing their bells, constant gun salutes, grandstands, refreshment booths with free drinks, illuminations, fireworks and captured Swedish banners and flags – everything but the kitchen sink. As Charles himself could not be put on display, the next best thing was to include the litter on which he had been borne during the Battle of Poltava, mounted on a special chariot. That was followed by serried ranks of captured Swedish officers, marching two by two, ending with Charles's first minister Piper and his senior generals – Rehnskiöld, Lewenhaupt, Schlippenbach, Hamilton and Stackelburg – also on foot. Last but by no means least came the tsar-conqueror himself, mounted on the steed that had carried him at Poltava.[56]

The kings have left, long live the king!

By this time, Augustus was firmly back in the Polish saddle. Like everyone else in Europe, he had been following the progress of Charles's Russian invasion with keen interest, not to say immense pleasure. For the time being, a return to Poland could only be a dream, but its translation into reality could be prepared. No sooner had the Swedes left Saxony than plans for revenge were being formed and the longer they were gone the bolder those plans became. Money was borrowed, recruits were mustered and trained, horses were bought, weapons and ammunition were stockpiled and a militia was organized for home defence.[57] It is certain that from 1708 Augustus was intending to abrogate the Treaty of Altranstädt and return.[58]

With every step Charles and his army marched eastwards, the more optimistic the mood in Dresden became. Well before the news of Poltava arrived on 23 July 1709, Augustus had decided the time was ripe for a return. Preparations were begun to restore the Grand Alliance of 1699. The first to be enlisted was Frederick IV of Denmark, who in the autumn of 1708 had embarked on what was essentially a jaunt to Italy, including of course the Venetian carnival. On his way back the following summer, he called in at Dresden. He found his host in an expansive mood, as Augustus unleashed the full splendour of his court (an episode that will be dealt with later in a different context).[59] The two were closely related, Augustus's mother being the daughter of Frederick III, who was Frederick IV's grandfather.

A close relationship, good relations and a good time paved the way for a treaty of alliance, signed at Dresden on 28 June, or in other words *before* Poltava had been fought, let alone reported. The declared purpose was to restore the 'balance of power' in the north by returning to Denmark the provinces lost to Sweden during the previous century and restoring Augustus to the Polish throne.[60] Following their junketing at Dresden, Frederick IV and Augustus travelled on to Berlin to seek the support of Frederick I of Prussia (r. 1688–1713). He had territorial ambitions too, but hitherto had steered clear of any involvement in the Northern War (although he was heavily involved in the War of the Spanish Succession in the west). The bruising misfortunes of his two visitors at the hands of the Swedes also counselled caution. All he was prepared to sign, on 15 July 1709, was a treaty of neutrality with no commitment to active intervention. It was benevolent neutrality, however, as he showed when he agreed to prohibit Krassow and his Swedish army from entering Prussian territory but allowed Augustus to do so en route to Poland.[61] Prussian plans for a grand redistribution of the Swedish Baltic empire were put on hold, if only for the time being.

With his neighbours safely on board or neutralized, Augustus was now ready to return. On 30 August he joined his expeditionary force of around 11,000 at Guben, near the Brandenburg frontier. From there he issued a manifesto defending his past conduct, denouncing the Peace of Altranstädt as illegal, and claiming that he was returning at the invitation of his loyal Polish subjects.[62] As the Danish historian Christian von Sarauw acidly remarked: 'there was a lie in every line'.[63] True to form, Augustus celebrated his re-entry into Poland with ostentatious display. In addition to his regular guards regiment he was escorted by a new '*Garde des Chevaliers*', an elite force in a decorative if not a military sense. Designed to attract nobles from all over Europe, it accepted anyone able to pay for the sumptuous uniform: a scarlet jacket with blue lapels and gold buttons, a blue velvet cloak trimmed with gold braid, adorned with a gold star, and bearing on the front the motto '*Jehova vexillum meum*' (Jehova is my banner) and on the back a red cross edged in gold. Every *chevalier* was attended by an esquire, grooms, lackeys and eight to ten horses.[64] It was almost as if Augustus was flaunting his distance from his cousin Charles's austere puritanism.

Events in Poland during Charles's Russian adventure had demonstrated that King Stanisław was kept in power only by the military force of his Swedish masters. So it was no surprise that the return of Augustus did not meet much opposition.[65] When news of Poltava and Perevolotjna filtered back to Poland, the magnates knew that Augustus would be coming back from the west and Tsar Peter would be coming back from the east, so they hurried to abandon King Stanisław's sinking ship.[66] The szlachta even seemed prepared to accept the presence of Saxon troops, as protection against the Swedes.[67] Augustus now consulted senators and leading lights of the Sandomierz Confederation on how best to secure the restored regime.[68] The answer was a general council convened in Warsaw in January 1710, which confirmed Augustus as the rightful king and declared Stanisław's rule to have been illegal. An amnesty was granted to any of the latter's supporters who submitted.[69]

Ex-king Stanisław was now so isolated that he abandoned what remained of his Polish army and sought the protection of the Swedish General Krassow, with whose army he withdrew to Pomerania.[70] He now had plenty of time on his hands to reflect on the folly of his decision to accept election at the behest of his admirer, Charles XII. In 1704 he had been one of the most powerful, prosperous and respected magnates in the Commonwealth. Five years later he was a despised fugitive, his estates in ruins, his future uncertain, his past a nightmare. In the bleak assessment of Richard Butterwick, his brief reign had been 'little more than a façade for Swedish pillage'.[71] It was only after several more years of anxiety and privation that he found himself, by a series of happy accidents, Duke of Lorraine and father-in-law of King Louis XV of France.[72]

Not much foresight was needed to spot that what really mattered in the autumn of 1709 was the return not of Augustus and his gorgeous guards but of Tsar Peter and his seasoned veterans. On 20 September Peter sailed down the Vistula to Warsaw, where a reception committee of senators congratulated him on his victory and thanked him for having restored their rightful king and their liberties.[73] During Augustus's absence from Poland, Peter had built up his own party of loyalists, who now flocked to greet him as he made his way across Poland to meet Augustus at Toruń. Back in July his ambassador had signed a treaty with Augustus at Dresden, but Peter had delayed ratification. Brimful of the victor's confidence, Peter wanted more. The essential content of the treaty signed on 26 September was simple: Russia was to keep all the territory taken from Sweden, while Poland was to be restored to the *status quo ante bellum*. Both powers were to combine in the war against Sweden, to restore its 'proper borders'. That might seem to give precious little to Augustus, although in truth it was all he deserved, given his feeble effort during the first six years of the war and eventual defeat. However, what really mattered to him was the secret article agreed on 20 October, which stated: 'the Principality of Livonia with all its cities and places are to pass to his Royal Polish Majesty, as Elector of Saxony, with succession to his heirs'.[74] That was what he had been seeking all along, in the belief that a hereditary principality would also make the Polish Crown hereditary in the House of Wettin. Ominously, however, no date was mentioned for the transfer to Augustus.[75] As events were to show, Peter had not the slightest intention of making over his prized conquest to his faithless ally, although Augustus seems to have been blissfully unaware of a possibility which should have been seen as a probability.

For the time being, Augustus could luxuriate in success. He was back in Poland and back on the throne. Of his enemies, Charles was in exile in the Ottoman Empire and Stanisław was in exile in Pomerania. The great magnates who had caused him so much trouble in the past had either submitted or fled. The international situation was also promising. Just as Peter and Augustus were conferring on the latter's luxurious red-painted yacht on the Vistula at Toruń, the Grand Alliance was winning another victory against the French at Malplaquet. Making a notable contribution was the Saxon contingent, which included Augustus's twelve-year-old illegitimate son Moritz (better known later as Maurice de Saxe, who would become the most successful French general of Louis XV's long reign).[76] With France losing the War of the Spanish Succession, there was no prospect of Sweden obtaining any material assistance from its traditional ally. Determined to keep the two major European wars apart, in March 1710 the Grand Alliance concluded a convention at The Hague to render the Holy Roman Empire neutral, thus making it impossible for Swedish forces to take action against Poland.[77]

The icing on the cake came in 1711 when Emperor Joseph I died of smallpox, for that elevated Augustus, as Elector of Saxony, to be 'Imperial Vicar' (*Reichsvikar*). Together with the Elector of the Palatinate, he administered the Holy Roman Empire of the German Nation during the interregnum, which in this case lasted from 17 April until 12 October. Augustus certainly made the most of his six months at the pinnacle of European royalty. One of his first actions was to have the imperial insignia displayed on the tower of the Church of the Holy Cross in Dresden, whose bells pealed at noon for half an hour every day in homage to his new status.[78] At the 'Zwinger', the representational arena being created next door to the Dresden Palace, the imperial double eagle was added to the Saxon and Polish coat of arms. The central iconographic motif of the complex was Hercules (Augustus) bearing the weight of the globe (the Holy Roman Empire) while deputizing for Atlas (the emperor).[79] Among the many privileges the office of *Reichsvikar* conveyed was the right to confer patents of imperial nobility. It was typically Augustan that he should have taken the opportunity to elevate Adolf Magnus von Hoym, the former husband of his mistress Constantia, from imperial baron (*Reichsfreiherr*) to imperial count (*Reichsgraf*). It cannot have been often that the office was used to reward a cuckold for his complaisance. Other more respectable recipients of the same promotion were the senior ministers Jakob Heinrich von Flemming and Friedrich Vitzthum von Eckstädt. More seriously, Augustus also found himself in joint command of the imperial army fighting in the War of the Spanish Succession.[80]

Back in the Royal Palace in Warsaw, Augustus appeared to be the monarch of all he surveyed. Long gone were the wretched days of defeat and humiliation of 1706. Yet if it was not quite the case of '*plus ça change, plus c'est la même chose*', so many problems remained unresolved. The Great Northern War continued on its meandering, sclerotic path, as inconclusive as it was destructive. Had the great Battle of Poltava really resolved anything? If it was 'one of the decisive battles of the century' (Franklin Daniel Scot) or even one of *The Fifteen Decisive Battles of the World* (the title of Sir Edward Shepherd Creasy's influential book of 1851), why did the war not end for another *twelve years*?[81] Inside Poland–Lithuania, a decade of what amounted to civil war had left wounds so deep and raw that they would fester for years to come. Reconciliation would need very careful handling of Polish sensibilities. Alas, on his return to Poland, Augustus was to provide a trailer for the remark about the restored Bourbons after 1815, usually attributed to Talleyrand: 'they have learnt nothing, and have forgotten nothing'.[82]

How the Great Northern War Was Won and Lost

How the Great Northern War was won by Russia

The post-Poltava phase of the war (1709–21) presents a challenge of unusual severity to historians. There were so many events in so many places with such transient results that any coherent thread eludes discovery. It can be assumed with some confidence that those who have attempted a complete narrative – the work of James Frederick Chance springs to mind – will not have been rewarded by many readers, or at least not by many who persevered very far.[1] Revealingly, the best English-language study of the war devotes sixty-six pages to the period before Poltava and just three to the rather longer second part of the conflict.[2] For the biographer of Augustus, more equitable attention is required. In what follows, I have eschewed the often inconsequential comings and goings of the various sovereigns, ministers and diplomats in favour of an analysis of the reasons for the outcome. This involves revisiting the earlier period, for it was then that the die was cast. Of necessity, Augustus himself will play something of a bit part, upstaged by the two superstars, Charles XII and Tsar Peter. To mix the metaphors, he became the grist between two millstones.

One augury of the final result could be found right at the start, in the summer of 1700, when Charles overwhelmed the Danes in a lightning campaign.[3] It was to prove the only successful Swedish amphibious exercise of the war.[4] Although it demonstrated the advantages of a combined operation of both land and sea forces, subsequently Charles had eyes only for the military dimension. The ghastly experience of crossing the Baltic in the autumn of the same year, when the equinoctial gales dispersed much of his fleet and condemned him to a prolonged agony of seasickness, alienated him not just from sea travel but from the maritime sector as a whole.[5] In part, this was a personal aversion. Fourteen years after this first (and last) unhappy experience on the ocean wave, when he found himself trapped in the Ottoman Empire after Poltava, he insisted on returning overland, despite its dangers. Whatever the origin, this prioritizing of dry land had fatal consequences. Many were the causes of his downfall, but top of the list must stand his obtuse failure to recognize the importance of the navy.

His thalassophobia would have been less damaging if it had not been countered by the equally passionate thalassophilia of his great enemy, Tsar Peter. All of the latter's better biographers agree that everything to do with the sea was an early and enduring passion.[6] In 1689, at the age of seventeen, he went to work in a recently constructed shipyard at Pereslavl, north of Moscow, serving as a simple carpenter and returning during the winter of 1691–2 to work on a warship.[7] This hands-on approach to learning about the details of ship construction was repeated at Archangel (then Russia's only maritime port) in 1693 and again in 1694 when he laid the keel of a new ship, took part in sea trials, commissioned a 44-gun battleship and ordered the construction of additional dockyards on the Solombala peninsula.[8] The determination to make Russia a great naval power was also the main motive for his 'Grand Embassy' to the west in 1697–8. One day after his arrival in Amsterdam, on 18 August 1697, he was already hard at work in a Zaandam dockyard, helping to build a frigate. Disappointed that he could learn only practical skills from the Dutch, in January the following year he crossed to England to acquire the theoretical and mathematical knowledge he still lacked.[9] To enlarge his experience to include the construction of galleys, it had been his intention to complete his European tour in Venice, the Venetians being the acknowledged master-builders of shallow-water craft. News of the revolt of the *streltsi* in Moscow aborted that last expedition,[10] but his interest in vessels able to operate in the Baltic archipelagos remained very much alive.

In the course of his journey, Peter had been busy recruiting maritime personnel, from simple seamen to shipbuilders and admirals. The most important newcomer was Cornelius Cruys, a Norwegian with Dutch naval experience, whose task in Russia was to organize the recruits – sixty officers, 115 petty officers and 350 seamen – as the foundation of a new naval force.[11] At this stage – 1698 – the Ottomans were the enemy, the centre of operations was at Voronezh and the main target was the Black Sea. When that war came to an end in 1700 and attention swivelled to the north, Peter's maritime strategy made the necessary adjustment. He now concentrated on what he rightly saw as the key to Swedish control of the eastern Baltic – the province of Ingria, in particular the River Neva, running from Lake Ladoga to the Gulf of Finland. Only seventy-four kilometres in length, it is nonetheless the fourth-largest river in Europe in terms of water flow, pouring into the Gulf of Finland so vigorously that the current is still visible a mile from shore.[12]

Ceded to Sweden by the Treaty of Stolbova in 1617, Ingria formed the barrier cutting off Russia from the Baltic.[13] For that reason, it had been regarded by King Gustavus Adolphus as the most important of all the territorial gains made by that landmark treaty. In a speech to his Estates after its signature, he stressed the future danger posed to Sweden by Russia, should it ever begin to realize its potential, and therefore the imperative necessity of keeping it severed from the Baltic.[14] Best remembered for his brilliant victories on land, Gustavus Adolphus was also the only King of Sweden to command his navy at sea, using combined naval–military operations to brilliant effect: 'successful combined operations were to be decisive for Swedish ability to gain control over the Baltic'.[15] In 1631 his chief minister, Axel Oxenstierna, laid down Swedish policy: 'it is essential that Your Majesty should above all things labour to create a powerful fleet at sea; a fleet of good ships, and most especially a fleet very numerous, so that you may be master of every nook and cranny of the Baltic'.[16]

Whether Peter was aware of Gustavus Adolphus's fears or not, he certainly set about justifying them. In the spring of 1700, or in other words even before he had declared war on Sweden, he ordered a survey of communications between Russian territory on the southern shore of Lake Ladoga and Nöteborg, the Swedish fortress at the exit of the Neva from the lake, and from there along the course of the Neva to the Gulf of Finland. In the aftermath of the disaster at Narva, Peter had other things to deal with first. It was not until the summer of 1702 that he moved against Nöteborg. To block Swedish reinforcements, fifty boats were dragged overland along a three-kilometre track cut through the forest and then refloated on the Neva to the west of the fortress. At the end of September, Peter arrived in person to organize the final assault. Despite stout resistance, the heavily outnumbered Swedish garrison surrendered on 13 October. This was a truly momentous event, as the tsar himself advertised when he renamed Nöteborg 'Schlüsselburg' (Key Castle) and had the actual keys to the town handed over by the Swedish commander embedded in the wall to show that the Baltic was now unlocked.[17]

Back in Stockholm there was consternation, for Nöteborg was only forty kilometres from the sea, as the crow flies, and only thirty from Nyenskans, the last Swedish fortress on the Neva. Their alarm was not shared by their king, who dismissed their fears that Peter would now build a port on the Baltic with the assurance that recapture would be simple.[18] In the event, the only Swede ever to set foot in Schlüsselburg arrived as a prisoner of war to perform forced labour on the fortifications or, much later, as a tourist. The winter brought only a brief respite. In the spring, Peter moved down the Neva to Nyenskans, which capitulated on 2 May 1703. Rather than establish his headquarters there, Peter decided to create a new fortified settlement further downstream, on the small island of Janissari, at the point where the Neva divides into multiple channels and flows into the Baltic. He named it St Petersburg.[19]

It was at this point that Peter made a decisive personal contribution to the durability of his eponymous creation, drawing on his long maritime training and experience. His careful reconnaissance of the western approaches revealed the strategic importance of a small island called Retusaari, because it commanded the only channel deep enough for battleships to proceed from the Gulf of Finland to the mouth of the Neva. From that channel, which was just 500 metres wide, across the shallow waters to the southern shore there ran a rocky outcrop only two metres below water-level. It was on this that Peter immediately set about sinking piles and building a battery, calling it 'Kronslott'.[20] By the following year it boasted an armament of fourteen heavy cannon. No wonder that Peter staged a boisterous festival lasting three days to celebrate its completion. Together with a matching battery on the island, Kronslott ensured that no enemy ship could get past. As the waters to the north and west of Retusaari were too shallow to allow Swedish warships to get close enough to mount a bombardment, the new St Petersburg was now invulnerable, as the failure of successive Swedish attempts to scotch it in the egg proved.[21] There are many candidates for the accolade 'point of no return' in the collapse of the Swedish Baltic Empire, but the building of Kronslott deserves to be included in any top ten. Advertising the sea change, the frigate that bore Peter to his new creation flew a redesigned standard on which the double-headed eagle now held in its claws maps representing not just the three seas hitherto controlled by Russia (Caspian, White, Azov) but a fourth – the Baltic.[22]

The earliest attempt to eject the Russians was launched on 8 May 1703 when Admiral Numers sent a brigantine and a yacht into the Neva estuary. It was promptly ambushed and overwhelmed by around 100 small Russian vessels. The brigantine was destroyed by its crew before it could be boarded, but the yacht was captured and sent up the Neva to Nyenskans in triumph. Peter awarded himself the Order of St Andrew to mark his active participation in the engagement.[23] As this incident revealed, his sustained efforts to build as many ships as quickly as possible was paying off. They were built at shipyards around Lake Ladoga, especially at Olonets on the eastern shore.[24] These were joined in 1703 by a new centre at St Petersburg, where serf labour, convicts, Cossacks and Swedish prisoners of war were drafted in to build wharves and dockyards.

Shipbuilding began at once, as did commerce, and before the year was out the first merchant vessel from the west docked to unload a cargo of wine and salt.[25]

It might well be asked what King Charles was doing to defend Swedish possessions around the Baltic. As we have seen,[26] the answer is 'not very much'. After his victory over Steinau's Saxons at Pułtusk in April 1703, he moved on to besiege Toruń, an operation that lasted six months, before going into winter quarters in Warmia for another six months. He then spent most of 1704 getting Stanisław Leszczyński elected King of Poland and 1705 getting him crowned. It was only in 1706, following his wild-goose chase to Lwów, that he decided to invade Saxony, where he remained for a year. Even then his next initiative took him not to the Baltic but to Ukraine and from there to exile in the Ottoman Empire. As this simple chronology reveals, Livonia, Estonia, Ingria and Finland came a long way down his list of priorities. All his efforts were concentrated on dethroning Augustus. During the six years spent chasing him around Poland, his real enemy, Peter, was busily creating a navy and conquering the Swedish Baltic empire.

Waging war against two enemies in widely separated theatres was always going to be demanding. Charles made it more difficult by neglecting to appoint a single commander to coordinate the eastern campaign, delegating his authority to four subordinates – Carl Magnus Stuart in Courland, Abraham Cronhjort in Ingria, Henning Rudolf Horn in Narva and Wolmar Anton von Schlippenbach in Livonia. This was a recipe for the internecine conflict that duly ensued, not to mention the inevitable disputes of all of them with the civilian authorities. The most far-sighted was Stuart, who had supervised Charles's military education before his accession and was 'one the ablest and most knowledgeable of all the Swedish generals' (Arnold Munthe). Early in 1703 – at a time when Nyenskans was still in Swedish hands – Stuart came up with a sensible plan for halting any further Russian advance. He did not bother to send it to Charles, however, because all his previous communications had either taken so long to reach their destination that they were overtaken by events, or had never arrived at all. So he sent it to the Defence Commission in Stockholm, hoping they would take action. But they felt unable to comment on matters of such gravity and sent it back across the Baltic to Schlippenbach in Livonia and the governors of Reval and Riga for their comments. As the response was negative, the commission adopted the classic bureaucratic solution – and filed it. In the meantime, Nyenskans had fallen and the construction of St Petersburg was under way.[27]

This account of the naval dimension must now be truncated before Augustus completely disappears over the horizon. The key events can be identified readily – control of Lake Ladoga was achieved in 1702 and of Lake Peipus in 1704, the latter leading to the fall of the key port and fortress of Narva in the same year.[28] In 1710, the transfer of Russian land forces from Ukraine after Poltava brought five great prizes, all won by combined operations – Reval (which had been Swedish for 150 years), the island of Ösel, Riga, Kexholm and Viborg (which had been Swedish for four centuries). Those last two prepared the way for the conquest of Finland. This surge of Russian expansion was made possible by a rapid increase in naval strength. In the early stages of the war, Peter concentrated on building galleys and other small vessels suitable for actions close in shore. Later, the emphasis moved to constructing battleships cap-able of confronting the main Swedish fleet in open water. In 1708–9 five small 50-gun ships had been laid down, followed by six medium-sized ships at St Petersburg in 1711–12 and eleven more in 1714–16, some of them carrying 96 guns.[29] In addition battleships and frigates were bought from the Dutch Republic, England and Hamburg.[30] Yet it was the galley fleet which won the first major battle against the Swedes, on 7 August 1714 at Gangut off the Hanko peninsula.[31] This was a total rout, all the Swedes involved being killed or cap-tured. The result was the conquest of the Åland Islands and the withdrawal of the last remaining Swedish forces from Finland. In the view of Kirill Alekseyevich Naryshkin, the first commandant of St Petersburg, the victory had 'opened the door to Sweden'.[32] If that proved to be an exaggeration, it certainly marked the end of

Swedish naval predominance in the Baltic. Yet despite the brilliance of the Gangut victory, it was not the battles which proved decisive but the sieges and captures of fortresses, beginning with Narva in 1704 and reaching a climax with Stralsund in 1715. They were all made possible by the operations combining shallow-water craft with land forces.

The course of events in the maritime sector of the Great Northern War showed what many had long suspected, namely that the Swedish empire was inherently fragile. It had been put together when its most important rivals had been weakened by the 'Time of Troubles' (1598–1613) in the case of Russia, the 'Deluge' (1648–67) in the case of Poland and the Thirty Years War (1618–48) in the case of the Habsburg emperor.[33] With a homeland population of barely one and a quarter million, sooner or later this fundamental demographic weakness had to make itself felt. On the insistence of Charles, the limited resources available were concentrated on the land war in Poland. Repeated entreaties from the naval commanders and governors of the Baltic fortresses for more men, money and matériel were ignored. Complaints rained in that the seamen had not been paid for months or even years, that they lacked proper clothing and footwear, were permanently malnourished, and so on. It cannot often happen that a group of naval officers, who had received just three months' pay in two years, 'pleaded to be dismissed so that they could go into the countryside and beg'.[34] Moreover, the chief role assigned to the navy was auxiliary, the ferrying of supplies, soldiers and prisoners of war to and fro across the Baltic.[35] A further self-inflicted wound was Admiral Hans Wachtmeister's prioritizing capital ships over the shallow-water craft the Russians were using to such devastating effect.[36] This choice did allow the Swedish fleet to play a defensive role against the Danes but not to go on the offensive against the Russians to regain what had been lost. By the closing stages of the war, even that was no longer possible. When peace was signed in 1721 there were only twenty-seven Swedish battleships in service – and half of them were unseaworthy.[37] By contrast, Tsar Peter commanded a fleet of thirty-four ships of the line, fifteen frigates and a huge number of galleys, a total which outnumbered the Swedish and Danish fleets combined.[38]

How Augustus (and Poland) lost the Great Northern War

This was an episode which highlighted the role of individual personalities in history. Of course Tsar Peter had able assistants, but this was his very own achievement. The transformation from humiliated coward to alpha warlord had been astonishingly rapid. In 1700 he had panicked and run away from the enemy at Narva. In August 1716 he took command of the combined Russian, Danish, Dutch and British fleets off Copenhagen and cruised in triumph in the face of his enemy.[39] When the war eventually came to an end, he was the undisputed monarch of all he surveyed, his colossal physical stature – he was six foot eight (2.03 metres) – matched by his hegemonic political status. Conversely, his task had been made much easier by the personal flaws and failures of his chief opponent, King Charles, whose obsessively obtuse pursuit of Augustus and consequent neglect of his navy had delivered up the Swedish empire on a plate. What both men had in common was an autocratic power of command, deriving partly from their political inheritance and partly from their personal charisma. If Charles's regime was absolutist rather than despotic, even those of his ministers who realized that his strategy was taking their country to disaster never dared to press the point.

How different was the fate of poor Augustus, to whom it is high time to return. He had his masterful moments too, but they paled by comparison with his fellow sovereigns. One cannot imagine him personally wielding a sword in the beheading of mutinous soldiers, or arranging for his son to be tortured to death, as Peter did. Nor would he ever have followed Charles in his merciless application of some of the more brutal teachings of the Old Testament. Even as a hereditary ruler in Saxony his authority was restricted by tradition, the Estates, independent-minded ministers, the constitution of the Holy Roman Empire and his own moral sense. In Poland he always found himself swimming laboriously in the treacle (or rather the golden syrup) of the szlachta's 'golden liberty' (*złota wolność*). When push came to shove, influence on events during the Great Northern War depended on a state's ability to mobilize military and naval resources. Augustus never had enough of the former and none at all of the latter. Saxony was landlocked and Poland might as well have been, given the lack of interest taken in maritime matters by those who mattered.

As the population of Poland–Lithuania was in the order of ten million (it fluctuated considerably depending on the incidence of plague and war), it was remarkable that there was no permanent Polish naval establishment. Even the Habsburgs managed a flotilla on the Danube (put to good use by Prince Eugene in the wars against the Turks) and a warship or two at Trieste.[40] Admittedly, the geography was not favourable. The Polish coastline was meagre, for East Prussia was sovereign Prussian territory after 1657 and Courland, although a Polish fief, was ruled by the dukes of the Kettler dynasty.[41] That left just a short coastal stretch around Połąga in Lithuania and West or 'Royal' Prussia, extending around the western part of the Gulf of Danzig from Gdynia to Braunsberg (Braniewo) and including two ports with the capacity for ocean-going vessels – Elbing (Elbląg) on the Vistula lagoon and Danzig (Gdańsk) on the Baltic.

The latter was by far the most important, indeed was the most populous and prosperous city in the entire Polish–Lithuanian Commonwealth. That its budget was *twenty times* that of the Polish state in the first half of the seventeenth century testified both to its own strength and the weakness of its host.[42] Its population of around 40,000 was almost double that of Warsaw.[43] But Danzig was Polish only in a limited sense, for its inhabitants were predominantly German by language and Lutheran by religion. In the view of one Polish historian, the late Piotr S. Wandycz, it was more like a Dutch than a Polish city, a state-within-a-state, with its own currency, diplomatic corps and military force.[44] It also sent its own representatives to the Sejm, a privilege dating from its original acceptance of Polish suzerainty following its secession from the state of the Teutonic Knights in 1454. Although loyal to its new ruler, the city always thought of itself as a 'free member'.[45] A sense of being part of a wider German cultural community also persisted. In a sermon preached in the Church of the Holy Trinity (St Trinitaskirche) on the occasion of Augustus's coronation, the pastor, Samuel Schelwigen, celebrated the close relationship of the people of Danzig with their new king, thanks to their common German origin, and gloried in the fact that henceforth 'we Germans will be ruled by a German'.[46]

As might be expected from a city run by merchants, there was no enthusiasm in Danzig for the presence of a naval force that would disrupt trade by attracting enemy action.[47] It was a distaste shared by the landed interest that ruled the country. It is difficult to imagine an ethos less conducive to maritime endeavour than the Sarmatian culture of the szlachta.[48] Moreover, as the seventeenth century progressed, there was little sign of any weakening of its attachment to land and its values, a serf economy, militant baroque Catholicism, religious intolerance and to political decentralization. Aversion to anything smacking of urban life had been given classic formulation by Jan Zamoyski c.1600: 'in Western Europe real cities prosper because the burgher estate has many rights there. But because their happiness is the result of the violation of noble privileges and freedom, I prefer not to have [cities] at such a price. The happiness of the people cannot be measured on the basis of handicrafts, or by walls and great buildings, of which we have no shortage anyway.'[49] Towards the end of the century, this sort of axiom had become even more exclusive. Stanisław Orzechowski stated in his popular tract *Domina Palatii – Regina Libertas* that only nobles had all three qualities of true Sarmatian citizens, namely freedom, truthfulness and faith, for the peasants had no freedom, the merchants and burghers no truthfulness and other commoners very often pursued 'unworthy activities'.[50]

The other Baltic states naturally did all they could to keep Poland away from the sea. When the two Vasa Kings of Poland – Sigismund III (r. 1587–1632) and Władysław IV (r. 1632–48) – started to build a fleet in the 1630s in pursuit of their Swedish interests, they were soon checked. In 1635 the Treaty of Stuhmsdorf (Sztum) included a ban on Polish naval assistance to any of Sweden's enemies. An attempt to include a ban on any future naval construction failed, but the Swedes need not have worried. Two years later, the Danes took pre-emptive action by simply putting to sea and destroying the Polish vessels.[51] Opposition from Danzig and a refusal by the Sejm to provide the necessary finance ensured that this short-lived naval adventure was not renewed. The remaining ships were sold in 1642–3. Thus ended what Urszula Augustyniak judged to have been 'the last attempt to maintain a fleet in the service of the Commonwealth'.[52]

That is a little too negative, for there was one brief flurry of maritime activity during the Great Northern War. Augustus had come to the throne with an ambitious plan for reviving Poland's fortunes in every sector. His interest in, and knowledge of, the Baltic had been fostered by his visits to his grandfather's court at Copenhagen.[53] In February 1697 – in other words, after he had decided to become a candidate for the Polish throne but before the election – he composed a treatise entitled 'How to promote Poland's prosperity and reputation with regard to its neighbours' (*Umb Pohlen in Flor und in ansehung gegen seine nachbarn zu setzen*).[54] There was nothing original about his economic programme, which came straight out of the mercantilist textbook: the encouragement of native manufacturing to keep money in the country, the expansion of commercial relations with other states, the attraction of wealthy immigrants, the abolition of the exemption from customs dues currently enjoyed by the privileged orders, the removal of internal customs barriers, and the construction of a navy and sea ports.[55] This might look like an election manifesto, but in fact was a serious project. Composed in his own hand, it was not published and did not see the light of day until unearthed by a Polish scholar,

Stanisław Piotrowicz, in the Dresden archives early in the twentieth century. As he remarked, it was a much-needed corrective to the conventional image of Augustus as a 'muscle-bound drunkard, womaniser and charlatan'.[56]

In the spring of 1698, following his election, Augustus travelled to Danzig to thank the city for its support and to investigate what help he might expect for his commercial and naval plans. The response was disappointing, the Danzigers being instinctively opposed to anything that might dilute their current comfortable domination of Polish overseas trade. So other options had to be considered – the revival of an old Vasa plan for a new port at Władysławowo at the base of the Hel peninsula north of Danzig; the resumption of work begun on port facilities at Palanga on the Lithuanian coast; or even new ventures in Courland and Livonia. That he was in earnest was shown by his determined pursuit of an ambitious plan for a company to trade with the Mediterranean presented to him in 1698 by a sea captain called Johann Friedrich von Thilow. Saxon diplomats were told to organize the necessary agreements with Denmark and Sweden, the gatekeepers of the Baltic. Unsurprisingly, the Swedes vetoed a proposal deemed incompatible with their monopoly of the region's commerce. Also predictably, all these schemes fell victim to the outbreak of a war in which there was minimal Polish naval involvement.[57] All that was achieved was the issue of letters of marque for a few privateers operating from Danzig against Swedish merchant shipping.[58]

In short, in a war in which naval power was proving decisive, Augustus and his two states were thrown back on their land forces to make an impact. This was certainly possible, as was demonstrated by the Prussians, who had no navy to speak of but a formidable army, growing rapidly after 1713 under their new king, Frederick William I (r. 1713–40). In many ways the polar opposite of Augustus, he combined extreme personal parsimony with lavish expenditure on his army. There was never any prospect of Saxony or Poland emulating that combination. In the stop–go war that unfolded in and around the Baltic after Poltava, Augustus's modest armies were often present but never dominant, for the good reason they were simply not big enough. Both his states were recovering from a decade of over-exertion and devastation, inflicted by a war in which their Prussian neighbour sensibly had stayed neutral. Although the natural buoyancy of the Saxon economy soon began to generate a good revenue stream, Augustus's priority when it came to expenditure was always on his representational culture rather than the sinews of war, and he never did believe in putting something by for a rainy day. As he told Frederick William when he came to call in 1730: 'when Your Majesty collects a ducat, you just add it to your treasure, while I prefer to spend it, so that it comes back to me threefold'.[59] Neither lived to see that boast refuted when Augustus's son fell victim to the awesome weapon forged by Frederick William and wielded after 1740 with such devastating effect by his son Frederick ('the Great').

Why the Great Northern War lasted so long

At the close of the previous chapter, it was asked why the war should have continued for another twelve years after the Poltava / Perevolotjna debacle, especially given its catastrophic nature. After most military catastrophes the defeated army usually manages to maintain some kind of identity, and even to fight another day. In this case the Swedish army in Ukraine just disappeared off the face of the earth, the individual survivors packed off to hard labour in Russia.[60] So dominant had the apparently invincible Charles been that the total collapse of the Swedish war effort now seemed only a matter of time. As one German observer commented: 'Now what has happened has happened, and cannot be altered. That which the Swedes achieved in such a short time to the astonishment of the whole world through so many campaigns, battles, and victories, is suddenly, in the blink of an eye, transformed, demolished.'[61]

Peter was well aware of the significance of the destruction of the Swedish army, finding time on the very day of the victory to write to

Admiral Fyodor Apraksin that Poltava had cemented the foundations of St Petersburg.[62] The rest of Europe also grasped that a sea
change in the European states system had occurred. The most
famous philosopher of the day, Leibniz, wrote to the Russian envoy
in Vienna in August 1709: 'You can imagine how the great revolution
in the north has astounded people. It is being said that the tsar will be
formidable to the whole of Europe, that he will be a sort of Turk of
the North.'[63] As the bulk of the victorious Russian army moved back
from Ukraine to Poland, the commanders of the Swedish army
there, General Ernst Detlef von Krassow and King Stanisław, withdrew to Pomerania. That left the Swedish garrisons in the Baltic
fortresses highly vulnerable. In the course of 1710 they fell like nine-
pins: Elbing in January, Viborg in June, Pernau in August, the island
of Ösel and Reval in September. The conquests were assisted by a
wave of bubonic plague, which decimated all sides but affected most
the outnumbered Swedish garrisons.[64] The collapse of Swedish
power in the region was dramatized by the fate of the mortally ill
commander of the Reval garrison, Diedrich Friedrich von Patkull,
whose dying hand was too weak to sign the capitulation.[65]

Yet any hope that the Great Northern War might now come to
an end was soon dashed. When Charles was killed nine years later,
in December 1718, it was still in progress, indeed had another three
years to run. Part of the reason was that Charles was down but not
out after Poltava. His main army may have been dead or imprisoned,
but there were still 8,000 Swedish troops in Poland under Krassow,
3,000 in Courland, 13,000 in Livonia and Estonia, 14,000 in Finland
and 18,000 in Sweden itself.[66] Moreover, the remaining Swedish contingents showed that, man for man, they were still the most effective
fighting force in the Baltic theatre. A spectacular demonstration was
the repulse of the ill-advised invasion of Scania launched by Frederick IV of Denmark in November 1709. The hero of the hour was
Magnus Stenbock, who showed exceptional enterprise and strategic
insight in organizing resistance. After withdrawing his heavily outnumbered forces – they only amounted to 3,000 – and allowing the
invaders to occupy most of the province, he regrouped, reinforced

and then returned, crushing the Danish invaders at Helsingborg on 28 February 1710. Inflicting 50 per cent casualties, he forced the evacuation by sea of the survivors, who slaughtered the several thousand horses they could not take with them.[67] As Otto Haintz commented, the Swedes had delivered a 'masterclass' in how to combine political, military and naval resources.[68] Indeed, this success prompts speculation as to what they might have achieved if their king had fled into exile at the beginning of the war rather than halfway through it.

This episode barely rates a mention in most accounts of the Great Northern War, although it might have proved the turning point. If the Danes had achieved their goal of seizing the main Swedish naval base at Karlskrona, the war would probably have ended shortly thereafter. As it was, thanks to Stenbock's heroics, the Swedish navy remained an insuperable barrier to final allied success, still able to supply the remaining Swedish garrisons across the Baltic and still able to protect the grain convoys on which the homeland relied for subsistence. In a maritime region such as the Baltic, it was control of the sea which still mattered most. The Russian galleys had proved invaluable in picking off Swedish fortresses in Karelia and Ingria, but it was the Swedish battle fleet which still ruled the high seas and blockaded the Russian capital ships in the Gulf of Finland.[69] That was not affected by Charles's defeat at Poltava, when he was so far to the south as to be closer to the Black Sea than the Baltic. Not even the Russian naval victory at Gangut brought a sea change.[70] It was not until the appearance of the British Royal Navy in the Baltic in 1716 that the balance swung the other way.[71]

This reflection is intended to guard against too teleological a narrative in the wake of Poltava. Even more so was the attack of hubris to which Tsar Peter succumbed when the Ottomans declared war in November 1710. Over-reaching himself, Peter took the offensive, marching south in the following spring with an army of around 38,000. His strategic objective was to make the Danube a defensive moat, behind which the two Danubian Principalities (Moldavia and

Wallachia) could be organized as Russian colonies and serve as a springboard for a further drive through Bulgaria to Constantinople.[72] It all went horribly wrong. Although his army got a long way south, deep into Moldavia, by the time it reached Stănileşti on the River Pruth (today's border between Moldova and Romania) drought and a plague of locusts left it facing starvation. Having fatally underestimated the Ottoman response, it now found itself surrounded by a huge enemy army of perhaps 120,000. What then ensued 'may deservedly be looked on as one of the most surprizing and extraordinary events that ever happened', as the British ambassador put it.[73] Sultan Ahmed III was in a position not just to dictate terms but to eliminate Tsar Peter and his army altogether. In the event a settlement was reached, by which Peter undertook to return the fortress of Azov on the Don, to refrain from interfering in Poland or the Crimea and to allow Charles, a refugee since the defeat at Poltava, to return to the north unmolested.[74] Those terms were hard enough, for they meant the abandonment of Peter's Black Sea ambitions for the time being; but simple survival had been paramount and was greeted with a mighty sigh of relief.

So the 'once in a millennium opportunity' to put an end to Russia as a great power was passed up.[75] In the annals of European counterfactuals, the 'miracle on the Pruth' (Reinhard Wittram) deserves a high ranking. Explanations of the great escape include Russian bribery of the venal Ottoman negotiators; opposition from the Janissaries and Sipahis, who hated fighting in such an inhospitable area; a simple error of judgement on the part of the grand vizier; and reluctance to be used as the tool of King Charles, who was disliked and distrusted by the Ottomans.[76] It was Charles who was the real loser. Although the Ottomans declared war on Peter once more, in October 1712, they did so without enthusiasm and the crisis came and went without any fighting.[77] Moreover, relations between Charles and his increasingly reluctant hosts then deteriorated to the point of an armed clash in January–February 1713. With a war against Venice planned, there was no prospect of the Ottomans intervening in the north for the foreseeable future.[78]

Back in the north, the war had ground to a halt. In both 1711 and 1712 the allied Danish, Saxon and Russian forces made no progress in Pomerania, as the key Swedish fortresses of Stettin and Stralsund held out successfully. All the familiar problems of coalition warfare emerged, with the various combatants prioritizing their own divergent interests. The Danes, for example, used their artillery to conquer Bremen and Verden rather than send it to besiege the Pomeranian fortresses.[79] At the end of 1712, the impasse was broken when the enterprising Stenbock obeyed a direct order from Charles (still in exile at Bender) to scrape together an army in Sweden, take it across the Baltic and link up with Charles coming from the south. Once again, the Swedish soldiers showed their superiority by defeating a joint Saxon–Danish army at Gadebusch in western Mecklenburg on 20 December. Although a brilliant victory, in the long run it served only to advertise the increasingly desperate Swedish position, for the successful landing of Stenbock's little army had been swiftly followed by the total destruction of the accompanying supply convoy by the Danish navy.[80] So, despite his victory, Stenbock was now trapped. Not strong enough to turn south-east to Poland, as he had been ordered, he turned west, hoping to find refuge in Holstein. Along the way he did manage to burn Altona to the ground, in one of the most notorious atrocities of the war, but was then driven further and further west by an allied army until obliged to take refuge in the Danish fortress of Tönning at the mouth of the Eider in January 1713.[81] With no prospect of being evacuated by sea, Stenbock's army capitulated in May. The episode showed that although the Danes might have lost every battle on land, they still had the final say, thanks to their naval superiority.

In short, by early 1713 Charles XII had lost one army in Ukraine and another in Holstein. Both disasters were his personal responsibility. It was thanks to his 'completely stupid decision'[82] to send Stenbock across the Baltic that the way was opened for the Russian conquest of Finland, a Swedish possession for the best part of four centuries. Nothing daunted by his narrow escape on the Pruth in

1711, Tsar Peter switched his attention to this softer target. Once again this was a combined operation, with an army marching along the southern coast in close cooperation with waterborne forces. It was the task of the galleys to occupy the Finnish archipelago and get in behind the Swedish defensive positions.[83] Just such a landing at Sandviken in May 1713 forced the Swedish commander Karl Gustav Armfeldt to abandon the coast and retreat inland to the province of Tavastia.[84] The Russian advance was now relentless. Helsingfors (Helsinki) was taken without a fight, followed in August by the largest Finnish city, Åbo (Turku). In February 1714, a victory on land at Storkyro (Isokyrö) in the north-west extended control to the eastern shore of the Gulf of Bothnia, sending 30,000 Swedish refugees fleeing across to the homeland.[85] By now it very much looked as if the net was closing, for Turku is only just over 150 miles from Stockholm across the water, the strait interrupted by the Åland Islands, which were added to the haul following the naval victory at Gangut in August.[86]

Meanwhile, the stalemate in northern Germany had shown signs of breaking up. At long last, in September 1713, the important fortress and port of Stettin at the mouth of the Oder fell to a combined force of Russians and Saxons. The problem of future ownership was resolved by assigning it to Prussia 'for possession and sequestration' until a final peace between all combatants was concluded.[87] This ingenious solution prevented arguments among the allies, neutralized both the town itself and its Pomeranian hinterland, and took Frederick William I of Prussia away from his carefully guarded neutrality and towards the anti-Swedish coalition. For his part, he gained possession of a long-desired prize without having to fire a shot. Of course, legally it was only to be Prussian for the duration of the war, but Frederick William could reasonably expect that possession would prove nine-tenths of the law. The likelihood that Charles XII would be either willing or able to pay the 400,000 talers cost of repossession decreed by the agreement was vanishingly remote.[88]

And so it proved when the next spark in the slow-burning war ignited at 2 a.m. on 11 November 1714, when the released Charles and a small escort knocked on the town gate of Stralsund after an epic fifteen-day ride across Europe from the Ottoman Empire.[89] The town now became the centre of the Great Northern War, for that was where he stayed and took command. He soon acquired two more enemies in 1715, Prussia entering the war at long last in April with Hanover following in October. The latter accession was more formidable than it looked, for in August 1714 Georg Ludwig, Elector of Hanover had also become George I King of England. That did not mean that his new kingdom would join the war as an active belligerent, for no British troops could be used in the service of 'any dominions or territories which do not belong to the Crown of England, without the consent of Parliament'. As events were to prove, the wily King George found ways of using the Royal Navy to promote his Hanoverian interests in the Baltic without breaking the letter of the law.[90]

Allied forces had been blockading or besieging Stralsund for several years without result. Surrounded by a chain of islands, notably Rügen, Germany's largest island, its position on the Strela Sound enjoyed good natural protection. The first stage in overcoming it was naval control. That was achieved by two sea battles fought by the Danes, in April and July 1715, which severed Charles's connections with Sweden. No help could be expected from the Maritime Powers of the kind that had proved so important back when the war began in 1700.[91] With his usual cross-grained knack of alienating potential allies, Charles was foolishly supporting the Jacobites against George I and encouraging Swedish privateering against Dutch and British shipping.[92] As a result the Danes were receiving invaluable, if technically non-belligerent, assistance from the Royal Navy. When Admiral Norris sailed back to British waters in the autumn of 1715, on the orders of George I he left behind eight of his best battleships. There is general agreement that without their intimidating presence in the waters off Stralsund the town could not have been captured.[93]

Once again, it was a combined operation that delivered the *coup de grâce.* At the beginning of November, a joint Saxon–Prussian force, led by the formidable Prince Leopold von Anhalt-Dessau, crossed the Bay of Greifswald, quickly conquered Rügen and established control of the fortress of Altefähr directly across the water from Stralsund. Once that had been achieved, it was only a matter of time before the defenders succumbed. Given Charles's obstinacy, further blood-soaked heroics on both sides were required before the surrender was signed on 23 December. In yet another of the hair-raising episodes that marked his career, Charles had left the doomed fortress the night before in an open rowing boat, dodging both enemy ships and the rapidly thickening ice floes, to rendezvous with a Swedish warship waiting in the bay.[94] Although he then returned to Sweden, he did not go back to his capital (indeed, he never saw it again), but stayed on the coast and promptly set about planning his next adventure, which turned out to be the invasion of Danish-ruled Norway.

Now all that was left of the Swedish Baltic empire was the minor outpost of Wismar, whose defenders were starved into submission in April 1716. Although it could not be claimed that Augustus had played a leading role in this extended drama, a Saxon force had always been present during the Pomeranian campaigns and could even claim a leading role in the final act at Stralsund. In the verdict of the most recent history of the Great Northern War, 'the victory at Stralsund was the achievement of Saxony'. Frederick William I of Prussia, not a man to offer praise easily and especially not to non-Prussians, wrote that the Saxon General August von Wackerbarth had been largely responsible for the conquest. Yet the city was then taken over by the Danes and was eventually returned to Sweden at the peace. As per usual, Augustus came away empty-handed.[95] In truth, all three allies had been needed – the Danes for their navy, the Prussians for their soldiers and the Saxons for their artillery as well as their soldiers. Their cooperation was commemorated by a handsome medal displaying three royal portraits and a Latin inscription: 'Here can be seen three Fredericks, Frederick William King of Prussia, Frederick Augustus King of Poland, Frederick King of Denmark', and on the obverse a depiction of Stralsund with the motto 'Stralsund, besieged and captured by Danes, Saxons and Prussians: who can steal it back?'.[96] This emblematic unity was flawed by a dispute about which of the victors should take control of Stralsund. Having made the most effective contribution, the Saxons expected to be given priority. In the event, a deal between the Prussians and the Danes left the latter in command.[97]

But this was only a trio of allies singing in harmony, not a quartet. Conspicuous by his absence was the *basso profondo* of Tsar Peter. Although that was due to a decision by his ambassador in Poland, Prince Grigori Dolgoruki, to keep Russian soldiers away, the divisions among the allies soon widened further. When a Russian force did try to join in the later capture of Wismar, the Prussians told them to go away.[98] As this tiff revealed, now that Charles was back in Sweden and his empire conquered, the adhesive formed by 'my enemy's enemy is my friend' began to dissolve. All the major players on the allied side – Augustus, George I, Frederick William, Frederick IV of Denmark and Tsar Peter – were strong characters with a depressing capacity for personal hatreds. They also, of course, had their own national agendas. The last thing wanted by the first four rulers named was to see Swedish hegemony in the Baltic replaced by Russian. Allied to squabbling about who was to get what, that ever-strengthening anxiety postponed any general settlement for year after year. A climactic moment came in the autumn of 1716 when it did begin to look as though a final solution was near. Peter masterminded a great concentration of military and naval resources at Copenhagen, in preparation for what was intended to be a war-ending invasion of Scania. It looked terrific. When Peter ordered the combined fleet to weigh anchor on 16 August, the armada comprised sixty-nine battleships – twenty-three Danish, twenty-one Russian, nineteen British and six Dutch, not to mention 400 merchant support vessels.[99]

It may well have been 'the noblest fleet of sail ever to appear in the Baltic' (Robert Massie), but it achieved nothing. An object lesson in the accuracy of Clausewitz's dictum 'everything in war is very simple, but the simplest thing is difficult',[100] everything that could go wrong did go wrong. Crucially, Peter's reconnaissance of the Scanian coast convinced him that an invasion would be resisted fiercely, not least because the ship in which he was travelling came under withering fire from the shore. The terrible mauling the Danes had received at the hands of Stenbock when invading Scania in 1709 was also fresh in the memory.[101] However, the main reason for the volte-face may have to be sought deeper in Peter's psyche. The Russian historian Boris Akunin has argued convincingly that Peter did not lack personal courage in the face of enemy action, as he had shown on numerous occasions, most notably at Poltava. What he did fear was the shame of *personal failure*. It was this that led him to absent himself from Narva on the eve of the battle in 1700; it was this that prompted him always to delegate command on the battlefield; and it was this that made him blink when having to confront Charles and his defences in the summer of 1716.[102] Whatever the reason, on 17 September Peter suddenly announced that the season was now too advanced and the invasion would have to be postponed.[103] Great was the resentment among his allies, already disturbed by rumours that in reality his martial ardour had been dampened by peace feelers put out by Charles, who of course was well aware of the divisions among his enemies.[104]

9.

Out of the Swedish Frying Pan into the Russian Fire

Augustus loses control of Poland – again

In Poland, meanwhile, Augustus had lost control. When he returned in 1709 the future looked tolerable, if not promising: his great enemy Charles XII was *hors de combat*; the anti-king Stanisław Leszczyński had fled to Pomerania; the opposition Polish magnates had retired to their estates or left the country; the majority of the szlachta at least accepted his return.[1] The general council of the Sandomierz Confederation, meeting at Warsaw in February 1710, provided a legal trapping for the restored regime by declaring the reign of Stanisław to have been illegal and welcoming Augustus as the rightful king. More substantively, there was recognition of the need to form a standing army 36,000-strong and to provide adequate financing through fiscal reform.[2] That looked as though the lessons of the previous decade had been learnt, prompting Józef Gierowski's comment that the council's resolutions 'marked the highest flight of reform in the period of the two Saxon kings'.[3] Although he did not add 'which is not saying very much', he would have been justified in doing so. Moreover, they did not move from paper to practice. Although Stanisław Leszczyński stayed deposed and Augustus unchallenged, neither the army of 36,000 nor the fiscal reforms ever did materialize. To achieve full legitimacy they first had to be approved by a full Sejm, which did not meet until April 1712 and then decided nothing. Prorogued until the following December, it was killed off by the *liberum veto*. So ended what Henryk Olszewski judged to have been the last occasion, in this period at least, when a compromise between king and szlachta could have been arranged and fiscal–military reform introduced.[4]

As to who was responsible for the rupture of the Sejm, historians' verdicts are divided between two candidates – Adam Mikołaj Sieniawski and Ludwik Pociej. They had three things in common – they were both Grand Hetmans, the former of Poland and the latter of Lithuania, and they both stood to lose power and profit if the reform programme went through.[5] They both looked to Tsar Peter for support, and he was happy to oblige. He had considered making Sieniawski king following the abdication of Augustus in 1706 and had forced through the appointment of Pociej as hetman in 1709.[6] During the turmoil of the years which followed they helped to sabotage any chance of a settlement between Augustus and the opposition, so that Russian intervention, lightly disguised as 'mediation', became inevitable.[7] Along the way, they added to the prevailing instability by their individual feuds – Sieniawski with the clergy and Pociej with his second-in-command, the Lithuanian Field Hetman Stanisław Ernst von Denhoff.[8]

Augustus should have known by now what to expect from Polish politics, but it has to be said that he did not help himself. The experiences of 1697–1706 should have warned him that both magnates and szlachta were hypersensitive about anything impinging on their treasured 'golden liberties'. In time, they might have been wooed away to a more constructive attitude to their country's problems, in the same way that the Tory squires of England were eventually brought to accept a parliamentary monarchy, but patience and time were assets Augustus did not possess. He was already well into middle age by the standards of the time and suffering from the diabetes that would eventually kill him. His top priority was making the Polish throne hereditary in the House of Wettin by securing the succession of his son Frederick Augustus, born in 1696.[9] In the Counter-Reformatory world of the Polish nobility, an absolute *sine qua non* for a king was Catholicism. That seemed an insuperable obstacle, for the crown prince had been brought up in Saxony as a strict Lutheran by his devout mother and grandmother. As recently as 1710 they had arranged for his confirmation, in the course of which he had sworn an oath to remain faithful to the Protestant religion. This was probably a pre-emptive strike, occasioned by rumours from Rome that Prince Frederick Augustus was about to convert.[10] His father had not been informed in advance and was suitably enraged, not least because he had been telling the Pope that he was himself doing all in his power to direct his son to the True Faith.[11]

Augustus extricated his son from his Lutheran minders with a characteristic act of bravado. On 24 May 1711, as he was taking leave of courtiers gathered at the Great Garden in Dresden before setting off for Poland, he asked his son whether he would like to come too. Frederick Augustus jumped at the chance to travel, jumped into the royal carriage, and away they went.[12] As Augustus smugly reported to the Pope later that day, his heir's rescue from heresy had begun. The conversion took more than a year, facilitated during the winter of 1711–12 by a sojourn in Italy, mixing recreation at the Venice carnival with religious instruction in Bologna. As his subsequent career was to demonstrate, Frederick Augustus was amiable, weak-willed, indolent, eager to please and a connoisseur of the visual arts and music. Every now and again during his physical and spiritual journey around northern Italy he showed a spark of Protestant resistance, but eventually succumbed. On 27 November 1712 at Bologna in the private chapel of the papal legate, Cardinal Cassano, he was received into the Catholic Church. He then embraced his new faith with all the habitual zeal of the convert.[13] To guard against the predictable protests from Protestant Europe, especially Saxony, for the time being the news was kept secret, although rumours were already circulating.[14] As we shall see later, it had to be revealed when spiritual salvation was rewarded with a secular prize of corresponding appeal.[15]

As it was well known that Augustus's commitment to any form of Christianity was lukewarm, the Polish nobles could guess why he was encouraging his son to apostasize.[16] Unfortunately, this triggered one of the most vehement of their atavistic reactions. No right was guarded more fervently by the szlachta than the freedom to choose their king, so nothing was better calculated to mobilize resistance than an attempt by the current incumbent to choose his successor in advance (*vivente rege* was the shorthand phrase used). It was this issue more than any other which had prompted King John II Casimir (Jan Kazimierz) to abdicate in 1668.[17] So the scene was set for confrontation when it was included on Augustus's agenda when he returned in 1709. Other objectives included the abolition of the *liberum veto*; the reorganization of Sejm committees to improve cooperation with the king; the creation of royal councils; fiscal centralization; the formation of a court partly by the use of patronage; and a closer union between Saxony and Poland.[18] Augustus was not so naïve as to suppose that this could be achieved by persuasion alone and looked to coercion. He had the necessary instrument to hand in the shape of the Saxon army, released from the west by the ending of the War of the Spanish Succession in 1713, supplemented by troops brought from Pomerania. He could also justify their appearance by reference to a new invasion threat from the Ottomans.[19] As Russian troops were withdrawn in accordance with the Pruth treaty, their places were taken by 'Saxons' (although in terms of ethnic origin they were a disparate collection, including many Poles recruited locally).[20]

A debate has raged ever since as to just how duplicitous Augustus was being. The most negative version – advanced by Antoni Prochaska in 1917 – held that Augustus brought in the Saxons in the full knowledge that their behaviour would provoke an insurrection. Its repression by the army would then be extended to a *coup d'état* to impose an absolutist regime. It was the patriotic reaction to this fell scheme, Prochaska concluded, which led to its frustration by the formation of the Tarnogród Confederation in 1715.[21] There was certainly something in this, for Augustus was indeed seeking to strengthen monarchical authority, and his ministers did draft a scheme for imposing reform from above.[22] Whether that is the whole story is a different matter. The Tarnogród Confederation was more than just a negative reaction on the part of the szlachta; it was also the result of two positive initiatives, the first by supporters of ex-King Stanisław, the second by Tsar Peter, acting through the two hetmans Sieniawski and Pociej.[23] Most important was the simple fact that Augustus was so distrusted by his Polish subjects that they could easily convince themselves that he really was planning a *coup d'état*. It was also widely suspected that Augustus would use his Saxon army to carve out a new hereditary possession for his dynasty in Pomerania.[24]

Also real – all too real – was the impact of armies on the population. Even after active campaigning had moved away north-west to Pomerania the burden continued, although now inflicted by the Polish army, notoriously unpaid, unfed and undisciplined. Józef Gierowski's chapter dealing with this episode is titled 'The harm of all harms – home-grown soldiers' (*krzywda nad wszystkie krzywdy – żołnierz domowy*).[25] It got even worse when they found themselves having to compete with the Saxon army when it arrived in 1713. Claiming that Saxony was too impoverished to finance it, Augustus decreed that it should be fed and supplied from Polish resources, organized by a Saxon commissariat based in Warsaw.[26] This would have been unpopular in any circumstances; in a country already devastated by more than a decade of incessant warfare it proved to be intolerable. As the Great Northern War had progressed, the marauding armies of the numerous belligerents brought with them not just the usual horrors of war but also bubonic plague.[27] Outbreaks in Kraków and Poznań in 1707 spread to Warsaw the following year and from there to the whole country in 1709–11, killing tens of thousands as it went. Simultaneous bovine epidemics decimated livestock, the loss of draught animals being especially serious. Fields lay untilled, while lack of manure reduced the yield of those crops that could be grown. Harrowing reports of abandoned farms, deserted villages and depopulated towns flowed in from every quarter. One response was flight, a diaspora of desperate peasants in all directions – Brandenburg, East Prussia, Silesia, Hungary, Wallachia, even Russia and the Ottoman Empire. Hetman Sieniawski was reluctant to send the army to the borderland regions lest it unleashed another wave of refugees.[28]

The Tarnogród Confederation and the Treaty of Warsaw

Reaction from noble landowners was not long delayed. In 1714 the szlachta of Lesser Poland formed a confederation to protect themselves and their peasants from the depredations of Saxon foragers.[29] Over the next year, sporadic skirmishes between Saxons and Poles gathered momentum. A point of no return seems to have been an incident on 28 April 1715 near Opatów, north-west of Sandomierz, when the *starosta* Jan Bonaventura Turski and two companions were killed. This 'distressing but essentially trivial incident' was then used by the anti-Augustan party to spread the insurrection far and wide.[30] It led to the foundation of a confederation at Vilnius on 23 August and a general confederation at Tarnogród, between Kraków and Lwów, on 26 November.[31] Led by the energetic Stanisław Ledóchowski as marshal, the latter became a nationwide movement aimed primarily at the expulsion of the Saxons and a second dethronement of Augustus. Military operations ensued without any clear verdict being reached, although plenty of atrocities were committed by both sides and the civilian population suffered most.[32] In February 1716 the confederation rejected a mediation attempt by the Pope, whom they believed – correctly – to be on Augustus's side. They turned instead to Tsar Peter, who was more sympathetic, given his reluctance to see Augustus's authority in Poland enhanced.[33] The confederates even made an approach to Jakub Sobieski, but were told that the approval of the Austrians would be required, and anyway Tsar Peter had decided that he would rather weaken Augustus than replace him.[34]

By the autumn of 1716 Augustus was in dire straits. The confederates had taken Poznań in July and Toruń in September. Help then reached him in the nick of time from an unaccustomed quarter – military victory. On 5 October at Kowalewo Pomorskie, about twenty-five kilometres north-east of Toruń, a Saxon army commanded by General Adam Heinrich von Bose crushed a larger army of confederates. The latter did not distinguish themselves, offering little resistance and then fleeing in panic, leaving more than 1,000 dead, wounded and captured. The most important result was a signal improvement in Augustus's position in the mediation currently being supervised by the Russian ambassador, Prince Grigori Dolgoruki. An armistice was signed on 10 October and a settlement – the Treaty of Warsaw – on 3 November.[35] It is a good question as to who was the winner. Two well-placed observers chose Augustus. The Prussian envoy Georg Friedrich von Lölhöffel told Frederick William I: 'a splendid basis has been laid for absolutist rule' and his Russian colleague Grigori Dolgoruki's comment on the Sejm convened to approve the settlement was that 'he had never seen in Poland a king so mighty and full of authority as at this Sejm; he was like a sovereign'.[36]

Augustus had certainly made some gains. First and foremost, the worst-case scenario – dethronement – had been banished, never to return. Royal authority benefited from a ban on confederations and the reduction of the powers of the *sejmiki*, especially in fiscal and military matters. As a result, the long period often labelled by Polish historians 'Government by *Sejmiki*' had come to an end. Most important in the authoritative view of Józef Gierowski was provision for a standing army of 24,000, supported for the first time by permanent taxes, to be paid by all property-owners, with no exemptions for szlachta land.[37] Other privileged casualties were the hetmans, whose quasi-independent status was abruptly halted, along with their manifold opportunities for embezzling state revenues.[38] Other senior officers of state also had their wings clipped, notably the marshals and treasurers. On the debit side for Augustus, the Treaty of Warsaw put an end to his ambitions to turn the personal link between Saxony and Poland into a real union. In future, Saxon ministers were to be barred from interfering in any Polish business, domestic or foreign; the Saxon army was to be withdrawn forthwith, apart from a modest troop of lifeguards; the king was not to spend more than three months in any year in Saxony or to make any appointments affecting Poland while he was away.[39] He probably cared less about the further restrictions placed on non-Catholics, notably their exclusion from the officer corps.[40]

It was some measure of the stagnation of Polish politics since 1697 that the Treaty of Warsaw could be dubbed 'the only major item of reform to emerge from the Saxon era' by the pre-eminent anglophone historian of the period.[41] One Polish historian has gone further, writing that there was to be no more comprehensive reform of the state before the great (if short-lived) revolution of 3 May 1791.[42] Alas, most of the positive changes turned out to be illusory. Even the modest size of the national army was never achieved, for the good reason that the pay of the officers had not been taken into account when the sums were being calculated. Once that was done, the projected 24,000 fell by a quarter to 18,000, a derisory total when compared with the giant that Prussia was becoming and the leviathan that Russia already was.[43] The arrangement by which taxes were paid directly to individual regiments, bypassing the central treasury, proved predictably 'fatal'.[44] If the *sejmiki* never did regain their previous dominance, the restrictions on their deliberations were of short duration, being abolished in 1726.[45] Cowed for a while, the hetmans were soon back to their old ways, causing mayhem.[46] More generally, the reform programme devised by Augustus and his ministers, envisaging – among other things – urban growth, the abolition of internal customs barriers, the development of mining, monetary reform and the secularization of Church property, never got beyond the planning stage.[47] In the bleak verdict of Urszula Augustyniak, the next forty years were 'a period of permanent crisis and legislative atrophy' (*okres permanentnego kryzysu i zaniku ustawodawstwa*).[48]

The return of the Russians and the 'Silent Sejm'

As if all that were not enough, there was always the return of the Russians to lower spirits further. Although barred from Poland by their treaty with the Ottomans, Peter was able to send the troops back in 1716 in response to appeals for mediation from both sides in the civil war. Nothing could have been more welcome to him.

He had already tightened his grip on the region by taking control of the Duchy of Courland in 1710 by marrying his niece, Anna Ivanovna, to Duke Frederick William, who conveniently died the following year, leaving the Russians firmly in control.[49] In 1716 he married another niece, Catherine Ivanovna, to another Baltic prince, the supremely disagreeable Karl Leopold, Duke of Mecklenburg-Schwerin.[50] Once the Treaty of Warsaw had been negotiated and ratified in January 1717 by representatives of the Tarnogród Confederation and King Augustus, it still needed to be approved by the Sejm. This was accomplished on 1 February by the famous 'Silent Sejm', so called because, instead of the usual cacophony of contestation, almost nothing was said beyond the simple exposition of the terms of the Treaty of Warsaw. Among them was confirmation of the cardinal 'golden liberties', including – crucially – the *liberum veto*.[51]

This was certainly an episode of great significance both in the life of Augustus and in the history of Poland. It marked the end of any attempt to turn the country into an absolute monarchy on the lines of Louis XIV's France or Frederick William I's Prussia (not that either of those polities was very absolutist). More controversial has been the view that it also marked a watershed in Polish history. On one side there are those historians who believe it was the turning point, leading to the partitions and the elimination of the Polish state. For Antony Polonsky, for example, the events of 1717 had turned the country into a 'Russian protectorate', while the wording preferred by Norman Davies was 'Russian supremacy', which 'has persisted in one form or another to the present day'.[52] Heidi Hein-Kircher and Michael G. Müller saw this as the moment when Poland lost its capacity for independent action in foreign policy.[53] That was not the view Tsar Peter took at the time. The Treaty of Warsaw was not a Russian diktat. Dolgoruki was not present when the negotiations between the two parties were conducted and the settlement concluded.[54] Moreover, Peter failed in his aim to have Russia recognized as the 'guarantor power' of the treaty. There was more to this than met the eye, for such a status would have authorized intervention later if the terms of the treaty were deemed to have been broken. Dolgoruki certainly tried his best, but he failed. Both Augustus and the Tarnogród Confederation opposed it so adamantly that he had to give way. Yet that was what had prompted Peter to agree to the mediation in the first place.[55]

These semantic technicalities probably did not matter much. Despite the Pruth 'hiccup', Tsar Peter was very much in control of Polish affairs, as the simple act of mediation showed.[56] For his part, Augustus was finding the Russian yoke intolerable. He had known for some time that he had been double-crossed over the division of the Swedish spoils. At his meeting with Peter at Toruń in 1709 he had been promised that he would receive hereditary possession of Livonia.[57] Peter probably never intended to honour that commitment. As the years passed, and his domination of the Baltic grew, it was gently laid to rest in the capacious graveyard of his broken promises. Added to that basic grievance was the increasingly dictatorial tone he adopted, treating his erstwhile ally like a subordinate.[58] Augustus was also well aware that during his enforced exile from 1706 to 1709, Peter had put together his own party of Polish supporters, dependent on his patronage and ready to do his bidding.[59] After the Treaty of Warsaw the Russian army was supposed to go home, its mission accomplished. As month after month passed it showed no signs of doing so, indeed it was reinforced until there were around 40,000 Russian soldiers eating the Poles out of house and home.[60] Even when they did start to withdraw, in 1719, it proved to be a protracted process. The British envoy James Jefferyes reported to London that every time Tsar Peter was told they must leave, he ordered their commander to delay their departure by another week.[61] At least the anger at Russian exactions could be channelled by Augustus into support for himself. The Sejm at Grodno, which began in October 1718, proved to be his most successful. The Treaty of Warsaw was approved, as was action to enforce the removal of the Russian troops, and a grant for the army. Russian-inspired attempts by the opposition to collapse it were frustrated.[62]

The victory of Peter the Great and the failure of Augustus

Fortunately for Augustus, he was not the only one to oppose growing Russian domination. Especially hostile, and especially powerful, was George I. As Elector of Hanover he was greatly alarmed by the Russian takeover of Mecklenburg, which bordered his own territories. As King of England he was anxious to prevent any power gaining hegemony in the Baltic, the main source of the 'naval stores' needed to build ships for the Royal Navy and the British merchant marine. In both his royal and electoral capacities he dreaded the prospect of Russian domination of Mecklenburg resulting in control of exits from the Baltic to the North Sea.[63] Less directly affected but also anxious were the Austrians, alienated by the support Peter had given to the Hungarian insurgents, his intensifying rapprochement with Prussia, and his links with Cardinal Alberoni, the troublesome first minister of Philip V of Spain.[64] All three allies were encouraged to form an anti-Russian bloc by Peter's abrupt abandonment of the planned invasion of Sweden in September 1716 amid rumours that he was seeking a separate peace with Charles XII at the expense of his allies.[65] The rumours turned out to be correct, albeit not confirmed until the spring of 1718 when negotiations between Swedish and Russian representatives began on the Åland Islands.

Meanwhile, the allied response had been proceeding at the leisurely pace dictated by mutual distrust and quadruped communications. It was not until 5 January 1718 that a treaty was signed at Vienna by Jakob Heinrich von Flemming for Augustus, as both Elector of Saxony and King of Poland; Philipp Ludwig von Sinzendorf for Emperor Charles VI; and François Louis de Pesme de Saint-Saphorin (he was Swiss by origin) for George I as Elector of Hanover.[66] Amid the usual blather about 'the pacification of the North' and 'the tranquillity of the Empire', the essential clauses were aimed squarely at Russia. Poland and especially Danzig (the recent target of Russian bullying) were to be protected. Russian troops were to be withdrawn and not allowed to return, even if only in transit. Secret articles also committed the signatories to armed resistance if Prussia intervened in Mecklenburg to assist Russia. A combined armed force amounting to 32,000 was to be made available for enforcement of all this. Saint-Saphorin also committed George to sending a fleet, although he did so without the knowledge of the British ministers and so was certainly acting *ultra vires*.[67]

This treaty should have liberated both Augustus and Poland. As Władysław Konopczyński observed, no previous Polish king had succeeded in securing such powerful support against Russia.[68] Alas, the ink was barely dry on the treaty before its provisions began to unravel. The first piece of bad news was also paradoxical, namely that Charles XII had been killed on 30 November 1718 while besieging Fredriksten in Norway.[69] Any rejoicing at the demise of such a destructive figure would have been natural but, for Augustus at least, should have been tempered by the reflection that the *raison d'être* of the Triple Alliance had just diminished, if it had not disappeared entirely. It had been mobilized by the threat of a diplomatic revolution creating a Swedish–Russian alliance and now that had dissipated. Indeed, the Saxon minister Flemming told a colleague that if the news had arrived twenty-four earlier, the Austrians would not have signed.[70] They had more than enough on their plate already, being still at war with the Turks.

In Sweden the death of the autocrat led to both a palace coup and a constitutional revolution. The immediate victim was Georg Heinrich von Görtz, who had dominated Swedish foreign policy ever since Charles's return from the Ottoman Empire in 1714. It was he who had initiated the rapprochement with Tsar Peter and had organized the negotiations on the Åland Islands. All that fell abruptly to earth, as did Görtz's severed head when he was executed by the new regime. After a brief struggle for power in Stockholm, Charles's younger sister Ulrika Eleonora and her husband Frederick of Hessen-Kassel had taken control. With their impoverished and depopulated country in a state of collapse after nearly two decades of war, their overriding priority was peace. A settlement with Great Britain/Hanover followed in 1719 at the cost of Sweden losing the north German territories of Bremen and Verden, and with Prussia in 1720 at the cost of Stettin and western Pomerania up to the River Peene, including the islands of Usedom and Wolin.[71] The issue that had started it all was also laid to rest when the Holstein-Gottorp territories in Schleswig were allocated to Frederick IV of Denmark.[72] At home, the hard lesson taught by Charles's absolutist regime led to the transformation of Sweden into a limited monarchy and the beginning of an 'Age of Liberty' that was to last until 1772.

Only Augustus came away empty-handed. The Treaty of Vienna that had looked so promising in January 1719 turned out to be just another disappointment. His main problem was the inability to get it ratified. Partly this was due to the opposition of the hetmans, whose wings had been clipped by the Treaty of Warsaw but not amputated. Their special bugbear was Flemming, to whom military control had passed and whom they saw as Augustus's evil genius. Fuelled by resentment at their loss, they were willing collaborators of Tsar Peter, only too pleased to take the Russian rouble. Protected by their life-tenure, they could also take revenge on Augustus with impunity. They were not the only ones on Peter's payroll, for his ambassador, Grigori Dolgoruki, was also paying large sums to a number of influential magnates.[73] Together this venal elite group ensured that enough of the szlachta rejected ratification.

Peter was employing both stick and carrot. The latter was the gradual withdrawal of Russian troops, beginning in February 1719. The former was the threat of violence. Peter let it be known that he did not need a regular army in Poland to wreak havoc, for he had plenty of irregular Tatars and Cossacks to bring fire and sword across the border.[74] Dolgoruki also mounted a propaganda campaign, spreading rumours that the Treaty of Vienna contained secret articles pledging support for the establishment of a hereditary absolute monarchy and the cession of Polish territory, that an Austrian army would soon be invading, and that Poland would be drawn into Austria's wars. A letter from Peter to Augustus upbraiding him for his ingratitude and threatening retaliation was also circulated.[75] The campaign of disinformation was aided and abetted by the Prussian envoy, Friedrich Wilhelm Posadowski.[76]

The threat of a return to the horrors of war clinched it. Poland had been even more devastated than Sweden, so no wonder the szlachta would do anything for a quiet life. By the summer of 1719 the last Russian soldiers had gone (albeit not very far), the war around the Baltic was petering out, so why risk reigniting a conflagration? More generally, it was Augustus's long-standing inability to win the trust of his Polish subjects that prepared his misfortunes. The failure of his second reign in Poland showed he had not learned the lessons of the first: 'Augustus had only himself to blame for squandering the great opportunity he had in 1710 to work with the Commonwealth's system to introduce important reforms.'[77] His Polish subjects never believed he had their interests at heart and saw their involuntary participation in the Great Northern War as a Saxon project (and, *mutatis mutandis*, the Saxons saw the war as a Polish project).[78] If they did serve him, it was only for as long as their personal interest told them to do so. Consequently, when Tsar Peter sought to annul the Vienna settlement, he had an easy task. After the Warsaw Sejm from 30 December to 23 February 1720 had failed to ratify the treaty, its renewal in September 1720 was broken and the treaty was lost. As the author of the most authoritative account of the episode, Urszula Kosińska, concluded, 'the Sejm failed because the Russian and Prussian representatives conspired with the hetmans', but they could do so only because Augustus was so distrusted.[79]

The failure of the Triple Alliance created by the Treaty of Vienna left Poland perilously isolated. The British, who had only ever been loosely linked via Hanover, were now preoccupied with the financial scandal of the 'South Sea Bubble'.[80] Exasperated by the refusal of the Poles to ratify the treaty, Emperor Charles VI was looking for a rapprochement with Tsar Peter. In October 1720 he stated that participation in a northern alliance would be conditional on Poland ratifying the treaty, which he must have known was not going to happen. That shift in Vienna would lead eventually, in 1725, to de facto recognition by the Austrians of Russian hegemony in Poland and eastern Europe.[81] Most seriously of all, the Prussians concluded a treaty with Tsar Peter at Potsdam in February 1719, aimed at blocking any political change in Poland. Similar agreements followed with Sweden in 1724 and Austria in 1726, putting 'a band of steel' around Poland.[82] In short, everyone was agreed that Poland must be kept weak.[83] This was perhaps the ultimate rebuke to the advocates of the szlachta's precious 'golden liberties', showing that the latter were also cherished by the country's enemies. For Augustus, the unkindest cut came in the late summer of 1721 when Tsar Peter made sure that he and Poland were excluded from the negotiations leading to the Peace of Nystad and the formal end of the Great Northern War. That was Augustus's punishment for trying to break free from Russian tutelage.[84] Technically, Sweden remained at war with Saxony until 1728 and Poland until 1732.[85]

Polish historians have rightly seen 1719–20 as crucial years in the unravelling of the Polish–Lithuanian Commonwealth. Three penetrating assessments deserve quotation here. The first two were written by scholars whose biographies had much in common – both were born in Kraków within a year of each other, left the country in their teens, were educated at Cambridge, and did not return to Poland. Lucjan Lewitter's contribution is perhaps the most entertaining: 'after this fiasco, Augustus II and the Poles went their separate ways, he promoting the interests of the House of Wettin, the *szlachta*, lulled by a false sense of security, eating, drinking, making merry and cultivating their garden of anarchy, ignorance and religious intolerance'.[86] Piotr S. Wandycz also found a telling metaphor: 'If Augustus's policy of creating a coalition to oppose Russia had succeeded, the position of the Commonwealth would have been greatly improved. Poland was turning into a wayside inn open for unwanted and non-paying guests.'[87] Finally, in the same vein is Władysław Konopczyński's verdict: 'There were long declamations about liberty and grievances, and means of rectifying the same, but no one was ready to shed a drop of blood in defence of the former and to satisfy the latter. In such circumstances, Augustus's political anti-Russian plan was stranded on the shoals of ill-timed pacifism. Russia's triumph was complete.'[88]

Augustus may have been relieved at having to settle for a quiescent position in the European states system. A eunuch can be happy in a harem (although the priapic Augustus might not have liked that metaphor much). The end of the war meant that he could now devote all his prodigious energy to what he really excelled at – representational culture. The conclusion of the Treaty of Vienna came in the same year as the greatest achievement of his reign in this department – the festivities surrounding the marriage of his only son and heir, Frederick Augustus. It was celebrated in truly spectacular fashion over two weeks in September 1719 in Dresden as 'the European wedding of the century'. It will be argued in the final two chapters that festivities such as this, together with more durable creations, entitle him to be viewed as one of the great artists, whatever his manifest political incompetence.

10.

Augustus the Artist: the Wedding of the Century

The wedding of the century

Just as Augustus's international position was subsiding into passivity, things began to look up on the dynastic front. The vehicle was his only legitimate child, Frederick Augustus, born in October 1696. In many ways he had turned out to be the ideal son and heir for not only had he survived to adulthood – by no means certain at a time when bubonic plague and smallpox were endemic – he had turned out to be an unusually obedient son. Crucially, he had offered little resistance to the order to convert to Catholicism, despite a qualm or two occasioned by his rigorously Lutheran upbringing.[1] When asked whether he was troubled by the anguish suffered by his deeply pious mother and grandmother over his apostasy, he replied insouciantly: 'I don't care what all the women in the world might think.'[2] It was an obviously advantageous move for him because it opened up a much richer choice of marriage partners. Since the Reformation, the Wettins had been confined to the Lutheran princely families of the Empire, although Augustus's own father had managed to win a scion of the Danish royal family. As still just a younger son when he himself entered the marriage market, Augustus had to settle for the junior Bayreuth branch of the Brandenburg Hohenzollerns.

But now that he was a king ('Ay, every inch a king,' he might have added), Augustus had greater ambitions for his son. Indeed they could not have gone higher, for his eye was fixed on Archduchess Maria Josepha von Habsburg, daughter of the late Holy Roman Emperor Joseph I, who had died of smallpox in 1711 without a male heir. As his brother, who succeeded as Charles VI, was also failing in this all-important task, the Habsburg Monarchy faced an uncertain future. To guard against the inevitable scramble for spoils when his own end came, in 1716 Emperor Charles issued a document known as the 'Pragmatic Sanction', which ruled that, if he left no male heir, all the Habsburg hereditary possessions would pass to his eldest daughter. (There was no question of the elective office of Holy Roman Emperor also being included, for women were explicitly excluded by Salic Law.) It was a good and confusing question as to whether the two daughters of Joseph I took precedence over any daughters of his younger brother. That was why the Pragmatic Sanction was needed, to stop the lawyers getting involved when Charles died. In the event, of course, the matter would be decided not by lawyers but by armies, but that is another story. In the meantime, the two Habsburg ladies, born in 1699 and 1701 respectively, were clearly highly desirable prizes in the royal marriage stakes. As the son of the Elector of Saxony and King of Poland, and a declared Catholic after 1717, young Frederick Augustus was as well placed as most European princes. Although not obvious at the time, he later proved to have three qualities conspicuously lacking in his father, namely the desire and ability to sire legitimate children (five boys and six girls, surviving to adulthood), uxorious fidelity (never a whiff of scandal) and piety (he made amends for his heretical background with deep devotion to traditional Catholicism).

In his courtship of the archduchess, Frederick Augustus benefited from having the Saxon diplomatic establishment to conduct negotiations with Vienna. There is no need to follow them in any detail.[3] For a few months in 1716, Charles VI was the proud father of a male heir, but alas he died the same year. The birth of a healthy daughter, Maria Theresa, in 1717, gave the Pragmatic Sanction new relevance. An important potential obstacle to the Saxon match was removed in February 1719 when the late Emperor Joseph I's two daughters, Maria Josepha and Maria Amalia, formally renounced any claim to the Habsburg inheritance. Emperor Charles and his advisers were also well aware that a Habsburg princess in the Electoral Palace in

Dresden would increase Austrian and Catholic influence both in Saxony and the Holy Roman Empire as a whole.[4]

As the conclusion of the Treaty of Vienna the previous month had shown,[5] Augustus still possessed military and political assets badly needed by Austria, so the slow-moving matrimonial mills could now begin to grind a little faster. The end came quite quickly: the marriage contract was signed on 12 August 1719 and the wedding took place a week later. It was a fairly low-key affair, performed in the chapel of the Favorita Palace, one of the Habsburg summer residences just outside Vienna. The high spots included the presentation of congratulatory addresses from the Estates of Lower and Upper Austria, together with decorative purses containing 'an amount of ducats'; an opera – *Sirita* – by Antonio Caldara; and some fancy '*Schau-Gerichte*' (defined as 'decorative confectionery centrepieces in an architectural or sculptural form used for formal banquets'). They featured a triumphal arch festooned with the bride's virtues, plus four celebrations: of the Peace of Passarowitz, which had brought the victorious war against the Turks to an end the previous year; the union of the dynasties of Habsburg and Wettin; the emperor and the Holy Roman Empire; and the Roman Catholic Church, incorporating, rather fancifully it might be thought, King Augustus.[6] Shortly afterwards, the happy couple left Vienna for Dresden.[7]

By Habsburg standards, the wedding was definitely modest compared with some of the extravaganzas staged in Vienna in the past. Legendary were the festivities surrounding the marriage of Emperor Leopold I in 1666, which lasted (off and on) for almost *two years* and acquired the reputation of being the 'the festivity of the century'.[8] But Leopold had been marrying the Infanta Margarita of Spain, another Habsburg, and so avoided the whiff of *mésalliance* which hung about any union that was not Habsburg–Habsburg. Indeed, Margarita was Leopold's niece and had referred to him as 'uncle', even – so it was rumoured – in bed.

The precedence, ritual and etiquette of the Viennese court combined to make it plain that the Saxon bridegroom and his family were being done a favour by Europe's senior dynasty. Augustus had already been on the receiving end of Habsburg pretensions when spending time in Vienna in the 1690s. As the Wettins could trace their origins appreciably further back than the Habsburgs, this condescension rankled. It was an added spur to using the welcome of Maria Josepha to her new home at Dresden to show that she was moving to a court just as splendid as anything on offer in Vienna. To this project Augustus brought all his energy, imagination, enterprise and resources. In the process he created what was arguably not only the wedding of the century but also 'perhaps the greatest baroque festivity' of all time.[9]

He started as he meant to go on.[10] The new Duchess of Saxony arrived at Pirna on the River Elbe, twenty-five kilometres south-east of Dresden, on the evening of 31 August. After a rest-day to recover from the journey, and now joined by Prince Frederick Augustus, on 2 September she embarked on a resplendent new gondola named *Bucentauro*, specially created by the theatrical designer Alessandro Mauro. As the name suggests, this was based on the Venetian gondola from which the doge conducted the annual 'marriage of the sea' ceremony. Every square inch was covered with gilt ornamentation, the three-room cabin was lined with mirrors, the decks were lined with red velvet, the prow was in the form of a fabulous fish (rather like a dolphin with an elongated snout).[11] Propelled by twenty oarsmen dressed 'in the Dutch style' in yellow jackets and white stockings, accompanied by a flotilla of fifteen newly purchased Dutch yachts crewed by sailors in white and red uniforms, *Bucentauro* proceeded down the Elbe to the *Vogelwiese* (Meadow of the Birds, today the suburb of Blasewitz) just outside the city. Along the way, the duchess was entertained by a band of musicians drawn from the court orchestra.

Happily, the weather was perfect. After a cruise of just an hour, the newlyweds arrived at 10 a.m., to be greeted by a twelve-gun salute. Waiting on shore, standing outside a marquee of golden silk was King Augustus, dressed in the Polish royal costume of purple and red, covered in jewels valued at two million talers (or about 25 per cent of the annual Saxon budget). He was accompanied by a formidable array of aristocrats – seven princes, 200 counts, 200 barons and 500 untitled nobles. A band played. After suitable refreshments had been served, the procession to Dresden began, escorted by 6,000 foot soldiers including twenty-four generals. As more than 100 richly decorated carriages were involved, drawn by four or six horses according to the rank of the occupants, it is no surprise that three hours were needed for the short journey to the city. The gala coach of the princess was drawn by eight white horses, preceded by a black bodyguard (*Leibmohr*) commanding twenty-four additional black guards clad in white satin with red turbans.[12] At the Pirna Gate a triumphal arch had been erected, designed by Augustus's star architect Matthäus Daniel Pöppelmann, where drummers and trumpeters greeted the royal party. Two more triumphal arches had been erected on the Old Market, one of them referring to an earlier Wettin–Habsburg marriage (in 1431).[13] The streets were lined with 1,300 citizens, all dressed in red and grey uniforms. Outside the palace the Saxon Estates were drawn up, also in uniform, as were the hunting personnel, complete with hunting horns. The frequent reference in the detailed official description to music of various kinds being played and salutes being fired suggests that this was a very noisy affair.

The route through Dresden to the palace was, of course, carefully arranged to make the most favourable visual impression on the new resident. The gala coach was driven into the inner courtyard, to be greeted by forty-eight trumpeters and four drummers. Further progress up the 'English Staircase' and through the full panoply of state rooms can still be followed in the numerous high-quality engravings later published by Augustus to ensure that the event would gain maximum impact as widely as possible. The sequence of rooms presented a progressively richer, more lavishly decorated spectacle, incorporating paintings, sculptures and other *objets d'art* advertising the wealth of the Wettins, until a climax was reached in the state bedroom (*Paradeschlafzimmer*), where Augustus and his queen were waiting.[14] It can be assumed with some confidence that the new arrivals heaved a mighty sigh of relief when allowed to retreat to the private apartments prepared for them.

Augustus in charge

They would have been sensible to seize every moment of relaxation on offer, for a full month of festivities followed.[15] The programme has been recounted many times.[16] To avoid the sense of fatigue, not to say tedium, inseparable from a seemingly endless list of banquets, balls, operas, ballets etc., only the more important aspects will be isolated and discussed in what follows. Pride of place must be taken by the role played by Augustus personally. On this point a rare unanimity rules: he was his own patron, designer, impresario, producer and director, right down to the seating arrangements. It had always been so. From his first major undertaking – the carnival of 1695 – he brought to the creation of his festivities a degree of personal involvement that outstripped even that of Louis XIV. The Dresden archives teem with plans and sketches in his own semi-legible hand, marked 'created by His Royal Majesty himself' or 'from ideas of His Royal Majesty'.[17] Such is his reputation for self-indulgent hedonism that it is often forgotten that he was also a knowledgeable, experienced and well-read connoisseur with an enviable capacity for hard work, organization and sustained application. The excellent education provided in his youth by the architect Wolf Caspar von Klengel was then supplemented by the keen interest he took in the great buildings of western and southern Europe he visited on the grand tour, as the tutor who accompanied him recorded.[18] Back in Saxony he continued his studies through the illustrated publications acquired for his library. During the first visit to Poland in 1697–8, he sent home for a collection of designs and a crate of architectural books, to be brought by the architect Johann Friedrich Karcher.[19]

If the imperious Augustus was always in charge of his various projects, he was assisted by a team whose talents he recognized and encouraged. It included the architects Matthäus Daniel Pöppelmann,

Georg Bähr and Zacharias Longuelune, the sculptor Balthasar Permoser, the interior decorator Raymond Leplat, the painter Louis de Silvestre, the jeweller and goldsmith Johann Melchior Dinglinger, the cabinetmakers Peter Hoese and Johann Christoph Schwartze, the porcelain painter Johann Gregorius Höroldt, the porcelain modeller Johann Joachim Kändler, the enameller Georg Friedrich Dinglinger, the actor, dancer and impresario Angelo Costantini, and many more. A special category has to be reserved for Johann von Besser, the master of ceremonies (*Zeremonienmeister*) who turned Augustus's ideas for the 1719 festivities into a detailed programme.[20] Although Augustus took a close interest in every last detail of the smallest item of jewellery, for example, it was architecture which took pride of place. Displayed on one of the pavilions erected for the 1719 celebrations was the aphorism: 'Princes gain immortality through great buildings as much as through great victories' (which might be thought especially welcome to a prince with such a modest military record).[21] As he put it: 'we, from our special love of the art of building, wherein we are particularly wont to amuse ourselves, have before now created various designs, put them down on paper and ordered our architects in our own person to put them into complete execution . . . and have reserved the final say once and for all to ourselves as master'.[22]

Augustus may have been in charge, but he was anything but a dictator. The substantial surviving documentation shows him conferring, discussing, adapting, even deferring to the specialists. In the 1720s he succeeded in mediating between the older Italianate baroque school headed by Pöppelmann and the more French classicist style favoured by Longuelune. This willingness to consult prompted Walther Hentschel to conclude: 'for his architects, Augustus was the ideal patron'.[23] It was a verdict endorsed by another East German art historian, Monika Schlechte: 'what distinguished Augustus as a builder was his interest, his expertise, his love of a combination of the arts and both his decisiveness and his flexibility when dealing with architects'.[24] Although not unique in this regard, he provided generous travel scholarships for selected artists. Pöppelmann was sent to Prague, Vienna, Rome and Paris; in 1714 a group of musicians went to Paris and Venice where they also played for the crown prince on his grand tour; the flautist Johann Joachim Quantz spent many months in Naples and Paris in 1725.[25] Pöppelmann's instructions were 'to view the current style of the building of palaces and gardens and especially to have the plans he is taking with him scrutinized by the leading architects and artists'.[26] The influence of what he saw, especially in Vienna and Rome, can be seen in the Dresden Zwinger.

The Zwinger

The Zwinger was at the centre of the 1719 festivities. It was also Augustus's greatest single creation. At the risk of over-egging the pudding, it can also be hailed as the apotheosis of baroque representational culture, for its essential function was display, the arena in which the court festivities were performed. Its name derives from the space between the outer and inner fortification walls, now devoted to pleasure because no longer thought to be needed for military purposes.[27] It started in 1709 as a festive site for the lavish entertainment of Frederick IV, King of Denmark, but was only intended to be a temporary structure, built mainly of wood. In 1710 Pöppelmann was commissioned to replace it with an orangery, to feed Augustus's passion for fruits of the south.[28] As was often the way with Augustus's schemes, it soon mushroomed, for the following year turned out to be an *annus mirabilis*. The stroke of good fortune was the sudden death of Emperor Joseph, for during any interregnum the Elector of Saxony was *ex officio* one of two *Reichsvikare* or regents (the other was the Elector Palatine). This entitled him to create imperial peerages, among the beneficiaries being his fourteen-year-old illegitimate son Maurice, now styled 'Count of Saxony' but better known later as the 'Maréchal de Saxe'.[29]

Although his spell at the pinnacle of European royalty came to an end in October 1711, when Charles VI was elected emperor, Augustus gave it a three-dimensional memorial in the shape of the

Zwinger. The connection was made explicit by Pöppelmann in the Preface to his illustrated review of the complex.[30] Never before, he proclaimed, had a *Reichsvikar* been simultaneously both king and elector. Paying tribute to his employer's enlightenment (*lumières*), perfect knowledge of the fine arts, intelligence, good taste and magnificence, he also provided a helpful exegesis of the complex frontispiece. Much was made of the splendours of Saxony, the River Elbe and the combination of the Holy Roman Empire, Saxony and Poland. Special emphasis was laid on the appearance of Hercules, complete with club, as 'the inseparable companion of glory' and standing in front of an orange tree representing the Garden of the Hesperides. Just as Hercules had relieved Atlas of the burden of holding up the sky and earth, so had Augustus taken on the weight of the Holy Roman Empire during the interregnum. Indeed, Hercules is 'the central figure of the Zwinger's iconology'.[31] All the arts combined with nature and science to pay homage to the ruler of this modern version of the ancient world's most famous garden. Although Augustus was not the first European monarch to borrow Herculean imagery, he was one of the most consistent. As soon as he succeeded as elector, he commissioned the Augsburg medallist Philipp Heinrich Müller to design a medal with his image and on the obverse Hercules with club and lionskin in front of a silhouette of Dresden. Many such images were to follow.[32]

Dominating the central Wall Pavilion was a statue of Hercules–Augustus by Balthasar Permoser, one of the most important German baroque sculptors. In Dresden since 1690, he was nearly sixty when work began on the Zwinger.[33] Together with Pöppelmann, with whom he enjoyed a cordial relationship, he created 'a palatial complex that can be celebrated as one of the last and finest achievements of the European Baroque'.[34] Permoser can only have been responsible personally for a limited number of the 450 free-standing figures in the complex, but he was in charge of the large workshop, directing a team of sculptors in matters of subject, style and technique.[35] As a result the Zwinger achieved the organic quality that was at the heart of the baroque.[36] This was well put by Siegfried Asche: 'the sculptures of the Zwinger grow organically from the building, like plants they spread from or grow back into the architectural forms'.[37] The massive Polish crown adorning the gate to the bridge over the moat on the west side is a particularly striking example of the happy marriage between architecture and sculpture.[38]

It was on the central space, 116 metres long by 107 metres wide, flanked by pavilions and raised terraces for spectators, that many of the festivities of 1719 took place.[39] The programme had been worked out very carefully in advance by master of ceremonies Besser, although – needless to say – he had to put up with Augustus constantly looking over his shoulder.[40] The inspiration was not Versailles, as has sometimes been assumed, but the festivities staged by previous pleasure-loving electors, with his grandfather Johann Georg II to the fore.[41] In 1678 the latter had celebrated a gathering of the Wettin clans with festivities taking up most of the month of February. This was well known to Augustus because every last detail had been recorded in the festival book to end them all – Gabriel Tzschimmer's *The Most Serene Reunion*, which ran to two volumes comprising 562 folio pages and nearly fifty engravings, thirty of them large-format.[42] For connoisseurs of European festivals, Dresden impressed by size and extravagance but was rather old-fashioned, if not retro. In particular, Augustus's penchant for mock-tournaments in full armour was deemed out of date.[43] Not that he cared. Much more *à la mode* was 'Tilting at the Ring' (*Ringrennen*), helpfully described by Helen Watanabe-O'Kelly, the doyenne of festival studies, as an equestrian contest in which riders sought to prick with a lance a ring suspended between two cords. The ring itself was sometimes subdivided into different zones, with extra points being awarded for hitting a particular part or for removing the ring altogether.[44] Ladies also competed, although in carriages rather than on horseback, and accompanied by 'cavaliers' to provide an escort and assistance with the steering. Prizes were distributed with a liberal hand.[45]

While its beauty, novelty and location next door to the palace made the Zwinger the main arena, there were several other sites. The all-important firework display was staged in the 'Holland Palace' on the right bank of the Elbe, to allow the pyrotechnics to be mirrored in the dark waters of the river and a naval narrative to be introduced to the explosions and illuminations. Once again, Augustus went back to his grandfather's model to choose the subject, in this case Jason's quest for the Golden Fleece (it was no coincidence, of course, that Augustus himself was member of this, the most glamorous of Europe's orders of chivalry).[46] It must have been a very noisy evening, opening with a fanfare from sixty-four trumpeters and a salvo from fifty heavy cannon.[47] A battle on the river between the fleets of the Argonauts and King Aeëtes of Kolchis, to the accompaniment of rockets and artillery, ended with victory for the former, when a final pyrotechnic spectacular displayed the name and titles of Maria Josepha: Jason had won the Golden Fleece, and Crown Prince Augustus had won his Habsburg bride.[48] A good impression of the dazzling show can be gained from the engraving produced by Johann August Corvinus for the commemorative album.[49]

Music

It will have become clear that music was a constant accompaniment to the court festivities, across a wide spectrum of genres from the drumrolls and fanfares of the outdoor events, through the aural wallpaper (*Tafelmusik*) of mealtimes, to the high-end sophistication of operas and ballets, all justifying Ortrud Landmann's authoritative description of Dresden court life as 'permeated with music' (*musikdurchtränkt*).[50] Augustus was particularly fond of the 'Janissary music' played by a special band to accompany festivities with a Turkish theme. Perhaps dating from his military service in Hungary against the Ottomans in the 1690s, his Turcomania was much in evidence in 1719. When his son and Maria Josepha arrived in Dresden, the first things they saw were nine specially commissioned tents *à la turque*. As Augustus made his way back to the city after their reception, he was preceded by a soldier in full armour bearing a horse tail, the symbol of Ottoman authority, guarded by four native Turks of imposing height wearing Turkish costume and turbans. Throughout the festivities he was accompanied by a battalion of Turkish-clad Saxon soldiers, selected the previous year for their impressive physique and ordered to grow long moustaches. The climax was a 'Turkish Festival' on 17 September at what had been the Queen Mother's Palace in the Italian Garden, known henceforth as the 'Turkish Palace' and the 'Turkish Garden' respectively.[51]

In the culturally competitive world of the Holy Roman Empire, music ranked high as a prestige marker, nowhere more so than in Thuringia and Saxony. In the Electorate of Saxony there was a long tradition of musical excellence, personified by the long career of Heinrich Schütz (1585–1672), who served three successive electors. Augustus had been given a sound musical education by his father's *Kapellmeister* Christoph Bernard and was described as '*un grand amateur de musique*'.[52] Like most imperious rulers he knew what he liked, although his taste fluctuated between French and Italian models before settling with the latter. That was mainly thanks to the influence of his son and heir, who had been deeply bitten by the Italian opera bug during his extended grand tour. Not as gifted musically as some of his fellow rulers – Emperor Leopold I being the star – Augustus demonstrated his commitment in the practical way of supporting financially a musical establishment distinguished by both quality and quantity.[53] He inherited a good orchestra and made it better. By the end of his life, it had the reputation of being 'the most famous European orchestra'.[54] Among the virtuosi were the violinists Jean Baptiste Volumier (also spelled Woulmyer), Johann Georg Pisendel and Francesco Maria Veracini, the organist Christoph Petzold, the theorbist Sylvius Leopold Weiss, the double bassist Jan Dismas Zelenka, the flautists Pierre-Gabriel Buffardin and Johann Joachim Quantz, the oboist Johann Christoph Richter and the pantaleonist Pantaleon Hebenstreit, who invented the eponymous instrument (a large dulcimer). All these instrumentalists were eminent enough to deserve inclusion in *The New Grove Dictionary of Music and Musicians* and several of them were composers too.[55] This was a modern orchestra with modern instrumentation and modern working practices, for each orchestral player was allowed to confine himself to just one instrument.[56] In short, Augustus had created a musical environment of high quality. It has been eloquently evoked by David Charlton:

> Let your imagination conjure up an orchestra without rival for its instrumental virtuosity that also includes some of the finest musicians of the day, many of whom are composers. Contemporary composers who write music of unprecedented virtuosity for 'their' ensemble and create their own variation of the concerto form, the *concerto per molti strumenti* as Chamber concerti, Sonatas for up to ten soloists, Solo Concerti for up to five soloists and gigantic Concert Suites with different soloists in each movement. An orchestra that, due to its excellence, also inspires the most celebrated composers of the day to compose highly virtuosic works.[57]

Packed into the month of September 1719 was a full range of musical performances: ballets (performed between the acts of operas), opera-ballets (Johann Christoph Schmidt's *Les Quatres saisons*), serenatas (Johann David Heinichen's *La Gara degli dei*), and three full operas (Antonio Lotti's *Giove in Argo, Ascanio* and *Teofane*). Conspicuous by its absence was any religious music, apart from the High Mass attended by Augustus and the newlyweds on the day after their arrival. The architectural focus was not the church but the new opera house, constructed immediately adjacent to the Zwinger at huge cost in just eleven months by a labour force working twenty-four-hour shifts, supplemented by specialist craftsmen, many hired from out of state.[58] The finished product was the biggest in Germany, with an auditorium seventy metres long and twenty-eight metres wide and a stage forty-three metres deep and twenty-three metres wide or 989 square metres (larger than most modern stages).[59] The orchestra stalls and three rows of eighteen boxes each could accommodate an audience of 2,000. Needless to say, there was a huge royal box on the central axis, although in practice Augustus preferred to sit in the stalls close to the stage or in a stage box.[60] The acoustics were excellent.[61]

To perform in this extravagant space, a company of international stars had been formed. The main recruiting agent was the bridegroom. Whatever Frederick Augustus's later shortcomings as ruler of Saxony and Poland, as a young man he lacked nothing when it came to appreciating Italian opera and its practitioners. During his prolonged stay in Venice, he had got to know both very well. From 1716 he lodged with his agent, the merchant Bianchi, whose wife was a distinguished singer and whose house was a lively musical centre.[62] Although Augustus initially did not share his passion for Italian music, he did authorize the eye-watering expenditure needed to assemble singers and instrumentalists capable of meeting the challenge posed by the most demanding (and expensive) of musical genres – *opera seria*. Among them were the leading composer of opera Antonio Lotti, his equally famous wife Santa Stella (soprano), Margherita Durastanti (another star soprano), the celebrated contralto Antonia Maria Novelli Laurenti ('La Coralli'), the top castrato 'Senesino' (Francesco Bernardi), the violinist Francesco Maria Veracini, the theorbo virtuoso Silvius Leopold Weiss and the bass Giuseppe Maria Boschi. Since much of Italian operatic music was not scored, it was essential to have musicians experienced in improvisation, especially in recitative (which explains the presence of the theorbist).[63] By the time the festivities began the company comprised three sopranos, three contraltos, a soprano castrato, an alto castrato, a tenor and two basses.[64] As spectacle was so important, the set designers Alessandro and Girolamo Mauro had also been hired, together with their team of carpenters and painters.[65]

With these resources available, Augustus and his master of ceremonies, Johann von Besser, had devised a repertoire of corresponding splendour. They also gave the familiar 'Festival of the Seven Planets' genre a political flavour. In the introduction to Heinichen's *La Gara degli dei* (The Competition of the Gods), Mercury addresses the assembled gods:

The fame of the wedding that unites Frederick [Augustus] with Maria [Josepha], Saxony with Austria, has already reached you in heaven. Now Jupiter has convoked you at the banks of the river Elbe to honour the arrival of the happy couple.

The goddess Diana then expresses the hope that the Roman goddess of childbirth, Lucina, will extend her favour to the new bride, so that Germany will be populated with a new breed of heroes. Mars concurs enthusiastically:

> Yes, yes, may new heroes emerge from this fecund womb, and establish once more courage and glory in the world. Does not Mars expect from these dynasties [the Wettins and the Habsburgs] mighty warriors to emulate the feats of their ancestors? So that Austria and Saxony will rise to shine in the firmament with ever growing splendour.[66]

The same point was made at much greater length in the climax of the whole festivities, namely the performance of *Teofane*, a grand *opera seria* written specially for the occasion, with music by Antonio Lotti, libretto by Stefano Pallavicino, ballet music by Jean Baptiste Volumier, choreography by Charles Duparc and sets by Alessandro Mauro.[67] Among the top brass in the audience were a number of musicians attracted by the reputation of the ensemble and well able to appreciate its quality, namely Pier Francesco Tosi, Georg Philipp Telemann and Georg Friedrich Handel, who had travelled from Vienna, Hamburg and London respectively.

This was a long evening, lasting from seven in the evening until two o'clock the next morning. The set changes took so long that the royal party was served a meal at their seats.[68] The quality of the music, singing and dancing, the visual spectacle, not to mention the sense of being present at a great occasion, kept the audience enthralled:

All the arts and sciences seem to have united in this breath of air. The extraordinary payments which the king grants the players have attracted the best and most excellent masters of this art to Dresden from Italy, the great school of music. When Senesino and Berselli sing, to Lotti's directions, however, one hears everything beautiful and tender that music has to offer. The whole orchestra is manned by the best instrumentalists. The stage is actually smaller than the one in Vienna, but its complement is incomparable.[69]

Although there is no recording of *Teofane* yet, it is possible to follow the intricacies of the plot through Handel's very similar *Ottone, re di Germania*. It recounts the wooing and winning of the Byzantine princess Teofane by the German Emperor Otto. Although set in the late tenth century, in Dresden the topicality (Teofane = Maria Josepha, Otto = Crown Prince Frederick Augustus) was obvious. Handel must have been impressed by what he saw and heard in Dresden, for he took the libretto back with him to England. In 1722 he had this adapted by Nicolo Haym, omitting the local Dresden references. First performed the following year, it became one of Handel's most successful operas, not least because three members of the Dresden cast performed – Senesino, Margherita Durastanti and Giuseppe Maria Boschi.[70] What the London audience did not see was the closing scene in the Temple of Hymen where 'Germania' invokes the shades of Ottone and Teofane and repeats the prediction first made in *La Gara degli dei* that Frederick Augustus and Maria Josepha would bring forth a race of heroes to make Germany renowned throughout the world.[71] In the event, the happy couple exceeded even the most optimistic forecasts, producing eleven children surviving to adulthood. If there were no heroes among them, they did include a son-in-law of the Empress Maria Theresa, a Queen of Spain, a Queen of France, an Electress of Bavaria and two Electors of the Holy Roman Empire.

As we have seen, when the wedding took place in Vienna, Frederick Augustus was made to feel that he was a very lucky man to be marrying a Habsburg. The post-nuptial festivities at Dresden deftly reversed the pecking order. In *Teofane* it was Ottone (Frederick Augustus

Wettin) who was the dominant masculine hero and Teofane (Maria Josepha Habsburg) who was the submissive female.[72] The relative merits of the two families had been subtly advertised on the previous day when the tournament on the Old Market staged for the 'Festival of Mars' concluded with a speech reminding everyone that on that day – 12 September – in 1683 the Elector Johann Georg III, Augustus's father, had led in person the allied left wing in the great victory over the Ottomans at Vienna.[73] Left unspoken was the memory of the Habsburg Emperor Leopold having fled Vienna to the safety of Passau when the Ottomans first approached.

In the libretti of the 1719 works, Augustus had to take a back seat to his son and daughter-in-law. For his next – and last – operatic extravaganza, his persona moved to the centre of the stage. This was in 1731 with a performance of *Cleofide* by Johann Adolf Hasse, a composer even more esteemed than Lotti.[74] The title page of the published libretto made it crystal-clear who was in charge:

CLEOFIDE
Drama per Musica
Da rappresentarsi nel Reggio Teatro di Core
Per Commando della Sacra Real Majestà
Di

FEDERICO AUGUSTO
Re delle Polonie, Elettor di Sassonia,
Sempre Grande e Invittissimo
Il mese di Settembre dell' Anno
M DCC XXXI
La Musica è del famosissimo Signor
Giovanni Adolfo Hasse,
detto il Sassone,
Maestro di Capella di S.M. di Polonia, Elettore di Sassonia

Dresda
Presso di Giovanni Conrado Stössel di Corte S.M. di Polonia, Elettorale di Sassonia

CLEOFIDE
Opera
to be performed in the Royal Court Theatre
At the command of His Majesty
By the Grace of God

FREDERICK AUGUST
King of Poland, Elector of Saxony,
Always Great and Invincible
In the month of September of the year
1731
The music is by the most illustrious
Johann Adolf Hasse
known as 'The Saxon'
Master of the Chapel of His Majesty of Poland, Elector of Saxony

Dresden
Printed by Johann Conrad Stössel, Royal Court Printer of His Majesty of Poland, Elector of Saxony

Figure 1. *The title-page of the original libretto of* Cleofide

It would be difficult to find a better example of the patron-centred nature of representational culture. Augustus's typeface is twice the size of the composer's and there is relentless insistence on the royal nature of the exercise – 'Royal Court Theatre . . . His Majesty by the Grace of God . . . King of Poland, Elector of Saxony . . . '. It was work he owned, was performed in his theatre, was applauded only when indicated, and was attended only by those he invited. Indeed, the first performance had been private, exclusive to the royal family and a select few courtiers. The claim by a man dethroned by Charles XII in 1706, and restored only by courtesy of Peter the Great, to be 'Always Great and Invincible' must surely have made even the most loyal lips curl. Even more outrageous was the association he clearly intended between himself and the opera's main character, Alexander the Great. So when the latter forgives King Poros and graciously allows him to claim the eponymous Cleofide as his bride, Augustus was pointing to his own magnanimous abstention from adding the Russian Empire to Saxony–Poland.[75] If the singers on stage did not swivel to face Augustus when nominally singing '*O Grande! O Magnanimo!*' in praise of Alexander, they were missing an obvious opportunity to ingratiate themselves with their real target.[76]

Hunting and baiting animals in the theatre of cruelty

Beyond the play-acting of the tournaments and *opera seria*, there was plenty of real violence on offer during the festivities, although the targets were not human. It could not be otherwise with a man like Augustus in charge, because one of the things he really loved was killing animals. An excellent marksman, he liked to take pot-shots at anything that caught his eye when out riding, as evinced by the numerous claims for compensation that had to be met. His targets included his courtiers' hats. During his sojourn at Moritzburg in 1694, for example, he paid for six hats, one walking stick, eighteen geese and four pigs. On his way through his dominions to receive homage after his succession he despatched seven cows, three sheep, two horses and numerous geese.[77] Augustus was simply an incorrigible show-off, always drawing attention to himself. Although his sobriquet 'the Strong' was a posthumous award,[78] there were plenty of anecdotes circulating during his lifetime of his exceptional strength and his delight in displaying it. If stories of the bull wrestled to the ground in a Madrid bullring or the head of an ox severed with one stroke of his sword were invented by the mendacious scandal-monger Baron Pöllnitz, there were credible eyewitness accounts of the breaking of a horseshoe or the rolling-up of a silver plate with one hand.[79]

Sniping at livestock was one thing, quite another was the slaughter occasioned by the various forms of hunting. With very few exceptions, all European rulers of the period regarded hunting not as a recreational leisure pursuit but as an essential part of their kingship.[80] In Dresden in 1719, it was not separate from court culture but an integral part of the festivities. On 18 September a grand spectacle was organized on the River Elbe. At one o'clock in the afternoon Augustus and his party arrived on a magnificent boat specially constructed for the occasion and enjoyed a good lunch in the tented village. There then appeared, floating downstream, a quite extraordinary vessel, more stage than boat, bearing an orchestra and a group of singers, its prow formed by four 'water-horses', its stern a raised platform in the shape of an enormous scallop shell. The meticulous illustration by Zacharias Longuelune does not reveal any obvious means of propulsion, so presumably it was towed into position in front of the royal marquee. A serenata was then performed – *Diana on the Elbe* – with music by Heinichen and libretto by (probably) Pallavicino.[81] The modern editor suggests that Maria Josepha was not presented as the personification of Venus because she simply did not look the part ('extraordinarily ugly' was the verdict of Princess Wilhelmine of Prussia, Frederick the Great's sister).[82] The choice of Diana, however, was entirely appropriate, for both she and her equally plain husband were known to be passionately fond of hunting. In the serenata, Diana announces that she has sent 1,000 beasts from her forest, to swim rather than run, happy to lose their lives at such illustrious hands.[83] That was something of an exaggeration, as it appears that it was 'only' about 400 animals who were driven into the river to provide sport for the royal party. Although called a 'water hunt' (*Wasser-Jagd*), it was really just a slaughter. The deer and wild boar had been gathered in advance in an enclosure upstream. From there they were driven into the water by the huntsmen and their dogs, funnelled through the central arch of the bridge, and forced to swim down to be shot from the shore or from boats. Any managing to get ashore were despatched by dogs, huntsmen or spectators.[84] Among those enthusiastically delivering the *coup de grâce* was the newly wed Crown Princess Maria Josepha.[85]

Killing animals within the precincts of Dresden could only be conducted in an arena. Out in the country, the hunting centre was at Moritzburg in the Friede forest (*Friedewald*) twelve kilometres north of Dresden. Two kinds of hunting took place there. The first and most popular form was known as 'managed' or 'organized' hunting (*eingerichtete/eingestellte Jagd*), whose other sobriquets revealed its nature – 'main hunting' (*Hauptjagd*), 'parade hunting' (*Prunkjagd*), 'festive hunting' (*Festinjagd*) or, because it was so popular in the Holy Roman Empire, 'German hunting'.[86] Fortunately, a contemporary account of a hunt of this type held at Moritzburg in 1718 has survived, together with an excellent illustration. Particularly revealing is the fact that the actual hunt was only one part of a ceremonial panoply. It was also a celebration of Augustus's sexual conquest of his current *maîtresse en titre*, Maria Magdalena von Dön-hoff, of whom more later.[87] The three-day festivity began with a grand procession of 200 hunt servants divided into four groups, each representing one corner of the earth and dressed accordingly, bearing fruits and plants of the region. As usual with any of Augustus's shows, there was plenty of music, the highlight being a French song of welcome hailing Augustus as the man who tamed the wild beasts. Rowing races on the lake were followed by a duck shoot, a banquet, fireworks and illuminations. The climax was the appearance of a flotilla manned by appropriately clad and blacked-up 'Moors', the narrative being that an African envoy was arriving to worship Augustus as the Sun God and bearing gifts of exotic flora and fauna, including lions, tigers, bears, apes and parrots.[88]

On day two there was a managed hunt, with huge numbers of game driven into a pond inside a fenced enclosure where they were mown down by the waiting guns. As usual, there was no discrimination between the sexes when it came to killing. This was followed by a session of pig-sticking, or the skewering of wild boar with lance or knife, a sport which later became associated with British officers in India but was also popular earlier in the German lands. Augustus was a devotee, renowned for his fearless skill.[89]

The final day was devoted to a *Parforce* hunt, involving the chase across open country of a single stag by huntsmen and a pack of hounds until it was immobilized by exhaustion and despatched by a knife. On this occasion, three 'especially handsome stags' were hunted in turn.[90] Amazingly, one actually got away, probably the only survivor of the innumerable animals put to death during the three days of bloodletting.

That *parforce* hunt would have been accepted by the hunting fraternity in France and England. They would not have regarded any form of managed hunt, whether aquatic or not, as hunting at all. Also unacceptable would have been another activity much in vogue in Dresden, namely the 'fight-hunt' (*Kampf Jagd*). This took place in an enclosed space such as the courtyard of the palace, a fenced-off section of the Old Market or at the headquarters of the hunting administration (*Jägerhof*), where a grandstand was erected for special occasions. Wild animals of various kinds were released simultaneously and encouraged to fight each other to the death. In 1709, during the visit to Dresden of Frederick IV of Denmark, for example, a lion, six bears, seven wild boars, an aurochs, a bison, a Polish ox and two horses were pitched against each other. To get them in a suitably aggressive frame of mind, they had been tortured in advance by the application of red-hot irons, mutilation of their ears, the firing of darts into their skin and the infliction of other goads. To 'the agreeable sound of hunting horns and bugles' they were then released into the arena to do battle.[91] The result was disappointing: 'the fight did not proceed in a very exciting manner because the animals did not do much to each other', it was recorded regretfully, apart from the aurochs throwing a bear in the air and piercing a horse with its horn, and a bear killing a boar.[92]

Two other related activities need to be noted. The first was especially popular in Saxony for reasons that have never been addressed, let alone explained. This was fox-tossing (*Fuchsprellen*), which usually took place in the courtyard of the palace with courtiers spectating from the surrounding windows. It was very simple: foxes (and other animals) were repeatedly tossed high in the air from a net or blanket until they died. Not requiring too much physical strength, it was popular with the ladies too, often joined by a male 'cavalier', the couple wearing matching 'his-and-hers' hunting dress (usually green).[93] Augustus was a keen tosser, directing that a special space for fox-tossing should be added to the plans for the reconstruction of the Jägerhof.[94] In a grand session he organized in 1728 for the visit of Frederick William I of Prussia, no fewer than 200 foxes were tossed to death. That was followed by the release of a herd of wild boars for pig-sticking and, as a climax, a final tossing of two badgers, two beavers and six wild cats. The royal Prussian visitor distinguished himself by shooting 150 pheasants and partridges at a shoot in the Grand Garden.[95] The worst shot of the entire gathering was the Prussian Crown Prince Frederick. It would be cheering to think that he missed deliberately: he was one of the very few European sovereigns ever to record his disapproval of hunting, in his treatise *Anti-Machiavel*, published in 1740 just before he came to the throne.[96]

Although it might seem impossible to find an activity more offensive to modern sensibility, a final form of *Jagd* certainly qualifies. This was the 'driven hunt' (*Treibjagd*) staged on 26 September at the 'Plauenscher Grund', a deep valley south of Dresden. It was even more straightforward than fox-tossing. Deer, bears and boars were simply driven over the high cliff to fall to their death, watched from below by a large crowd of spectators. As with the other festivities, it was carefully recorded visually and publicized as an engraving. The artist cannot have been present, for he depicted the animals just falling off the cliff. In reality, it was made much more entertaining: a platform was built projecting over the valley but left open, the end concealed with a pile of brushwood, so that the unwitting animals rushed out over the edge, appearing to be jumping rather than just tumbling. The second victim seen falling in the illustration was a bear, which spotted what was happening and tried to turn back, alas too late.[97] As is also shown, groups of peasants had gathered on the surrounding cliffs to watch their masters and mistresses enjoying themselves. Far from being disgusted at the spectacle, they cheered as each animal went over the edge. A hostile verse written after the event lamented the screams of the wounded creatures that survived the fall but added:

> That was fine for the peasants who applauded
> The killing of so many wild beasts
> And even wanted more to suffer the same frightful end
> So much damage had they caused [to their crops].[98]

The peasants' anger would have been better directed at Augustus and his hunt officials, who had promoted the overpopulation of game and prevented its control. As in most parts of Europe, there were draconic laws to preserve the nobility's sport. Pet dogs were crippled or hobbled by chains to prevent them chasing; humans were confined to footpaths or excluded from the forests altogether; there was a ban on collecting any form of food that might sustain game – nuts, acorns, wild fruit etc.; compensation was rarely paid for damage inflicted on crops; and so on and so forth.[99] So severe were the penalties that only the very brave, stupid or desperate tried their hand at poaching. The wedding festival was almost over by the time of the massacre at the Plauenscher Grund, but the hunting continued unabated. The court then moved to Moritzburg, where more hunts of various kinds were organized.[100] There were also plenty of other forms of entertainment, including balls, banquets and lots of music, including a new sinfonia by Heinichen (in F major, '*di Moritzburg*') performed as table music.[101]

Private and public

As the presence of the crowd of cheering peasants indicated, the festivities of 1719 were not socially exclusive. Of course the social hierarchy was preserved, whatever the venue. The peasants were no more likely to watch from the royal pavilion than a burgher was to sit in a box at the opera. Nevertheless, the whole community was involved in many of the events. Their participation was not entirely voluntary. To make the biggest possible show when Maria Josepha arrived, Augustus ordered the governor of Dresden, Count August Christoph von Wackerbarth, to recruit a civil guard of 1,600 to line the streets as the procession made its way to the palace. Their muskets were issued from the arsenal, but they were expected to pay for their own uniform – black tricorn hat, grey coats with red lapels, white spats, ammunition pouches and belts. Unsurprisingly, both the cost and requirement to attend rehearsals aroused opposition, with Wackerbarth reporting a 50 per cent refusal rate. As the city's tradesmen all depended to a greater or lesser extent on the custom of the court, not too much coercion was needed to make 1,200–1,300 eventually see sense.[102] Like all pre-industrial residential cities, the political and social culture of Dresden was deferential.

Over the next month, banquets or performances in theatres were confined to the court, although the plain people of Dresden could gain admission to the upper tier of the cavernous opera house. Indeed they were needed to ensure a full house. They could also watch the firework displays, the aquatic hunt on the Elbe, the processions through the streets which preceded the tournaments and the tournaments themselves if they took place on the Old Market or in the Great Garden. There was also room for them in the grandstands erected at the Zwinger and the Jägerhof.[103] This was a common feature of Saxon festivities and not confined to 1719. Johann Michael von Loen's description of the carnival of 1723, for example, makes it clear that the whole community was involved in what sounds like a gigantic street party.[104] Dresden is special, wrote an anonymous visitor in 1728, because the common people are admitted to all the court festivities.[105] For once, there is corroboration for an observation of Baron Pöllnitz: 'when the king is present, the people participate in almost all the entertainments of the court, most of the festivities staged by the king being public. The shows and the masquerades are open to everyone well-dressed; no one has to pay and all can enjoy themselves as they see fit.'[106] A more jaundiced observer, Julius Bernhard von Rohr, agreed that the 'riff-raff' (*Pöbel*) were allowed to attend the festivities but added that, as their pleasure never went beyond 'guzzling and boozing' (*Fressen und Saufen*), they were allocated special tables.[107]

There was direct plebeian involvement when the last of the planetary festivals was held on 26 September. This was for Saturn, held at the Plauen Gorge and prefaced by the 'driven hunt' already described. After watching the animals perish by being forced to jump off the cliff, the company moved to an illuminated structure shaped like a mountain. Never one to miss an opportunity for self-display, Augustus had the high table at dinner arranged to form the letter 'A' and every place setting was adorned with a sugar loaf shaped like an ore mountain.[108] The after-dinner entertainment was a parade of 1,600 miners, marching out of the darkness with their lamps, bearing the tools of their trade and richly decorated symbols of the ore they mined. They also brought with them a working model of a blast furnace, which was then used to melt metal from which medals were struck. Technological exercises were intermingled with theatrical representations, after which the miners sang eight verses on the theme 'Good luck!' (*Glück auf!*) to the happy couple before being treated to a mock-peasant wedding with much jollification and beer. This was another festivity shared with the public, for 'thousands' were said to have been present.[109]

Augustus paid a rather back-handed compliment to his subjects by organizing at the Zwinger, as part of the 1719 festivities, a mock-plebeian fair and tavern (*Wirtschaft*), the latter best defined as 'a role play in which the ruler and his consort play the inn-keeper and his wife and entertain the members of the court dressed up as visiting foreigners, peasants, etc.'.[110] On 20 September, the Zwinger was turned into what was surely the most lavish beer garden of all time. Doors opened to the general public at 2 p.m. 'and everyone was admitted', as the official account put it.[111] At 6 p.m., as the autumn light began to fade, the main party arrived, headed by a band of twenty-four musicians, followed by senior officials dressed as cooks and servants, and high-ranking courtiers wearing what was thought to be peasant clothing. Then came Augustus and Queen Christiane Eberhardine, lightly disguised as the innkeeper of the 'White Eagle' and his lady, the latter accompanied by her little dwarf attendant.

This was not just an excuse to pretend that the world had been turned upside down (for one evening only!), it was also advertised as a '*Wirtschaft* of the nations' (*Nationenwirtschaft*). Among other things, this designation allowed Augustus to indulge his taste for exotic clothing. A carefully choreographed procession was led by the Prince of Hessen dressed as a Turk, together with nine identically clad companions, followed by groups, also of ten pairs each, of Egyptians, French, Spanish, Moors, Africans, Indians, Poles, Hungarians and Germans, all in appropriate outfits. ('My pen finds it impossible to describe the sumptuousness of their clothes and the opulence of their jewellery.')[112] A crowd of German peasant boys in green uniforms with red lanyards brought up the rear. The poet laureate (Johann von Besser) then addressed each of the group leaders and their ladies in turn with short eulogistic verses. To his employer, 'The Inn Keeper (His Majesty the King)' he declaimed:

> That is a good tavern-keeper! That is a rich man,
> Who can organize a fair and a *Wirtschaft* like this,
> And make his garden look like Heaven,

By illuminating the darkness with a hundred eyes.
Tell me! Does not every lamp and every lantern,
Shine forth as a sign of glory and a star of joy?

Mine host of the 'White Eagle' and his team had certainly laid on a great variety of entertainments. There was an Italian troupe presenting 'The Strength of Hercules', a company performing *commedia dell'arte*, tightrope walkers, cock-fighting, a puppet show, waxworks (a sultan reclines in his seraglio, surrounded by his concubines), aquatic fun in the Bath of Diana, acrobats, fortune tellers, ballad singers (with songs celebrating victory over the Turks) and a lottery. The last-named offered prizes to the value of 60,000 talers to the ladies participating, but of much lower value to their male cavaliers. Sixteen tables were laid out for dinner for the top brass. Although barely credible, it is recorded that 65,572 lights turned night into day.[113] Needless to say, there was much music and a ballet. The jollifications continued until three in the morning.[114]

This extravaganza also had a commercial purpose. Not for nothing was it the 'Festival of Mercury', who was the god of commerce and wealth among his other attributes. So the *Wirtschaft* (another meaning of the German word is 'economy') was used by Augustus to advertise Saxon enterprise. Sixty booths had been erected, selling all manner of locally produced goods – ornaments, gold and silver ware, dolls, toys, tools, etc. Pride of place, of course, was taken by porcelain, Augustus's greatest contribution to Europe's luxury trades. In the next chapter the perspective will be widened from the events of 1719 to embrace Augustus's whole career as entrepreneur, builder, architect, town planner, landscape designer – and artist.

Augustus the Artist: Refashioning the Environment

The refashioning of Dresden

If nothing else, the wedding celebrations at Dresden in 1719 showed that Augustus was the most flamboyant ruler in the Holy Roman Empire, if not Europe. In one important respect, however, he fell behind his colleagues. The problem was his residence, large and imposing and beautifully located on the River Elbe, but dating from the sixteenth century and hopelessly out of date by contemporary standards. This was a time when more – and bigger – princely palaces were being built across Germany than ever before – Nymphenburg and Schleissheim in Bavaria, Herrenhausen in Hanover, Mannheim in the Palatinate, Wilhelmshöhe in Hessen-Kassel, Ludwigsburg in Württemberg, Brühl (Cologne), Bruchsal (Speyer), Mainz, Bamberg and Würzburg, just to name a few. Particularly galling must have been the knowledge that the detested Hohenzollerns were building a colossal new palace in the centre of Berlin (from 1689 to 1713). An added spur to emulation was the devastating fire which broke out in the Dresden Palace during the night of 25–6 March 1701, which burned for two days and left about half of the building a ruin.[1]

It was not for want of planning that a replacement never rose from the ashes. Together with his architects, especially Matthäus Daniel Pöppelmann, Augustus considered one plan after another, each more ambitious than the last.[2] He knew that the Habsburgs were considering a similar project and sent Pöppelmann down to Vienna to consult their chief architect, Johann Bernhard Fischer von Erlach, who had also produced a grandiose design for a new palace at Schönbrunn.[3] Neither progressed from the drawing board, and for the same simple reason – lack of money. With a ruinously expensive war to fight in the east and the crippling cost of the Swedish occupation in 1706–7, there was nothing left for non-essentials. And when the war started to fade away after 1717, there were the upcoming wedding festivities ready to absorb every last penny. It was not until 22 February 1717 that Augustus finally bit the bullet and announced that the Dresden Palace would have to be left as it was, albeit extensively remodelled to provide a greater degree of comfort and beauty.[4] Pöppelmann was sent to Vienna again, but this time it was to look at interiors only.[5]

In bringing the existing palace up to scratch, minds were concentrated by the deadline of the great wedding. With a Habsburg archduchess due to arrive in September 1719, no expense was spared in turning the fire-damaged relic into a baroque paradise. Fortunately, Augustus had at his disposal the highly efficient building department he had inherited and then expanded.[6] Its staff of around 100 included many specialist craftsmen.[7] Now that the devastation inflicted by the notorious air raids of 13–15 February 1945 has been repaired, it is possible to appreciate just how much was achieved.[8] The state rooms are decorated with a sumptuous profusion of silk wall hangings, golden textile pilasters, marble, gilt stucco forms, mirrors, furniture and ceiling frescoes that pay tribute to the imagination of the designer, Raymond Leplat, and the extravagance of his patron.[9] One example of the opulence must suffice, namely the colossal silver fire screen in the audience chamber created by Albrecht and Lorenz II Biller of Augsburg. The figures depicted are Vulcan and Venus, with Cupid alluding to the latter's adultery by holding the helmet of Mars.[10] If it was not created with Augustus in mind, it was certainly a most appropriate choice of topic. The erotic theme was continued by overdoors depicting 'Leda and the Swan' and 'Venus and Adonis' by Louis de Silvestre. More principled was the same artist's ceiling fresco presenting Augustus as 'Hercules casting discord, envy and hatred to the ground and protecting wisdom, truth, justice and strength'.[11]

If the exterior of the Dresden Palace could not be radically altered, it was transformed by the addition of the Zwinger, originally conceived as part of the planned rebuild and discussed in the previous chapter.[12] Its context was also complemented by being part of the transformation of Dresden that occurred during Augustus's reign. This was partly informal, the result of the local elites following their ruler's example by building grand town houses. The claim has been made by one of the city's historians that no other central European city boasted so many noble residences, although that must surely exclude Prague and Vienna.[13] Thanks to their broad acres, mineral resources and even, occasionally, entrepreneurial ventures, many Saxon nobles could afford to keep up an establishment in Dresden as well as a country estate. If they overcame their distaste for Augustus's apostasy and immorality, his court had a great deal to offer in the way of entertainment and patronage. Dresden had always been a *Residenzstadt* – a community whose economic *raison d'être* was the residence within its walls of the ruler, his court, his administration and his servants – and Augustus made it even more so. Not all the nobles lived like a grandee such as Count Flemming, who even maintained his own musical establishment.[14] After Augustus bought Flemming's Holland Palace, he built another on Pirna Street.[15] Both ambition and style filtered down from the nobility to the *haute bourgeoisie*, so much so that a recent history of baroque Dresden has a chapter entitled 'A city "filled with beautiful palaces": the baroque houses of the burghers'.[16]

Private initiative was encouraged by public direction, employing a combination of stick and carrot. Building ordinances issued by Flemming and Wackerbarth in 1708 and 1720 regulated such matters as height (the limit was 17.5 metres), appearance (only gentle colours – *gelinde Farben* – for façades), natural lighting (no overhanging roofs), hygiene (proper drainage) and fire precautions (compulsory conversion from wood to stone within a specified period). Any house-owner unable to make the necessary changes was obliged to sell to someone who could. The incentives offered were loans, tax rebates and fiscal holidays.[17] Although very interventionist, this programme did eventually make a beautiful city a pearl among European cities, as the justly celebrated *vedute* of Bernardo Bellotto reveal. The same approach with the same results was applied to right-bank Dresden, almost completely destroyed by fire in 1685 and with much left derelict. When Augustus succeeded in 1694 there were only twenty-three houses intact.[18] In the course of his reign, 'Altendresden', as it was known, was reborn and turned into an elegant city quarter. It was thanks to his direction that the High Street (*Hauptstrasse*) leading from the Elbe bridge to what is now Albert Square was complemented by another running back to the river from the latter to the Japanese Palace (previously known as the Holland Palace). With his habitual immodesty, Augustus named it 'King Street'. As he instructed, it was to be broad, straight and lined with linden trees, the houses were to be uniform in height and general appearance (bright colours in this case), and were to be lower than the palace at the end. Pöppelmann issued builders with models.[19]

In the last year of his life Augustus renamed rebuilt Altendresden simply 'New Town' (*Neustadt*), to emphasize that it was no longer a separate community with a different name but was now united with the main city on the left bank. Linking the two was the great bridge, rebuilt between 1727 and 1731 and for many contemporaries the greatest of Augustus's achievements.[20] Pöppelmann was the designer, the municipal mason Johann Gottfried Fehre the engineer. Stone bridges across wide rivers were still relatively rare at a time when most crossings were made by ferry. It was said that Prague had the broadest, Regensburg the strongest and Dresden the longest, but after the Augustus Bridge had been completed, Dresden had the broadest, the strongest, the longest – and the most beautiful. It was now 437 metres long and eleven metres wide.[21] More than a convenience for travellers, whether on foot or in carriages, or a place of recreation where the public could sit on the '*rondelles*' (the alcoves above the pillars) and admire the view, it was also envisaged as an artery linking the two communities and binding them into the Elbe landscape.[22] Augustus being Augustus, he wanted to have his statue on the bridge, to compete with statue of Henry IV on the Pont Neuf in Paris and of Frederick William the Great Elector of Brandenburg on the Long Bridge in Berlin, but the engineers advised against. He had his way eventually, albeit posthumously when an extraordinary golden equestrian statue was placed on the New Town market square at the end of the bridge.[23]

Since the middle of the eighteenth century, the view from the bridge has been dominated by the immediately adjacent Catholic 'Court Church', designed by Gaetano Chiaveri and built in 1739–55, commissioned by the devoutly Catholic convert Augustus III. A more appealing view opens up if one's eyes swivel left to the Church of Our Lady (Frauenkirche), aesthetically superior and the achievement of the reign of his markedly less devout if nominally Catholic father.[24] A replacement for a dilapidated medieval structure, this was built at the initiative of the city council and was designed not by one of Augustus's architects but by Georg Bähr, the municipal master carpenter. He may have come from a plebeian family (his father was a weaver), never travelled abroad and been self-taught, but he created one of the most beautiful baroque churches in central Europe, which is saying something.[25] Among its splendours was a magnificent new organ built by Gottfried Silbermann, the most celebrated organ-builder of his age. For its inauguration in 1736 Johann Sebastian Bach came from Leipzig to put it through its paces, and also to demonstrate the excellent acoustics of the new building in a two-hour concert attended by 'a great many other personages and artists'.[26] It should be noted that Silbermann was based at Freiberg in Saxony and a prolific manufacturer: as well as the forty-five organs he built for Saxon churches, in 1732 he was also responsible for the first fortepiano to be made in Germany.[27] If the Frauenkirche was not Augustus's own project, he certainly had an impact on its construction, not least by overruling his building officials, who wished to veto the town council's choice of Bähr.[28] He also received the architect 'in a gracious and friendly manner', as Bähr put it, and supported his plan for a high dome.[29] What he did not do was to provide much in the way of finance, donating just 7,300 talers in three instalments, a drop in the ocean given that the total cost was 230,000.[30] It was his successor who made completion possible by diverting all the money collected in Saxony for the relief of Protestants expelled by the Archbishop of Salzburg, thus deftly alleviating the injury inflicted on the True Faith by the erection of a new Protestant church by harming another group of heretics.[31]

The residential landscape

The shape of the church, central with a high dome, was a wholly intentional reference to Santa Maria della Salute in Venice, which Augustus knew very well. The Frauenkirche was to play the same role in Dresden, dominating the cityscape, with the Elbe taking the role of the Grand Canal.[32] The success of this exercise in pictur-esque town planning is evident in Bellotto's *veduta*. The Dresden vista was also integrated in a wider context, what Heinrich Magir-ius has termed 'a residential landscape'. That term was not used by Augustus himself, although he might well have done so when he referred proudly to the twenty-four palaces situated within a radius of three Saxon miles (about thirty kilometres).[33] That was roughly the limit of what could be travelled on a round trip in the course of a day's excursion. The central axis was the Elbe Valley running from south-east to north-west, its natural beauties combining with the ease of river transport. To his possession at Meissen in the north and Königstein in the south, Augustus added a hunting lodge at Hubertusburg (which his son later turned into a palace); a country retreat with ornamental gardens at Übigau, bought from Count Flemming; a residence at Elsterwerda, which he bought from his minister Baron Woldemar von Löwendahl; a residence added to the existing stud at Graditz, designed by Pöppelmann; a residence with extensive gardens at Großsedlitz, which he bought from his minis-ter Count Wackerbarth; and a summer palace at Pillnitz.[34]

The most interesting was the last-named, not least because it expressed in bricks and mortar the importance enjoyed by princely mistresses, albeit only fleetingly. In 1694 Augustus's brother, Elector Johann Georg IV, bought the residence and estate for his teenage lover Magdalena Sibylla von Neitschütz, although both died the same year.[35] In 1706 Augustus gave it to his new *maîtresse en titre* Constantia von Cosel (of whom more later). After her flight in 1716 and eventual incarceration it passed back to Augustus, who began a major rebuild in 1720. Its position certainly invited development, being close to Dresden, immediately adjacent to the river, with a flight of steps leading down to the water's edge and framed by a picturesque setting of hills and vineyards.[36] Quite unlike any other of the Saxon residences, by the time of Augustus's death it consisted of two quite separate buildings, the Water Palace and the Hill Palace, divided by a baroque garden (a third wing linking the two was added much later). Also unusual, indeed unique at the time of its construction, was the strong oriental flavour of both exterior form and interior decoration: 'it was here that the fashion for chinoiserie first found architectural expression in Germany'.[37] It was to gain posthumous fame as the place from which the eponymous declaration was issued on 27 August 1791 by Emperor Francis II and the Prussian King Frederick William II, calling on the European sovereigns to combine to restore liberty to the embattled King of France, which has been blamed (wrongly) for causing the wars of the French Revolution.

Pillnitz was a place for summer pursuits, where courtiers played outdoor games including 'Riding at the Ring', archery, skittles and croquet.[38] In June 1725 it was the scene of the marriage of one Augustus's daughters, Augusta. Her mother was Countess Cosel, currently languishing in prison at Stolpen Castle following her disgrace, but Augustus clearly did not believe in punishing the innocent, for he laid on a spectacular mock-peasant celebration.[39] A whole village comprising thirty-eight wooden houses was erected to house the singers, dancers and actors. There was also a mayor's house, a lunatic asylum, stocks on the village green, a pub, artisan workshops, and so on. During the three weeks it lasted, the wedding guests could experience bonfires, agricultural

Johann Georg Schreiber, *The Market at Leipzig* (1710)

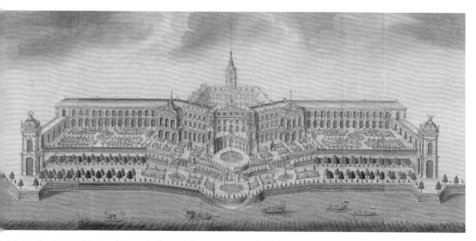

Matthäus Daniel Pöppelmann's design for a new royal palace at Warsaw

18. Samuel Theodor Gericke,
*Augustus II, Frederick I of Prussia
and Frederick IV of Denmark* (1709)

19. Louis de Silvestre, *The Reception of the Electoral Prince Frederick Augustus
by King Louis XIV of France at Fontainebleau on 27 September 1715*

20. Johan David Swartz,
Charles XII of Sweden (1706)

21. Jean-Marc Nattier,
Peter the Great (1717)

Feu d'Artifice, tiré vis à vis du Palais de Hollande, representant le Combat naval d'Acté et de Jason, avec l'Enlevement de la Toison d'or. Par où se termine la fête, a laquelle presida le Soleil.

22. Johann August Corvinus, *The Firework Display on the Elbe Behind the Holland Palace on 10 September 1719*

23. The Old Market at Dresden showing the crowds watching the tournament 12 September 1719. The triumphal arch designed by Pöppelmann is on the left

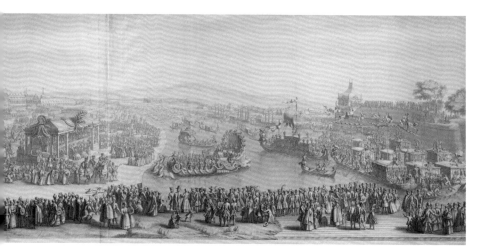

Detail of Zacharias Longuelune's pen-and-ink drawing of the serenata 'Diana on the Elbe', performed on 18 September 1719. It was subsequently published as an engraving in an album illustrations recording 'the wedding of the century'

25. Carl Heinrich Jacob Fehling, The 'Driven Hunt' at the Plauenscher Grund on 26 September 1719

26. Dresden, the Church of Our Lady (Frauenkirche) designed by Georg Bähr and built 1726–43

27. The interior of the church

Dresden, the 'Augustus Bridge' built in 1727–31, pictured before demolition and rebuilding in 1907

Bernardo Bellotto, *Dresden From the Right Bank of the Elbe Below the Augustus Bridge* (1748)

30. Augustus's son and heir, Augustus III. Portrait by Pietro Antonio Rotari (*c.* 1755)

31. His wife, Maria Josepha *née* Habsburg. Portrait by Louis de Silvestre (1720s)

32. Augustus as the Golden Horseman at the New Town end of the bridge named after him. It was created by the metalsmith Ludwig Wiedemann after a design by the court sculptor Jean-Joseph Vinache (1732–4)

pursuits such as threshing, a duck shoot on the Elbe and hare-coursing in the palace garden with the court dwarf playing the role of chief huntsman. There was much more strange jollity, but that is quite enough to be going on with.[40]

The most impressive of the palaces built by Augustus around Dresden was undoubtedly Moritzburg in the Friede forest eleven kilometres north of the city. Between 1723 and 1733 Augustus transformed both the building and the surroundings to form 'the most important baroque complex in Saxony'.[41] Even those who find the baroque florid or the building's function (hunting) offensive must surely derive some aesthetic pleasure from this matchless combination of landscape, architecture, water and forest. Understandably, it is one of the most photographed palaces in Germany. The usual team of Pöppelmann, Longuelune, Leplat and Permoser excelled themselves in creating the total work of art (*Gesamtkunstwerk*) Augustus was seeking. As with other building projects, in large measure they were the faithful executors of his original ideas, the autograph sketches of which have survived.[42] To the fore outside are the sculptures Augustus loved so much, the work of a team directed by Permoser.[43] Much more than just a centre for hunting, it also served as an important location for court festivities, the lakes adding another dimension.[44] In addition there were extensive greenhouses for exotic plants, a menagerie and an aviary.[45] The interior is remarkable for the chapel, the first Catholic place of worship to be established in Saxony since the Reformation; the biggest collection of stag antlers in the world; and some remarkable – and surprisingly beautiful – painted leather wall coverings.[46]

Luxury goods

Augustus left nothing to chance. Every last detail of his festivities was carefully planned and recorded, with the result that recreating the scale of his extravaganza does not have to rely on the subjective impressions of awestruck (or hostile) contemporaries but can be documented by the meticulous records kept by the court marshal's office. For example, it would be so easy to overlook the particular attention paid to details such as colour schemes. One example must suffice. For the 'Riding at the Ring' held in 1709, the following colours were specified for the dresses of the twenty-four ladies competing: lemon, 'aurora', 'isabella', straw, coffee, purple, poppy, grey-violet (*gridelin*), cerise, rose-pink, nude, three different shades of blue, five different shades of green, three shades of yellow, white and carmoisine.[47] It need hardly be added that Augustus was in a class of his own when it came to vestiary variety and opulence. For each day of the festivities of 1719 he wore a different outfit, with a matching combination of jewels, including diamonds, rubies, sapphires, emeralds and semi-precious stones too numerous to list.[48] As in so many other respects, he was not an innovator, for his grandfather, Elector Johann Georg II, had not only started the Saxon fashion for jewel-encrusted clothing but had given seven-year-old Augustus his first diamond buckles and buttons.[49] Augustus himself had got off to a quick start on his succession as elector. In April 1695 the court journal noted: 'this afternoon Chamberlain Spiegel returned home from Leipzig and brought back all sorts of wonderful things from France.'[50] Surprisingly, perhaps, he was well behind the times when it came to style, instructing his valet Montargon, who was in Paris in 1717 buying him luxury goods, to send back a mannequin doll dressed in 'the kind of coat known as a rhinegrave, worn by the late King of France at grand ceremonies such as a wedding'.[51] Old-fashioned or not, Augustus wore a succession of rhinegraves throughout the 1719 festivities.

As the great day approached, the pace of acquisitions increased. In October 1718 four carriages and five waggons arrived in Dresden from Paris laden with luxury goods.[52] There were also plenty of home-grown products available too for over the past century Saxony's wealth had combined with the extravagant tastes of its rulers to encourage the development of its own luxury sector. Manufactories to cater for representational needs such as glass, mirrors, clocks, bijouterie, stone-cutting, medals, furniture, carpets, pictures and tapestry all flourished.[53] Especially prized was Saxon glass, famous for its clarity and hard surface, comparable with the best of Bohemia and Venice. Those qualities allowed the elaborate engraving of drinking vessels of various kinds with coats of arms and scenes of hunting and classical mythology.[54]

Two other branches of native art and enterprise deserve mention. The first is goldsmithing. Augustus was doubtless extremely lucky to have inherited the great genius of baroque goldsmithing, Johann Melchior Dinglinger, for he had arrived in Dresden two years before Augustus became elector. But it was Augustus who early recognized his genius, selected him for valuable commissions and made him court jeweller in 1704.[55] As usual in Augustan Dresden, the artefacts were often a collaborative venture, involving Dinglinger's own brother Georg Friedrich as enameller, Balthasar Permoser, Gottlieb Kirchner and Paul Heermann as sculptors, Christoph Hübner as jewel-cutter, Raymond Le Plat as painter and – last but by no means least – Augustus as designer and coordinator as well as financier.[56] Even those who find baroque *objets d'art* too florid can surely appreciate the exquisite and wonderfully imaginative creations housed in the Green Vault in the Dresden Palace.[57] Here there is space for only one, with several masterpieces competing for selection – the Gold Coffee Set, *The Bath of Diana*, *Obeliscus Augustalis*, the Weissenfelser Hunting Trophy, the Apis-Altar, just for a start – but pride of place must surely go to *The Court at Delhi on the Birthday of the Grand Mogul Aureng-Zeb* (*Der Hofstaat zu Delhi am Geburtstag des Großmoguls Aureng-Zeb*) containing 165 figures adorned with around 3,000 diamonds and other precious stones. This was very much Augustus's project, for he had studied the accounts of the court of the long-lived Aureng-Zeb (1618–1707) written by the French travellers Jean-Baptiste Tavernier and François Berthier and knew exactly what he wanted.[58] The Dinglinger brothers with eleven assistants worked on the project for seven years from 1701 at a cost of 54,485 talers.[59] All the details were discussed by patron and artist, better described as 'the two collaborators'. As one historian of the episode has written, 'here sat two poets composing in gold and precious stones'.[60]

Although Augustus's failure to pay his bills on time often took Dinglinger to the brink of insolvency, overall he did very well in Dresden during his long life, among other things buying a large house for 4,000 talers in cash, grand enough to accommodate Peter the Great of Russia when he came to visit in 1712. Dinglinger declined payment from the court authorities when his Russian guests departed, although he did ask for the repair of the damage they had caused. He also owned a vineyard and villa at Loschwitz outside Dresden.[61] As he married five times, accumulating twenty-three children, both a large fortune and plenty of space proved essential (his brother Georg Friedrich only married twice but fathered twenty-two children). His relations with Augustus were close, socially as well as professionally. When King Frederick IV of Denmark visited Dresden in 1709, Augustus took him to dine *chez* Dinglinger on the latter's roof garden. Another indication of the goldsmith's elevated status was his portrait by the court painter Antoine Pesne, which was also published as an engraving.[62]

Porcelain

In the second major branch of domestic manufacture, Augustus also enjoyed two strokes of good fortune. The first was the presence in Saxony of the Lusatian noble Ehrenfried Walther von Tschirnhaus, one of the most gifted natural scientists of the age. An inveterate traveller and correspondent, he had met and consulted some of the leading lights of the European scientific community, including Huygens, Newton, Boyle and Leibniz and was a member of the French Royal Academy of Science. Among his special interests were ceramics and the associated creation of high temperatures using burning mirrors. In 1703 he was charged by Augustus with the supervision of Johann Frederick Böttger, a young fugitive from Prussia who claimed to be able to transmute metal into gold and was being kept prisoner while his experiments progressed. He was, of course, a fraud so far as the gold-making was concerned, but he also proved to be a highly skilled intuitive chemist with brilliant experimental techniques. To abbreviate a long story that has been told many times, Tschirnhaus and Böttger, with the assistance of the mining expert Gottfried Pabst von Ohain and the physician Jacob Bartholomaei, discovered the secret of making porcelain, the first Europeans to do so. Their work was facilitated by the local presence of ample supplies of essential raw materials, namely kaolin clay, alabaster and wood.[63] The first successful experiment was completed by Böttger on 7 July 1708, followed on 20 March 1709 with the addition of a corresponding glaze. The good news was conveyed to Augustus a week later.[64]

Brought to Europe from Japan and China since the sixteenth century, porcelain was both greatly prized and highly priced. As Böttger told a government commission in 1709, it met three basic human desires, being beautiful, rare and useful. In particular, it had enjoyed a mutually supportive relationship with the rapid growth in popularity of tea and coffee, for it is both non-porous and translucent, does not burn the hand or the mouth and does not assume an external smell or taste.[65] When Böttger finally confessed to Augustus in December 1709 that he could not create gold, the blow had been softened in advance by the wholly authentic claim, made earlier in the year, that he could manufacture white porcelain.[66] That may have been a little premature, for the first products were not white but brown and classified better as 'vitrified stoneware' than porcelain proper, and it was this that was on sale at the Leipzig fair in 1710. By 1713, however, substantial quantities of white porcelain objects were on sale there and an export market was forming.[67]

As the proximity of all these dates suggests, Augustus was quick to exploit his new asset. Partly this was due to a private passion.[68] As he observed to Flemming: 'don't you know those who have caught the craze (*maladie*) for oranges or porcelain can never have enough of one or the other and always want to have more?'[69] He had been closely involved at every stage, although the main motive was undoubtedly his lust for the gold Böttger the alchemist promised to deliver. Once the by-product became the main product, all his formidable energy was brought to bear. Already in 1708, local officials were ordered to send to Dresden samples of clay that might be found suitable for transmutation into 'white gold'.[70] In 1710, at the Leipzig New Year's fair, he hosted a gathering of German princes, including Frederick I of Prussia and his crown prince, entertaining them to a banquet at which they could eat off plates made at Meissen (to which the operation had moved for extra security) and presenting them with choice items to take home. The decree announcing the formation of the Royal Saxon Porcelain Manufactory was dated 23 January 1710, translated into French, Dutch and Latin and published in the press across Europe, signalling that the Chinese and Japanese monopoly had been broken. At the 'Blue Angel' inn at Leipzig, the display of Meissen porcelain attracted large crowds.[71] The business was expanded rapidly. By the end of the following year, the labour force numbered more than thirty and over 12,000 pieces were ready for sale.[72] By the time Augustus died in 1733 there was a shop in Dresden and agents in thirty-nine towns across Europe.[73]

It was not all plain sailing. There were many technical issues to address, especially in connection with glazing and painting. On the organizational side, Böttger proved to be an increasing liability, prone to fits of depression and bouts of drunken debauchery. Following his death in 1719 at the age of thirty-seven, a commission reported that during his last years he had been almost permanently intoxicated.[74] Overall, the enterprise flourished. Once again, Augustus benefited from his ability to select, retain and encourage top-quality artists. Three deserve special mention. The first is Johann Jakob Irminger, the court goldsmith, who was entrusted with the artistic direction. It was he who devised a new repertoire of forms and decorative schemes, created a large library of moulds and frequently travelled to Meissen from Dresden to provide training. Böttger's tribute was that 'he made good artists out of poor potters'.[75] The second was Johann Gregorius Höroldt, who arrived in 1720 and revolutionized the art of painting on porcelain. So successful was he that five years later he had attracted ten journeymen and five apprentices, increasing to twenty-five and eleven respectively by 1731.[76] In the course of the 1720s Höroldt and his team moved beyond their Asian models by using new colours (yellow, dark blue, sky-blue, peach, gunmetal, aquamarine, grey, purple and red) and choosing new subjects (many introduced at the suggestion of their Paris agent, who knew what would sell best).[77] Most famous of all was Johann Joachim Kändler, 'the greatest porcelain modeller of the century' in the view of the Victoria and Albert Museum.[78] In 1723, aged seventeen, he was sent to Dresden to be apprenticed to the court sculptor Benjamin Thomae. His work on the Green Vault caught the eye of Augustus, who in 1731 sent him to Meissen as court model master with a handsome salary and free lodging.[79]

There is no need to extol the qualities of the porcelain created under Augustus's aegis. A subjective appreciation can be achieved by anyone with access to an internet browser to provide an almost inexhaustible supply of high-quality illustrations. A more objective standard can be supplied by auction house prices. For example, in September 2021 the sale by Sotheby's in New York of the Margarethe and Franz Oppenheimer Collection yielded a total of over $15,000,000, the prize item being a mantel clock case of 1727 which sold for $1,593,000.[80] How Augustus would have relished that news item! When setting up the business, he had announced his ambition to have Saxon products recognized as superior to the Asian originals. In a decorative scheme for a planned ceiling fresco, Saxon and Japanese manufacturers were to be depicted disputing before Minerva which of their creations was superior. As Saxony takes first prize, their outraged – but envious – Japanese competitors are shown packing their own wares back on to their ship. In the event, this was not executed, but the same message was later given three-dimensional form in the bas-relief by Thomae on the gable of the main portal of the Japanese Palace, showing Saxons claiming superiority by appropriate gestures. As this suggests, Augustus did not lack self-confidence. At the *Wirtschaft* during the festivities of 1719, a

display of Asian porcelain was placed opposite native products positively to invite comparison.[81] Indeed, so good were Meissen copies
of the Chinese originals that an elaborate fraud was attempted by
Augustus's Parisian agent Rodolphe Lemaire, acting in cahoots with
the Saxon minister von Hoym, to pass off Saxon porcelain as Chinese.[82] Shortly after Augustus died, the ubiquitous traveller Johann
Georg Keyssler reported that Meissen porcelain was famous all over
Europe and 'produces a very advantageous Trade'.[83]

Collections

Among the many assets Augustus inherited from his cultured ancestors was a well-stocked 'Art Chamber' (*Kunstkammer*). An eclectic
mixture of the weird and wonderful and scientific–technological as
well as aesthetic objects, it was more like a chamber of curiosities
than an art gallery. As well as the 'unicorn's horn' boasted by most
such collections (it was of course a narwhal's tusk), the largest
number of exhibits were tools and scientific instruments. There was
also a well-organized subsection of armour.[84] Although some
progress had been made towards creating a more coherent catego-
rization, it was Augustus's achievement to create a modern museum
structure. This began in 1709–10 with the removal of several thousand items from the old *Kunstkammer* in the attic storey of the
Electoral Palace to the first floor of the stable building on the New
Market. That began an odyssey whose many intervening stations do
not need to be charted here.[85] An important step was taken almost
immediately with the separation of prints and drawing to form a
dedicated print gallery (*Kupferstichkabinett*), the first in Germany,
with its own curator (Johann Heinrich von Heucher).[86]

As might be expected from everything that has gone before in
this chapter, Augustus was not content with organizing past acquisitions. With his habitual enthusiasm for spending, from the start he
set about making additions, including several large collections for
the new print gallery.[87] Also as usual, he made his own luck by

appointing able assistants. One of the most important was the long-lived Raymond Leplat (1664–1742), a Fleming from Ghent, who served as 'Ordonnateur du Cabinet' throughout the reign.[88] This involved two key tasks. Firstly, he was the chief interior decorator, designing not only the decor of the new or remodelled buildings but also individual objects, such as the enormous bed, measuring seventeen by eight and a half metres, for the new state bedroom in the main palace.[89] A second heavy responsibility was acting as the purchasing agent for Augustus's various collections. In 1698–9, for example, he was sent to Paris to buy bronze statues and 'other objects' equipped with a credit of 3,000 talers. In the event, he spent more than ten times that sum (38,792), which provides a fair indication of Augustus's sense of budgetary control. However, he certainly got value for money, one of Leplat's acquisitions – for 2,200 talers – being Nicolas Poussin's *Realm of Flora*, a masterpiece that can still be admired in the Dresden Old Masters Picture Gallery.[90] He was also responsible for recruiting in Paris Louis de Silvestre as court painter and François Coudray as court sculptor. His greatest acquisition was made in 1728, when 160 pieces of antique sculpture were acquired in Rome from the estate of Cardinal Flavio Chigi and thirty-two from Cardinal Alessandro Albani.[91] The former included a number of more modern pieces, including a skull created by the greatest of all baroque sculptors, Gian Lorenzo Bernini.[92] At the end of the reign, Leplat composed his own memorial by publishing an album of the antique marbles in the royal collection, illustrated with 230 high-quality engravings.[93]

As the purchase of the Poussin indicated, Leplat was also involved in the purchase of paintings, as were other Saxon officials and local agents in all the main European art-dealing centres.[94] From Paris came Giorgione's *Sleeping Venus*, from Antwerp Rubens' *Diana Returning from the Hunt*, from Prague Rubens' *Leda and the Swan*, from Venice Palma Vecchio's *Resting Venus*, just to mention some of the most spectacular. In 1711 Augustus bought from Count Wackerbarth a large collection of mainly Dutch and Flemish pictures and Wackerbarth continued to buy more for him.[95] Although one might have expected Augustus to have had a special liking for the erotic Italian paintings representing Venus, Diana or Leda, it has been suggested that his personal taste was more for the less arousing art of the Netherlands.[96] Both genres were suitable for representational purposes, to impress visitors with the excellence of his taste and the depth of his pocket. Good care was taken to have the most prestigious works displayed on the walls of the state rooms of the palaces. In 1718, or in other words in time for his heir's wedding festivities, a great gallery sixty-two metres long and nine metres wide was created in the south wing of the Electoral Palace.[97] There were plenty of paintings available to fill it, for Leplat's inventory completed in 1722 listed 1,928 items.[98] To encourage home-grown talent and provide a pool of artists to work on his various projects and to create a pictorial record of his reign, Augustus founded an Academy of Painting in 1705.[99]

Paintings were important, but porcelain was a passion. With the Great Northern War declining in importance, at least so far as he was concerned, Augustus could indulge himself more liberally. In 1717 there were two major accessions. The first cost him nothing in money terms, because he negotiated a barter deal with Frederick William I of Prussia. It said a good deal about the two kings' respective priorities: Augustus exchanged a force of 600 cavalry for 151 monumental Chinese vases.[100] In the same year, Pietro Taparelli, Count von Lagnasco, of Piedmontese origin but long in Augustus's military service, went on an official buying spree in The Hague and Amsterdam, sending back seventy crates of Chinese and Japanese porcelain.[101] To house his enormous and constantly growing collection, Augustus bought a palace. This was the Holland Palace built in 1715–16 by his chief minister and friend Flemming, from whom he bought it in May 1717. Two years later it played an important part in the wedding festivities, as the venue for the inauguration of the 'Festival of the Seven Planets' with Heinichen's serenata *La Gara degli dei* and the great firework display which followed. It also provided an appropriate setting for the display of porcelain. Although Augustus used the building as an occasional residence, it was primarily an exhibition centre. In 1721, when the first inventory was compiled, there were more than 25,000 pieces of porcelain on display in eighteen rooms, a spectacle unique in Europe.[102] Unsurprisingly, the collection soon outgrew its host. In 1727 Augustus embarked on a full-scale rebuilding project which more than doubled the palace's size. By then he had accumulated 21,000 East Asian pieces and 20,000 of Meissen manufacture.[103] And he went on buying; in 1730 his order list to Meissen included 100 bowls, fifty bird cages, fifty dozen teacups and saucers and 200 bowls.[104] It was 'the most comprehensive porcelain collection in the world'.[105]

Among other things, the Japanese Palace served as a storeroom for porcelain to be used as gifts to rulers and their ministers to oil the cogs of diplomacy. Among the recipients were Vittorio Amadeo of Savoy, Cardinal Fleury of France, Tsarina Catherine I of Russia, the King of Denmark and the Queen of Prussia.[106] This was porcelain as the continuation of foreign policy by other means. It was a highly prized prestige object and for many years Saxony enjoyed a virtual monopoly of European manufacture. Until Augustus's explosive arrival on the scene, the dynasty most closely associated with collecting porcelain had been the Hohenzollerns of Brandenburg–Prussia, starting with the Dutch wife of Frederick William the Great Elector. Having stolen a march on his detested rival, Augustus strove to stay ahead. In 1727 he launched an industrial espionage operation, sending a top draughtsman off to view the Prussian collections at Potsdam and Charlottenburg and to make secret drawings of both the actual pieces (all of them East Asian, of course) and the way in which they were displayed. In other words, Cordula Bischoff concludes, 'the Japanese Palace was a gigantic piece of Saxon propaganda'.[107]

The Japanese Palace was undoubtedly a cultural coup, but the greatest of his creations was the 'Green Vault' (*Grünes Gewölbe*), which its long-serving director, Dirk Syndram, has claimed as 'the largest collection of treasure in Europe'.[108] It had started life in the middle of the sixteenth century when Elector Moritz added a new wing to the Dresden Palace, including a suite of four vaulted strongrooms, whose green walls gave the collective name to the suite. Although Augustus took an early interest in a space close to his private apartments, where he could view his special treasures, it was not until the 1720s that a major reconstruction took place. As with all his major building projects, it was he who provided the ideas and his expert team of Pöppelmann as architect, Permoser as sculptor and Leplat as decorator who turned them into reality.[109] As Syndram has pointed out, his specification was essentially that of a modern museum (exhibition rooms, a technical facility, a cloakroom, a foyer, a large storeroom and service rooms for the curators).[110]

Progress through the eight rooms was carefully modulated and choreographed in a 'dramaturgical progression' (Syndram), the decor of each so arranged not only to show the exhibits at their best but also to create a cumulative experience in which the whole became much more than a sum of the parts. To put it another way, the museum did not just contain works of art, it was a work of art itself. It was here that the major objects described earlier in this chapter could be seen to their best advantage, their intrinsic quality enhanced by cabinets, mirrors, varied lighting and sculptured walls. Keyssler was deeply impressed, writing that 'the green room' made a bigger impact than even the *Tribuna* at Florence because of the way it was organized.[111] A more recent tribute from Thomas W. Gaehtgens praised the originality of the Green Vault: 'Augustus the Strong inaugurated a new era in the presentation of works of art and curiosities'.[112]

Traditionally, a prince's *Kunstkammer* was a *réserve secrète*, a place of mystery, where he alone, perhaps with a few favoured companions, could enjoy priceless treasures in glorious seclusion. That was not Augustus's way. From at least 1721, the plain people of Dresden – if decently dressed – could gain admission, although the size of the rooms obviously placed a limit on numbers admitted at any one time.[113] A concern for public access was also apparent in 1720 when Augustus separated the various scientific items from the collections in which they were currently incorporated and sent them to form a

'House of Knowledge' (*Haus der Wissenschaft*) in the former residence of the governor of Dresden (*Regimentshaus*) on Jew Court
(*Judenhof*), adjacent to the New Market.[114] When Count von Manteuffel was appointed to be its director the following year, Augustus
explained in his letter of appointment his motive:

> For some time, on our own initiative, we have been intending to
> demonstrate how much we seek to promote scholarship in our
> lands, by increasing the size of our libraries and by providing other
> means of promoting intellectual endeavour and the practical arts
> and sciences, and to show by personal example how much we wish
> to see them flourish, not just to satisfy our own curiosity but also to
> assist all those who are involved in their advancement.[115]

In 1728, when the collection was moved to the Zwinger, he added
that its purpose was to be a source of pride for his regime, to encourage the sciences and the arts, and to serve the public good (*dem
publico zum besten*).[116] The pavilion in which it was now housed was
named The Palace of Sciences (*Palais des Sciences*, using French
rather German).[117]

Practical assistance was given to the promotion of science in 1731
when Augustus sent an expedition to North Africa, led by the bot-
anist Johann Ernst Hebenstreit. The original object was to obtain
wild animals for Augustus's zoo at Moritzburg, or in other words
the motive was more representational than scholarly. For many
other rulers of the period, a collection of exotic fauna was highly
regarded both as a means of extravagant display and to serve as victims of the animal fights and baiting described in the previous
chapter.[118] In this, as in everything else, Augustus was keen to out-
shine his princely competitors. In the Jägerhof at Dresden and at
Moritzburg he assembled a large collection – lions, 'tigers' (often in
reality leopards), lynx, meerkats, polar and brown bears, apes and
monkeys of various kinds (baboons were especially prized), arctic
foxes, ostriches, vultures, and so on. Some were purchased at the
Leipzig fairs, some by Saxon diplomats. Augustus's man in Berlin

showed enterprise by snapping up the royal lions for the bargain price of 1,000 talers when Frederick William I dispersed his father's collection.[119] Others came as presents: in 1731, for example, Augustus received from Frederick I of Sweden a lion, two lionesses, a tiger and an 'Indian cat'.[120] Given the transport problems, there was a very high rate of attrition as the wretched creatures were moved from court to court. Of a herd of reindeer that set out from Lapland for Dresden in 1715, only five survived, together with their Norwegian officer and Finnish attendant.[121]

The African expedition, however, had a more elevated purpose. Its scholarly credentials were shown by the identity of the man chosen to lead it. Hebenstreit had been recommended by Augustus's personal doctor, Johann Heinrich von Heucher, a distinguished scientist who was a Fellow of the Royal Society of London and was also in charge of the electoral natural history collection.[122] Setting off in the autumn of 1731, the party of seven travelled first to Marseilles, from where they crossed to Algiers. After a hazardous journey into the interior, they travelled by sea east along the North African coast to Annaba, inland to Constantine, by sea to Tunis and then Lampedusa, Tripoli and Malta, before returning to Tunis. Along the way they were busily collecting samples animal, vegetable and mineral.[123] The original plan to follow up with further expeditions to Senegal and the Cape of Good Hope had to be aborted when Augustus died and his successor cancelled the project. The explorers arrived back in Dresden on 12 September 1732. Their surviving collection of live specimens was small – a lioness, a leopard, a hyena, two donkeys, a jackal, various sheep, two apes, three meerkats, two porcupines, seven ostriches, four guineafowl, 'a bird known as a Damoiselle', an eagle, two vultures, fifteen doves, two 'African cats' and one 'Eydexe'.[124] More impressive was the huge amount of plants, trees, minerals, fossils, skeletons and inscriptions (from Roman ruins). Everything had been recorded meticulously in word and image (a specialist draughtsman had been in the party).[125] The entry in the official 'Court Calendar' announcing the project had stated that 'the public' expected great things to result and also that it would set the seal on Augustus's immortality.[126] If neither hope was fulfilled, what was one of the first scientific expeditions to Africa deserves to be set against the sponsor's usual reputation for self-indulgent hedonism.

Mistresses

Despite this rather belated scholarly initiative, Augustus's court culture was nothing if not sensual. It has also had the reputation of being sexual. The 'fact' most often cited about him is that he fathered an enormous number of illegitimate children. 'Some 300' is the estimate found in one standard history of Poland (which has been translated into both Polish and German), with the highest – from an eminently respectable scholar – being 355. The most popular is 354, for the good reason that this is the figure conveyed in everyone's original source (although usually filtered through secondary or even tertiary works), namely the memoirs of Wilhelmine, Margravine of Bayreuth and sister of Frederick the Great.[127] For good measure, she added that Augustus's priapic example was followed by the rest of his court. Augustus might well have gloried in this posthumous reputation for virility but would have known that it was false, as his actual score was just eight.[128] In other words, he was outclassed by several contemporary rulers, including Charles II of England and Louis XIV of France.

On the other hand, Augustus was certainly both highly sexed and uninhibited by any moral scruples. As noted in Chapter 1, he had got off to an early start, aged sixteen, with a lady of his father's court, Countess Marie Elisabeth von Brockdorff – not that there was (or is) anything unusual in a young prince taking advantage of his privileged position.[129] His marriage in January 1693 to Christiane Eberhardine of Brandenburg-Bayreuth, when he was still the younger son and not expected to succeed to the Electorate, did not alter the promiscuous habits consolidated during his grand tour. The English diplomat George Stepney, who claimed to know Saxony and Augustus 'as well as any Englishman can know them', reported that he was 'continually in frolics and debauches'.[130] In 1695 he added that Augustus was about to leave to take the waters at Carlsbad, accompanied by his ordinary mistress, his extraordinary mistress and there would be a third waiting for him when he got there.[131] His promiscuity was advertised to the world when, in one and the same month, October 1696, his wife gave birth to what proved to be their only child (the future Augustus III) and his mistress, Aurora von Königsmarck, gave birth to his first bastard (the future French military hero, the Maréchal de Saxe). In fact, by then Aurora was no longer his first-choice mistress, for during his sojourn in Vienna he had begun a relationship with Anna, Countess Esterle, whom he brought with him when he returned to Dresden, rather belatedly, in December to meet his two new sons.

Aurora von Königsmarck was undoubtedly the most accomplished of Augustus's numerous mistresses, combining beauty, brains and accomplishments.[132] She arrived in Dresden in 1694, seeking the help of Augustus in locating her brother, Count Philipp Christoph von Königsmarck, who had mysteriously gone missing in Hanover. As he had been conducting an illicit affair with the wife of the elector's eldest son (the future King George I of England), it was generally supposed that he had been 'disposed of'.[133] She had a special claim for assistance because Augustus had offered Count Philipp a senior rank in his officer corps in lieu of a gambling debt of 30,000 talers.[134] Augustus could not help her quest (her brother's body was almost certainly lying at the bottom of the River Leine in Hanover), but he could give other forms of assistance and Aurora quickly became his first *maîtresse en titre*. She was also the best, in the sense that she caused the least trouble and, possibly, gave the greatest pleasure. Impeccably discreet, she withdrew from Dresden to give birth, aware that Augustus's wife was also expecting at about the same time. She also succeeded in establishing good relations with the latter and even with Augustus's mother, the dowager electress, to the extent that the three ladies appeared together in one of Augustus's carnival pageants.[135] The sight of wife, mother and mistress acting in harmony must be judged a tribute to their man's eirenic skills.

Eight years older than her lover, Aurora's reign in the bedroom did not last long, especially not after the arrival of Countess Esterle. Yet she stayed at court, well integrated in Dresden high society. In 1698, for example, she was one of only five ladies invited by the Viceroy, Prince Fürstenberg, to dine with Tsar Peter of Russia when he visited (Augustus was away in Poland).[136] As we have seen, she was also used by Augustus as an emissary to Charles XII in 1702.[137] It has to be acknowledged that Augustus was good to her, lavishing attention and extravagance on her during her time in the sun and finding a comfortable sinecure for her to relieve the pain of redundancy. This was the post of prioress of the aristocratic foundation at Quedlinburg, which brought both status and a good income. Alas, most of the latter had to be spent on their rakish if gifted son, whom Augustus both recognized and ennobled.[138]

In terms of sexual relations, the longest-surviving mistress was probably Fatima. Accounts of her origin and early life are so various that almost nothing can be believed. What does seem reasonably certain is that she was of Turkish origin, was part of the booty seized during the campaigns of the 1690s, was passed from hand to hand by the military, and ended up with Count Jan Jerzy Przebendowski, who was related to Flemming through marriage and was a key supporter of Augustus during the Polish election.[139] It was almost certainly in the Przebendowski household that Augustus first met her.[140] In 1702 she gave birth to a boy, who was given the revealing first names 'Frederick Augustus'. A girl, Maria Aurora, followed in 1706. In the meantime, part of Fatima's duties had been acting as nanny for little Maurice, the son of Augustus and Aurora von Königsmarck.[141] Probably because of her lowly social status and ethnic origin, Fatima had to wait longer for Augustus's largesse. It was not until 1706 that he found a good husband for her, in the shape of Johann Georg von Spiegel, a senior official in the administration of the royal domains in Poland.[142] The two children had to wait until 1724 before they were legitimized and ennobled as count and countess. Frederick Augustus ended his military career as a Saxon field marshal and was responsible for the stubborn six-week defence of Pirna in 1756 at the beginning of the Seven Years War, frustrating Frederick the Great's intended blitzkrieg. Maria Aurora married first the Polish Count Bielinski and then, after their divorce, the Piedmontese Count Claude von Bellegarde.[143]

Entitled by her high birth and imperious personality to expect more extravagant reward was Ursula Katharina, Countess of Alten-bockum, whose father was high steward (*Truchsess*) of Lithuania. In 1695, at the age of fifteen, she married the Polish magnate Jerzy Dominik Lubomirski, who was fifteen years older. When she caught Augustus's eye, she was already the mother of two sons. As a Pole she seemed to offer Augustus another means of integration with his new kingdom, although it turned out that the strait-laced ladies of Warsaw would not accept her and she had to move to Dresden.[144] If he also hoped that her close family relationship to Cardinal Radzie-jowski would bring political dividends, he hoped in vain.[145] That there was real passion at play is suggested by the exertions required to make her his own. First the feelings of the cuckolded husband had to be soothed by the application of lucrative posts (commander of the guard, court chamberlain); then intensive lobbying in Rome was needed to secure papal approval of a divorce; and a similar operation had to be launched in Vienna to induce Emperor Leopold to issue a grand title of imperial nobility (Princess of Teschen).[146]

Augustus must have wondered whether all the effort had been worthwhile. The princess gave him another son, in May 1704, who was recognized, christened as Johann Georg, ennobled and later pro-vided with a military career, but there were no political dividends and Augustus's wandering eye was soon on the move again. Indeed, he was incapable of being faithful, continuing a sporadic relationship with Fatima as well as indulging in shorter-term occasional flings. As the English diplomat George Stepney observed, 'the first woman that offers is sure of his caresses', although in many cases he did not wait for an offer.[147] He was certainly proactive when he next fell in love, less than a year after the birth of Johann Georg. The object of his passion was Constantia von Hoym née Brockdorff, the wife of Adolf Magnus Baron (later Count) von Hoym, a senior official in the Saxon administration. Both partners had a chequered past or present: Constantia had secretly given birth to a child out of wedlock before she met von Hoym, while the latter kept a live-in mistress in his palace in Dresden and continued to do so after the marriage.[148] Unusually, Constantia declined the first advance from Augustus, made on his behalf by the Viceroy, Prince Fürstenberg, early in 1705. In view of her later conduct it can be assumed that she was just raising the stakes, a high-risk strategy but one which soon paid off. Certainly she drove a hard bargain when she succumbed in May: Hoym's consent to a divorce was to be bought (as both parties were Protestants, no papal approval was needed); she herself was to receive an annual grant of 100,000 talers (almost as much as the queen received for her establishment); Augustus's current liaison with the Princess of Teschen was to be broken off; and any children were to be legitimized and ennobled as princes and princesses.

The most arresting concession was Augustus's promise to marry her when the queen died. In December 1705, a further document was drafted stating that Augustus would marry her morganatically as soon as her divorce was finalized 'in the same way as the kings of France and Denmark and other sovereigns in Europe have done', but it is not certain that Augustus ever ratified it.[149] Once Constantia was installed as *maîtresse en titre*, however, Augustus opened his purse strings as far as they would go. He bought Count Haugwitz's residence on the Taschenberg, adjacent to the Electoral Palace, added two more buildings to it and had an enormous new palace built by Pöppelmann (it is now the Kempinski Hotel). He also gave her the 'Turkish Garden' outside the Wilsdruff Gate, together with the villa there, and in 1707 the palace and estate at Pillnitz.[150] It goes without saying that a title of imperial nobility – Countess von Cosel – was secured from the emperor.[151] She bore three children to Augustus, their paternity proclaimed by their names – Augusta, Frederica and Frederick Augustus.

Needless to say, the relationship did not prove to be permanent, although it did last longer than most. Augustus remained incorrigibly promiscuous. Early in 1706 Constantia unwisely paid a surprise visit to Warsaw, where she found that Augustus was still seeing the Princess of Teschen, that Fatima was pregnant again and that he was also having an affair with Henriette Duval, the daughter of a local wine-dealer.[152] It was also in 1706 that Fürstenberg complained that she was meddling in government business. More serious was the opposition organized by Flemming, whose star was in the ascendancy but who was not yet first minister. In the meantime, Constantia ruled the roost as *maîtresse en titre* and managed to retain Augustus's affection despite his extra-extramarital escapades. By all accounts, she was bright, witty, entertaining and well able to keep up with Augustus in his outdoor pursuits, being a good shot and horsewoman. It was not until 1712 that her position began to crumble. A bad blow was the death of the first minister Count August Ferdinand von Pflugk, for the ensuing government reshuffle put Flemming and his supporters in charge.[153] All seemed well in the autumn of that year, as she accompanied Augustus to the Michaelmas fair at Leipzig. It was noticed that Augustus dined with her but then went out on the town, her state of advanced pregnancy (she gave birth at the end of October) doing nothing to keep him by the fireside. They then went their separate ways, Augustus to Warsaw, Constantia back to Dresden. It was now that her enemies struck, presenting at the Polish court the beautiful and voluptuous Countess Dönhoff. According to Johann Michael von Loen, she had a limited intellect but was lively, very agreeable, great company, liked to laugh a lot and had no interest in government business.[154] Not yet twenty, she was also much younger than Constantia von Cosel. Augustus quickly succumbed and, unusually, did not return to Saxony for the carnival season.

In the summer of 1713 Constantia attempted a bold stroke, setting off for Warsaw unannounced. Forewarned by Flemming that she was on her way, Augustus sent a courtier and a company of guards to intercept her and tell her to return. Although that clearly marked the end of the relationship, the aftermath was protracted and messy. Excluded from her palace in Dresden, she was confined to the estate at Pillnitz, from where she conducted a lengthy correspondence with Flemming, her main concern being a proper financial settlement for her children. As she pathetically pointed out in one letter, it was not her fault 'if another pleases him more than I do' (*sy dautre lui plaise mieux que moi* (sic)).[155] In December 1715 she escaped from what was in effect imprisonment at Pillnitz, evaded the posse sent to detain her and made her way to Berlin. After first resisting Augustus's request for her extradition, in the autumn of 1716 Frederick William I ordered her to be handed over. She was taken straight to Stolpen Castle, thirty kilometres east of Dresden, and was placed in confinement that was both close and solitary. There she remained for the next forty-nine years until she died in 1765 at the age of eighty-four. This brutal treatment, which was so at odds with the generosity shown by Augustus to his other redundant mistresses, cannot be satisfactorily explained. It seems to have centred on a document containing Augustus's imprudent promise of marriage, which she would not – or could not – hand over. That she had meddled in the factional conflicts inseparable from any court, that she had supported the Protestant group opposing the Polish connection, and that her sharp tongue had made many personal enemies does not explain the severity of her treatment. Especially mystifying is her continued incarceration after Augustus's death – indeed she outlived his son.

At least the sins of the mother were not laid on her children. Augusta Constantia was married to the Saxon Grand Falconer Major-General Count Friedrich von Friesen and Maria Aurora to the Polish Crown Grand Treasurer Count Anton Moszyński. Both received dowries of 100,000 talers from Constantia's estate and both were integrated into the courts of both Augustus and his son, as was their brother Frederick Augustus.[156] Augustus also showed generosity in the case of Anna Karolina, the daughter he fathered in 1707 with Henriette Duval. Although her early history is obscure, it is certain that she was found in Paris in 1724 by her half-brother Frederick Augustus, son of Fatima, and was taken to meet her father in Poland. There could be little doubt about her paternity, given her very striking resemblance to Augustus.[157] He made amends for years of neglect, or possibly simple ignorance, by recognizing her as his daughter, making her a countess, giving her the Blue (Potocki) Palace in Warsaw, marrying her to Duke Karl Ludwig of Holstein-Beck and generally making a fuss of her.[158]

Logan Pearsall Smith did not have Augustus in mind when he observed that 'a virtuous king is a king who has shirked his proper function: to embody for his subjects an ideal of illustrious misbehaviour absolutely beyond their reach', but he might have done.[159] There is no need to continue with Augustus's amatory exploits. Many more names could be listed, including several he failed to impregnate. What does need to be stressed, however, is that this was more than just gratification on the part of a libidinous man with the power to attract or command consent. No doubt boasting was part of it. Flemming, who knew him better than anyone, wrote in a character sketch in 1722: 'among his pleasures, his favourite was sex, from which however he did not derive as much pleasure as he would have others believe'.[160] Also important was the use he made of his virile reputation to lend an erotic aura to the festivities. His mistresses were not to be kept tucked away for private pleasures, they were to be paraded in public as integral contributors to the court spectacles.

The surrender of his first *maîtresse en titre*, Aurora von Königs-marck, to his advances, after initial resistance, was advertised to the world by a great 'Festival of Diana' at Moritzburg. That Diana was the goddess of hunting was entirely appropriate, her association with inviolable chastity less so. More in keeping with the occasion was the later appearance of Augustus as Pan and later as a Turkish sultan, reclining in a seraglio. There was certainly an impressive and imaginative attention to detail when lavishing gifts on his new love. As she took her place next to him at the banquet, she found her place setting decorated with a bouquet of precious stones – diamonds, rubies, emeralds and pearls. At another banquet held in her honour at a 'Festival of Fishing' an enormous pie was carried in, which Aurora cut with a correspondingly huge wooden knife. Out stepped the court jester to present her with a costly present and to drink the health of the happy couple. After dining they repaired to the lake, to be transported in a boat shaped like a swan. When its net was pulled it, it was found to contain a large fish with a golden ring in its mouth inscribed 'Aurora' which Augustus then tenderly placed on her finger.[161]

Moritzburg was out in the country, but the same flaunting of extramarital sexual conquest was also paraded on the streets of Dresden. Constantia von Cosel provided a good example when she starred in the 'Riding at the Ring' staged especially for ladies on 6 June 1709, as part of the lavish ceremonies organized to greet Frederick IV King of Denmark. Twenty-four ladies were each accompanied by knights, one to steer the carriage and two on horseback as guards, all allocated in advance by lot. 'Quite by chance', Constantia happened to draw King Frederick as the coachman and King Augustus as one of the guards. It was her group, in pink costumes, that was seen leading the parade in one of the twenty-eight large-format coloured illustrations commissioned to record the event.[162] Also present, as spectators, were Augustus's wife and other members of his family.[163] As we have seen, Constantia's replacement, Maria Magdalena von Dönhoff, was the honorand of another great festivity, organized at Moritzburg in August 1718.[164]

Poland

This chapter and its predecessor have been concerned almost exclusively with Saxony, and Dresden in particular. It was there that Augustus unfolded his representational and artistic ambitions to the full. Whatever is concluded about the value of his regime from a political or military point of view, it is difficult to deny its enormous impact. His reign in Poland, by contrast, came and went without commensurate effect. Although three years have to be deducted, from his abdication in 1706 until the return in 1709, in terms of days spent, he was actually longer in Poland than in Saxony.[165] On the other hand, much of that time was so disrupted by civil conflict and foreign war, and so restricted by shortage of funds, that any thought of replicating the kind of extravagant court culture promoted in Dresden could not be contemplated. Even when there was no actual fighting, the intensity of factional feuding made for inhibiting instability. The one major architectural similarity between the two capitals was negative, namely the conception but eventual abandonment of a grandiose scheme for a new palace. The existing Warsaw Royal Palace was very much the property of the nation, majestic but old-fashioned, its main institutional purpose being the housing of the two chambers of the Sejm. Much more modern and impressive were the palaces of the magnates – Morsztyn, Radziwiłł, Sanguszko and Krasiński. Indeed, for the first decade and more, Augustus owned no property in his Polish capital and only started to make purchases after 1712.[166]

Revealingly, his three major contributions to the city were all prefixed with the adjective 'Saxon' – the Saxon Palace (formerly the Morsztyn Palace), the Saxon Garden and the Saxon Axis. Moreover, most of the architects involved were familiar names from Saxony – Pöppelmann, Longuelune and Naumann.[167] The directors of the Warsaw building authority were successively Burchard Christoph von Münnich, a Saxon major-general, and Johann Daniel von Jauch, also a Saxon officer who, among other things, had been in charge of Dresden's street lighting.[168] It has to be borne in mind that Warsaw was a small city, even by central European standards, the population in 1710 being only around 10,000 (Dresden was three times as big).[169] Combined with low rates of literacy, a much less developed economy and a sparsely populated hinterland, this meant a correspondingly small public sphere. The moral climate also appears to have been inimical to display. Many Polish ladies showed their disapproval of Augustus parading his mistresses by boycotting his carnivals.[170] So, although Augustus maintained a splendid court when he was in town, the environment could not compete with the fleshpots of Dresden.[171]

Augustus the artist

Augustus was a self-indulgent, selfish, unscrupulous spendthrift and voluptuary. It has been the argument of these last two chapters that he was also a great artist, arguably the greatest of his age. He never designed a building, painted a picture, sculpted a statue, composed a symphony or wrote a libretto. What he did do was to provide the initiative, organization, driving force and funds to make all those genres flourish and to be combined in such a way that they became a culture that was greater than its individual parts: a *Gesamtkunstwerk*. He knew what he was doing and made sure that posterity would know too. He was not just having a good time, although of course sheer enjoyment was a very important part of his project. To appreciate this fully, there has to be a perspectival shift on the part of the observer. It does not involve approval. It is possible to be outraged by the parasitic and exploitative nature of the aristocratic society (what Marxist historians used to call 'feudal-absolutist') from which it came or to be repelled by the excesses of baroque decoration. All that is needed is a willingness to recognize that past cultures can be approached not only hermeneutically but also as 'presence', for themselves, on their own terms, not ours.[172] The axiomatic privileging of interpretation, the assumption that there must be something beyond what is seen or heard to be brought to the surface, amounts to an involuntary lobotomy.[173] There is no need to belabour the point. Any visitor to Dresden and its 'residential landscape', whether accessed on the spot or virtually, will find a plethora of evidence to support the insight conveyed by Erna von Watzdorf in her monumental study of Johann Melchior Dinglinger: 'to the very core of his being, Augustus was an artist'.[174]

Epilogue: The Posthumous Triumph

After a quarter of a century of turmoil at home and abroad, Augustus's last years were relatively peaceful. The ending of the War of the Spanish Succession in 1714 and the Great Northern War in 1721 left all European powers, great and small, pacified by exhaustion. Surprisingly durable cooperation between France and Great Britain following the death of Louis XIV in 1715 ensured that most international disputes could be resolved – or at least smothered – by negotiation. The brief and ill-fated adventure in the Mediterranean launched by the ambitious Queen of Spain in 1719–20 was the exception that proved the rule. Epitomizing the beneficial torpor of international relations during the 1720s was the Congress of Cambrai, which was planned to assemble in 1722, did not actually start until 1724, got nowhere and was terminated a year later without deciding anything.[1]

That did not mean that Augustus was inactive. On the contrary, as usual he had a number of irons in the fire.[2] The two most important were attempting to secure the imperial inheritance on the death of Charles VI, who had no male heir, and ensuring the succession of his son to the Polish throne. Also as usual, he failed in both. There was an obvious disabling flaw at the heart of the two projects. The Austrian support necessary for the second was ruled out by the first, for he could not accept the Pragmatic Sanction which assigned the Habsburg lands in their entirety to Charles VI's eldest daughter, Maria Theresa.[3] The Austrians of course were well aware of the dilemma. Despite the matrimonial alliance of 1719, they continued to regard Augustus with deep mistrust. They were right to do so, for Augustus was always toying with the idea of joining France in an anti-Austrian alliance.[4] In July 1732, in what proved to be the last major foreign policy initiative of his life, he teamed up with the

285

Bavarians (who had similar designs on the Habsburg inheritance) in a tripartite defensive alliance with France against Austria. The partition scheme to be implemented on Charles VI's death envisaged allocating Silesia, Bohemia and Moravia to Saxony.[5]

He was no more successful in winning the support of Prussia, another key player in any new northern crisis. On a personal level, Augustus enjoyed a good relationship with Frederick William I. Despite sharply differing attitudes to extravagance (Frederick William was a miser in anything other than military spending), they shared a taste for coarse discourse and drunken carousing.[6] At Dresden in February 1728 they formed an 'Anti-Sobriety Society', whose declared objective was a war on temperance and which ejected any member failing an intoxication test.[7] Shared debauches did not prevent Augustus from asserting Polish interests against Berlin when the occasion arose.[8] Nor were the Prussian king's wits befuddled when the interests of his state were at stake. An obvious axiom of Prussian policy was the need to keep both Poland and Saxony weak. The prospect of a permanent union between the two which might add Polish quantity to Saxon quality and create an east European hegemon was a nightmare.[9] For the same reasons, the Russians were also opposed to a continuation of the union. Augustus's earlier attempts to wriggle free from Russian control were not forgotten.[10] The death of Peter the Great in 1725 made no difference for none of his three successors – Catherine (r. 1725–7), Peter II (r. 1727–30) and Anna (r. 1730–40) – changed Russian policy in this regard.

This aversion of all three eastern powers to the election of another Saxon led to Austria proposing Prince Emanuel, the brother of King John of Portugal, as its preferred candidate. He was the right sort of age (b. 1697), a Catholic and had fought with distinction in the Austrian army against the Turks. An added attraction was his lack of any fortune or power base of his own to allow independent action once on the throne. As the impoverished younger scion of a minor dynasty, he was the ideal puppet (although the puppet-masters might well have fallen out over which string to pull). This appealing combination led to the negotiation of an agreement in December 1732 that became known as the 'League of the Three Black Eagles' (after the heraldic devices of Austria, Prussia and Russia), or more mundanely as the 'Löwenwold Treaty' after the Russian chief negotiator.[11] As things turned out, it was never ratified, let alone implemented.

Waiting in the wings was another candidate for the Polish throne. Indeed, in his own estimation he was already king. This was Stanisław Leszczyński, elected and crowned in 1704–5 at the behest of Charles XII,[12] but chased out following the latter's defeat at Poltava in 1709. Since then, he had lived quietly as a Swedish pensioner at Zweibrücken and then as a French pensioner at Wissembourg in Alsace. His fortunes suddenly revived in 1725 when his 22-year-old daughter, Maria, was selected by the French prime minister, the Duc de Bourbon, to be the wife of fifteen-year-old King Louis XV. Although the main purpose of the match was to produce the badly needed heir to the French throne, her father's status as Polish anti-king-in-exile was a potential added bonus. With Augustus still hale and hearty, that was something for the future, although the next French prime minister, Cardinal Fleury, told his diplomats to start preparing the ground for Leszczyński's restoration.[13] As Augustus's health began to fail in the late 1720s, the Marquis de Monti stepped up his lobbying, buying friends and financing a pamphlet campaign to promote Leszczyński as the only guarantor of the szlachta's golden liberties.[14]

Pride of place among the recipients of Monti's largesse was the Archbishop of Gniezno, Teodor Potocki, the leader of the most powerful clan in the Commonwealth. Even by the standards of the Polish magnates he was exceptionally slippery, a veritable Archbishop of Bray. He was appointed to his first preferment, the bishopric of Chełm, despite reservations about his 'excessive propensity for cupidity'.[15] His subsequent odyssey neatly charted the fluctuations of Polish politics: after first supporting Jakub Sobieski in the 1697 election, he switched to Augustus when his success seemed certain; following the Peace of Altranstädt, he moved to the

Swedish camp and the new King Stanisław; with equal rapidity he was back with Augustus after Poltava, his eventual reward being the Archbishopric of Gniezno and the Primacy (in the latter capacity he would preside over any interregnum). His admission to the Austrian payroll in 1726 for an annual 'gratuity' of 6,000 talers did not inhibit subsequent and repeated requests to the French for money and for help in securing a cardinal's hat.[16]

The Potocki clan's main rivals were the Czartoryskis. An ancient but hitherto under-resourced Lithuanian family, they struck it rich when August Aleksander Czartoryski married Maria Zofia Sieniawska, the richest heiress in the country, who inherited one fortune from her father, Count Adam Mikołaj Sieniawski; a second from her mother, Elżbieta Lubomirska; and a third from her first husband, Count Stanisław Ernst von Denhoff.[17] The last-named haul alone comprised thirty-five towns and 235 villages.[18] To wealth was added brains in the attractive shape of Augustus Alexander's formidable sister Konstancja, who had the good sense to marry the talented and energetic Stanisław Poniatowski. It was he who directed the family interests as a kind of *consigliere*, an appropriate term given that the clan was known at the time as 'the family' (*Familia*).[19] He died in 1762, two years before his son, also called Stanisław, became King of Poland.

Although broadly speaking the Potockis were the more conservative and the Czartoryskis the more inclined to reform, these two groupings were more about power and patronage than policy.[20] Fortunately, there is no need to follow the enervating quarrels over who got which post. Into this Namierite world of politics without principles there erupted in 1724 a fierce religious conflict. Known as 'The Tumult at Toruń' (*Tumult toruński*) in Poland or, more excitedly, as 'The Bloody Assizes at Torun' (*Thorner Blutgericht*) in the German-speaking world, it began as a protest by Catholics at the failure of Protestants to remove their hats and kneel as a statue of the Virgin was carried past in procession. Reaction followed, ending with an attack on the Jesuit College, including the desecration of Catholic symbols. The heavy hand of the Catholic authorities came down very hard. Ten Protestants, including the city's mayor, were beheaded in public in the Old Town Square. An eleventh saved his life by converting to Catholicism. In addition, the only Protestant church in the city was handed over to the Catholics (the first Mass was celebrated the day after the executions), the Protestant school was closed and Catholics were given parity on the town council.[21]

What might have been acceptable in early-seventeenth-century Europe, when twenty-three Bohemian Protestants had been executed on the Old Town Square of Prague, now caused outrage in Protestant Europe and uneasiness among many Catholics. Even the papal nuncio Santini intervened to seek clemency. The passive role played by the King of Poland has never been satisfactorily explained.[22] The most popular view is that he was seeking political gain by pandering to the anti-Protestant prejudices of the szlachta.[23] Although it is certain that any intervention to save the Toruń ten would have caused uproar in Poland, there does not appear to be any solid evidence that this was what stayed his hand, although Karin Friedrich has written that Augustus 'endorsed' the judgment of the court and Władyslaw Konopczyński claimed that he took action to frustrate the nuncio's attempted intervention.[24] What does seem clear is that after the event Augustus sought privately to present himself as being powerless to intervene in the face of Polish laws, Polish 'stubbornness' and Polish 'fanaticism'.[25] The Saxon ministers also informed the Reichstag of the Holy Roman Empire that Augustus's hands had been tied by 'the Polish system' and that the Polish king had no constitutional authority to impose his will in judicial cases.[26] Whatever the rights and wrongs of the episode, the real loser was the Polish Commonwealth for the affair was a public relations disaster at a time when national image was starting to be important. In the judgement of the affair's most recent historian: 'in the long term, the notoriety of the Thorn case affected the European perceptions of Poland by tarnishing the Commonwealth with an image of intolerance and backwardness, which probably facilitated the justifications and public acceptance of the partitions of Poland by Russia, Prussia and Austria later in the century'.[27]

The other major episode of the 1720s was much more to Augustus's liking. In 1717, with the Great Northern War winding down and the Habsburg marriage winding up, he had sharply reduced the size of the Saxon army to release resources for the upcoming nuptials and subsequent representational expenditure. At the same time, however, he had set about improving military efficiency by introducing improved equipment, weaponry and uniforms, with special attention paid to officer training. This also involved important civilian spin-offs, for the expanded engineering corps under Jean de Bodt was also involved in bridge-building, land surveys and river regulation.[28] With the economy expanding rapidly in the 1720s, funds became available for an increase in numbers too, eventually reaching 27,000.[29] If dwarfed by the great host currently being created by his Prussian neighbour, it was a respectable force compared with the military establishments of other middling states of the Holy Roman Empire.

In 1728 Augustus paid a visit to Frederick William I at Berlin and Potsdam and was mightily impressed by the military manoeuvres laid on for his benefit (and intimidation, it can safely be conjectured).[30] On his return home he set about preparing his own version, which was to be so much bigger and more impressive that its like would never have been witnessed in Europe. The next two years were spent in preparation, with Augustus bringing to the task all his fabled energy and organizational genius. It was an exercise that has been written up many times, not least because of the care taken by its creator to capture every last detail in word and image. A huge commemorative volume containing 100 illustrations and weighing fifteen kilos was published after the event.[31] The site chosen was near the village of Zeithain, close to the River Elbe, thirty kilometres north of Meissen. Construction work began in 1729 with roads and bridges repaired, widened and strengthened. An army of around 500 peasants and 250 miners doubling as builders was put to work, clearing a greenfield site four kilometres by five and constructing what was in effect a new town, complete with streets, squares, gardens, abattoirs, bakeries, inns and shops. Warehouses were constructed on the Elbe for the huge stocks of provisions needed for the planned four weeks of manoeuvres and attendant jollifications. An army of catering staff was recruited – eighty-nine cooks (including specialist chefs from Paris), twenty-eight sous-chefs, forty-three kitchen maids, twenty-three 'roasting boys', and so on. Every spare room in every peasant cottage in the vicinity was booked for bed and breakfast.[32] Over 1,000 tents and marquees were erected to accommodate the hordes of visitors.[33]

The exercise began at the end of May 1730 with the arrival of the guest of honour, Frederick William of Prussia, accompanied by a retinue of 150 officers, including his detested son Frederick (who shortly afterwards tried to run away from his father's tyranny). In the days which followed, the entire Saxon army – now amounting to around 30,000 men – was put through its paces in columns, lines and squares, fighting mock-battles, including a defended crossing of the Elbe complete with a naval bombardment. Although later derided as mere play-acting, there was a serious side to the proceedings, the main purpose being to show the Prussians that Saxony was an ally worth having.[34] That was emphasized by the presence of a host of other imperial dignitaries and Polish magnates. The entire Order of the White Eagle, founded by Augustus in 1705, was on display – twenty-one German and fifteen Polish knights in their resplendent uniforms.[35] But of course the *après manoeuvre* was not neglected. At the theatre built specially for the occasion there were operatic performances featuring three castrati and two female sopranos hired from Venice, Italian comedies, ballets and also firework displays, hunting and sumptuous banquets – all the usual court entertainments, in other words.[36]

Although trivial in itself, worth mentioning as an illustration of Augustus's exhibitionism is the giant cake baked at the camp. As usual with Augustus, there were no half-measures: the specially constructed brick oven took eight days to reach the required temperature; the dough was made of a ton (*20 Zentner*) of flour, 305 litres (*326 Kannen*) of milk and 3,600 eggs. Eight horses pulled it on an extended cart to the oven where it was baked for six hours, by which time it was eighteen metres (16 *Ellen*) long and 6.9 metres (6 *Ellen*) wide. Also a candidate for the *Guinness Book of Records*, had it existed, was the giant knife used to cut it. This was all well publicized in the European press, of course, for example in the popular French-language *Mercure historique et politique* published at The Hague.[37] Augustus was a showman, the P. T. Barnum of his day.

Two years later, Augustus held a similar camp for the benefit of his Polish subjects at Czerniaków, just outside Warsaw, albeit on a more modest scale.[38] Within the strict limits imposed by the Polish constitution and the 1717 agreement,[39] he had taken a number of initiatives to improve the country's military potential. Young Poles were sent to train at the Dresden cadet academy, a Polish equivalent was established in 1730 and the training and weaponry of the army were modernized.[40] It was to no avail. Such was the distrust felt by most szlachta for Augustus's political objectives that *any* measure appearing to increase the country's military capability was interpreted as a preparation for an absolutist *coup d'état*.[41] Those fears had been exacerbated recently by the abortive attempt of Augustus's illegitimate son Maurice to become Duke of Courland, a Polish fief. A soldier and womanizer of European renown, Maurice was less adept at politics. Although it was Augustus who intervened to put a stop to his adventure, that did not stop the hypersensitive Polish szlachta from seeing it as part of a fell plot against their liberties.[42]

Overall in the course of his reign, Augustus divided his time more or less equally between Saxony and Poland, although towards the end he was spending far more time in less contentious Dresden.[43] But it was in Warsaw that he died. Given his lifestyle and the prevalence of endemic disease, it was a tribute to his physical robustness that he lived so long. His Achilles heel proved to be a toe, damaged when he dropped a marble dish on it during his grand tour and aggravated during the Dresden carnival of 1697 when he fell off his horse. Reappearing during the wedding festivities in 1719, the toe came back to plague him with increasing vehemence during the 1720s, by which time he was suffering from what was likely diabetes.[44] In January 1727, when travelling from Grodno to Warsaw, he became so ill that he had to stop at Białystok, where his enterprising doctor saved his life by amputating the now-gangrenous toe.[45] Augustus then rallied and returned to his old ways, as he showed by his carousing with Frederick William I when he visited the following year, including the foundation of the Anti-Sobriety Society.

It was not until the autumn of 1732, when he had to watch the Czerniaków manoeuvres sitting down, that what proved to be the terminal phase began. He returned to Dresden for the carnival, visited the New Year fair at Leipzig and then set out for Warsaw. At Krossen he stopped to confer with the Prussian minister Friedrich Wilhelm von Grumbkow. A drinking bout ensued in which each man tried – and failed – to tempt the other into indiscretions about their respective foreign policy agenda. On arrival in Warsaw on 16 January 1733, Augustus seemed to rally but then went rapidly downhill, dying just after 5 a.m. on Sunday, 1 February. The body was embalmed, dressed in a suitably gorgeous outfit, displayed for a week and then removed to Kraków. In accordance with Polish custom, it could not be buried there until the coronation of a successor. His entrails were interred in an urn and buried in the Capuchin Church in Warsaw. In accordance with the direction in his will, his heart was taken back to Dresden, where in a metaphysical sense it had always been.[46]

Minus these two body parts, what remained of Augustus was eventually laid to rest in the Wawel Cathedral in Kraków on 15 January 1734.[47] Two days later, his son was crowned King of Poland as Augustus III. It was a triumph both posthumous and undeserved, but a triumph it undoubtedly was. It was undeserved because Augustus's strenuous efforts to secure the succession had alienated rather than attracted Polish opinion. That was shown immediately after his death by the rush of support for Stanisław Leszczyński. The Convocation Sejm held in May–June 1733 ruled out a Saxon candidacy by affirming that the next king must be a native Pole, which in effect was a collective vote for Leszczyński.[48] He was indeed elected on the Wola field just outside Warsaw on 12 September, with about 13,000 szlachta present and voting.[49] By that time, however, decision-making had passed to the great powers, with Austria and Russia in the van. Neither had the slightest intention of allowing the French *barrière de l'est* to be resurrected with a French puppet on the throne. Their original alternative, Prince Emanuel of Portugal, soon fell by wayside for want of support from the Polish Electorate.[50] That left them receptive to approaches from the Saxon diplomats, lobbying hard for Augustus junior. They came bearing irresistible gifts – for Charles VI the recognition of the Pragmatic Sanction he craved, and for Tsarina Anna the Duchy of Courland (a Polish fief) for her lover Ernst Johann von Biron. Also offered was a commitment to the Commonwealth's traditional constitution, thus guaranteeing continuing Polish weakness, and an informal assurance from Saxon diplomats that their master would prove much less 'problematic' than his father.[51] The deal to make Augustus the Austro-Russian candidate was struck on 19 August, by which time a Russian army of around 30,000, commanded by General Peter Lacy, had already crossed the frontier. They could not stop Leszczyński's election, but they could stage their own. On 5 October, outside an inn at the village of Kamień, a gathering of 3,000–4,000 szlachta elected Augustus.[52]

The sword would now decide. It was an unequal contest from the start. The Polish army supporting Leszczyński, commanded by Józef Potocki, offered little resistance; a small French flotilla proved reluctant to engage and ended up surrendering; an anticipated Swedish army did not materialize.[53] King Stanisław himself and most of his supporters withdrew hurriedly to Danzig and from there to Königsberg. They took refuge there courtesy of Frederick William I, who was exacting revenge for being ignored and left empty-handed by his Austrian and Russian allies. By the end of 1734 it was all over, and international diplomacy now took control. 'The War of the Polish Succession', as it was misleadingly called, was really a European war between Austria and France, allied to Spain and Sardinia. As the latter bloc achieved military victory, it was the

French who determined the peace settlement. So far as Poland was concerned, this meant the recognition of Augustus III as King of Poland, with Stanisław Leszczyński being compensated with the Duchy of Lorraine (which on his death was to pass to France). In a fine illustration of the marginal importance of the Polish dimension, King Stanisław was neither consulted nor even informed of his impending abdication and demotion to ducal status.[54]

Conclusion

By any standard, Augustus has to be judged a dismal failure in Poland, although not in Saxony. When elected king, his intention was to transform Poland into a prosperous, stable, well-governed and powerful state, the dominant power in eastern Europe.[1] None of those objectives were achieved, although progress was certainly made once the Great Northern War petered out. The economy revived, domestic peace was restored as a *modus vivendi* was reached between king and nobility, and social and cultural life flourished, with Warsaw emerging as a true capital city.[2] But beneath a thin veneer of normality, the old problems lurked. As the civil war which erupted after Augustus's death demonstrated, if anything Poland was now less stable than when he himself came to the throne. It was also more obviously impotent, for it was only thanks to the Russian army that his son secured the Polish throne. Left to themselves, the Poles would have chosen Stanisław Leszczyński. Abandoned by their French allies, who were always more interested in gains in the west, they had to submit to Russian *force majeure*. It was not to be the last such occasion.

When Augustus III died on 5 October 1763, the Polish–Lithuanian Commonwealth was still the largest country in Europe outside Russia. By 1795 it had disappeared from the map altogether, partitioned in three stages – 1772, 1793 and 1795 – by Austria, Prussia and Russia. In the same way that knowledge of the French Revolution has distorted everything that happened in France before 1789, so has the eventual fate of Poland cast a long backward shadow. Especially after nationalism got into its stride, the 'Saxon era' was consigned to outer darkness. In Robert Frost's striking image, 'The partitions squat like an incubus over Polish historiography.'[3] For Polish patriots seeking to explain their nation's extinction, the sixty-six years of rule by two Germans were an inviting target. For Kazimierz Jarochowski, writing in the middle of the nineteenth century, it was a period of 'misery and horror' (*nieszczęście i zgroza*), so upsetting that most scholars avoided it altogether 'in the same way that superstitious peasants shun a suicide's grave at midnight'. By 1763, he concluded, everything was in place for Poland's doom and defeat.[4]

If nationalism sharpened hostility to Augustus father and son, the simultaneous advance of middle-class morality pilloried the former as the arch-villain: 'a debauched, unbridled, treacherous circus performer masquerading as a monarch and leader' was Władysław Konopczyński's verdict. The reign of this 'immoral and dissolute egoist', he added, was characterized by degeneration, selfishness, moral depravity and licentious hedonism, 'a moral plague leading to the systematic poisoning of society'.[5] Augustus was treated almost as roughly by nineteenth-century German historians, especially those with a pro-Prussian agenda. In his hugely successful *History of the Eighteenth Century*, the Heidelberg Professor and Prussian Privy Councillor Friedrich Christoph Schlosser branded Augustus as a worthless, unscrupulous, unprincipled, treacherous voluptuary.[6] Even the Saxon historian Theodor Flathe (1827–1900) saw Brandenburg–Prussia as destined by Providence (*Schicksal*) to take charge of the German mission, replacing Saxony whose unworthy rulers were weak, lazy, addicted to pleasure and subservient to the Austrians.[7] Most serious was the treatment of Saxon history in general, and Augustus in particular, by the Berlin scholar Paul Haake, whose overriding objective was to show how the Hohenzollerns of Prussia triumphed over the Wettins of Saxony in the struggle for mastery in Germany.[8] Paradoxically, that made Augustus perversely admirable, for by involuntarily shrinking Saxony to second-rate status he opened the way for Frederick the Great's march to glory.[9] As with much of the German writing on Augustus as King of Poland, Haake's books and articles were disfigured by crude Polonophobia.[10] An honourable exception to these uncritically negative depictions was Ranke, who discerned 'extra-ordinary personal qualities' in Augustus including an aptitude for whatever he embarked on (*was er angriff, dazu hatte er Geschick*).[11]

By the time Haake died in 1950, the historiographical landscape of both Saxony and Poland had changed radically following their annexation by the Soviet Empire. With nationalism proscribed, international solidarity was the order of the day. To the fore in the revisionist project which now developed were Henryk Olsz-ewski (1932–2021) of Poznań, Józef Gierowski (1922–2006) of Kraków and Jacek Staszewski (1933–2013) of Toruń. They dis-tanced themselves from those predecessors who had demonized the Saxon period 'simply because the two kings had been German', as Gierowski put it.[12] The 'black legend', they pointed out, had been created by mendacious scandalmongers such as Pöllnitz and propagated by Prussians eager to evade their respon-sibility for Poland's decline and fall.[13] In 1961 Olszewski argued that the problems afflicting Augustus were more his inheritance than his creation and, moreover, that his reign saw green shoots of reform which were to mature later under Stanisław Ponia-towski.[14] More recently, Urszula Kosińska has sounded a more negative note. In her study of Augustus's foreign policy during the closing years of his reign she was sharply critical of his use of Russian intervention for his own selfish purposes, concluding: 'it was then that the basic methods of Russian diplomacy to influ-ence the Polish lords and maintain control over the country were developed'.[15] Although her strictures were well deserved, the revisionists had a good case when they pointed out that the sea change in Polish history that brought the decline of what had once been the best-governed and most vital state in eastern Europe long predated Augustus's election.

Many are the candidates for the status of 'point of no return'. Was it Zebrzydowski's *rokosz* of 1606–7, Khmelnytskyi's rising of 1648 and the 'Deluge' (*Potop*) which followed? The abortive Treaty of Hadziacz of 1658? The Treaty of Perpetual Peace of 1686 which confirmed the cession of left-bank Ukraine plus Kiev to Russia? Or was it a longer-term development such as the rise of the magnates, the decline of the towns, the depression of the serfs, the growing intolerance of the Counter-Reformation, or even 'the complete collapse of civic morality [that] had set in towards the end of the reign of Jan III Sobieski'?[16] The best case has been made by Robert Frost for the mid-seventeenth century: 'It was above all the failure immediately to reform the political system during John Casimir's reign [1648–68] which ensured that recovery was impossible, for it was henceforth very much in the interests of the Commonwealth's neighbours to block any political reform which might lead to its military revival: they therefore signed a series of treaties agreeing to preserve its political system . . . [it was then that] the vital psychological shift took place.'[17]

The victory at Vienna in 1683, which seemed to herald a return to the palmy days of the previous century, was a false dawn, soon overshadowed by military failure in Moldavia and a diplomatic debacle only three years later. Augustus was never going to be the man to reverse the downward spiral. He would have needed to be a combination of Henry VII (who tamed the English magnates), Henry VIII (who anchored the English gentry to the monarchy by expropriating the English Church) and Elizabeth I (who inspired the English nation), but, alas, he proved to be more of a Stuart than a Tudor. His overriding dynastic concern to conquer a principality in Moldavia, Livonia, Pomerania or wherever and then to turn Poland into a hereditary monarchy was so much at odds with the szlachta's most treasured political principles and interests that fierce resistance was guaranteed. In truth, he had never really tried to assimilate with his Polish subjects, not even learning their language.[18] If trust is the lubricant which oils the wheels of state, Poland under Augustus was doomed to repeated grating breakdowns.

More contentious was the role he played in the seismic changes in the European states system during his reign. As we have seen, Augustus made an important if not decisive contribution to the success of Tsar Peter by keeping Charles XII busy in Poland between

1700 and 1706. Moreover, the Saxon army made a powerful contribution to the conquest of the Swedish Baltic empire after 1709, most notably at Stralsund.[19] If Charles had been able to concentrate on Peter in 1700, he might well have dealt him a terminal blow. On the other hand, the demographic and socio-economic foundations of Sweden's empire had always been too shallow to sustain a permanent structure. Their collapse was hastened less by Augustus's fitful interventions than by Charles XII's egregious follies and Peter's endurance, strategic insight and ruthless exploitation of his country's colossal potential. There was to be no going back. Even under his short-lived successors Catherine, Peter II, Anna and Ivan VI, Russia remained a major player in European affairs: there was a Russian army on the Rhine in 1735.

Nor could Augustus have done much, if anything, to impede the advance of the two other eventual participants in the partitions of Poland. In Brandenburg, the reforms of Frederick William the Great Elector, the acquisition of the royal title by Frederick I and the intensive militarization imposed by Frederick William I, created a mighty weapon which Frederick II would use to make Prussia a great power and secure the sobriquet 'The Great' for himself. It was he who masterminded the first partition in 1772.[20] Also beyond Augustus's reach was the Habsburg Monarchy, the least enthusiastic of the partitioning powers because linked to Poland by family ties and religion. Much more important targets for Vienna were France, at least until the 'diplomatic revolution' of 1756, the Ottoman Empire and, of course, Prussia. It was the existential threat presented by the last-named after 1740 that prompted a wave of modernizing reforms. However defective the latter may have been, they ensured that the Habsburg Monarchy would be predator rather than prey.

In all three cases – Russian, Prussian and Austrian – the need to compete in the international states system was met by the creation of 'fiscal-military states' whose chief characteristics have been defined by the coiner of the phrase, John Brewer, as 'high taxes, a growing and well-organised civil administration, a standing army and the determination to act as a major European power'.[21] The sharp end was a big army. Yet Poland was a territorial giant (the largest country in Europe outside Russia) but a military midget. Even after the modest changes introduced in 1717, it met none of Brewer's tests. Indeed, the size of the army actually fell to around 18,000.[22] It might be objected that to compare a constitutional monarchy such as Poland with three autocracies is misleading. The obvious answer is the case of England, which after 1688 created the fiscal-military state par excellence, demonstrating in the process that a parliamentary regime could maximize resources more efficiently than any absolute monarch. However attractive the Polish szlachta's attachment to their golden liberties and aversion to anything smacking of top-down government might seem, the awkward fact remains that they refused to allow their ruler the resources necessary to organize their defence. So Frederick the Great could violate their neutrality at will during the three Silesian wars (1740–63) and then play a leading role in the partition of 1772.

Against these long-term structural weaknesses Augustus struggled in vain, even if it has to be conceded that his struggles were short-lived and inept. Yet it is also worth remembering not only that Poland's territorial integrity remained intact during the reigns of the two Saxon kings, but also that Augustus was the first King of Poland since time out of mind to (re)gain territory (by the Treaty of Karlowitz of 1699). If enough has been written in previous chapters to present him 'warts and all' (O. Cromwell), it ought to be added that not all Poles viewed him as the ogre of the black legend. If one can disregard the hyperbole of contemporary sycophants such as David Fassmann, who hailed Augustus as 'the most glorious hero of our age . . . one of the greatest and best potentates ever to draw breath . . . he dazzled with the beauty of Absalom, the wisdom of Solomon, the good nature and justice of David, and the strength of Samson',[23] there were other more sober contemporary tributes that have to be taken seriously. In 1740 the Danzig historian Gottfried Lengnich, for example, praised him for his courtesy, humanity, tenacity and good nature, singling out his attempts to repopulate

Poland and to promote its economy.[24] A popular rhyme making the rounds after the end of the Saxon era ran:

> In the time of the Saxons what we felt
> Was eat and drink and let out the belt.[25]

A posthumous tribute was paid by the makers of the constitution of 3 May 1791 when they specified in article seven that when the current King Stanisław (Poniatowski) died, 'the dynasty of the future kings of Poland shall begin with the person of Frederick Augustus, present-day Elector of Saxony, to whose male successors *de lumbis* [from the loins] we reserve the throne of Poland. The eldest son of the reigning king shall succeed his father to the throne.'[26] How Augustus's shade, wherever it might have been located, would have relished that provision! In the event, Frederick Augustus did get to rule Poland, albeit only as Napoleon's puppet 'Grand Duke of Warsaw'.

Augustus was not the stuff of which historiographical heroes are made. He was undoubtedly a rascal, self-indulgent, recklessly extravagant, unprincipled, ruthless in the pursuit of sensual pleasure – not to mention all the other pejorative epithets directed by the wagging fingers of indignant moralizers. But he was also a great risk-taker, never dull, lived in exciting times, was always trying this or that, and if not larger than life then certainly brimful with vitality. In the world of politics his mercurial personality led to disappointment followed by failure followed by recovery followed by disappointment, and so on. It was in the cultural sphere that all his manifold flaws became assets, elevating him to iconic status, the cynosure of baroque culture. Viewing the Dresden skyline from the banks of the Elbe outside the Japanese Palace (or Bellotto's *veduta* of the same scene), even the most hostile of his critics can surely repeat the epitaph carved on the tomb of Sir Christopher Wren in St Paul's Cathedral: '*Si monumentum requiris circumspice*' (If you seek his monument, look around you).

Acknowledgements

I acknowledge with gratitude all those who have helped me with advice, criticism and information, especially Ilya Berkovich, Robert Frost, William Godsey, Lothar Höbel, Michael Middeke, James Pullen and Adam Storring, and with special thanks to Richard Butterworth, Simon Dixon and Simon Winder, who heroically read a first draft and saved me from all manner of mistakes and misjudgements. I take full responsibility for those that remain. I am also deeply indebted to Cecilia Mackay, peerless picture researcher.

Further Reading

As the books and articles I have cited are all recorded in the Notes, I shall confine myself here to a selection of those which I have found most useful, choosing mainly books and trying to confine myself to no more than twenty titles in each language (English, German, Polish, Swedish, French and Russian). Scholars aggrieved at not finding their work listed below will (probably) find it in the footnotes.

Adamson, John, *The Princely Courts of Europe: Ritual, Politics and Culture Under the Ancien Régime 1500–1750* (London, 1999)

Akunin, Boris, *Istoriia rossiiskogo gosudarstva. Aziatskaia evropeizatsiia* (Kiev, 2017)

Aleksiun, Natalie, Daniel Beauvois, Marie-Élizabeth Ducreux, Jerzy Kloczowski, Henryk Samsonowicz and Piotr Wandycz, *Histoire de l'Europe du Centre-Est* (Paris, 2004)

Arnold, Ulli and Werner Schmidt (eds), *Barock in Dresden: Kunst und Kunstsammlungen unter der Regierung des Kurfürsten Friedrich August I. von Sachsen und Königs August II. von Polen, genannt August der Starke, 1694–1733, und des Kurfürsten Friedrich August II. von Sachsen und Königs Augusts III. von Polen, 1733–1763* (Leipzig, 1986)

Augustyniak, Urszula, *Historia Polski 1572–1795* (Warsaw, 2008)

Bäumel, Jutta, *Auf dem Weg zum Thron. Die Krönungsreise Augusts des Starken* (Dresden, 1997)

Beauvois, Daniel, *Histoire de la Pologne* (Paris, 1995)

Becker-Glauch, Irmgard, *Die Bedeutung der Musik für die Dresdener Hoffeste bis in die Zeit Augusts des Starken* (Kassel and Basle, 1951)

Behre, Göran, Lars-Olof Larsson and Eva Österberg, *Sveriges Historia 1521–1809: Stormaktsdröm och Småstatsrealiteter* (Stockholm, 1985)

Berling, Karl, *Das Meissner Porzellan und seine Geschichte* (Leipzig, 1900)

Further Reading

Bespalov, Alexander, *Severnaia Vojna. Karl XII i shvedskaia armiia. Put' ot Kopengagena do Perevolochnoi 1700–1709* (Moscow, 1998)

Bill, Stanley and Simon Lewis (eds), *Multicultural Commonwealth: Poland–Lithuania and its Afterlives* (Pittsburgh, 2023)

Blettermann, Petra, *Die Universitätspolitik Augusts des Starken, 1694–1733* (Cologne and Vienna, 1990)

Bobylev, V. S., *Vneshniaia politika Rossii epokhi Petra I* (Moscow, 1990)

Bömelburg, Hans-Jürgen, 'Sarmatismus – zur Begriffsgeschichte und den Chancen und Grenzen als forschungsleitender Begriff', *Jahrbücher für Geschichte Osteuropas*, NS, 57, 3 (2009)

Bonnesen, Sten, *Peter den Store* (Stockholm, 1928)

— *Studier över August II:s utrikespolitik 1712–1715* (Lund, 1918)

Bring, Samuel E. (ed.), *Karl XII till 200-årsdagen av hans död* (Stockholm, 1918)

Buganov, V. I., *Petr velikii i ego vremia* (Moscow, 1989)

Burdowicz-Nowicki, Jacek, *Piotr I, August II i Rzeczpospolita 1697–1706* (Kraków, 2010)

Butterwick, Richard, 'Catholicism and the enlightenment in Poland–Lithuania', in Ulrich L. Lehner and Michael O'Neill Printy (eds), *A Companion to the Catholic Enlightenment in Europe* (Leiden, 2010)

— *The Constitution of 3 May 1791. Testament of the Polish–Lithuanian Commonwealth* (Warsaw, 2021)

— *The Polish–Lithuanian Commonwealth. Light and Flame* (New Haven and London, 2020)

Carlson, Fredrik Ferdinand, *Sveriges historia under konungarne af pfalziska huset*, pt 7: *Carl XII.* (Stockholm, 1881)

Castelluccio, Stéphane (ed.), *Le Commerce du luxe à Paris au XVIIe et XVIIIe siècles* (Bern etc., 2009)

Corvisier, André, *Arts et sociétés dans l'Europe du XVIIIe siècle* (Paris, 1978)

Cynarski, Stanisław, 'The shape of Sarmatian ideology', *Acta Poloniae Historica*, 19 (1968)

Czok, Karl, *August der Starke und Kursachsen* (Leipzig, 1987)

Danielson, Johann Richard, *Zur Geschichte der sächsischen Politik 1706–1709* (Helsingfors, 1878)

Davies, Norman, *God's Playground*, vol. 1: *The Origins to 1795* (Oxford, 2005)

Des Roches de Parthenay, Jean-Baptiste, *The History of Poland under Augustus II* (London, 1734)

Dixon, Simon, *The Modernisation of Russia 1676–1825* (Cambridge, 1999)

Doubek, Katja, *August der Starke* (Hamburg, 2015)

Faber, Martin, *Sarmatismus: Die politische Ideologie des polnischen Adels im 16. und 17. Jahrhundert* (Deutsches Historisches Institut Warschau, Quellen und Studien, vol. 35) (Wiesbaden, 2018)

Fester, André (ed.), *Das Residenzschloss zu Dresden*, vol. 3: *Von barocker Prachtentfaltung bis zum großen Schlossumbau im 19. Jahrhundert* (Petersberg, 2020)

Feygina, S. A., *Alandskii kongress: vneshniaia politika Rossii v kontse Severnoy Voyny* (Moscow–Leningrad, 1959)

Flemming, Stephan, 'Mit Konversion und Bestechung zur Krone. Die Bemühungen Augusts des Starken um den polnischen Thron', *Neues Archiv für sächsische Geschichte*, 90 (2019)

Flipczak-Kocur, Anna, 'Poland–Lithuania before partition', in Richard Bonney (ed.), *The Rise of the Fiscal State in Europe* (Oxford, 1999)

Forberger, Rudolf, *Die Manufaktur in Sachsen vom Ende des 16. bis zum Anfang des 19. Jahrhunderts* (Berlin, 1958)

Förster, Friedrich, *Friedrich August II. der Starke, Kurfürst von Sachsen und König von Polen, geschildert als Regent und Mensch* (Potsdam, 1839)

Forycki, Maciej, *Stanisław Leszczyński* (Poznań, 2016)

Friedrich, Karin, *The Other Prussia: Royal Prussia, Poland and Liberty, 1569–1772* (Cambridge, 2000)

Frost, Robert I., ' "Everyone understood what it meant": The impact of the Battle of Poltava on the Polish–Lithuanian Commonwealth', *Harvard Ukrainian Studies*, 31,1/4

— 'The nobility of Poland–Lithuania, 1569–1795', in H. M. Scott (ed.), *The European Nobilities in the Seventeenth and Eighteenth Centuries*, vol. 2: *Northern, Central and Eastern Europe* (London and New York, 1995)

— *The Northern Wars: War, State and Society in North-Eastern Europe, 1558–1721* (Harlow, 2000)

— *The Oxford History of Poland–Lithuania*, vol. 1 (Oxford, 2015)

Fürstenau, Moritz, *Zur Geschichte der Musik und des Theaters am Hofe zu Dresden*, vol. 2 (Dresden, 1862)

Gierowski, Józef, 'August II Wettyn', in Irena Kaniewska (ed.), *Królowie elekcyjni leksykon biograficzny* (Kraków, 1997)

— 'The eclipse of Poland', in J. S. Bromley (ed.), *The New Cambridge Modern History*, vol. 6: *The Rise of Great Britain and Russia* (Cambridge, 1970)

— *Rzeczpospolita w dobie złotej wolności (1648–1763)* (Krakow, 2001)

Gillberg, Christopher, 'Karl XII tycks ha uppfyllt de flesta kritierna för Aspergers syndrom', *Läkartidningen*, 48 (2002)

Glaeser, Michael, *By Defeating My Enemies: Charles XII of Sweden and the Great Northern War 1682–1721* (Warwick, 2020)

Glete, Jan, *Swedish Naval Administration, 1521–1721* (Leiden, 2010)

Göse, Frank, Winfried Müller, Kurt Winkler and Anne-Katrin Ziesak (eds), *Preussen und Sachsen. Szenen einer Nachbarschaft* (Dresden, 2014)

Grauers, Sven, 'Karl XII', *Svenskt Biografiskt Lexikon*, https://sok.riksarkivet.se/sbl/Presentation.aspx?id=12357

Grześkowiak-Krawicz, Anna, *Queen Liberty: The Concept of Freedom in the Polish–Lithuanian Commonwealth* (Leiden and Boston, 2012)

Gurlitt, Cornelius, *August der Starke. Ein Fürstenleben aus der Zeit des deutschen Barocks*, 2nd edn, 2 vols (Dresden, 1924)

Haake, Paul, *August der Starke* (Berlin and Leipzig, 1927)

— *August der Starke im Urteil seiner Zeit und der Nachwelt* (Dresden, 1922)

— 'Die Jugenderinnerungen König Augusts des Starken', *Historische Vierteljahrschrift*, 3 (1900)

— 'Die Türkenfeldzüge Augusts des Starken 1695 und 1696', *Neues Archiv für Sächsische Geschichte und Altertumskunde*, 24 (1903)

— 'Die Wahl Augusts des Starken zum König von Polen', *Historische Vierteljahrschrift* 9 (1906)

Haintz, Otto, *König Karl XII. von Schweden*, 2 vols (Berlin, 1958)

Hartmann, Hans-Günther, *Moritzburg. Schloß und Umgebung in Geschichte und Gegenwart* (Weimar, 1989)

Hassinger, Erich, *Brandenburg–Preußen, Schweden und Rußland 1700–1713* (Munich, 1953)

Hatton, Ragnhild, *Charles XII of Sweden* (London, 1968)

Held, Wieland, *Der Adel und August der Starke. Konflikt und Konfliktaustrag zwischen 1694 und 1707 in Kursachsen* (Cologne, Weimar and Vienna, 1999)

Hentschel, Walter, *Die sächsische Baukunst des 18. Jahrhunderts in Polen*, 2 vols (Berlin, 1967)

Hertzig, Stefan, *Das barocke Dresden. Architektur einer Metropole des 18. Jahrhunderts* (Petersberg, 2013)

Hiltebrandt, Philipp, 'Die polnische Königswahl von 1697 und die Konversion Augusts des Starken', *Quellen und Forschungen aus italienischen Archiven und Bibliotheken*, 10 (1907)

Hochedlinger, Michael, *Austria's Wars of Emergence: War, State and Society in the Habsburg Monarchy 1683–1797* (London, 2003)

Hoffmann, Klaus, *Johann Friedrich Böttger. Vom Alchemisten zum weißen Porzellan* (Berlin, 1985)

Hughes, Lindsey, *Peter the Great: A Biography* (New Haven and London, 2004)

Ingrao, Charles, *The Habsburg Monarchy 1618–1815*, 2nd edn (Cambridge, 2000)

Jarochowski, Kazimierz, *Dzieje panowania Augusta II od śmierci Jana III do chwili wstąpienia Karola XII na ziemię Polska* (Posnań, 1856)

Jaworski, Rudolf, Christian Lübke and Michael G. Müller, *Eine kleine Geschichte Polens* (Frankfurt am Main, 2000)

Jędruch, Jacek, *Constitutions, Elections and Legislatures of Poland 1493–1993: A Guide to Their History* (New York, 1998)

Jespersen, Knud J. V., 'Rivalry without victory: Denmark, Sweden and the struggle for the Baltic, 1500–1720', in Göran Rystad, Klaus-Richard Böhme and Wilhelm M. Carlgren, *In Quest of Trade and Security: The Baltic in Power Politics, 1500–1990* (Lund, 1994)

Jonasson, Gustaf, *Karl XII:s polska politik 1702–1703* (Stockholm, 1968)

Kalisch, Johannes and J. Gierowski (eds), *Um die polnische Krone: Sachsen und Polen während des Nordischen Krieges 1700–1721* (Berlin, 1962)

Kamiński, Andrzej, 'The *szlachta* of the Polish–Lithuanian Commonwealth and their government', in Ivo Banac and Paul Bushkovitch (eds), *The Nobility of Russia and Eastern Europe* (New Haven and London, 1985)

Kappeler, Andreas, *Kleine Geschichte der Ukraine* (Munich, 1994)

Keller, Katrin (ed.), *'Mein Herr befindet sich gottlob gesund und wohl': Sächsische Prinzen auf Reisen* (Leipzig, 1994)

Further Reading

Kersken, Norbert, 'Geschichtsbild und Adelsrepublik. Zur Sarmaten-theorie in der polnischen Geschichtsschreibung der frühen Neuzeit', *Jahrbücher für Geschichte Osteuropas*, 52 (2004)

Kłoczowski, Jerzy, 'The Polish Church', in William J. Callahan and David Higgs (eds), *Church and Society in Catholic Europe of the Eighteenth Century* (Cambridge, 1979)

Kneifel, Eduard, *Geschichte der Evangelisch-Augsburgischen Kirche in Polen* (Niedermarschacht über Winsen / Lube, n.d.)

Kollmann, Nancy Shields, *The Russian Empire 1450–1801* (Oxford, 2017)

Konopczyński, Władyslaw, *Dzieje polska nowożytnej*, vol. 2: *1648–1797* (Warsaw, 1936)

— *Polska a Szwecja od pokoju oliwskiego do upadku Rzeczpospolitej 1660–1795* (Warsaw, 1924)

Koroliuk, V. D., 'Izbranie Avgusta II na pol'skii prestol i russkaia diplomatiia', *Uchenye Zapiski Instituta Slavianovedeniia*, 3 (1951)

Koroluk, W. D., *Polska i Rosja a wojna północna* (Warsaw, 1954)

Kozińska, Urzula, *August II w poszukiwaniu sojusznika. Między aliansem wiedeńskim i hanowerskim (1725–1730)* (Warsaw, 2012)

— *Sejm 1719–1720 a sprawa ratyfikacji traktatu wiedeńskiego* (Warsaw, 2003)

Kriegseisen, Wojciech, *Between State and Church. Confessional Relations from Reformation to Enlightenment: Poland – Lithuania – Germany – Netherlands* (Frankfurt am Main, 2011)

Kroll, Frank-Lothar and Hendrik Thoss (eds), *Zwei Staaten, eine Krone. Die polnisch–sächsische Union 1697–1763* (Berlin, 2016)

Larsson, Olle, *Stormaktens sista krig* (Lund, 2009)

Lehnstaedt, Stephan, *Der Große Nordische Krieg 1700–1721* (Stuttgart, 2021)

Lewitter, L. R., 'Poland under the Saxon kings', *New Cambridge Modern History*, vol. 7: *The Old Regime, 1713–1763*, ed. J. O. Lindsay (Cambridge, 1957)

Liljegren, Bengt, *Karl XII. En biografi* (Lund, 2000)

Link-Lenczowski, Andrzej, *Rzeczpospolita na Rozdrożu 1696–1736* (Kraków, 1994)

Litak, Stanisław, *Od Reformacji do Oświecenia. Kościół katolicki w Polsce nowożytnej* (Lublin, 1994)

Lukowski, Jerzy, *Disorderly Liberty: The Political Culture of the Polish–Lithuanian Commonwealth in the Eighteenth Century* (London, 2010)

Further Reading

— 'Political ideas among the Polish nobility in the eighteenth century (to 1788)', *The Slavonic and East European Review*, 82, 1 (January 2004)

Magirius, Heinrich, *Die Dresdner Frauenkirche von Georg Bähr: Entstehung und Bedeutung* (Berlin, 2005)

Markiewicz, Mariusz, *Historia Polski 1492–1795* (Kraków, 2005)

McKay, Derek and H. M. Scott, *The Rise of the Great Powers 1648–1815* (London, 1983)

Moine, Marie-Christine, *Les Fêtes à la cour du roi soleil 1653–1715* (Paris, 1984)

Molchanov, N. N., *Diplomatiia Petra Pervogo* (Moscow, 1984)

Monier, F. M., *Histoire de Pologne depuis son origine jusqu'en 1795*, vol. 1 (Paris, 1807)

Munthe, Arnold, *Karl XII och den ryska sjömakten*, 3 vols (Stockholm, 1924–7)

Murphy, Curtis G., *From Citizens to Subjects: City, State, and the Enlightenment in Poland, Ukraine, and Belarus* (Pittsburgh, 2018)

Muszyński, Jadwig (ed.), *Rzeczpospolita w dobie wielkiej wojny północnej* (Kielce, 2001)

Nekrasov, G. A., *Voenno-morskie sily Rossii na Baltike v pervoi chetverti XVIII v.* (Moscow, 1969)

Nordberg, J. A., *Histoire de Charles XII roi de Suède*, vol. 4 (The Hague, 1748)

Oakley, Stewart P., *War and Peace in the Baltic 1560–1790* (London, 1992)

Olszewski, Henryk and Edmund Cieślak (eds), *Changes in Two Baltic Countries: Poland and Sweden in the XVIIIth Century* (Poznań, 1990)

— *Doktryny Prawno-ustrojowe Czasów Saskich, 1697–1740* (Warsaw, 1961)

Opalinski, Edward, 'Die Freiheit des Adels. Ideal und Wirklichkeit in Polen–Litauen im 17. Jahrhundert', in Ronald G. Asch (ed.), *Der europäische Adel im Ancien Régime. Von der Krise der ständischen Monarchien bis zur Revolution (ca. 1600–1789)* (Cologne, Weimar, Vienna, 2001)

Oredsson, Sverker (ed.), *Tsar Petr i Korol' Karl. Dva pravitelia i ikh narody* (Moscow, 1999)

Pavlenko, N. I., *Petr I* (Moscow, 2000)

Piwarski, Kazimierz, *Hieronim Lubomirski. Hetman Wielki Koronny* (Kraków, 1929)

Querengässer, Alexander, *Der kursächsische Militär im Großen Nordischen Krieg* (Paderborn, 2019)

310

Réau, Louis, *L'Europe française au siècle des lumières* (Paris, 1951)

Rexheuser, Rex (ed.), *Die Personalunionen von Sachsen–Polen 1697–1763 und Hannover–England 1714–1837: ein Vergleich* (Wiesbaden, 2005)

Rostworowski, Emanuel, 'War and society in the noble Republic of Poland–Lithuania in the eighteenth century', in Gunther E. Rothenberg, Béla K. Király and Peter F. Sugar (eds), *East Central European Society and War in the Pre-Revolutionary Eighteenth Century* (New York, 1982)

Rulhière, Claude, *Histoire de l'anarchie de Pologne et du démembrement de cette république*, vol. 1 (Paris, 1807)

Sachsen und Polen zwischen 1697 und 1765. Beiträge der wissenschaftlichen Konferenz vom 26. bis 28. Juni 1997 in Dresden, Saxonia. Schriftenreihe des Vereins für sächsische Landesgeschichte e.V., vols 4–5 (Dresden, 1998)

Salvadori, Philippe, *La Chasse sous l'ancien régime* (Paris, 1996)

Šapoka, Mindaugas, *Warfare, Loyalty and Rebellion: The Grand Duchy of Lithuania and the Great Northern War, 1709–1717* (London, 2017)

Schmidt, Werner and Dirk Syndram (eds), *Unter einer Krone. Kunst und Kultur der sächsisch–polnischen Union* (Leipzig, 1997)

Schnitzer, Claudia and Daniela Günther (eds), *Constellatio Felix: Die Planetenfeste Augusts des Starken anlässlich der Vermählung seines Sohnes Friedrich August mit der Kaisertochter Maria Josepha 1719 in Dresden* (Dresden, 2014)

Schuster, O. and F. A. Francke, *Geschichte der sächsischen Armee von deren Errichtung bis auf die neueste Zeit*, vol. 1 (Leipzig, 1885)

Shirokorad, B., *Severnie voiny Rossii* (Moscow, 2001)

Sjöström, Oskar, *Fraustadt 1706. Ett fält färgat rött* (Lund, 2009)

Skinner, Barbara, *The Western Front of the Eastern Church: Uniate and Orthodox Conflict in 18th-century Poland, Ukraine, Belarus, and Russia* (DeKalb, 2009)

Skrzypietz, Aleksandra, *Jakub Sobieski* (Poznań, 2015)

Skworoda, Pawel, *Wojny Rzeczypospolitej Obojga Narodów ze Szwecją* (Warsaw, 2007)

Solov'ev, S. M., *Istoriia Rossii s drevneishikh vremen*, vol. 7 (Moscow, 1962)

Sponsel, Jean Louis, *Der Zwinger, die Hoffeste und die Schloßbaupläne zu Dresden* (Dresden, 1924, reprint Dresden 2019)

Staszewski, Jacek, *August II. Kurfürst von Sachsen und König von Polen. Eine Biographie* (Berlin, 1996)

— *August II Mocny* (Warsaw, 1998)

— 'Elekcja 1697 roku', *Acta Universitatis Nicolai Copernici, Historia*, XXVIII (Torun, 1993)

— *O Miesce w Europie. Stosunki Polski i Saksonii z Francją na przełomie XVII i XVIII wieku* (Warsaw, 1973)

— *Die Polen in Dresden des 18. Jahrhunderts* (Osnabrück, 2019)

Stevens, Carol B., *Russia's Wars of Emergence 1460–1730* (Harlow, 2007)

Stone, Daniel, *The Polish–Lithuanian Commonwealth* (Seattle and London, 2001)

Svensson, Sven, 'Tsar Peters motiv för kriget mot Sverige', *Historisk Tidskrift*, 51 (1931)

Syndram, Dirk and Martina Minning (eds), *Die kurfürstlich–sächsische Kunstkammer in Dresden: Geschichte einer Sammlung* (Dresden, 2012)

Syndram, Dirk, *Das Schloss zu Dresden: von der Residenz zum Museum* (Munich, 2001)

Tarlé, Evguéni [*sic*], *La guerre du Nord et l'invasion suédoise en Russie*, 2 vols (Moscow, 1966)

Tazbir, Janusz, *Kultura szlachecka w Polsce. Rozkwit – Upadek – Relikty* (Warsaw, 1978)

— 'Recherches sur la conscience nationale en Pologne au XVIᵉ' et XVIIᵉ' siècle', *Acta Poloniae Historica*, 14 (1966)

Tel'pukhovskii, B. S., *Severnaia voina 1700–1721* (Moscow, 1946)

Teter, Magda, *Jews and Heretics in Poland: A Beleaguered Church in the Post-Reformation Era* (Cambridge, 2006)

Tollet, Daniel, *Histoire des Juifs en Pologne du XVIᵉ siècle à nos jours* (Paris, 1992)

Vozgrin, V. E., *Rossiia i evropeiskie strany v gody severnoi voiny: istoriia diplomaticheskikh otnoshenii v 1697–1710 gg.* (Leningrad, 1986)

Wagner, Marek, *Bitwa pod Kliszowem 19 lipca 1702 roku* (Oświęcim, 2003)

Watanabe-O'Kelly, Helen, *Court Culture in Dresden. From Renaissance to Baroque* (Basingstoke, 2003)

— 'Festival books in Europe from Renaissance to rococo', *The Seventeenth Century*, 3, 3 (1988)

— 'Joseph und seine Brüder: Johann Georg II und seine Feste zwischen 1660 und 1679', in *Zur Festkultur des Dresdner Hofes* [no editor listed], *Dresdner Hefte*, 8, 1 (1990)

Further Reading

Watzdorf, Erna von, *Johann Melchior Dinglinger: Der Goldschmied des Deutschen Barock*, 2 vols (Berlin, 1962)

Weintraub, Wiktor, 'Tolerance and intolerance in Old Poland', *Canadian Slavonic Papers*, 13, 1 (Spring 1971)

Wimmer, Jan, *Polska–Szwecja. Konflikty zbrojne w XVI–XVIII wieku* (Oświęcim, 2019)

— *Wojsko Rzeczpospolitej w dobie wojny północnej (1700–1717)* (Warsaw, 1956)

Wolke, Lars Ericson, *Sjöslag och rysshärjningar Kampen om Östersjön under stora nordiska kriget 1700–1721* (Stockholm, 2012)

Wünsch, Thomas, *Der weiße Adler. Die Geschichte Polens vom 10. Jahrhundert bis heute* (Wiesbaden, 2021)

Zernack, Klaus, *Polen und Russland. Zwei Wege in der europäischen Geschichte* (Berlin, 1994)

Ziekursch, Johannes, 'August der Starke und die katholische Kirche in den Jahren 1697–1720', *Zeitschrift für Kirchengeschichte*, 24, 1 (1903)

Notes

Introduction

1 Before we start, a note on names is needed: the main actor in what follows was born on 12 May 1670 and christened Frederick Augustus. On 27 April 1694 he succeeded his elder brother as Elector of Saxony and was titled Frederick Augustus I. In June 1697 he was elected King of Poland, taking the title Augustus II. To posterity he became better known as 'Augustus the Strong', although this sobriquet was a posthumous award. For the sake of clarity and simplicity, I shall refer to him throughout as 'Augustus'.

2 The Wettins could date their genealogy with confidence to the tenth century, making them – in English parlance – 'pre-Conquest', and so could be as proud as the Thornes of Ullathorne. Heinrich Wettin had been invested with the margraviate of Meissen by Emperor Henry IV in 1089 – Reiner Gross, *Die Wettiner* (Stuttgart, 2007), p. 23; Jutta Bäumel, 'Der Kurhut und das sächsische Kurschwert', in Werner Schmidt and Dirk Syndram (eds), *Unter einer Krone. Kunst und Kultur der sächsisch–polnischen Union* (Leipzig, 1997), p. 374.

3 József Andrzej Gierowski, *Rzeczpospolita w dobie złotej wolności (1648–1763)* (Krakow, 2001), p. 338; Anon., 'Die letzten Tage Augusts des Starken', *Archiv für Sächsische Geschichte*, 9 (1871), p. 335. This reproduces in full a document entitled '*Das Ableben Ihrer Königl. Maj. in Pohlen und Churf. Durchl. Zu Sachsen, Herrn Augusts 1733*'.

4 See below, pp 146–7.

5 The full form of the country which Augustus ruled from 1697 until his death in 1733 was 'The Polish–Lithuanian Commonwealth'. Apart from being unacceptably cumbersome, it does not easily allow the use of an appropriate adjective or other cognates. I shall refer to it simply as 'Poland', distinguishing between Poland and Lithuania when needed. As Richard Butterwick has informed me (in a private communication), the title was never definitively fixed, the full version was a construction of historians and the simple form 'Poland' was used by contemporaries.

6 https://web.archive.org/web/20170303190424/http://www.marx2mao.com/M&E/EBLB52.html

Notes

7 T. C. W. Blanning, *The Culture of Power and the Power of Culture: Old Regime Europe 1660–1789* (Oxford, 2002), pp. 5–7.

8 Christophe Pincemaille, 'La guerre de Hollande dans le programme iconographique de la grande galerie de Versailles', *Histoire économie et société*, 4, 3 (1985), p. 313; Édouard Pommier, 'Versailles, l'image du souverain', in Pierre Nora (ed.), *Les Lieux de mémoire*, 7 vols (Paris, 1984), vol. 2, p. 208.

9 I referred to this anecdote in my history of Europe in the period – *The Pursuit of Glory: Europe 1648–1815* (London, 2007), p. 430, but have mislaid the source. It is more than likely, of course, that Parisian cuisine was the cause.

10 Philip Mansel, *King of the World: The Life of Louis XIV* (London, 2019), p. 351.

11 Philippe Salvadori, *La Chasse sous l'ancien régime* (Paris, 1996), p. 193.

12 Ibid., p. 201.

13 Ibid., p. 213.

14 Dominique Bouhours, *Entretiens d'Ariste et d'Eugène* (Paris, 1671), p. 38. This is available online at https://gallica.bnf.fr/ark:/12148/bpt6k122907n.texteImage#. Extracts are reprinted in Ruth Florack, *Tiefsinnige Deutsche, frivole Franzosen. Nationale Stereotype in deutscher und französischer Literatur* (Stuttgart and Weimar, 2001), pp. 164ff. although she appears to be using a later edition.

15 Louis Réau, *L'Europe française au siècle des lumières* (Paris, 1951), p. 17.

16 Alain Rey, 'Linguistic absolutism', in Denis Hollier (ed.), *A New History of French Literature* (Cambridge, Mass., and London, 1989), p. 12. It has also been suggested that a contributory reason was the inability of the French negotiator, the maréchal de Villars, to understand Latin: André Corvisier, *Arts et sociétés dans l'Europe du XVIIIe siècle* (Paris, 1978), p. 21.

17 Two influential examples are Norbert Elias, *The Court Society* (Oxford, 1983) and Peter Burke, *The Fabrication of Louis XIV* (New Haven and London, 1992). See also the discussion in R. L. M. Morris, *Court Festivals of the Holy Roman Empire, 1555–1619* (Turnhout, 2020), pp. 29–30.

18 John Adamson, 'The making of the Ancien Régime court 1500–1700', in John Adamson, *The Princely Courts of Europe: Ritual, Politics and Culture under the Ancien Régime 1500–1750* (London, 1999), p. 8. This brilliant essay is by far the best analysis of the old-regime courts.

19 Marie-Christine Moine, *Les Fêtes à la cour du roi soleil 1653–1715* (Paris, 1984), p. 42.

20 William Ritchey Newton, *L'Espace du roi. La cour de France au château de Versailles 1682–1789* (Paris, 2000), p. 19.

21 Shakespeare, *The Merchant of Venice*, Act. I, scene 1.

22 Cesare de Seta, 'Grand tour: the lure of Italy in the eighteenth century', in Andrew Wilton and Ilaria Bignamini (eds), *Grand Tour: The Lure of Italy in the*

Eighteenth Century (London, 1996), p. 13. 'Grand tour' was first used in Richard Lassels's *Voyage or Compleat Journey through Italy* (1670).

23 James Boswell, *The Life of Samuel Johnson*, ed. R. W. Chapman and J. D. Fleeman, new edn (Oxford, 1976), entry for 11 April 1776. Johnson himself never did have the means to visit Italy, his foreign travels being confined to France and Scotland.

24 T. C. W. Blanning, 'The Grand Tour and the reception of neo-classicism in Great Britain in the eighteenth century', in Werner Paravicini and Rainer Babel (eds), *Grand Tour: Adeliges Reisen und Europäische Kultur vom 14. bis zum 18. Jahrhundert, Francia*, Beiheft, vol. 60 (2005), https://perspectivia.net/receive/ploneimport_mods_00009716

25 Ellis Dye, 'Goethe and individuation', in Larry H. Peer and Christopher R. Clason (eds), *Romantic Rapports: New Essays in Romanticism Across the Disciplines* (Rochester, NY, 2017), p. 160.

Chapter 1: The Gilded Cage

1 Paul Haake, *August der Starke* (Berlin and Leipzig, 1927), p. 18.

2 Paul Haake, 'Die Jugenderinnerungen König Augusts des Starken', *Historische Vierteljahrschrift*, 3 (1900), pp. 397–8. Augustus seems to have been right, at least about his brother's physical weakness, as the tutor accompanying him on his grand tour in 1685 was told that 'in view of his rather weak constitution', special attention should be paid to his health – Katrin Keller (ed.), *'Mein Herr befindet sich gottlob gesund und wohl': Sächsische Prinzen auf Reisen* (Leipzig, 1994), p. 22.

3 Friedrich August Freiherr von O'Byrn, 'Christian, Herzog zu Sachsen-Weissenfels, kursächsischer Generalfeldmarschalllieutenant', *Archiv für sächsische Geschichte*, Neue Folge, 6 (1880), p. 85.

4 Theodor Flathe, *Geschichte des Kurstaates und Königreiches Sachsen*, vol. 2: *Von der Mitte des sechszehnten bis zu Anfang des neunzehnten Jahrhunderts* (Gotha, 1870), p. 265.

5 Detlef Döring, 'Johann Georg III. 1680–1691 und Johann Georg IV. 1691–1694', in Frank-Lothar Kroll (ed), *Die Herrscher Sachsen. Markgrafen, Kurfürsten, Könige 1989–1918* (Munich, 2004), p. 169.

6 Theodor Flathe, 'Johann Georg IV', *Allgemeine Deutsche Biographie*, vol. 14 (Leipzig, 1881), p. 385.

7 Eduard Vehse, *Geschichte der Höfe des Hauses Sachsen*, vol. 4 (Hamburg, 1854), p. 193.

Notes

8 Quoted in Tony Sharp, *Pleasure and Ambition: The Life, Loves and Wars of Augustus the Strong 1670–1707* (London and New York, 2001), p. 64.

9 K. G. Helbig, 'Die Gräfin von Rochlitz. Nach archivalischen Nachrichten', *Zeitschrift für deutsche Culturgeschichte*, Neue Folge, II (1873), p. 193.

10 Friedrich Förster, *Friedrich August II. der Starke, Kurfürst von Sachsen und König von Polen, geschildert als Regent und Mensch* (Potsdam, 1839), p. 7.

11 Helbig, 'Die Gräfin von Rochlitz', p. 195. Helbig worked through the previously unexploited papers of Magdalena's private secretary, Christoph Heinrich Engelschall, and concluded that Johann Georg was unaware of the corruption of his mistress and her mother. See also Hans-Joachim Böttcher, *Johann Georg IV. Von Sachsen und Magdalena Sibylla von Neitschütz* (Dresden, 2014), p. 75.

12 Sharp, *Pleasure and Ambition*, p. 54.

13 This is not to be taken literally: a 'ton of gold' was another way of saying '100,000 talers'. It is still a very large fortune.

14 Vehse, *Geschichte der Höfe des Hauses Sachsen*, vol. 4, p. 208.

15 Vehse – ibid., p. 209 – maintained that it was popular pressure that made Augustus charge her with witchcraft, but Vehse was not entirely reliable and I know of no corroboration.

16 Cornelius Gurlitt, *August der Starke. Ein Fürstenleben aus der Zeit des deutschen Barock*, 2nd edn, 2 vols (Dresden, 1924), vol. 1, p. 44; Böttcher, *Johann Georg IV. Von Sachsen*, p. 175.

17 C. C. C. Gretschel, *Geschichte des sächsischen Volkes und Staates*, vol. 2 (Leipzig, 1847), p. 465.

18 Helbig, 'Die Gräfin von Rochlitz', p. 195.

19 Theodor Flathe, 'Johann Georg III., Kurfürst von Sachsen', *Allgemeine Deutsche Biographie*, vol. 14 (1881), p. 383.

20 Anglophone sources usually give the figure as 9,000; Germans prefer 10,000 or 10,500 or even 11,000 – the actual figure was 10,379 (3,222 cavalry and 7,157 infantry) – O. Schuster and F. A. Francke, *Geschichte der sächsischen Armee von deren Errichtung bis auf die neueste Zeit*, vol. 1 (Leipzig, 1885) p. 99.

21 Flathe, 'Johann Georg III', p. 383.

22 Schuster and Francke, *Geschichte der sächsischen Armee*, p. 108.

23 John P. Spielman, *Leopold I of Austria* (London, 1977), p. 107; Frank-Lothar Kroll and Hendrik Thoss (eds), *Zwei Staaten, eine Krone. Die polnisch–sächsische Union 1697–1763* (Berlin, 2016), p. 60 n. 5.

24 Holger Schuckelt, 'Die Rolle Sachsens in den Türkenkriegen des 16. und 17. Jahrhunderts', in Claudia Schnitzer and Holger Schuckelt (eds.), *Im Lichte des Halbmonds: das Abendland und der türkische Orient* (Dresden, 1995), p. 173.

25 Ibid., pp. 100–101.

26 The Augustinian monk Abraham a Sancta Clara maintained that Leopold had defeated all his enemies on his knees, for it was the power of prayer which brought victory – Anna Coreth, *Pietas Austriaca. Ursprung und Entwicklung barocker Frömmigkeit in Österreich* (Munich, 1959), p. 15 n. 52.

27 Charles Ingrao, *The Habsburg Monarchy 1618–1815*, 2nd edn (Cambridge, 2000), p. 109.

28 Coreth, *Pietas Austriaca*, p. 56.

29 R. G. Helbig, 'Kurfürst Johann Georg der Dritte in seinen Beziehungen zum Kaiser und zum Reich', *Archiv für sächsische Geschichte*, 9 (1870–71), p. 106.

30 Leopold's failure to remove his hat when greeting the Polish contingent was also regarded as marking a serious lack of respect – Daniel Stone, *The Polish–Lithuanian Commonwealth* (Seattle and London, 2001), p. 209.

31 Gierowski, *Rzeczpospolita w dobie złotej wolnośći*, pp. 161–2. As Gierowski reasonably complains, Austrian and German historians have always talked down the importance of the Polish contribution in general and of Sobieski in particular, although it might be objected that Polish historians have often been guilty of the opposite. According to Mariusz Markiewicz, the disparaging began at once with Austrian diplomats – *Historia Polski 1492–1795* (Kraków, 2005), p. 584.

32 Klaus-Peter Matschke, *Das Kreuz und der Halbmond: die Geschichte der Türkenkriege* (Düsseldorf, 2004), p. 375.

33 Schuster and Francke, *Geschichte der sächsischen Armee*, p. 108.

34 Schuckelt, 'Die Rolle Sachsens in den Türkenkriegen', p. 177. See also below, p. 287–8.

35 Constantin von Wurzbach, *Biographisches Lexikon des Kaiserthums Oesterreich*, vol. 15 (Vienna, 1923), p. 422.

36 For a high-quality reproduction see https://www.museodelprado.es/en/the-collection/art-work/louis-xiv-of-france/eb9b8bf3-4e26-4539-aff5-e368222c3f98

37 Marie-Claude Canova-Green, 'Warrior king or king of war? Louis XIII's entries into his *Bonnes Villes* (1620–1629)', https://research.gold.ac.uk/id/eprint/16144/. On the importance attached to the personal leadership of French kings see Joël Cornette, *Le Roi de guerre. Essai sur la souveraineté dans la France du Grand Siècle* (Paris, 1993), pp. 177–8.

38 Jacek Staszewski, *August II Mocny* (Warsaw, 1998), p. 26.

39 Franz Otto Stichart, *Das Königreich Sachsen und seine Fürsten* (Leipzig 1854), p. 222.

40 This account is taken from an article by Michael Strich, first published in *Historische Zeitschrift* in 1928, vol. 138 – 'Der Streit zwischen Kursachsen und Mantua um die erste Primadonna in Deutschland, nach archivalischen Quellen aus Dresden und München'. In an apologetic note, the editors expressed the hope that 'the serious readers' of the journal would have sufficient 'historical humour' to give the article a friendly reception. It was at their wish that the author had dispensed with footnotes, although the secure archival foundations of his work are clear. Also helpful is a more recent article by Michael Walter, 'Der Fall Salicola oder Die Sängerin als symbolisches Kapital', *LiThes: Literatur- und Theatersoziologie*, 4 (2011), 6, http://lithes.uni-graz.at/lithes/beitraege11_06/michael_walter_fall_salicola.pdf which makes a number of corrections of Strich's article, especially relating to dating. 'Margarita' has also been spelled 'Margherita' and 'Margerita'.

41 Flathe, *Geschichte des Kurstaates und Königreiches Sachsen*, vol. 2, p. 261. It is recorded that the closing years of the life of the architect Wolf Caspar von Klengel (who designed the palace in the Grand Garden in Dresden) were embittered by the loss of a son and son-in-law serving in the Peloponnese – Günter Passavant, *Wolf Caspar von Klengel (Dresden 1630–1691). Reisen – Skizzen – Baukünstlerische Tätigkeit* (Munich and Berlin, 2001), p. 58.

42 Walter, 'Der Fall Salicola', p. 34.

43 Several websites state this without equivocation, but neither *Sächsische Biografie* nor *Deutsche Biografie* record her – or anyone else – as being Fürstenhoff's mother.

44 Hermann Heckmann, 'Johann Georg Maximilian von Fürstenhoff', in *Sächsische Biografie*, http://www.isgv.de/saebi/

45 Jacek Staszewski, *Die Polen in Dresden des 18. Jahrhunderts* (Osnabrück, 2019), p. 52. The figure of 354 was invented by the imaginative Wilhelmine of Bayreuth, sister of Frederick the Great – *Memoiren der Markgräfin Wilhelmine von Bayreuth Schwester Friedrichs des Großen*, vol. 1 (Leipzig, 1926), p. 81. This is the confirmed score; it is possible, of course, that there were others of which contemporaries (and he himself) were unaware.

46 Katya Doubek, *August der Starke* (Hamburg, 2007), loc. 65.

47 Karl Czok, *August der Starke und Kursachsen* (Leipzig, 1987), p. 12.

48 Gross, *Die Wettiner*, p. 168.

49 Regrettably, the *Oxford English Dictionary* now also lists the latter, improper, sense, although two of the only three examples are from the *Texas Monthly* and *The Guardian*, neither of which can be viewed as authoritative.

50 Keller (ed.), *'Mein Herr befindet sich gottlob gesund und wohl'*, pp. 21–4.

51 Ibid., pp. 28–152.

52 Ibid., p. 186.

53 Friedrich August Freiherr O'Byrn, 'Ein sächsischer Prinz auf Reisen', *Archiv für sächsische Geschichte*, N.S., 6 (1880), p. 325.

54 Mansel, *King of the World*, p. 201. The best visual representation of Versailles is to be found in the sumptuously illustrated exhibition catalogue *Visitors to Versailles from Louis XIV to the French Revolution*, ed. Daniëlle Kisluk and Bertrand Rondot (New Haven and London, 2018), *passim*.

55 O'Byrn, 'Ein sächsischer Prinz auf Reisen', pp. 298, 300.

56 Eduard Bodemann (ed.), *Aus den Briefen der Herzogin Elisabeth Charlotte von Orléans an die Kurfürstin Sophie von Hannover* (Hanover, 1891), p. 85; also quoted in Haake, 'Die Jugenderinnerungen König Augusts des Starken', p. 4.

57 Keller (ed.), *Sächsische Prinzen auf Reisen*, p. 283.

58 Quoted in Katrin Keller, 'Friedrich August von Sachsen als Herrscher, Mann und Mythos. Ein Versuch über den Beinamen "der Starke"', in Wolfgang Schmale (ed.), *Mannbilder. Ein Lese- und Quellenbuch zur historischen Männerforschung* (Berlin, 1998), p. 111.

59 Staszewski, *August II Mocny*, p. 22.

60 The progress of the illness can be followed in detail in Keller (ed.), *Sächsische Prinzen auf Reisen*, pp. 235–49.

61 Karl Ludwig von Pöllnitz, *The Amorous Adventures of Augustus of Saxony containing several Transactions of his Life not mentioned in any other History Together with Diverting Remarks of the ladies of the Several Countries thro' which he travell'd* (London, 1750, reprinted 1929), pp. 22–3. It was first published in 1734, the year after death had safely disqualified its victim from seeking retribution. The original was published in 1734 in German as *Das galante Sachsen* and in French as *La Saxe Galante*, with the places of publication listed as Frankfurt am Main and Amsterdam respectively. 'Career' makes no sense – in the French edition it appears as '*carriere*' and in the German as '*Schrancken*' [barriers]. It is likely that '*carriere*' is a misprint of '*barriere*' and that what is meant is the untranslatable Spanish word '*callejón*', the area where the bullfighters prepare and take refuge.

62 Staszewski, *August II Mocny*, p. 21.

63 The document – *Eigenhändige Aufzeichnungen König Augusts II. von Polen zu seiner Jugendgeschichte, etwa 1680 bis 1690* – is reprinted in full in Keller (ed.) *Sächsische Prinzen auf Reisen*, pp. 388–9.

64 Ibid., p. 388.

65 O'Byrn, 'Ein sächsischer Prinz auf Reisen', p. 321.

66 David Fassmann, *Des glorwürdigsten Fürsten und Herrn, Herrn Friedrich Augusti, des Großen, Königs in Pohlen und Churfürstens zu Sachsen* (Leipzig, 1734), p. 18.

67 Ibid.

68 Staszewski, *August II Mocny*, p. 24.

69 Ibid., p. 26.

70 Keller (ed.), *Sächsische Prinzen auf Reisen*, p. 368.

71 O'Byrn, 'Ein sächsischer Prinz auf Reisen', p. 323.

72 Keller (ed.), *Sächsische Prinzen auf Reisen*, p. 364.

73 Volker Bauer, *Die höfische Gesellschaft in Deutschland von der Mitte des 17. bis zum Ausgang des 18. Jahrhunderts. Versuch einer Typologie* (Tübingen, 1993), p. 4.

74 Adamson, *The Princely Courts of Europe*, p. 315 n. 24.

75 Ibid., p. 12; Jeroen Duindam, *Vienna and Versailles: The Courts of Europe's Dynastic Rivals, 1550–1780* (Cambridge, 2003), pp. 86–9.

76 Adamson, *The Princely Courts of Europe*, p. 14.

77 Bodemann (ed.), *Aus den Briefen der Herzogin Elisabeth Charlotte von Orléans*, p. 11.

78 Ibid., p. 208.

79 Helen Watanabe-O'Kelly, 'Joseph und seine Brüder: Johann Georg II. und seine Feste zwischen 1660 und 1679', in *Zur Festkultur des Dresdner Hofes* (no editor listed), *Dresdner Hefte*, 8, 1 (1990), p. 29.

80 https://www.chateauversailles.fr/decouvrir/histoire/grandes-dates/fetes-plaisirs-ile-enchantee

81 The full text is available online at https://gallica.bnf.fr/ark:/12148/btv1b8 626216h/f11.image.r=.langEN

82 *The Pleasures of the Enchanted Island* was influenced by a festival staged at Munich in 1662 – Helen Watanabe-O'Kelly, 'Festival books in Europe from Renaissance to rococo', *The Seventeenth Century*, 3, 3 (1988), p. 190.

83 Christian Horn, *Der aufgeführte Staat. Zur Theatralität höfischer Repräsentation unter Kurfürst Johann Georg II. von Sachsen* (Tübingen and Basel, 2004), p. 75. When this type of festivity was imported to France, it was known as a 'Hôtelière allemande' – Hermann Bauer, *Barock. Kunst einer Epoche* (Berlin, 1992), p. 133.

84 Helen Watanabe-O'Kelly, *Court Culture in Dresden: From Renaissance to Baroque* (Basingstoke, 2003), p. 131.

85 Watanabe-O'Kelly, 'Festival books in Europe', p. 188.

86 Dirk Syndram, *Das Schloss Zu Dresden: von der Residenz zum Museum* (Munich, 2001), p. 39.

87 Steffen Delang, 'Das Dresdener Schloss in der zweiten Hälfte des 17. Jahrhunderts', in *Das Dresdener Schloss. Monument sächsischer Geschichte und Kultur* (Dresden, 1989), p. 68.

88 Syndram, *Das Schloss Zu Dresden*, p. 44.

89 Kathrin Reeckmann, *Anfänge der Barockarchitektur in Sachsen. Johann Georg Starcke und seine Zeit* (Cologne, Weimar and Vienna, 2000), p. 1. Also up to date was the palace built by Starcke in the 'Grand Garden' (ibid., ch. 4), but it was the Electoral Palace which set the tone for both a domestic and international audience.

90 Elias, *The Court Society*, p. 81.

91 Ulli Arnold, *Die Juwelen Augusts des Starken* (Munich and Berlin, 2001), *passim*. See also below pp. 272–3

92 Dirk Syndram, ' "Shopping à Paris" à la demande d'Auguste le Fort', in Stéphane Castelluccio (ed.), *Le Commerce du luxe à Paris au XVIIe et XVIIIe siècles* (Bern etc., 2009), p. 268.

93 Mansel, *King of the World*, p. 233. 'To say that Louis XIV had a passionate love of diamonds is a true understatement' – Michèle Bimbenet-Privat, 'Les pierreries de Louis XIV objets de collection et instruments politiques', in Bernard Barbiche and Yves-Marie Bercé (eds), *Études sur l'ancienne France offertes en homage à Michael Antoine* (Paris, 2003), p. 81.

94 Karl Czok, 'Die Personalunion als Problem des Monarchen', in Karl Czok and Volker Titel (eds.), *Leipzig und Sachsen. Beiträge zur Stadt- und Landesgeschichte vom 15.–20. Jahrhundert. Siegfried Hoyer zum 70. Geburtstag* (Beucha, 2000), p. 48; Haake, 'Die Jugenderinnerungen König Augusts des Starken', p. 398.

95 See above, pp. 23–4

Chapter 2: The Polish Election

1 Paul Haake, 'Die Türkenfeldzüge Augusts des Starken 1695 und 1696', *Neues Archiv für Sächsische Geschichte und Altertumskunde*, 24 (1903), p. 135.

2 Oswald Redlich, *Österreichs Großmachtbildung in der Zeit Kaiser Leopolds I.* (Gotha, 1921), p. 581.

3 Staszewski, *August II Mocny*, p. 40.

4 Haake, 'Die Türkenfeldzüge Augusts des Starken', p. 137.

5 Lothar Höbelt, 'From Slankamen to Zenta: The Austrian war effort in the east in the 1680s and 1690s', in Colin Heywood and Ivan Parvev (eds.), *The Treaties of Carlowitz (1699): Antecedents, Course and Consequences. The Ottoman Empire and Its Heritage* (Leiden, 2020), p. 154. The fullest accounts are to be found in ibid., *passim*; Redlich, *Österreichs Großmachtbildung*, pp. 581–96; Schuster and Francke, *Geschichte der sächsischen Armee*, pp. 113–34; and Staszewski, *August II Mocny*, pp. 28–43. It is difficult to track the progress of the imperial army, or lack of it, because almost every place name has

several different spellings. In an attempt to introduce some sort of clarity, I have included the modern accepted version in brackets after each contemporary reference.

6 Höbelt, 'From Slankamen to Zenta', pp. 161, 176.

7 Ivan Parvev, *Habsburgs and Ottomans Between Vienna and Belgrade (1683–1739)* (Boulder, 1995), p. 123.

8 C. von Duncker, 'Friedrich Graf von Veterani', *Allgemeine Deutsche Biographie*, vol. 39 (Leipzig, 1895), pp. 657–8. It is stated that this article is based on the Austrian Military Archives (Kriegsarchiv).

9 Onno Klopp, *Das Jahr 1683 und der folgende große Türkenkrieg bis zum Frieden von Carlowitz* (Graz, 1882), p. 500.

10 'The best and most experienced commander left in Hungary' – Spielman, *Leopold I of Austria*, p. 163.

11 Redlich, *Österreichs Großmachtbildung*, p. 585.

12 Max von Turek, 'Türkenkriege der Österreicher', in Bernhard von Poten (ed.), *Handwörterbuch der gesamten Militärwissenschaften*, vol. 9 (Leipzig, 1880), p. 196.

13 Schuster and Francke, *Geschichte der sächsischen Armee*, p. 131.

14 Augustus was a useful whipping boy because his failure highlighted the brilliant success of Prince Eugene, who succeeded him. The most severe of his Austrian critics was Alfred Ritter von Arneth in his biography of Prince Eugene – Alfred Ritter von Arneth, *Prinz Eugen von Savoyen*, vol. 1: *1663–1707* (Vienna, 1864), pp. 93–5.

15 Staszewski, *August II Mocny*, p. 42; Haake, 'Die Türkenfeldzüge Augusts des Starken', p. 153.

16 Redlich, *Österreichs Großmachtbildung*, p. 583. See also Spielman, *Leopold I of Austria*, p. 163.

17 Redlich, *Österreichs Großmachtbildung*, pp. 583–4.

18 Max Braubach, *Prinz Eugen von Savoyen: Eine Biographie*, vol. 1 (Munich, 1963), p. 221.

19 H. Manners Sutton (ed.), *The Lexington Papers: Or, Some Account of the Courts of London and Vienna; at the Conclusion of the Seventeenth Century* (London, 1851), p. 208. Spielman commented that Augustus and Caprara spent more time fighting each other than the Ottomans – Spielman, *Leopold I of Austria*, p. 163.

20 Braubach, *Prinz Eugen von Savoyen*, vol. 1, p. 419 n. 6.

21 Arneth, *Prinz Eugen von Savoyen*, vol. 1, p. 95 and note 4 on p. 458.

22 Hans Uebersberger, *Russlands Orientpolitik in den letzten zwei Jahrhunderten*, vol. 1: *Bis zum Frieden von Jassy* (Stuttgart, 1913), p. 54. On the Duc de Croÿ's fiasco at the Battle of Narva in Estonia see below pp. 119–20.

23   Braubach, *Prinz Eugen von Savoyen*, vol. 1, p. 244.

24   Ibid., p. 245.

25   Jean Nouzille, 'La campagne décisive du Prince Eugène en Hongrie (1697)', *Dix-septième siècle*, 229 (2005), p. 632.

26   Derek McKay, *Prince Eugene of Savoy* (London, 1977), p. 45.

27   Nouzille, 'La campagne décisive du Prince Eugène en Hongrie', p. 636. Michael Hochedlinger, *Austria's Wars of Emergence: War, State and Society in the Habsburg Monarchy 1683–1797* (London, 2003), p. 165 gives the figure of 25,000 dead; McKay's estimate is 30,000 – *Prince Eugene of Savoy*, p. 45.

28   Bernhard Erdmannsdörffer, *Deutsche Geschichte vom Westfälischen Frieden bis zum Regierungsantritt Friedrichs des Großen 1648–1740*, 2 vols (Berlin, 1892–3), vol. 2, p. 99.

29   Arneth, *Prinz Eugen von Savoyen*, vol. 1, p. 105.

30   'Zenta finished what Vienna had begun' – Władysław Konopczyński, *Polska a Turcja 1683–1792* (Kraków and Warsaw, 2013; reprint of the original 1936 edition), p. 22.

31   Réau, *L'Europe française au siècle des lumières*, p. 290.

32   The higher figure is cited by Förster, *Friedrich August II. der Starke*, p. 57, the lower in Schuster and Francke, *Geschichte der sächsischen Armee*, p. 134.

33   Schuster and Francke, *Geschichte der sächsischen Armee*, p. 134. It might be noted that not even Prince Eugene had succeeded in conquering Temesvár – that had to wait until 1716 – Hochedlinger, *Austria's Wars of Emergence*, p. 165.

34   Paweł Jaskanis, 'Vorwort', in Paweł Jaskanis and Stella Rollig (eds), *Jan III. Sobieski. Ein polnischer König in Wien* (Munich, 2017), p. 8. See also, in the same volume, Martina Thomsen, 'Jan II. Sobieski und Prinz Eugen von Savoyen. Selbstinszenierung, Glorifizierung und Kommemoration zweier Türken-sieger', pp. 45–9. This is the lavishly illustrated catalogue of an exhibition staged in the Winter Palace of the Belvedere in Vienna in 2017.

35   Gierowski, *Rzeczpospolita w dobie złotej wolnośći*, pp. 171–2. There is a helpful map on p. 168.

36   Ibid., pp. 180–81.

37   Urszula Augustyniak, *Historia Polski 1572–1795* (Warsaw, 2008), pp. 728, 737–9; Jacek Burdowicz-Nowicki, *Piotr I, August II i Rzeczpospolita 1697–1706* (Kraków, 2010), p. 115; Andrzej Sulima Kamiński, *Republic vs. Autocracy. Poland–Lithuania and Russia 1686–1697* (Cambridge, Mass., 1993), p. 12.

38   Markiewicz, *Historia Polski 1492–1795*, p. 586.

39   Gierowski, *Rzeczpospolita w dobie złotej wolnośći*, p. 176.

40   Bernard O'Connor, *The history of Poland in several letters to persons of quality, giving an account of the antient and present state of that kingdom, historical,*

geographical, physical, political and ecclesiastical, vol. 2 (London, 1698), p. 188. For confirmation that Jakub was not conventionally handsome see the portrait by Henri Gascard in the Wilanów Palace Museum, also available online at https:// commons.wikimedia.org/wiki/File:Gascar_Jakub_Ludwik_Sobieski.jpg and which – like most royal portraits – is probably flattering.

41 Augustyniak, *Historia Polski 1572–1795*, p. 739.

42 Mark 6:14–29; *Polski Słownik Biograficzny*, also available online at https://bur. ur.edu.pl/ipsb-internetowy-polski-slownik-biograficzny, although for unexplained reasons, this entry is not available in the online edition.

43 Gierowski, *Rzeczpospolita w dobie złotej wolnośći*, p. 139.

44 Ibid., pp. 183–4.

45 Karl Theodor von Heigel, 'Die Beziehungen des Kurfürsten Max Emanuel von Bayern zu Polen 1694 bis 1697', *Sitzungsberichte der philosophisch-philologischen und historischen Classe der k.b. Akademie der Wissenschaften zu München* (1881), p. 198.

46 Andrzej Link-Lenczowski, *Rzeczpospolita na Rozdrożu 1696–1736* (Kraków, 1994), p. 1.

47 Kazimierz Jarochowski, *Dzieje panowania Augusta II od śmierci Jana III do chwili wstąpienia Karola XII na ziemie Polska* (Posnań,1856), pp. 6–8. Jarochowski's account was based mainly on the (Latin) account of Andrzej Chryzostom Załuski, the Bishop of Płock. He was present at Warsaw Castle, together with Radziejowski, Marysieńka and the two younger Sobieski sons, and so was an eyewitness to the events he recorded.

48 Ibid., p. 39.

49 Aleksandra Skrzypietz, *Jakub Sobieski* (Poznań, 2015), loc. 3975–6.

50 Ibid., loc. 3696; Heigel, 'Die Beziehungen des Kurfürsten Max Emanuel von Bayern', p. 198.

51 Kazimierz Piwarski, *Hieronim Lubomirski. Hetman Wielki Koronny* (Kraków, 1929), p. 72.

52 Kazimierz Piwarski, 'Das Interregnum 1696/97 in Polen, und die politische Lage in Europa', in Johannes Kalisch and J. Gierowski (eds), *Um die polnische Krone: Sachsen und Polen während des Nordischen Krieges 1700–1721* (Berlin, 1962), pp. 20–21.

53 Jacek Staszewski, 'Begründung und Fortsetzung der Personalunion Sachsen–Polen 1697 und 1733', in Rex Rexheuser (ed.), *Die Personalunionen von Sachsen–Polen 1697–1763 und Hannover-England 1714–1837: ein Vergleich* (Wiesbaden, 2005), p. 40.

54 Jarochowski, *Dzieje panowania Augusta II*, p. 20.

55 Skrzypietz, *Jakub Sobieski*, loc. 3863.

56 Markiewicz, *Historia Polski 1492–1795*, p. 590.

57 See above, p. 46

58 Józef A. Gierowski, 'August II Wettyn', in Irena Kaniewska (ed.), *Królowie elekcyjni leksykon biograficzny* (Kraków, 1997), p. 166.

59 Paul Haake maintained that there had been no mention of Poland in the treaty signed in July 1691, but Staszewski showed that it had been in the first draft – Jacek Staszewski, 'Elekcja 1697 roku', *Acta Universitatis Nicolai Copernici, Historia*, XXVIII (Torun, 1993), p. 73. See also, Detlef Döring, 'Johann Georg III. 1680–1691', p. 164.

60 Förster, *Friedrich August II. der Starke*, p. 29

61 Staszewski, *August II Mocny*, p. 48

62 Ibid., p. 55.

63 Ludwig von Pastor, *The History of the Popes, from the Close of the Middle Ages: Drawn from the Secret Archives of the Vatican and Other Original Sources*, vol. 22 (London, 1891), p. 678.

64 Ibid., p. ??.

65 Paul Haake, 'Die Wahl Augusts des Starken zum König von Polen', *Historische Vierteljahrschrift*, 9 (1906), p. 58; Lothar Schilling, 'Der Wiener Hof und Sachsen–Polen (1697–1764)', in *Sachsen und Polen zwischen 1697 und 1765. Beiträge der wissenschaftlichen Konferenz vom 26. bis 28. Juni 1997 in Dresden, Saxonia*. Schriftenreihe des Vereins für sächsische Landesgeschichte e.V., vols 4–5 (Dresden, 1998), pp. 119–20.

66 Karlheinz Blaschke, 'Flemming, Jakob Heinrich Graf von', in *Neue Deutsche Biographie* 5 (1961), pp. 239–40, https://www.deutsche-biographie.de/pnd119415410.html#ndbcontent. Władysław Konopczynski, 'Jakub Henryk Flemming 1667–1728', *Internetowy Polski Słownik Biograficzny*, https://www.ipsb.nina.gov.pl/a/biografia/jakub-henryk-flemming-1667-1728-koniuszy-litewski-etc.

67 A 'castellan' was a high-ranking provincial official, subordinate to the palatine but with a seat in the national Senate.

68 Urszula Kosinska, 'Introduction' to her edition of Jakub Henryk Flemming, *Mémoires concernant l'élection d'Auguste II pour roi de Pologne et les débuts de la guerre du Nord (1696–1702)* (Warsaw, 2017), p. 20.

69 Jarochowski, *Dzieje panowania Augusta II*, p. 86. Jarochowski had a very low opinion of Przebendowski: 'a man without conscience, honour and faith, a very perfect egotist – the cynic of his age, who served all the candidates to the Polish throne in turn, taking money from all of them and then cheating them too' – p. 77.

70 Ibid., p. 89.

71 Ibid., p. 96.

72 Johann Michael von Loen, 'Abbildung des Königs von Pohlen im Jahr 1723', *Des Herrn von Loen Gesammlete kleine Schrifften besorgt und heraus gegeben von J. C. Schneidern* (Frankfurt am Main and Leipzig, 1750), vol. 1, p. 188. This is reprinted in Keller, 'Friedrich August von Sachsen als Herrscher', pp. 105–8.

73 Bodemann (ed.), *Aus den Briefen der Herzogin Elisabeth Charlotte von Orléans*, p. 293.

74 Martin Faber, *Sarmatismus: Die politische Ideologie des polnischen Adels im 16. und 17. Jahrhundert* (Deutsches Historisches Institut Warschau, Quellen und Studien, vol. 35) (Wiesbaden, 2018), p. 263.

75 The full text is published in Haake, 'Die Wahl Augusts des Starken zum König von Polen', pp. 54–6. For Flemming's own account of his firm attachment to Protestantism see Kosinska (ed), *Mémoires concernant l'élection d'Auguste II*, p. 57.

76 Stephan Flemming, in 'Mit Konversion und Bestechung zur Krone. Die Bemühungen Augusts des Starken um den polnischen Thron', *Neues Archiv für sächsische Geschichte*, 90 (2019), p. 78, suggests that it more likely took place in the bishop's private quarters. This is the best account of the election proceedings.

77 Ibid., pp. 59–60.

78 Gurlitt, *August der Starke*, vol. 1, p. 124; Philipp Hiltebrandt, 'Die polnische Königswahl von 1697 und die Konversion Augusts des Starken', *Quellen und Forschungen aus italienischen Archiven und Bibliotheken*, 10 (1907), pp. 178, 182.

79 There is disagreement as to how much was actually sent, the sums varying from 240,000 to 3,000,000 *livres*: Piwarski, 'Das Interregnum 1696/97 in Polen', p. 25; Karl Gustav Helbig, 'Polnische Wirtschaft und französische Diplomatie 1692 bis 1697', *Historische Zeitschrift*, 1, 2 (1859), p. 396. Two Polish nobles who presented their bills prematurely to Nathaniel Hollowell of Danzig, partner of the French court banker Samuel Bernard, were turned away – Berndt Strobach, *Der Hofjude Berend Lehmann (1661–1730). Eine Biografie* (Berlin, 2018), p. 56.

80 Piwarski, 'Das Interregnum 1696/97 in Polen', p. 26.

81 Förster, *Friedrich August II. der Starke*, p. 32.

82 Haake, 'Die Wahl Augusts des Starken zum König von Polen', p. 63.

83 Jutta Dick, 'Der Hofjude Berend Lehmann (1661–1730). Ein Leben mit Grenzen', in Frank Göse, Winfried Müller, Kurt Winkler and Anne-Katrin Ziesak (eds), *Preussen und Sachsen. Szenen einer Nachbarschaft* (Dresden, 2014), p. 177.

84 Uwe Schirmer, 'Staatliche Wirtschaftspolitik in Kursachsen um 1700? Haushaltspolitik und Hoffinanz zu Beginn der Augusteischen Zeit', in *Sachsen und Polen zwischen 1697 und 1765*, p. 271.

85 Heinrich Schnee, *Die Hoffinanz und der moderne Staat. Geschichte und System der Hoffaktoren an deutschen Fürstenhöfen im Zeitalter des Absolutismus*, vol. 2: *Die Institution des Hoffaktorentums in Hannover und Braunschweig, Sachsen und Anhalt, Mecklenburg, Hessen-Kassel und Hanau* (Berlin, 1954), p. 178. Flemming, 'Mit Konversion und Bestechung zur Krone', p. 79 gives rather different figures.

86 There is a detailed list of his sales in Czok, *August der Starke und Kursachsen*, pp. 50–51. See also the full account in Schirmer, 'Staatliche Wirtschaftspolitik in Kursachsen um 1700', pp. 271–2.

87 Emil Lehmann, *Der polnische Resident Berend Lehmann, der Stammvater der israelitischen Gemeinde zu Dresden* (Dresden, 1885), p. 4

88 Alphonse Levy, *Geschichte der Juden in Sachsen* (Berlin, 1900), p. 50. Against these philo-Semitic actions should be set the intention he announced in his memorandum of February 1697 on how to make Poland a flourishing country once more (*Umb Pohlen in Flor und ansehen gegen seine nachtbarn zu setzen*) not to tolerate Jews – Doubek, *August der Starke*, p. 24.

89 Estimates vary, the highest being 100,000 – Strobach, *Der Hofjude Berend Lehmann*, p. 56.

90 https://commons.wikimedia.org/wiki/File:Altomonte_Election_Diet_in_1697.jpg Altomonte moved to Vienna in 1699 where he enjoyed a successful career, mainly as a painter of religious subjects, until his death in 1745 at what was then the very advanced age of eighty-eight.

91 Jean Le Laboureur, *Traité du royaume de Pologne*, printed as an appendix to his *Histoire et relation du voyage de la Royne de Pologne* (Paris, 1698), pp. 4–6. The date of publication makes it seem as if this was a contemporary report but the author states that he had been in Poland in the 1640s.

92 Władyslaw Konopczyński, *Dzieje polska nowożytnej*, vol. 2: *1648–1797* (Warsaw, 1936), p. 148.

93 The report, dated 31 May 1697, is reprinted in full in Haake, 'Die Wahl Augusts des Starken zum König von Polen', p. 57 n. 1.

94 Hiltebrandt, 'Die polnische Königswahl von 1697', p. 181.

95 Piwarski, 'Das Interregnum 1696/97 in Polen', p. 39; Flemming, 'Mit Konversion und Bestechung zur Krone', p. 83.

96 Staszewski, 'Begründung und Fortsetzung der Personalunion Sachsen–Polen 1697 und 1733', p. 42.

97 Flemming, 'Mit Konversion und Bestechung zur Krone', p. 84.

98 It is possible that the nuncio's support was won by a promise from Augustus to exchange an Ottoman pasha taken prisoner in Temesvár for the nuncio's nephew, the young Marquis Davia who was being held in Turkish captivity – Jutta Bäumel, *Auf dem Weg zum Thron. Die Krönungsreise Augusts des Starken* (Dresden, 1997), p. 32.

99   Dick, 'Der Hofjude Berend Lehmann', p. 179; Haake, 'Die Wahl Augusts des Starken zum König von Polen', p. 67; Strobach, 'Der Hofjude Berend Lehmann', p. 59.

100 Link-Lenczowski, *Rzeczpospolita na Rozdrożu 1696–1736*, p. 7.

101 Piwarski, 'Das Interregnum 1696/97 in Polen', p. 41.

102 Staszewski, *August II Mocny*, p. 70.

103 Förster, *Friedrich August II. der Starke*, p. 53.

104 Fassmann, *Des glorwürdigsten Fürsten und Herrn*, pp. 190–91.

105 Jean-Baptiste Des Roches de Parthenay, *The History of Poland under Augustus II* (London 1734), p. 138.

106 Jacek Jędruch, *Constitutions, Elections and Legislatures of Poland 1493–1993: A Guide to Their History.* (New York, 1998), p. 75 translated *pacta conventa* as 'Bill of Rights'.

107 Andrzej Rachuba, 'Radziejowski Augustyn Michał Stefan h. Junosza (1645–1705)', *Internetowy Polski Słownik Biograficzny*, https://www.ipsb.nina.gov. pl/a/biografia/michal-radziejowski-prymas-polski

108 Staszewski, *August II Mocny*, p. 63.

109 Johann Sebastian Müller, *Des Chur- und Fürstlichen Hauses Sachsen, Ernestin- und Albertinischer Linien Annales von Anno 1400 bis 1700* (Leipzig, 1701), quoted in Arnold, *Die Juwelen Augusts des Starken*, p. 15.

110 Staszewski, *August II Mocny*, p. 63.

111 For a detailed account of the coronation and the events before and after see Bäumel, *Auf dem Weg zum Thron*, *passim*.

112 Förster, *Friedrich August II. der Starke*, p. 50.

113 Anna Filipczak-Kocur, 'Elekcja i koronacja Augusta II Sasa w ówczesnych niemieckojęzycznych drukach ulotnych', in Kazimierz Bartkiewicz (ed.), *Polska–Saksonia w czasach Unii (1697–1763): prośba nowego spojrzenia* (Zielona Góra, 1998), p. 102.

114 Dirk Syndram, 'In royal splendour: princely luxury and art as a means of propaganda in the time of the Polish–Saxon union 1697–1763', in Maja Łagocka and Izabella Zychowicz (eds), *Splendour of Power: The Wettins on the Throne of the Polish–Lithuanian Commonwealth* (Warsaw, 2023), p. 18.

115 Strobach, *Der Hofjude Berend Lehmann*, p. 62.

116 Vehse, *Geschichte der Höfe des Hauses Sachsen*, vol. 4, p. 247.

117 Parthenay, *The History of Poland under Augustus II*, p. 132–3.

118 Stanley Wells, Gary Taylor, John Jowett and William Montgomery (eds), William *Shakespeare: The Complete Works*, 2nd edn (Oxford, 2005), *Richard II*, Act 2, scene 4, p. 354.

119 Staszewski, *August II Mocny*, p. 68.

120 Johannes Ziekursch, 'August der Starke und die katholische Kirche in den Jahren 1697–1720', *Zeitschrift für Kirchengeschichte*, 24, 1 (1903), p. 104.

Notes

121 Förster, *Friedrich August II. der Starke*, p. 54.

122 Jarochowski, *Dzieje panowania Augusta II*, p. 142.

123 Piwarski, *Hieronim Lubomirski*, p. 74.

124 Ibid., p. 77.

125 F. M. Monier, *Histoire de Pologne depuis son origine jusqu'en 1795*, vol. 1 (Paris, 1807), p. 296.

126 Skrzypietz, *Jakub Sobieski*, loc. 3821; Albert Waddington, *Histoire de Prusse*, vol. 2 (Paris, 1922), p. 112.

127 Hiltebrandt, 'Die polnische Königswahl von 1697', pp. 192–3.

128 Ibid., p 194. There were other more detailed clauses, for example one barring the Bishop of Cujavia from acting instead of the Primate in future elections. There is a complete list in Jarochowski, *Dzieje panowania Augusta II*, pp. 171–3.

129 Burdowicz-Nowicki, *Piotr I, August II i Rzeczpospolita 1697–1706*, p. 192; Rachuba, 'Radziejowski'.

130 Staszewski, *August II Mocny*, p. 54; Haake, 'Die Wahl Augusts des Starken zum König von Polen', pp. 53, 57 n.1.

131 Hiltebrandt, 'Die polnische Königswahl von 1697', p. 169.

132 W. D. Koroluk, *Polska i Rosja a wojna północna* (Warsaw, 1954), pp. 17–19; V. D. Koroliuk, 'Izbranie Avgusta II na pol'skii prestol i russkaia diplomatiia', *Uchenye Zapiski Instituta Slavianovedeniia*, 3 (1951), pp. 183–5, 210. The difference in spelling of the author is explained by the different conventions employed when transliterating 'В.Д. Королюк'.

133 L. R. Lewitter, 'Peter I and the Polish election of 1697', *Cambridge Historical Journal*, 12, 2 (1956), p. 132.

134 Ibid., p. 136. Although Jacek Burdowicz-Nowicki in his *Piotr I, August II i Rzeczpospolita 1697–1706*, pp. 73–5, speculates that Tsar Peter's despatch was neither intended to, nor actually did, exert an influence, his conclusion is qualified with adverbs such as 'probably' and 'perhaps'.

135 Bäumel, *Auf dem Weg zum Thron*, p. 44. The authoritative verdict of Urszula Kosinska is that Flemming was 'l'artisan majeur de la victoire électorale saxonne' – *Mémoires concernant l'élection d'Auguste II*, p. 9.

136 Shakespeare, *Julius Caesar*, Act 4, scene 2, Wells, Taylor, Jowett and Montgomery (eds), *William Shakespeare: The Complete Works*, p. 649.

137 Gierowski, *Rzeczpospolita w dobie złotej wolnóśći*, p. 217.

138 Cicero was referring to war in his fifth philippic against Mark Antony (*Quid est aliud omnia ad bellum civile hosti arma largiri, primum nervos belli, pecuniam infinitam*).

139 For anglophone readers there is a convenient translation in Parthenay, *The History of Poland under Augustus II*, pp. 94–7, https://ia800301.us.archive.

org/34/items/historypolandunoopartgoog/historypolandunoopartgoog.
pdf

140 Nancy Shields Kollmann, *The Russian Empire 1450–1801* (Oxford, 2017), p. 74.

141 Barbara Skinner, *The Western Front of the Eastern Church: Uniate and Orthodox Conflict in 18th-century Poland, Ukraine, Belarus, and Russia* (DeKalb, 2009), p. 99.

142 Jerzy Kloczowski, *A History of Polish Christianity* (Cambridge, 2000), p. 153.

143 *Polnischer Mercurius, Das ist: Kurtze und deutliche Nachricht von alle demjenigen was in Polen vor in und nach der Wahl Ihro Majestät des itzigen Königs fürgegangen ist* (Breslau, 1697).

144 See above, p. 32.

145 Bodemann (ed.), *Aus den Briefen der Herzogin Elisabeth Charlotte von Orléans*, p. 295.

Chapter 3: The Iron Cage

1 Robert I. Frost, '"Everyone understood what it meant": The impact of the Battle of Poltava on the Polish–Lithuanian Commonwealth', *Harvard Ukrainian Studies*, 31,1/4, p. 171.

2 *'Jede Epoche ist unmittelbar zu Gott, und ihr Wert beruht gar nicht auf dem, was aus ihr hervorgeht, sondern in ihrer Existenz selbst, in ihrem eigenen Selbst'*, *Über die Epochen der neueren Geschichte*, Theodor Schieder and Helmut Berding (eds), *Historisch-kritische Ausgabe* (Munich, 1971), pp. 59–60.

3 Daniel Beauvois, *Histoire de la Pologne* (Paris, 1995), p. 109.

4 Robert I. Frost, *The Northern Wars: War, State and Society in North-Eastern Europe, 1558–1721* (Harlow, 2000), p. 41.

5 Beauvois, *Histoire de la Pologne*, p. 111; Markiewicz, *Historia Polski 1492–1795*, p. 37.

6 Claude Rulhière, *Histoire de l'anarchie de Pologne et du démembrement de cette république*, vol. 1 (Paris, 1807), p. 20.

7 Thomas Wünsch, *Der weiße Adler. Die Geschichte Polens vom 10. Jahrhundert bis heute* (Wiesbaden, 2021), loc. 2137.

8 Jerzy Lukowski, *Disorderly Liberty: The Political Culture of the Polish–Lithuanian Commonwealth in the Eighteenth Century* (London, 2010), p. 24.

9 See above, p. 229.

10 Jerzy Lukowski, 'Political ideas among the Polish nobility in the eighteenth century (to 1788)', *The Slavonic and East European Review*, 82, 1 (January 2004), p. 7.

Notes

11 Ibid., p. 22; Staszewski, *August II Mocny*, p. 77. The extent of royal landholding has been estimated variously. The figure of 25 per cent is given by Andrzej Kamiński in 'The *szlachta* of the Polish–Lithuanian Commonwealth and their government', in Ivo Banac and Paul Bushkovitch (eds), *The Nobility of Russia and Eastern Europe* (New Haven and London, 1985), p. 19.

12 L. R. Lewitter, 'Poland under the Saxon kings', *New Cambridge Modern History*, vol. 7: *The Old Regime, 1713–1763*, ed. J. O. Lindsay (Cambridge, 1957), p. 367.

13 Curtis G. Murphy, *From Citizens to Subjects: City, State, and the Enlightenment in Poland, Ukraine, and Belarus* (Pittsburgh, 2018), loc. 1058; Markiewicz, *Historia Polski 1492–1795*, p. 40. In 1607 the anti-Crown party had pushed through a law 'On vacancies' which obliged a new king to distribute vacant posts and estates before the next Sejm met, to stop him using patronage to subordinate the members.

14 Anna Grześkowiak-Krawicz, *Queen Liberty: The Concept of Freedom in the Polish–Lithuanian Commonwealth* (Leiden and Boston, 2012), pp. 72–3. She also quotes Jakub Boczłowicz, writing in 1699: 'the common freedom is like a glass vessel whose whole hangs upon one event, and once dropped thou wilt see nought but broken shards' – like Humpty Dumpty, one might add.

15 Kamiński in 'The *szlachta* of the Polish–Lithuanian Commonwealth and their government', p. 19.

16 Frans Gunnar Bengtsson, *The Life of Charles XII: King of Sweden, 1697–1718* (London, 1960), p. 122; Wünsch, *Der weiße Adler*, loc. 2502; Lukowski, *Disorderly Liberty*, p. 9; Jan Chryzostom Pasek, *Memoirs of the Polish Baroque. The Writings of Jan Chryzostom Pasek, A Squire of the Commonwealth of Poland and Lithuania*, edited, translated, with an Introduction and notes by Catherine S. Leach (Berkeley, Los Angeles, London, 1976), p. xxxviii.

17 Gierowski, *Rzeczpospolita w dobie złotej wolności*, p. 11.

18 Edward Opalinski, 'Die Freiheit des Adels. Ideal und Wirklichkeit in Polen–Litauen im 17. Jahrhundert', in Ronald G. Asch (ed.), *Der europäische Adel im Ancien Regime. Von der Krise der ständischen Monarchien bis zur Revolution (ca. 1600–1789)* (Cologne, Weimar, Vienna, 2001) p. 91.

19 Grześkowiak-Krawicz, *Queen Liberty*, p. 17.

20 Markiewicz, *Historia Polski 1492–1795*, p. 145; Jerzy Lukowski, 'Poland–Lithuania', in Peter H. Wilson (ed.), *A Companion to Eighteenth-century Europe* (Oxford, 2008), p. 248.

21 Robert I. Frost, *After the Deluge: Poland–Lithuania and the Second Northern War, 1655–1660* (Cambridge, 2004), p. 14.

22 Józef Gierowski, 'The eclipse of Poland', in J. S. Bromley (ed.), *The New Cambridge Modern History*, vol. 6: *The Rise of Great Britain and Russia* (Cambridge, 1970), p. 681.

332

23 Ibid.

24 Wünsch, *Der weiße Adler*, loc. 2433.

25 Frost, *After the Deluge*, p. 15.

26 Erich Hassinger, *Brandenburg-Preußen, Schweden und Rußland 1700–1713* (Munich, 1953), p. 22; David M. Althoen, 'That noble quest: From true nobility to enlightenment society in the Polish–Lithuanian Commonwealth, 1550–1830', unpublished University of Michigan PhD dissertation, 2000, https://deepblue.lib.umich.edu/handle/2027.42/132526

27 Lewitter, 'Poland under the Saxon kings', p. 366.

28 Benedict Wagner-Rundell, *Common Wealth, Common Good: The Politics of Virtue in Early Modern Poland–Lithuania* (Oxford, 2015), pp. 47–9.

29 Józef Andrzej Gierowski, *The Polish–Lithuanian Commonwealth in the XVIIIth Century: From Anarchy to Well-organised State* (Kraków, 1996), p. 37.

30 Richard Butterwick, *The Polish–Lithuanian Commonwealth 1733–1795: Light and Flame* (New Haven and London, 2020), p. 44.

31 Piotr S. Wandycz, *The Price of Freedom: A History of East Central Europe from the Middle Ages to the Present*, 2nd edn (London and New York, 2001), p. 62. Martin Faber lowers the figure to 6–6.5 per cent – Faber, *Sarmatismus*, p. 30.

32 Maria Bogucka, *The Lost World of the 'Sarmatians': Custom as the Regulator of Polish Social Life in Early Modern Times* (Warsaw, 1996), p. 24.

33 Gierowski, *The Polish–Lithuanian Commonwealth in the XVIIIth Century*, p. 134; Grześkowiak-Krawicz, *Queen Liberty*, p. 20.

34 Grześkowiak-Krawicz, *Queen Liberty*, p. 12.

35 Frost, *After the Deluge*, p. 12.

36 Wünsch, *Der weiße Adler*, loc. 2336.

37 Lukowski, *Disorderly Liberty*, p. 10.

38 Wünsch, *Der weiße Adler*, loc. 2342.

39 Andrzej Rottermund, 'Nikt tak nie ograbił Polski jak Szwedzi', https://www.polskieradio.pl/5/3/Artykul/664603

40 Andrzej J. Zakrzewski, *W Kręgu Kultu Maryjnego: Jasna Góra w kulturze staropolskiej* (Częstochowa, 1995), p. 91.

41 Gierowski, *Rzeczpospolita w dobie złotej wolnośći*, p. 107; Frost, *After the Deluge*, p. 14.

42 Frost, *After the Deluge*, p. 14.

43 Gierowski, *Rzeczpospolita w dobie złotej wolnośći*, p. 175.

44 Antony Polonsky, 'Introduction', in Antony Polonsky, Jakub Basista and Andrzej Link-Lenczowski (eds), *The Jews in Old Poland 1000–1795* (London and New York, 1993), p. 2. See also Rudolf Jaworski, Christian Lübke and Michael G. Müller, *Eine kleine Geschichte Polens* (Frankfurt am Main, 2000), p. 164 '[Poland–Lithuania] became a backward state'.

45 Robert Frost, 'The impact of war: The Holy Roman Empire and Poland–Lithuania, *c.*1600–1806', in R. J. W. Evans and Peter H. Wilson (eds), *The Holy Roman Empire 1495–1806: A European Perspective* (Leiden, 2012), p. 248.

46 Geoffrey Hosking, *Russia: People and Empire: 1552–1917* (London, 1997), p. 78.

47 Frost, *The Northern Wars*, p. 158.

48 Augustyniak, *Historia Polski 1572–1795*, pp. 151, 165; Wünsch, *Der weiße Adler*, loc. 2587.

49 Mirosław Nagielski, 'Upadek staropolskiej sztuki wojennej w dobie wielkiej wojny północnej', in Jadwig Muszyński (ed.), *Rzeczpospolita w dobie wielkiej wojny północnej* (Kielce, 2001), p. 42.

50 Frost, *After the Deluge*, p. 5.

51 Emanuel Rostworowski, 'War and society in the noble Republic of Poland–Lithuania in the eighteenth century', in Gunther E. Rothenberg, Béla K. Király and Peter F. Sugar (eds), *East Central European Society and War in the Pre-Revolutionary Eighteenth Century* (New York, 1982), p. 167.

52 Anna Flipczak-Kocur, 'Poland–Lithuania before partition', in Richard Bonney (ed.), *The Rise of the Fiscal State in Europe* (Oxford, 1999), p. 444. In addition there was the *hiberna*, a supplementary tax levied on royal and ecclesiastical lands to support the Commonwealth's armies during winter – Wagner-Rundell, *Common Wealth, Common Good*, p. 58 n. 3.

53 Markiewicz, *Historia Polski 1492–1795*, p. 47.

54 Althoen, 'That noble quest', p. 13.

55 Flipczak-Kocur, 'Poland–Lithuania before partition', p. 477.

56 Pawel Skworoda, *Wojny Rzeczypospolitej Obojga Narodów ze Szwecją* (Warsaw, 2007), p. 234. The number of soldiers actually available for duty was much smaller – Jan Wimmer, *Polska – Szwecja. Konflikty zbrojne w XVI–XVIII wieku* (Oświęcim, 2019), pp. 231–2.

57 Nagielski, 'Upadek staropolskiej sztuki wojennej', pp. 38–9.

58 Marek Wagner, *Bitwa pod Kliszowem 19 lipca 1702 roku* (Oświęcim, 2003), loc. 1182.

59 Link-Lenczowski, *Rzeczpospolita na Rozdrożu 1696–1736*, p. 3.

60 Piwarski, *Hieronim Lubomirski*, pp. 28–30.

61 Wünsch, *Der weiße Adler*, loc. 2361; Augustyniak, *Historia Polski 1572–1795*, p. 726; Markiewicz, *Historia Polski 1492–1795*, pp. 573, 577.

62 Norman Davies, *God's Playground*, vol. 1: *The Origins to 1795* (Oxford, 2005), p. 362.

63 Wünsch, *Der weiße Adler*, loc. 2480.

64 Wagner, *Bitwa pod Kliszowem*, p. 877.

65 Jacek Staszewski, *O Miejsce w Europie. Stosunki Polski i Saksonii z Francją na przełomie XVII i XVIII wieku* (Warsaw, 1973), p. 18.

66 The term Sarmatism was used for the first time in 1765 by *Monitor Polski* and in a negative sense – Augustyniak, *Historia Polski 1572–1795*, p. 358. For a critical review of the historiography see Hans-Jürgen Bömelburg, 'Sarmatismus – zur Begriffsgeschichte und den Chancen und Grenzen als forschungsleitender Begriff', *Jahrbücher für Geschichte Osteuropas*, NS, 57, 3 (2009), pp. 402–8.

67 Janusz Tazbir, 'Recherches sur la conscience nationale en Pologne au XVIe' et XVIIe siècle', *Acta Poloniae Historica* 14 (1966), p. 20; *idem*, 'Sarmatyzm a barok', *Kwartalnik Historyczny*, 76, 4 (1969), p. 827. Dębołęcki also demonstrated that the Bible revealed that God had assigned to Poles dominion over Asia and Africa as well as Europe – Stanisław Cynarski, 'Sarmatyzm – ideologia i styl życia', in *idem, Polska XVII wieku – państwo, społeczeństwo, kultura*, (Warsaw, 1974), p. 230. The claim that a particular language had been chosen by God was advanced by many other European nations – Joanna Partyka, 'What language God spoke to Adam: A 17th century Polish theologian on the oldest language', https://europe-nations.estudosculturais.com/pdf/0016i.pdf.

68 Wojciech Zembaty, 'The elegant downfall of the Polish Sarmatians', https://culture.pl/en/article/the-elegant-downfall-of-the-polish-sarmatians.

69 Althoen, 'That noble quest', p. 35. On the development of the historiography of Sarmatism see Norbert Kersken, 'Geschichtsbild und Adelsrepublik. Zur Sarmatentheorie in der polnischen Geschichtsschreibung der frühen Neuzeit', *Jahrbücher für Geschichte Osteuropas*, 52 (2004), pp. 235–60.

70 Karin Friedrich, *The Other Prussia: Royal Prussia, Poland and Liberty, 1569–1772* (Cambridge, 2000), p. 76; Wünsch, *Der weiße Adler*, loc. 218, 2960–64.

71 Wandycz, *The Price of Freedom*, p. 76.

72 Quoted in Lukowski, 'Political ideas among the Polish nobility', p. 4.

73 Quoted in Lewitter, 'Poland under the Saxon kings', p. 371 and also, in a slightly different form, in Konstantin Symmons-Symonolewicz, *National Consciousness in Poland: Origin and Evolution* (Meadville, PA., 1983), p. 33. I have amalgamated the two.

74 Markiewicz, *Historia Polski 1492–1795*, p. 145.

75 Joanna Orzeł, 'Sarmatyzm', *Pasaż Wiedzy. Muzeum Pałacu Króla Jana III w Wilanowie* (1 April 2015), https://www.wilanow-palac.pl/kultura_sarmacka_4.html.

76 Genesis 9:25. There has been much debate as to what lay behind the apparently innocuous 'saw': was that all Ham did, or did he castrate or sodomize his father as well? Or did he have sex with his mother?

77 Robert Frost, 'The nobility of Poland–Lithuania, 1569–1795', in H. M. Scott, *The European Nobilities in the Seventeenth and Eighteenth Centuries*, vol. 2: *Northern, Central and Eastern Europe* (London and New York, 1995), p. 191.

78 Gierowski, *Rzeczpospolita w dobie złotej wolność*, p. 193.
79 Damien Tricoire, 'Die Erfindung der Gottesmutter Königin von Polen. Zur diskursiven Konstruktion eines katholischen Staates', in Yvonne Kleinmann (ed.), *Kommunikation durch symbolische Akte. Religiöse Heterogenität und politische Herrschaft in Polen–Litauen* (Stuttgart, 2010), p. 229.
80 Neal Ascherson, *Black Sea: Coasts and Conquests: From Pericles to Putin* (London, 2015), loc. 4228.
81 Janusz Tazbir, *Kultura szlachecka w Polsce. Rozkwit – Upadek – Relikty* (Warsaw, 1978), pp. 108–10.
82 Confusingly, Wojciech Dembołęcki believed that it was the Poles who descended from the Scythians – Partyka, 'What language God spoke to Adam'.
83 Stanisław Cynarski, 'The shape of Sarmatian ideology', Acta Poloniae Historica, 19 (1968), p. 8.
84 Zembaty, 'The elegant downfall of the Polish Sarmatians'.
85 Klaus Zernack, *Polen und Russland. Zwei Wege in der europäischen Geschichte* (Berlin, 1994), pp. 18–19.
86 Cynarski, 'Sarmatyzm – ideologia i styl życia', p. 227.
87 Tazbir, *Kultura szlachecka w Polsce*, p. 108. *Mutatis mutandis*, the Dutch depicted the devil wearing Spanish dress.
88 Althoen, 'That noble quest', p. 169.
89 The fullest description is to be found in O'Connor, *The history of Poland in several letters to persons of quality*, pp. 177–8. See also Marek Kepa, 'The Kontush sash: Polish noblemen's best fashion statement', *Culture.pl* (25 January 2017), https://culture.pl/en/article/the-kontush-sash-polish-noblemens-best-fashion-statement and Janusz Tazbir, 'Saramatyzm a barok', *Kwartalnik Historyczny*, 76, 4 (1969), p. 819.
90 Neal Ascherson has stressed the irony of the ensemble: 'This neo-Sarmatian outfit was actually the clothing of Poland's enemies, the oriental gear of Turk and Tatar warriors appropriated by those who boasted that they were the bastion of Catholic and European Christianity against the pagans – *Black Sea*, loc. 4250.
91 See plate 6.
92 Augustyniak, *Historia Polski 1572–1795*, p. 193.
93 Stanisław Litak, *Od Reformacji do Oświecenia. Kościół katolicki w Polsce nowożytnej* (Lublin, 1994), p. 91.
94 Markiewicz, *Historia Polski 1492–1795*, p. 91.
95 Natalie Aleksiun, Daniel Beauvois, Marie-Élizabeth Ducreux, Jerzy Kloczowski, Henryk Samsonowicz and Piotr Wandycz, *Histoire de l'Europe du Centre-Est* (Paris, 2004), p. 224.

96 Peter Paul Bajer, 'Short history of the Radziwiłł family', *Rocznik Muzeum i Archiwum Polonii Australijskiej*, 4 (n.d.), pp. 19–21.

97 Wojciech Kriegseisen, *Between State and Church. Confessional Relations from Reformation to Enlightenment: Poland – Lithuania – Germany – Netherlands* (Frankfurt am Main, 2011), p. 455.

98 Stone, *The Polish–Lithuanian Commonwealth*, p. 136.

99 Eduard Kneifel, *Geschichte der Evangelisch-Augsburgischen Kirche in Polen* (Niedermarschacht über Winsen/Lube, n.d.), p. 54.

100 Lukowski, *Disorderly Liberty*, p. 62.

101 Augustyniak, *Historia Polski 1572–1795*, p. 197.

102 Litak, *Od Reformacji do Oświecenia*, pp. 89–90.

103 Richard Butterwick, 'Catholicism and the enlightenment in Poland–Lithuania', in Ulrich L. Lehner and Michael O'Neill Printy (eds), *A Companion to the Catholic Enlightenment in Europe* (Leiden, 2010), p. 300. Butterwick's periodization of the Catholic Enlightenment sees it beginning 'later by at least a generation than in western Europe', i.e. after Augustus's death – ibid., p. 311.

104 W. H. McNeill, *Europe's Steppe Frontier 1500–1800* (Chicago, 1964), p. 36.

105 Jerzy Kłoczowski, 'The Polish Church', in William J. Callahan and David Higgs (eds), *Church and Society in Catholic Europe of the Eighteenth Century* (Cambridge, 1979), p. 126.

106 Augustyniak, *Historia Polski 1572–1795*, p. 366.

107 Cynarski, 'Sarmatyzm – ideologia i styl życia', p. 242.

108 Bożena Steinborn and Anna Brzyski, revised by Andrzej Szczerski, 'Polish architecture and art *c.* 1600–*c.* 1700', from *Oxford Art Online*, https://www.oxfordartonline.com/groveart/view/10.1093/gao/9781884446054.001.0001/oao-9781884446054-e-7000068337?rskey=evLpzK#oao-9781884446054-e-7000068337-div1-7000068352 See also Jan Białostocki, 'Sarmatism', from *Oxford Art Online*, https://doi.org/10.1093/gao/9781884446054.article.T076050

109 On the unfair comparison, see Richard Butterwick, *Poland's Last King and English Culture* (Oxford, 1998), ch. 1.

110 Augustyniak, *Historia Polski 1572–1795*, p. 23.

111 Jörg K. Hoensch, *Geschichte Polens* (Stuttgart, 1983), p. 159.

112 Bogucka, *The Lost World of the 'Sarmatians'*, p. 8.

113 Frost, *The Northern Wars*, p. 52.

114 Robert Frost, *The Oxford History of Poland–Lithuania*, vol. 1 (Oxford, 2015), p. 18. Admittedly, that was in the early fifteenth century, but conditions did not change much during the next two centuries.

115 Quoted in Kollmann, *The Russian Empire 1450–1801*, p. 1.

116 David Landes, *The Unbound Prometheus: Technological Change and Industrial Development in Western Europe from 1750 to the Present* (Cambridge, 1969), p. 46.

117 O'Connor, *The history of Poland in several letters to persons of quality*, p. 4. This passage is also quoted in Frost, 'The nobility of Poland–Lithuania, 1569–1795', p. 183; William Coxe, *Travels into Poland, Russia, Sweden and Denmark*, 4th edn, vol. 1 (London, 1792), p. 142. See also Le Laboureur, *Traité du royaume de Pologne*, p. 106, and the article 'Pologne' by L. de Jaucourt in Diderot and D'Alembert's *Encyclopédie*.

118 Augustyniak, *Historia Polski 1572–1795*, p. 280. For a similar revisionist view see Frost, *The Oxford History of Poland–Lithuania*, vol. 1, pp. 251–9 and Butterwick, *The Polish–Lithuanian Commonwealth*, pp. 64–9.

119 Gierowski, *Rzeczpospolita w dobie złotej wolności*, p. 292; Lewitter, 'Poland under the Saxon kings', p. 368.

120 Augustyniak, *Historia Polski 1572–1795*, p. 111.

121 Ibid., p. 229. On the *socha* see John Smith, *A System of Modern Geography*, vol. 1 (London, 1810), p. 248. According to Jerzy Topolski, 'Polish economy in the eighteenth century', in Edmund Cieślak and Henryk Olszewski (eds), *Changes in Two Baltic Countries: Poland and Sweden in the XVIIIth Century* (Poznań, 1990), p. 12, average annual yields in Polish agriculture *c*.1785 were still only 3–1 in the late eighteenth century.

122 Augustyniak, *Historia Polski 1572–1795*, p. 229.

123 Ibid., pp. 231–2.

124 Butterwick, *The Polish–Lithuanian Commonwealth*, p. 66.

125 Faber, *Sarmatismus*, p. 35. A 'middling szlachta' owned between one and ten villages.

126 Lukowski, *Disorderly Liberty*, p. 10.

127 Augustyniak, *Historia Polski 1572–1795*, pp. 242, 272–3.

128 Jan Wimmer, *Wojsko Rzeczpospolitej w dobie wojny północnej (1700–1717)* (Warsaw, 1956), p.15; Lewitter, 'Poland under the Saxon kings', p. 369.

129 Augustyniak, *Historia Polski 1572–1795*, p. 273.

130 Daniel Tollet, *Histoire des Juifs en Pologne du XVIᵉ siècle à nos jours* (Paris, 1992), p. 12.

131 Butterwick, *The Polish–Lithuanian Commonwealth*, p. 70; Antony Polonsky, 'Introduction', in Polonsky, Basista and Link-Lenczowski (eds), *The Jews in Old Poland 1000–1795*, pp. 4–5. It is estimated that today only around 20,000 people of Jewish origin remain in Poland, although 80 per cent of the world's Jewish population trace to Poland–Lithuania – Samuel Fiszman (ed.), *Constitution and Reform in Eighteenth-century Poland* (Bloomington and Indianapolis, 1997), p. 6.

132 Coxe, *Travels into Poland, Russia, Sweden and Denmark*, 4th edn, vol. 1 (London, 1792), p. 293. Coxe was travelling in 1775.

133 Wiktor Weintraub, 'Tolerance and intolerance in Old Poland', *Canadian Slavonic Papers*, 13, 1 (Spring 1971), p. 32.

134 Bernard D. Weinryb, 'On Bohdan Khmel'nyts'zkyi and the Cossack–Polish war', *Harvard Ukrainian Studies*, 1, 2 (1977), pp. 174–5. For a contrary view, arguing that the number has been exaggerated, see Shaul Stampfer, 'What actually happened to the Jews of Ukraine in 1648?', *Jewish History*, 17, 2 (2003), pp. 207–27.

135 Carsten Kumke, 'Zwischen der polnischen Adelsrepublik und dem Russischen Reich (1569–1657)', in Frank Golczewski (ed.), *Geschichte der Ukraine* (Göttingen, 1993), p. 65.

136 Polonsky, 'Introduction', p. 5.

137 Orest Subtelny, *Ukraine: A History* (Toronto, 1988), p. 124; Ewy Dubas-Urwanowicz and Jerzy Urwanowicz (eds), *Patron i dwór. Magnateria Rzeczpospolitej w XVI–XVIII wieku* (Warsaw, 2006), p. 147.

138 On the self-governing institutions of the Polish Jews see Murphy, *From Citizens to Subjects*, loc. 1088.

139 Augustyniak, *Historia Polski 1572–1795*, p. 229.

140 Andreas Kappeler, *Kleine Geschichte der Ukraine* (Munich, 1994), loc. 1287; Paul Johnson, *A History of the Jews* (London, 1995), loc. 5410.

141 Jürgen Heyde, *Geschichte Polens* (Munich, 2011), loc. 665.

142 Magda Teter, *Jews and Heretics in Poland: A Beleaguered Church in the Post-Reformation Era* (Cambridge, 2006), p. vi.

143 Gierowski, *Rzeczpospolita w dobie złotej wolności*, p. 297; on the effects of the war see Adam Teller, *Money, Power, and Influence in Eighteenth-Century Poland–Lithuania* (Stanford, 2016), pp. 31–2.

Chapter 4: The Great Northern War

1 See above, pp. 49–50.

2 Gierowski, *Rzeczpospolita w dobie złotej wolności*, p. 233.

3 A. N. Kurat, 'The retreat of the Turks, 1688–1730', in Bromley (ed.), *The New Cambridge Modern History*, vol. 6, p. 627; Derek McKay and H. M. Scott, *The Rise of the Great Powers 1648–1815* (London, 1983), p. 76. Previously the Turks had only made truces, since they believed they were engaged in permanent war with the 'unbelievers'.

4 Hochedlinger, *Austria's Wars of Emergence*, p. 153.

Notes

5 There is a strange error in a recent article devoted to the Peace, in which it is clearly stated that Kamieniec and Podolia were ceded *to* the Ottomans ('Den Osmanen wurde Kamieniec inklusive der total zerstörten Landschaft Podolienj zugesprochen') although this may be a mistake of the translator (from Hungarian into German) – Monika Molnár, 'Der Friede von Karlowitz und das Osmanische Reich', in Arno Strohmeyer and Norbert Spannenberger (eds), *Frieden und Konfliktmanagement in interkulturellen Räumen: Das Osmanische Reich und die Habsburgermonarchie in der frühen Neuzeit* (Stuttgart, 2013), p. 213.

6 Konopczyński, *Polska a Turcja 1683–1792*, p. 33.

7 Augustyniak, *Historia Polski 1572–1795*, p. 766; Davies, *God's Playground*, p. 367; Koroluk, *Polska i Rosja a wojna północna*, p. 86.

8 Markiewicz, *Historia Polski 1492–1795*, p. 595; Gierowski, *Rzeczpospolita w dobie złotej wolnośći*, p. 233.

9 There is a summary in Paul Haake, *August der Starke*, p. 13 and a much fuller account in Haake's article 'Die Wahl Augusts des Starken zum König von Polen', pp. 46–51.

10 Ibid., p. 50.

11 Staszewski, *August II Mocny*, p. 90.

12 Arnold Munthe, *Karl XII och den ryska sjömakten* (Stockholm, 1924), vol. 1, p. 29.

13 Reinhard Wittram, *Peter I. Czar und Kaiser. Zur Geschichte Peters des Großen in seiner Zeit*, vol. 1 (Göttingen, 1964), p. 206. See also Wittram's earlier article, 'Peter des Grossen Interesse an Asien', *Nachrichten der Akademie der Wissenschaften in Göttingen aus dem Jahre 1957, Philologisch-Historische Klasse* (Göttingen, 1957), p. 5, which states that Peter's commercial project dated back at least to 1693.

14 Koroluk, *Polska i Rosja a wojna północna*, p. 98.

15 Sven Svensson, 'Tsar Peters motiv för kriget mot Sverige', *Historisk Tidskrift* 51 (1931), pp. 449–51, 459.

16 For example: Gierowski, *Rzeczpospolita w dobie złotej wolnośći*, p. 236; Burdowicz-Nowicki, *Piotr I, August II i Rzeczpospolita 1697–1706*, pp. 178–9; Staszewski, *August II Mocny*, p. 91; V. S. Bobylev, *Vneshniaia politika Rossii epokhi Petra I* (Moscow, 1990), p. 17; Walther Mediger, *Mecklenburg, Russland und England–Hannover 1706–1721. Ein Beitrag zur Geschichte des Nordischen Krieges* (Hildesheim, 1967), pp. 158–9.

17 Staszewski, *August II Mocny*, p. 91.

18 S. M. Solovev, *Istoria Rossiia s drevneishikh vremen*, vol. 7 (Moscow, 1962) p. 605.

19 Doubek, *August der Starke*, loc. 600; Wittram, *Peter I*, vol. 1, p. 166.

20 The Great Northern War has been responsible for some of the great unreadables in European historiography. The best book in any language is Robert Frost's excellent *The Northern Wars: War, State and Society in North-Eastern Europe, 1558–1721*.

21 See map.

22 Frost, *The Northern Wars*, pp. 114–15.

23 Klaus Zernack, 'Schweden als europäische Großmacht der frühen Neuzeit', *Historische Zeitschrift*, 232, 2 (1981), p. 348; Göran Behre, Lars-Olof Larsson and Eva Österberg, *Sveriges Historia 1521–1809: Stormaktsdröm och Småstatsrealiteter* (Stockholm, 1985), p. 178.

24 Eli F. Heckscher, *An Economic History of Sweden*, Harvard Economic Studies, vol. 95 (Cambridge, Mass., 1954), p. 85; Ingvar Andersson, *Schwedische Geschichte von den Anfängen bis zur Gegenwart* (Munich, 1950), p. 266.

25 Klaus Zernack, 'Die skandinavischen Reiche vom 1654 bis 1722', in Theodor Schieder (ed.), *Handbuch der Europäischen Geschichte*, vol. 4, *Europa im Zeitalter des Absolutismus und der Aufklärung* (Stuttgart, 1968), p. 519.

26 Andrejs Plakans, *A Concise History of the Baltic States* (Cambridge, 2011), p. 109.

27 C. Schirren, review of Fredrik Ferdinand Carlson, *Carl XII*, vol. 1, *Göttingische gelehrte Anzeigen*, (3, 10 January 1883), pp. 23–6. Although 'only' a review, this is a substantial and scholarly piece of work.

28 Yella Erdmann, *Der livländische Staatsmann Johann Reinhold von Patkul* (Berlin, 1970), p. 66.

29 A. Fryxell, *Lebensgeschichte Karl's des Zwölften* (Brunswick, 1861), vol. 1, p. 110.

30 Wittram, *Peter I*, vol. 1, p. 214.

31 Ibid., pp. 203–10.

32 Johann Gustav Droysen, *Geschichte der Preußischen Politik*, 2nd edn, pt 4, 1: *Friedrich Wilhelm I. König von Preußen* (Leipzig, 1872), p. 135.

33 Bengt Liljegren, *Karl XII. En biografi* (Lund, 2000), p. 72.

34 Fryxell, *Lebensgeschichte Karl's des Zwölften*, vol. 1, p. 36. The episode with reindeer is referred to in Boris Akunin, *Aziatskaia evropeizatsiia. Tsar' Petr Alekseyevich* (Kiev, 2019), p. 119.

35 Ibid., p. 48.

36 Ibid., p. 50; Soloviev, *Istoria Rossii s drevneishikh vremen*, vol. 7, p. 617.

37 Bengtsson, *The Life of Charles XII*, p. 38. Hjärne had been Charles XI's personal physician and, among other accomplishments, was a Fellow of the Royal Society of London.

38 Nils Herlitz, 'Det Stora Nordiska Krigets Förhistoria och första år (1697–1700)', in Samuel E. Bring (ed.), *Karl XII till 200-årsdagen av hans död* (Stockholm, 1918), p. 93.

39 Ernst Carlson and F. Mewius (eds), *Die eigenhändigen Briefe König Karls XII* (Berlin, 1894), pp. xx–xxi, 6.

40 Ragnhild Hatton's repeated attempts to establish Charles's heterosexual credentials – for example by recording that 'he liked gallant stories as long as they were "not too coarse"' (*Charles XII of Sweden* (London, 1968), p. 376) – only serve to diminish them.

41 Christopher Gillberg, 'Karl XII tycks ha uppfyllt de flesta kritierna för Aspergers syndrom', *Läkartidningen*, 48 (2002), pp. 4837–8; Boris Akunin, *Istoriia rossiiskogo gosudarstva. Aziatskaia evropeizatsiia* (Kiev, 2017), p. 116.

42 Liljegren, *Karl XII*, p. 54. When the Russians captured Nöteborg in 1702 they offered to release him, but Boethius declined on the grounds that he was a Swedish prisoner.

43 This has achieved 'common knowledge' status. I have not been able to locate an authoritative citation, not that it matters much.

44 Bernhard Erdmannsdörffer, *Deutsche Geschichte vom Westälischen Frieden*, vol. 1, pp. 33–4. For the best recent discussion of the Schleswig-Holstein problem see Joachim Krüger, *Der letzte Versuch einer Hegemonialpolitik am Öresund. Dänemark–Norwegen und der Große Nordische Krieg (1700–1721)* (Berlin, 2019), pp. 17–19. The best map of Schleswig-Holstein is in Joachim Krüger, 'The Baltic Sea region by 1700. The time of the Great Northern War', in Ralf Bleile and Joachim Krüger (eds), *'Princess Hedvig Sofia' and the Great Northern War* (Dresden, 2015), p. 32.

45 Michael Glaeser, *By Defeating My Enemies: Charles XII of Sweden and the Great Northern War 1682–1721* (Warwick, 2020), p. 38; Knud J. V. Jespersen, 'Rivalry without victory: Denmark, Sweden and the struggle for the Baltic, 1500–1720', in Göran Rystad, Klaus-Richard. Böhme and Wilhelm M. Carlgren, *In Quest of Trade and Security: The Baltic in Power Politics, 1500–1990* (Lund, 1994), p. 165.

46 Hatton, *Charles XII of Sweden*, p. 102.

47 Herlitz, 'Det Stora Nordiska Krigets Förhistoria', pp. 90–93. On the abortive mission by the Danish diplomat Jul see V. E. Vozgrin, *Rossiia i evropeiskie strany v gody severnoi voiny* (Leningrad, 1986), pp. 58–9.

48 Liljegren, *Karl XII*, p. 68.

49 Otto Haintz, *König Karl XII. von Schweden* (Berlin, 1958), vol. 1, p. 26.

50 Ibid., p. 68.

51 Alexander Querengässer, *Der kursächsische Militär im Großen Nordischen Krieg* (Paderborn, 2019), p. 33; Wittram, *Peter I*, vol. 1, p. 213.

52 Fryxell, *Lebensgeschichte Karl's des Zwölften*, vol. 1, p. 112.

53 Fredrik Ferdinand Carlson, *Sveriges historia under konungarne af pfalziska huset*, pt 7: *Carl XII* (Stockholm, 1881), vol. 1, p. 239. No source or date is cited.

54 T. C. W. Blanning, 'The origins of great wars', in *idem*, *The French Revolution-ary Wars* (Harlow, 1986), p. 28; Geoffrey Blainey, *The Causes of War* (Melbourne, 1977), p. 53.

55 N. I. Pavlenko, *Petr I* (Moscow, 2000), p. 79.

56 Staszewski, *August II*, p. 82; Staszewski, *August II Mocny*, p. 98; Koroluk, *Polska i Rosja a wojna północna*, p. 127; Hatton, *Charles XII of Sweden*, p. 117.

57 Markiewicz, *Historia Polski 1492–1795*, p. 597.

58 Gierowski, *Rzeczpospolita w dobie złotej wolnośći*, p. 236.

59 Henryk Olszewski, *Doktryny Prawno-ustrojowe Czasów Saskich, 1697–1740* (Warsaw, 1961), p. 48.

60 Staszewski, *August II Mocny*, p. 108. Charles's chaplain, Jöran Nordberg, gave a similar account in his *Leben Carls des Zwölften Königs in Schweden mit Münzen und Kupfern*, vol. 1 (Hamburg, 1745), p. 126. For a very different account see Erdmann, *Patkul*, p. 81.

61 Fryxell, *Lebensgeschichte Karl's des Zwölften*, vol. 1, p. 112; Wimmer, *Wojsko Rzeczpospolitej w dobie wojny północnej*, p. 50.

62 Ibid.; Reinhard Wittram, *Baltische Geschichte; Die Ostseelande: Livland, Estland, Kurland, 1180–1918* (Munich, 1954), p. 104.

63 Carlson, *Sveriges historia*, p. 237; Erdmann, *Patkul*, p. 82.

64 Flemming did not marry Franciszka Izabela Sapieha until 1702 – Gintautas Sliesoriūnas, review of Kosińska (ed.), *Mémoires concernant l'élection d'Auguste II*, *Lithuanian Historical Studies*, 23 (2019), p. 195.

65 Wittram, *Peter I*, vol. 1, p. 221.

66 Hatton, *Charles XII of Sweden*, p. 117.

67 Querengässer, *Der kursächsische Militär im Großen Nordischen Krieg*, p. 33.

68 Frost, *The Northern Wars*, p. 229.

69 Lars Ericson Wolke, *Sjöslag och rysshärjningar Kampen om Östersjön under stora nordiska kriget 1700–1721* (Stockholm, 2012), p. 79; Liljegren, *Karl XII*, pp. 77–80. There is a helpful map showing the Sound and its channels on p. 78.

70 Ibid., p. 82. The treaty was signed at Traventhal but is always referred to, even by Swedes, as 'Travendal'.

71 V. I. Buganov, *Petr velikii i ego vremia* (Moscow, 1989), p. 70.

72 Herlitz, 'Det Stora Nordiska Krigets Förhistoria', pp. 124–5; Krüger, *Der letzte Versuch einer Hegemonialpolitik am Öresund*, pp. 97–8.

73 Wolke, *Sjöslag och rysshärjningar Kampen om Östersjön*, p. 81.

74 Ibid., pp. 111–12.

75 Förster, *Friedrich August II. der Starke*, pp. 99–100.

76 Querengässer, *Der kursächsische Militär im Großen Nordischen Krieg*, pp. 120–33.

Notes

77 Wimmer, *Wojsko Rzeczpospolitej w dobie wojny północnej*, p. 53.

78 Schuster and Francke, *Geschichte der sächsischen Armee*, p. 146.

79 B. Shirokorad, *Severnie voini Rossii* (Moscow, 2001), p. 157.

80 N. N. Molchanov, *Diplomatiia Petra Pervogo* (Moscow, 1984), p. 157; Soloviev, *Istoria Rossii s drevneishikh vremen*, vol. 7, p. 157; B. S. Telpukhovski, *Severnaia voina 1700–1721* (Moscow, 1946). The online edition is not paginated.

81 Wittram, *Peter I*, vol. 1, p. 233.

82 Liljegren, *Karl XII*, p. 85.

83 Ibid., p. 88; Fryxell, *Lebensgeschichte Karl's des Zwölften*, vol. 1, p. 85.

84 Liljegren, *Karl XII*, p. 89. 'The essence of Charles XII's religiosity [was] an unlimited trust in an all-powerful God and his ability to guide everything for the best. It was a faith founded in childhood and firmly held throughout life. This faith provides the inner explanation for his never-abandoned struggle for the continued existence of the Swedish empire – the kingdom was given to him by God – but also for his total indifference to the external dangers of warrior life' – Sven Grauers, 'Karl XII', *Svenskt Biografiskt Lexikon*, https://sok.riksarkivet.se/sbl/Presentation.aspx?id=12357

85 Figures vary. Those cited here are from ibid., p. 89. Others present a much wider discrepancy – Friedrich Förster, for example, who pits 8,000 Swedes against 80,000 Russians – *Friedrich August II. der Starke*, p. 102.

86 Fryxell, *Lebensgeschichte Karl's des Zwölften*, vol. 1, p. 90.

87 Liljegren, *Karl XII*, pp. 89–93.

88 Hatton, *Charles XII*, pp. 152–3.

89 Liljegren, *Karl XII*, p. 95.

90 Fryxell, *Lebensgeschichte Karl's des Zwölften*, vol. 1, p. 99.

91 Russian historians both before and after the Revolution were at pains to stress that there were good reasons for Peter absenting himself (for example Buganov, *Petr velikii i ego vremia*, p. 74) but they were patently whistling in the dark. A more recent biographer – N. I. Pavlenko – also finds his departure 'difficult to explain' but rejects any explanation smacking of cowardice because Peter had shown courage at Azov earlier and would do so again later – *Petr I*, pp. 82–3. The same line is taken by Alexander Bespalov in *Severnaia Voina. Karl XII i shvedskaia armiia. Put' ot Kopengagena do Perevolochnoy 1700–1709* (Moscow, 1998), p. 50. A more convincing account is provided by A. B. Shirokorad in *Severnie voini Rossii*, p. 159, who agrees that Peter ran away, observing that he was a complex character, capable of reckless courage as well as panic attacks. For an alternative and more convincing explanation see below, p. 208.

Notes

Chapter 5: Nemesis: Charles XII in Poland 1701–1706

1 Gierowski, *Rzeczpospolita w dobie złotej wolności*, p. 246.

2 Carlson, *Sveriges historia under konungarne af pfalziska huset*, p. 428; Vozgrin, *Rossiia i evropeiskie strany v gody severnoi voiny*, p. 95.

3 Förster, *Friedrich August II. der Starke*, p. 102; Molchanov, *Diplomatiia Petra Pervogo*, p. 168. For details of the agreement – and the conditions attached to it by the tsar – see Burdowicz-Nowicki, *Piotr I, August II i Rzeczpospolita 1697–1706*, pp. 262–3.

4 Christian von Sarauw, *Die Feldzüge Karl's XII*. (Leipzig, 1881), p. 67.

5 H. E. Uddgren, 'Fälttågen 1701–6', in Bring (ed.), *Karl XII till 200-årsdagen av hans död*, p. 221.

6 The best recent account is in Olle Larsson, *Stormaktens sista krig* (Lund, 2009), pp. 82–90. Also good are Bengt Liljegren, *Karl XII. En biofrafi*, pp. 99–103, including a good map on p. 101, and Querengässer, *Der kursächsische Militär im Großen Nordischen Krieg*, pp. 143–53, which also has excellent maps.

7 Wimmer, *Wojsko Rzeczpospolitej w dobie wojny północnej*, pp. 68–70.

8 See above, p. 112.

9 Fryxell, *Lebensgeschichte Karl's des Zwölften*, vol. 1, p. 127.

10 Gustaf Jonasson, 'Schweden, Sachsen und Polen 1697–1706', in *Sachsen und Polen zwischen 1697 und 1765*, p. 103.

11 See above, p. 101.

12 Frost, *The Northern Wars*, p. 257; Wimmer, *Wojsko Rzeczpospolitej w dobie wojny północnej*, p. 62. In an uncharacteristic error, Ragnhild Hatton dates Olkieniki as 18 November 1701 – Hatton, *Charles XII of Sweden*, p. 178.

13 Carlson, *Sveriges historia*, vol. 2, p. 28.

14 Sarauw, *Die Feldzüge Karl's XII*, p. 73.

15 Munthe, *Karl XII och den ryska sjömakten*, vol. 1, p. 82.

16 Sarauw, *Die Feldzüge Karl's XII*, pp. 74–5.

17 Schuster and Francke, *Geschichte der sächsischen Armee*, p. 150.

18 Wittram, *Peter I*, vol. 1, p. 248.

19 Władysław Konopczyński, *Polska a Szwecja od pokoju oliwskiego do upadku Rzeczpospolitej 1660–1795* (Warsaw, 1924), p. 40.

20 Bengtsson, *The Life of Charles XII*, p. 121. That is now the accepted view among Swedish historians at both an academic and a popular level – cf. Hugo Nordland, 'Karl XII:s eviga fälttåg', *Populär Historia*, 4 (2021).

21 *The Second World War: The Grand Alliance* (London, 1950), p. 607.

22 Fryxell, *Lebensgeschichte Karl's des Zwölften*, vol. 1, p. 130.

Notes

23 Gustaf Jonasson, *Karl XII:s polska politik 1702–1703* (Stockholm, 1968), p. 22. Oxenstierna's long letter was printed in its entirety in French translation in J. A. Nordberg, *Histoire de Charles XII roi de Suède*, vol. 4 (The Hague, 1748), pp. 59–67 and in German in *Leben Carls des Zwölften Königs in Schweden*, vol. 3, pp. 299–306.

24 Quoted in Liljegren, *Karl XII*, p. 79. 'That a streak of harshness, not to say ruthlessness, pervades Charles's conduct in certain situations is undeniable. This applies, for example, to his sentencing in various cases. He rarely took mitigating circumstances into account. He was consistent in his sentencing, but it was an abstract legal, Old Testament justice with little trace of humanity' – Sven Grauers, 'Karl XII', *Svenskt Biografiskt Lexikon*, https://sok.riksarkivet.se/sbl/Presentation.aspx?id=12357

25 Friedrich Ferdinand Carlson, *Karl der Zwölfte von Schweden* (Gotha, 1888), p. 232.

26 Munthe, *Karl XII och den ryska sjömakten*, vol. 1, p. 62 n. 1.

27 Ibid., pp. 106–7.

28 Fryxell, *Lebensgeschichte Karl's des Zwölften*, vol. 1, p. 107; Nils Herlitz, 'Karl XII:s Polska Politik 1701–1707', in Bring (ed.), *Karl XII till 200-årsdagen av hans död*, p. 142. That God was on the Swedish side was a constant theme of Swedish propaganda – Larsson, *Stormaktens sista krig*, p. 94.

29 Liljegren, *Karl XII*, p. 64.

30 The only luxury item he possessed was a gold-bound Luther Bible – ibid., p. 147.

31 Nordberg, *Leben Carls des Zwölften Königs in Schweden*, vol. 1, p. 273.

32 See below, p. 152.

33 Fryxell, *Lebensgeschichte Karl's des Zwölften*, vol. 1, pp. 143–5.

34 Charles Schefer (ed), 'Mémoire du Marquis de Bonnac sur les affaires du Nord de 1700 à 1710', *Revue d'histoire diplomatique*, 2 (1888), p. 111. Always keen to present her hero in the best possible (and heterosexual) light, Ragnhild Hatton explained Charles's lack of interest by suggesting that Aurora's looks had 'rather faded' – Hatton, *Charles XII of Sweden*, p. 179.

35 Gretschel, *Geschichte des sächsischen Volkes und Staates*, vol. 2, p. 537. He was eventually released in May 1702 – Nordberg, *Leben Carls des Zwölften Königs in Schweden*, vol. 1, p. 318.

36 Richard Martens, 'Die Absetzung des Königs August II. von Polen', *Zeitschrift des westpreussischen Geschichtsvereins*, 8 (1882), pp. 20, 66; Fryxell, *Lebensgeschichte Karl's des Zwölften*, vol. 1, pp. 148, 200.

37 Wagner, *Bitwa pod Kliszowem 19 lipca 1702 roku*, loc. 345, 362.

38 Quoted in Munthe, *Karl XII och den ryska sjömakten*, vol. 1, p. 81.

Notes

39 Fryxell, *Lebensgeschichte Karl's des Zwölften*, vol. 1, p. 132.

40 Carlson, *Karl der Zwölfte von Schweden*, p. 262

41 Carl von Clausewitz, *On War*, ed. and trans. Michael Howard and Peter Paret (Princeton, 1976), p. 111.

42 Quoted in Munthe, *Karl XII och den ryska sjömakten*, vol. 1, p. 471. 'It became increasingly clear that Charles had no strategic / political perspective' – Daniel Hohrath, 'Karl XII. (1682–1718)', in Stig Förster, Markus Pöhlmann and Dierk Walter (eds), *Kriegsherren der Weltgeschichte. 22 historische Porträts* (Munich, 2010), p. 136.

43 Wagner, *Bitwa pod Kliszowem*, p. 284.

44 Carlson, *Karl der Zwölfte von Schweden*, p. 237. Pastor Nordberg recorded that the locals were very impressed by this act of piety, even if performed by heretics – *Leben Carls des Zwölften*, vol. 1, p. 336.

45 Nordberg, *Leben Carls des Zwölften*, vol. 1, pp. 341–2.

46 Jonasson, *Karl XII:s polska politik 1702–1703*, pp. 61, 69–70.

47 Liljegren, *Karl XII*, p. 113. This verdict has been echoed by many historians, by Robert Frost, for example, who described it as 'stupid' (*töricht*) – Robert Frost, 'Sächsisch–polnische Personalunion und die Katastrophe des Großen Nordischen Krieges', in Hans-Jürgen Bömelburg (ed.), *Polen in der europäischen Geschichte*, vol. 2 (Stuttgart, 2017), p. 431.

48 Staszewski, *August II Mocny*, p. 74; Kamiński, *Republic vs. Autocracy*, p. 20.

49 Konopczyński, *Dzieje polska nowożytnej*, vol. 2, p. 155.

50 Gretschel, *Geschichte des sächsischen Volkes und Staates*, vol. 2, p. 536.

51 'List z gratulacjami zwycięstwa' – Wimmer, *Polska – Szwecja*, p. 231.

52 Martens, 'Die Absetzung des Königs August II. von Polen', p. 18; Herlitz, 'Karl XII:s Polska Politik 1701–1707', p. 151.

53 Hatton, *Charles XII of Sweden*, p. 182.

54 Skworoda *Wojny Rzeczypospolitej Obojga Narodów ze Szwecją*, p. 213.

55 Konopczyński, *Dzieje polska nowożytnej*, vol. 2, p. 36.

56 Herlitz, 'Det Stora Nordiska Krigets Förhistoria', p. 135.

57 Konopczyński, *Polska a Szwecja*, p. 36.

58 Hatton, *Charles XII of Sweden*, p. 158. Koroluk, *Polska i Rosja a wojna północna*, p. 140. On the meeting at Birże see above, p. 121.

59 Frost, *The Northern Wars*, p. 250.

60 Nordberg, *Leben Carls des Zwölften*, vol. 1, p. 346.

61 I have discussed this further in *The Pursuit of Glory*, pp. 207–17.

62 See below, pp. 211, 236, 283, 293.

63 See above, pp. 133 and below, pp 178–80. This misunderstanding has been promoted by both Swedish historians (Fryxell described him as 'an unlimited

Notes

Elector' – *Lebensgeschichte Karl's des Zwölften*, vol. 1, p. 151) and especially by their Polish colleagues (the worst offender was Jan Wimmer, who apostrophized him as 'a typical absolutist ruler' and viewed everything Augustus did as part of a grand project to establish *'absolutum dominium'* – Wimmer, *Wojsko Rzeczpospolitej w dobie wojny północnej, passim*. Honourable exceptions are Olszewski, *Doktryny Prawno-ustrojowe Czasów Saskich*, pp. 34–5 and Urszula Kosińska, *August II w poszukiwaniu sojusznika. Między aliansem wiedeńskim i hanowerskim (1725–1730)* (Warsaw, 2012), p. 81.

64   Fryxell, *Lebensgeschichte Karl's des Zwölften*, vol. 1, p. 137.

65   'Physically gigantic with a round red face' – Carlson, *Karl der Zwölfte von Schweden*, p. 238. For a good portrait see https://en.wikipedia.org/wiki/Michał_Stefan_Radziejowski#/media/File:Michał_Stefan_Radziejowski.PNG

66   Rachuba, 'Radziejowski' *passim*. Rachuba refers to Krzysztof Towiański as Radziejowski's 'relation', although many believed he was his son.

67   See above, pp. 56–7.

68   See above, pp. 112. For the payments made to them see Carlson, *Karl der Zwölfte von Schweden*, p. 239. From the loan raised by Charles in the Dutch Republic, Benedict received 3,000 talers, Radziejowski 20,000, his mistress 6,000.

69   Maciej Forycki, *Stanisław Leszczyński* (Poznań, 2016), p. 578; Włodzimierz Dworzaczek, 'Leszczyński Rafał', *Polski Słownik Biograficzny*.

70   Link-Lenczowski, *Rzeczpospolita na Rozdrożu 1696–1736*, p. 2; Skrzypietz, *Jakub Sobieski*, loc. 3863.

71   Konopczyński, *Dzieje polska nowożytnej*, vol. 2, p. 146; Wimmer, *Wojsko Rzeczpospolitej w dobie wojny północnej*, p. 20.

72   Piwarski, *Hieronim Lubomirski*, p. 82. He was appointed on 15 May, following the sudden death of Felix Potocki, who had succeeded Stanisław Jabłonowski on his death on 3 April.

73   Martens, 'Die Absetzung des Königs August II. von Polen', p. 23.

74   Wagner, *Bitwa pod Kliszowem*, p. 582.

75   On the period leading up to the battle, see Liljegren, *Karl XII*, p. 113; Querengässer, *Der kursächsische Militär*, pp. 186–90; Wagner, *Bitwa pod Kliszowem*, loc. 582ff.

76   The best accounts of the battle are to be found in Wimmer, *Wojsko Rzeczpospolitej w dobie wojny północnej*, pp. 217–23 and Wagner, *Bitwa pod Kliszowem*, loc. 2465ff.

77   Larsson, *Stormaktens sista krig*, p. 114.

78   Alexander Querengasser, 'The Battle of Kliszow 1702', in Stephen L. Kling (ed.), *Great Northern War Compendium* (St Louis, Missouri, 2015), vol. 1, p. 162; Fryxell, *Lebensgeschichte Karl's des Zweiten*, vol. 1, p. 160.

Notes

79 There is an excellent analysis of Charles as a battlefield commander by Gunnar Arteus in 'Karl XII i ego armiya', in Sverker Oredsson, (ed.), *Tsar Petr i Korol' Karl. Dva pravitelia i ikh narody* (Moscow, 1999), pp. 164ff. Arteus has a very low opinion of him as a strategist but judges him to have been 'one of the great captains of history' – ibid., p. 164. See also Querengässer, *Der kursächsische Militär im Großen Nordischen Krieg*, p. 198.

80 Ibid.

81 Piwarski, *Hieronim Lubomirski*, p. 88; Wagner, *Bitwa pod Kliszowem*, loc. 2465.

82 Ibid., p. 91. See also Martens, 'Die Absetzung des Königs August II. von Polen', p. 29.

83 Władysław Konopczyński, 'Early Saxon period 1697–1733', in W. F. Reddaway (ed.), *The Cambridge History of Poland* (Cambridge, 1941) p. 6; Haintz, *König Karl XII*, vol. 1, p. 62.

84 Piwarski, *Hieronim Lubomirski*, p. 90.

85 Ibid., p. 87.

86 Wimmer, *Wojsko Rzeczpospolitej w dobie wojny północnej*, p. 205.

87 Wagner, *Bitwa pod Kliszowem*, loc. 3136.

88 Wimmer, *Polska–Szwecja*, p. 235.

89 Ibid. See also his comment in *Wojsko Rzeczpospolitej w dobie wojny północnej*, p. 222, 'can only be called treason' (*nie można nazwać inaczej jak zdradą*).

90 Ibid. p. 221 – 'the treacherous actions of Hetman Lubomirski made an import-ant contribution to the Saxon defeat' (*Do klęski Sasów poważnie się przyczyniła zdradziecka postawa hetmana Lubomirskiego*). See also Gierowski, *Rzeczpospol-ita w dobie złotej wolnośći*, p. 251; Markiewicz, *Historia Polski 1492–1795*, p. 598; Monier, *Histoire de Pologne*, p. 504; Wagner, *Bitwa pod Kliszowem*, loc. 2465.

91 Wimmer, *Wojsko Rzeczpospolitej w dobie wojny północnej*, p. 223; Sarauw, *Die Feldzüge Karl's XII*, p. 104.

92 Ibid., pp. 225–6.

93 Carlson, *Karl der Zwölfte*, pp. 251, 254.

94 See above, p. 114.

95 Herlitz, 'Karl XII:s Polska Politik 1701–1707', p. 154.

96 A good visual aid to appreciating the extent of Charles's meanderings is one of the many maps available. The most accessible are probably those in Hatton, *Charles XII of Sweden*, p. 191 and Liljegren, *Karl XII.*, p. 104.

97 Martens, 'Die Absetzung des Königs August II. von Polen', p. 31.

98 Jonasson, *Karl XII:s polska politik 1702–1703*; Liljegren *Karl XII*, p. 122.

99 Förster, *Friedrich August II. der Starke*, pp. 129–30.

100 Carlson and Mewius (eds), *Die eigenhändigen Briefe König Karls XII.*, p. xxxvi.

101 Gunnar Arteus, 'Karl XII i ego armiya', p. 163.

Notes

102 Akunin, *Istoriia rossiiskogo gosudarstva*, p. 128. He added that, of all the mistakes made by Charles as a result of his over-confidence, the most egregious was his prolonged inaction before launching the campaign in the east – ibid., p. 151.

103 Carlson, *Karl der Zwölfte von Schweden*, pp. 342–3.

104 Parthenay, *Histoire de Pologne sous le règne d'Auguste II*. vol. 3 (The Hague, 1734), pp. 59–60; Liljegren, *Karl XII*, p. 130.

105 Munthe, *Karl XII och den ryska sjömakten*, vol. 1, p. 267.

106 Haintz, *König Karl XII*, vol. 1, p. 101. Even his most uncritical apologist, Ragnhild Hatton, conceded that it was 'a set-back' – Hatton, *Charles XII of Sweden*, p. 200. Another keen admirer, Christian von Sarauw, opined that Charles's expedition was 'inexplicable' – *Die Feldzüge Karl's XII.*, p. 324.

107 Fryxell, *Lebensgeschichte Karl's des Zweiten*, vol. 1, pp. 135–6.

108 Ibid., p. 195.

109 Soloviev, *Istoria Rossii s drevneyshikh vremen*, vol. 7, p. 502.

110 Frost, *The Northern Wars*, p. 267; Martens, 'Die Absetzung des Königs August II. von Polen', p. 97.

111 Skrzypietz, *Jakub Sobieski*, loc. 4271; Gretschel, *Geschichte des sächsischen Volkes und Staates*, vol. 2, p. 541. According to the Danish envoy, the scheme had been proposed by Patkul – Kasimir von Jarochowski, 'Patkuls Ausgang', *Neues Archiv für sächsische Geschichte*, 3 (1882), p. 209.

112 Hatton, *Charles XII of Sweden*, p. 198.

113 Parthenay, *Histoire de Pologne sous le règne d'Auguste II*, pp. 28–9; Carlson, *Karl der Zwölfte von Schweden*, p. 333.

114 Forycki, *Stanisław Leszczyński*, loc. 463, 558.

115 Carlson, *Karl der Zwölfte von Schweden*, p. 326.

116 Schefer (ed.), 'Mémoire du Marquis de Bonnac', p. 95; Sarauw also concluded that Stanisław had secured Charles's support thanks to his 'attractive appearance' (*sein anziehendes Aeussere*) and good manners – *Die Feldzüge Karl's XII*, p. 154.

117 'Par l'inclination qu'il a conçu pour ce palatin qui lui marquait un attachement particulier' – quoted in Pierre Boyé, *Stanislas Leszczyński et le troisième traité de Vienne* (Paris, 1898), p. 6.

118 Carlson, *Karl der Zwölfte von Schweden*, p. 325. Horn also told Charles that to select a native Pole would result in a powerless king and end in tragedy – ibid.

119 Pavlenko, *Petr I*, p. 107; Konopczyński, *Dzieje polska nowożytnej*, p. 159.

120 Parthenay, *Histoire de Pologne sous le règne d'Auguste II*, pp. 36–40.

121 Carlson, *Karl der Zwölfte von Schweden*, p. 338.

122 Liljegren, *Karl XII*, p. 128; Hatton, *Charles XII of Sweden*, p. 199.

Notes

123 Carlson, *Karl der Zwölfte von Schweden*, p. 339.

124 Frost, *The Northern Wars*, p. 269. 'Vicieuse dans toutes les circonstances, sans exception' – Parthenay, *Histoire de Pologne sous le règne d'Auguste II*, p. 41.

125 Fryxell, *Lebensgeschichte Karl's des Zwölften*, vol. 1, p. 215. If this improbable story is true, the child may have been one-year-old Maria, who twenty years later married Louis XV, king of France. The wedding took place on 25 August 1725.

126 Sarauw, *Die Feldzüge Karl's XII.*, pp. 159–60.

127 Fassmann, *Des glorwürdigsten Fürsten und Herrn*, p. 423. Released after two and a half years, he died in Vienna on his way back to Poland.

128 Parthenay, *Histoire de Pologne sous le règne d'Auguste II*, p. 59.

129 Parthenay (ibid., p. 59) valued the haul at 150,000 talers, Fryxell's (*Lebensgeschichte Karl's des Zwölften*, vol. 1, p. 217) more modest estimate was 50,000 talers, not that the monetary value matters much.

130 Kazimierz Jarochowski, 'Rada Senatu wyszogrodzka i zabiegi polityczno-dyplomatyczne po zajęciu Warszawy w miesiącu wrześniu 1704', in *idem*, *Odpowiadania i studia historyczne. Serya nowa* (Poznan, 1884), pp. 69–70.

131 See above, p. 54.

132 Munthe, *Karl XII och den ryska sjömakten*, vol. 2, p. 318.

133 Staszewski, *Die Polen in Dresden des 18. Jahrhunderts*, p. 145.

134 Fryxell, *Lebensgeschichte Karl's des Zweiten*, vol. 1, p. 225.

135 Markiewicz, *Historia Polski 1492–1795*, p. 602. See also Augustyniak, *Historia Polski 1572–1795*, p. 778.

136 Ibid., p. 177.

137 I have discussed this in relation to the armies of the French Revolution in *The French Revolution in Germany* (Oxford, 1983), ch. 3.

138 Gierowski, *The Polish–Lithuanian Commonwealth in the XVIIIth Century*, p. 105; Fryxell, *Lebensgeschichte Karl's des Zweiten*, vol. 1, pp. 217, 224.

139 Wimmer, *Polska–Szwecja*, p. 283.

140 Ibid., p. 195.

141 Jerzy Motylewicz, 'Obciążenia wojskowe w czasie wielkiej wojny północnej i ich wpływ na przemiany społeczne i etniczne w miastach ziemi przemyskiej', in Jadwiga Muszyńska (ed.), *Rzeczpospolita w dobie wielkiej wojny północnej* (Kielce, 2001), p. 227.

142 See above, p. 134.

143 Liljegren, *Karl XII*, p. 125.

144 Evguéni [*sic*] Tarlé, *La guerre du Nord et l'invasion suédoise en Russie*, 2 vols (Moscow, 1966), vol. 1, p. 60.

145 Liljegren, *Karl XII*, p. 125. Several other examples are listed here.

Notes

146 Tarlé, *La guerre du Nord*, vol. 1, p. 61; Larsson, *Stormaktens sista krig*, p. 117.

147 Schefer (ed), 'Mémoire du Marquis de Bonnac', p. 615.

148 Oskar Sjöström, *Fraustadt 1706. Ett fält färgat rött* (Lund, 2009), p. 43.

149 Telpukhovski, *Severnaia voina 1700–1721*. The online edition is not paginated.

150 Johann Reinhold von Patkul, *Berichte an das Zaarische Cabinet in Moscau von seinem Gesandschafts-Posten bey August II. Könige von Polen*, 2 vols (Berlin, 1792), vol. 1, p. 235.

151 Sten Bonnesen, *Peter den Store* (Stockholm, 1928), p. 131; Frost, 'Sächsisch-polnische Personalunion und die Katastrophe des Großen Nordischen Krieges', p. 433. On the Birze agreement see above, p. 109.

152 Vozgrin, *Rossiia i evropeiskie strany v gody severnoi voiny*, pp. 138–9.

153 V. D. Koroljuk, 'Der Eintritt der Rzeczpospolita in den Nordischen Krieg', in Kalisch and Gierowski (eds.), *Um die polnische Krone*, pp. 152–3.

154 Jozef Feldman, *Polska w dobie wielkiej wojny północnej 1704–1709* (Kraków, 1925), p. 2.

155 Geoffrey Hosking, *Russia and the Russians from the Earliest Times to the Present*, 2nd edn (London, 2012), p. 195.

156 Ibid., pp. 195–6.

157 Klaus Zernack, *Nordosteuropa: Skizzen und Beiträge zu einer Geschichte der Ostseeländer* (Lüneburg, 1993), p. 176.

158 Quoted in Janet Hartley, 'Russia as a fiscal-military state 1689–1825', in Christopher Storrs (ed.), *The Fiscal-military State in Eighteenth-century Europe. Essays in Honour of P. G. M. Dickson* (Farnham, 2009), p. 129.

159 William C. Fuller Jr, *Strategy and Power in Russia 1600–1914* (New York, 1992), p. 56.

160 See Patkul's correspondence of 1704 – Patkul, *Berichte an das Zaarische Cabinet*, vol. 1, pp. 305–12.

161 Herlitz, 'Karl XII:s Polska Politik 1701–1707', p. 166; Fuller, *Strategy and Power in Russia 1600–1914*, p. 78.

162 See above, p. 133.

163 Staszewski, *August II Mocny*, p. 160.

164 This account is based mainly on Hatton, *Charles XII of Sweden*, pp. 204–6; Wimmer, *Wojsko Rzeczpospolitej w dobie wojny północnej*, pp. 304–6; Bobylev, *Venshniaia politika Rossii epokhi Petra I*, pp. 25–7.

165 Kazimierz Jarochowski, 'Bitwa Wschowska, dnia 13 lutego 1706', in *idem*, *Odpowiadania i studia historyczne*, pp. 198, 208.

166 Wimmer, *Wojsko Rzeczpospolitej w dobie wojny północnej*, p. 305. Sjöström, *Fraustadt 1706*, p. 261; Sarauw, *Die Feldzüge Karl's XII*, pp. 192–3.

167 Ibid., chs 9–12.

168 Liljegren, *Karl XII*, p. 134.

169 Sjöström, *Fraustadt 1706*, p. 241; Liljegren, *Karl XII*, pp. 135–6. Olle Larsson pointed out – *Stormaktens sista krig*, p. 125 – that 260 Russian prisoners were sent off to Pomerania, so not all can have been massacred.

170 Sverker Oredsson, 'Karl XII', in *idem* (ed.), *Tsar Petr i Korol' Karl*, p. 51. This collection of nine essays was first published in Swedish as *Tsar Peter och kung Karl. Två härskare och deras folk* in 1998. For some reason, only the Russian translation is available in UK public collections.

171 Sarauw, *Die Feldzüge Karl's XII*, p. 201.

172 Carlson, *Karl der Zwölfte von Schweden*, pp. 388–90.

173 Jan Lindegren took the view that the Grodno episode represented one of Charles's greatest military achievements, if not the greatest ('*en av de största eller rent av den största militära framgången över huvud för Karl XII.*'), on account of the casualties inflicted on the Russians, but that seems grossly exaggerated – 'Karl XII', in Anders Florén, Stellan Dahlgren and Jan Lindegren, *Kungar och Krigare* (Stockholm, 1992), p. 193.

174 Parthenay, *Histoire de Pologne sous le règne d'Auguste II*, p. 159; Wimmer, *Wojsko Rzeczpospolitej w dobie wojny północnej*, p. 308.

175 Erdmannsdörffer, *Deutsche Geschichte vom Westfälischen Frieden*, vol. 2, p. 222.

Chapter 6: Augustus in Saxony

1 Wieland Held, *Der Adel und August der Starke. Konflikt und Konfliktaustrag zwischen 1694 und 1707 in Kursachsen* (Cologne, Weimar and Vienna, 1999), p. 205.

2 Arno Günther, 'Das schwedische Heer in Sachsen 1706–1707', *Neues Archiv für sächsische Geschichte*, 25 (1904), p. 236.

3 Förster, *Friedrich August II. der Starke*, p. 181.

4 This was the conclusion of Christian von Sarauw in *Die Feldzüge Karl's XII.*, pp. 204–9, based in part on Johann Richard Danielson, *Zur Geschichte der sächsischen Politik 1706–1709* (Helsingfors, 1878).

5 Haintz, *König Karl XII.*, vol. 1, p. 150.

6 Liljegren, *Karl XII.*, p. 139.

7 Sarauw, *Die Feldzüge Karl's XII*, p. 210.

8 Fryxell, *Lebensgeschichte Karl's des Zweiten*, vol. 1, pp. 251–2.

9 These obviously approximate figures were given by Sarauw in *Die Feldzüge Karl's XII*, pp. 218–19.

10 Ibid., p. 217. He was duly rewarded with the title of prince.

11 Haintz, *König Karl XII*, vol. 1, p. 156.

12 Zbigniew Chmiel, 'The Battle of Kalisz 1706', in Kling (ed.), *Great Northern War Compendium*, vol. 1, p. 219.

13 Sarauw, *Die Feldzüge Karl's XII*, p. 218.

14 Hatton, *Charles XII of Sweden*, p. 215. Hatton provides an admirably lucid account of the events leading up to the Battle of Kalisz, although her use of old style/Swedish dating can be confusing.

15 Jan Wimmer, 'Die Schlacht bei Kalisch am 29. Oktober 1706', in Kalisch and Gierowski (eds), *Um die polnische Krone*, p. 205.

16 Ibid., p. 204.

17 Sarauw, *Die Feldzüge Karl's XII*, p. 219.

18 Munthe, *Karl XII och den ryska sjömakten*, vol. 1, p. 65 n.1.

19 Bonnesen, *Peter den Store*, p. 139.

20 Nordberg, *Histoire de Charles XII*, vol. 4, p. 23.

21 Sarauw, *Die Feldzüge Karl's XII*, p. 210.

22 Danielson, *Zur Geschichte der sächsischen Politik 1706–1709*, p. 40.

23 Erdmann, *Patkul*, pp. 267–70; Jarochowski, 'Patkuls Ausgang', p. 284.

24 Jaroslav Goll, *Der Vertrag von Alt-Ranstaedt. Oesterreich und Schweden 1706–1707* (Prague, 1879), p. 9.

25 See above, p. 96.

26 Auguste Geffroy, *Lettres inédites du roi Charles XII* (Paris, 1853), p. 25.

27 M. Lorenz Hagens, *Feldpr. in der Armee Carls XII. Nachricht von der Hinrichtung Johann Reinhold von Patkul, Russischen Gen. Lieut. und Gesandten am sächsischen Hofe, mit Erläuterungen herausgegeben von J.C.L. Pr. Zu Br.* (Göttingen, 1783), p. xiv, https://digitale.bibliothek.uni-halle.de/vd18/content/pageview/4874336

28 Jarochowski, 'Patkuls Ausgang', p. 287. A second contemporary account – *Kurtze Beschreibung der merck- und denckwürdigen Execution Des tapffern und Welt-bekanten General Patkuls, Wie selbiger den 10. October. 1707. zu Casimir in Pohlen erbärmlich hingerichtet worden* – recorded that only three strokes were needed.

29 Tarlé, *La guerre du Nord*, vol. 1, p. 49.

30 Nordberg, *Leben Carls des Zwölften Königs in Schweden*, vol. 2, p. 40.

31 Erdmann, *Der livländische Staatsmann Johann Reinhold von Patkul*, p. 288.

32 An English translation of Hagen's account was published in London in 1761 – *Anecdotes concerning the famous John Reinhold Patkul: or, An authentic relation of what passed betwixt him & his confessor, the night before & at his execution. Tr. from the original manuscript, never yet printed*; Jürgen Luh, 'Die schwedische Armee in Sachsen 1706–1707', in Günther Kronenbitter, Markus Pöhlmann and Dierk Walter (eds.), *Besatzung: Funktion und Gestalt*

militärischer Fremdherrschaft von der Antike bis zum 20. Jahrhundert (Paderborn, 2006), p. 66.

33 Jarochowski, 'Patkuls Ausgang', p. 287. Less squeamish is Bengt Liljegren, *Karl XII. En biografi*, pp. 150–51.

34 Hatton, *Charles XII of Sweden*, p. 231.

35 Jarochowski, 'Patkuls Ausgang', p. 286.

36 Voltaire, *The History of Peter the Great* (New York, 1857), p. 176.

37 Parthenay, *Histoire de Pologne sous le règne d'Auguste II*, p. 177.

38 Ernst Carlson, *Der Vertrag zwischen Karl XII. von Schweden und Kaiser Joseph I. zu Altranstädt 1707* (Stockholm, 1907), p. 6.

39 Goll, *Der Vertrag von Alt-Ranstaedt*, p. 20.

40 Fryxell, *Lebensgeschichte Karl's des Zweiten*, vol. 1, pp. 69, 131; Skrzypietz, *Jakub Sobieski*, loc. 4435; Tarlé, *La guerre du Nord*, p. 41.

41 Gretschel, *Geschichte des sächsischen Volkes und Staates*, vol. 2, p. 557; Held, *Der Adel und August der Starke*, p. 208; Luh, 'Die schwedische Armee in Sachsen 1706–1707', p. 57.

42 Ibid., p. 60; Liljegren, *Karl XII*, p. 141. The conversion of two Saxon pounds of meat and half a pound of butter or bacon has been made on the basis that one Saxon pound = 467 grams. The 'beer' would most likely have been low-alcohol 'small beer'.

43 Günther, 'Das schwedische Heer in Sachsen 1706–1707', p. 246.

44 Czok, *August der Starke und Kursachsen*, p. 200; Józef Leszczyński, 'Die Oberlausitz in den ersten Jahren des nordischen Krieges (1700–1709)', in Kalisch and Gierowski (eds), *Um die polnische Krone*, p. 86.

45 Danielson, *Zur Geschichte der sächsischen Politik 1706–1709*, p. 60.

46 Werner Schmidt, 'Historische Voraussetzungen und Grundzüge', in Ulli Arnold and Werner Schmidt (eds), *Barock in Dresden: Kunst und Kunstsammlungen unter der Regierung des Kurfürsten Friedrich August I. von Sachsen und Königs August II. von Polen, genannt August der Starke, 1694–1733, und des Kurfürsten Friedrich August II. von Sachsen und Königs Augusts III. von Polen, 1733–1763* (Leipzig, 1986), p. 24.

47 Sven Grauers, 'Karl XII', *Svenskt Biografiskt Lexikon*, https://sok.riksarkivet.se/sbl/Presentation.aspx?id=12357.

48 Günther, 'Das schwedische Heer in Sachsen 1706–1707', pp. 248–9; Luh, 'Die schwedische Armee in Sachsen 1706–1707', p. 64.

49 Ibid., p. 244.

50 Skworoda, *Wojny Rzeczypospolitej Obojga Narodów ze Szwecją*, p. 225; Werner Schmidt, 'Historische Voraussetzungen und Grundzüge', in Rudolf Kötzschke and Hellmut Kretzschmar (eds), *Sächsische Geschichte* (Frankfurt am Main, 1965), p. 271.

Notes

51 Fassmann, *Des glorwürdigsten Fürsten und Herrn*, p. 481; Liljegren, *Karl XII*, p. 143.

52 Günther, 'Das schwedische Heer in Sachsen 1706–1707', p. 243; Fryxell, *Lebensgeschichte Karl's des Zweiten*, vol. 1, p. 265.

53 Luh, 'Die schwedische Armee in Sachsen 1706–1707', pp. 57–60.

54 Goll, *Der Vertrag von Alt-Ranstaedt*, p. 21.

55 Fryxell, *Lebensgeschichte Karl's des Zweiten*, vol. 1, p. 70.

56 Carlson, *Der Vertrag zwischen Karl XII. von Schweden und Kaiser Joseph I*, p. 5.

57 Ibid., p. 21.

58 Jaroslav Goll deals with this aspect in considerable detail in *Der Vertrag von Alt-Ranstaedt, passim*.

59 Charles W. Ingrao, *In Quest and Crisis: Emperor Joseph I and the Habsburg Monarchy* (West Lafayette, Ind., 1979), p. 55; Carlson, *Der Vertrag zwischen Karl XII. von Schweden und Kaiser Joseph I*, p. 18.

60 Sven Grauers, 'Karl XII', *Svenskt Biografiskt Lexikon*, https://sok.riksarkivet.se/sbl/Presentation.aspx?id=12357

61 Fryxell, *Lebensgeschichte Karl's des Zweiten*, vol. 1, p. 246.

62 Arno Herzig, *Geschichte Schlesiens. Vom Mittelalter bis zur Gegenwart* (Munich, 2015), pp. 694–6.

63 There is a helpful and richly illustrated article on the Silesian Gnadenkirchen on Wikipedia at https://de.wikipedia.org/wiki/Schlesische_Gnadenkirchen.

64 Gretschel, *Geschichte des sächsischen Volkes und Staates*, vol. 2, p. 561.

65 Karl von Weber, 'Anna Constance Gräfin von Cossell. Nach archivalischen Quellen', *Archiv für die sächsische Geschichte*, 9 (1871), p. 19.

66 Förster, *Friedrich August II. der Starke*, p. 191.

67 Weber, 'Anna Constance Gräfin von Cossell', p. 19. There is much about Mlle Duparc in Karl Ludwig von Pöllnitz, *La Saxe galante* (Amsterdam, 1734), pp. 339–57, but he is so unreliable that this is best treated as a historical novel very loosely based on fact.

68 Czok, *August der Starke und Kursachsen*, p. 59.

69 Reiner Gross (ed.), *Sachsen und die Wettiner: Chancen und Realität* (Dresden, 1990) (the proceedings of a conference held at Dresden 27–29 June 1989 and published as a special issue of *Dresdner Hefte*), p. 20.

70 Markus A. Denzel, 'Messestadt Leipzig. Marktplatz Europas in der Frühen Neuzeit', in Susanne Schötz (ed.), *Leipzigs Wirtschaft in Vergangenheit und Gegenwart: Akteure, Handlungsspielräume, Wirkungen (1400–2011)* (Leipzig, 2012), p. 99. See also the helpful map in Karlheinz Blaschke, 'Die Kurfürsten von Sachsen als Förderer der Leipziger Messe', in Hartmut Zwahr, Thomas Topstedt and Günter Bentele (eds), *Leipzigs Messen 1497–1997*, vol. 1 (Cologne, Weimar and Vienna, 1999), p. 65.

71 Werner Schmidt, 'Das augusteische Zeitalter Sachsens', in Schmidt and Syndram (eds), *Unter einer Krone*, p. 26; Czok, *August der Starke und Kursachsen*, pp. 62, 126–9.

72 Sheilagh C. Ogilvie, 'Proto-industrialisation in Germany', in Sheilagh C. Ogilvie and Markus Cerman (eds), *European Proto-industrialisation* (Cambridge, 1996), pp. 123–5.

73 Sheilagh C. Ogilvie, 'The beginnings of industrialisation', in S. C. Ogilvie (ed.), *Germany: A New Social and Economic History*, vol. 2: *1630–1800* (London, 1996), p. 576. Thuringia comprised the principalities ruled by the Ernestine branch of the Wettin dynasty.

74 Gierowski, *Rzeczpospolita w dobie złotej wolności*, p. 221.

75 Rudolf Forberger, *Die Manufaktur in Sachsen vom Ende des 16. bis zum Anfang des 19. Jahrhunderts* (Berlin, 1958), p. 299.

76 Karlheinz Blaschke, 'Die kursächsische Politik und Leipzig im 18. Jahrhundert', in Wolfgang Martens (ed.), *Leipzig. Aufklärung und Bürgerlichkeit* (Heidelberg, 1990), p. 23. As these figures are so arresting, I have deemed it prudent to cite the original German text: '*nur noch ein Viertel der Bevölkerung lebte als Bauern, zwei Fünftel machten die auf dem Lande lebende, gewerblich tätige Bevölkerung aus, während bereits ein Drittel aller Landesbewohner in den Städten wohnte*'.

77 Günter Vogler and Klaus Vetter, *Preussen von den Anfängen bis zur Reichsgründung* (Cologne, 1981), p. 82.

78 Czok, *August der Starke und Kursachsen*, p. 127.

79 Johannes Ziekursch, *Sachsen und Preußen um die Mitte des achtzehnten Jahrhunderts. Ein Beitrag zur Geschichte des österreichischen Erbfolgekrieges* (Breslau, 1904), pp. 29, 33.

80 See below, pp. 260–1.

81 Kretzschmar, 'Geschichte der Neuzeit seit der Mitte des 16. Jahrhunderts', in Rudolf Kötzschke and Hellmut Kretzschmar (eds), *Sächsische Geschichte* (Frankfurt am Main, 1965) p. 274; Czok, 'Die Personalunion als Problem des Monarchen', p. 63.

82 Anne-Katrin Ziesak, 'Leipzig', in Göse, Müller, Winkler and Ziesak (eds), *Preussen und Sachsen*, p. 84; Karl Czok, 'Leipzig und seine Messe im Augusteischen Zeitalter', in Zwahr, Topstedt and Bentele (eds), *Leipzigs Messen 1497–1997*, vol. 1, p. 183.

83 Forberger, *Die Manufaktur in Sachsen*, p. 300; Strobach, *Der Hofjude Berend Lehmann*, p. 46.

84 Joachim Menzhausen, 'Königliches Dresden', in Joachim Menzel and Jutta Kappel (eds), *Königliches Dresden. Höfische Kunst im 18. Jahrhundert* (Munich, 1990), p. 10.

85 Hazel Rosenstrauch, 'Leipzig als "Centralplatz" des deutschen Buchhandels', in Martens (ed.), *Leipzig. Aufklärung und Bürgerlichkeit*, p. 107.

86 Peter Beyer, 'Leipzigs Auseinandersetzung mit Frankfurt am Main (1706–1726)', in Zwahr, Topstedt and Bentele (eds.), *Leipzigs Messen 1497–1997*, vol. 1, p. 203.

87 Alberto Schwarz, 'Architektur und Stadtbild', in Detlev Döring (ed.), *Geschichte der Stadt Leipzig*, vol. 2: *Von der Reformation bis zum Wiener Kongress* (Leipzig, 2016), pp. 701–14; Karl Grosse, *Geschichte der Stadt Leipzig von der ältesten bis auf die neueste Zeit*, vol. 2 (Leipzig, 1898), pp. 271–2.

88 There is an excellent reproduction at https://www.paintingsbefore1800.com/PaintingsI/page5.html

89 Johann Limberg, *Denckwürdige Reisebeschreibung durch Teutschland, Italien, Spanien, Portugall, Engeland, Frankreich und Schweitz etc* (Leipzig, 1690), pp. 934–5.

90 Arnold Schering, *Musikgeschichte Leipzigs*, vol. 2, *Von 1650 bis 1723* (Leipzig, 1926), p. 304. The full text of the play can be found online at https://play.google.com/books/reader?id=EIJWxeyI3SoC&pg=GBS.PPi&hl=en_GB. It also contains some grossly offensive anti-Semitism. In 1706 a hippopotamus was on display – Wolfgang Schneider (ed.), *Leipzig. Streifzüge durch die Kulturgeschichte* (Leipzig, 1990), p. 169.

91 Detlev Döring, 'Vom Ende der schwedischen Besatzung (1650) bis zum Ende des Siebenjährigen Krieges (1763)', in Döring (ed.), *Geschichte der Stadt Leipzig*, vol. 2, pp. 75–6.

92 Czok, 'Leipzig und seine Messe im Augusteischen Zeitalter', p. 183. The Apel House is now known as the King's House. There is a good coloured illustration in Schneider (ed.), *Leipzig*, p. 189.

93 Schneider (ed.), *Leipzig*, p. 184.

94 For example Peter Burke, *Popular Culture in Early Modern Europe* (London, 1978), p. 29.

95 See also below, pp. ??. The influence of the literary historian Richard Alewyn's stimulating but erratic essay 'Das große Welttheater' has not been entirely beneficial. It can be found in Richard Alewyn and K. Sälzle, *Das große Welttheater. Die Epoche der höfischen Feste in Document und Deutung* (Hamburg, 1959), pp. 9–70.

96 See below, pp. 248–9.

97 Jacek Staszewski, 'Die sächsisch–polnische Union', in Schmidt and Syndram (eds), *Unter einer Krone*, p. 19.

98 Karl Czok, 'August der Starke. Sein Verhältnis zum Absolutismus und zum sächsischen Adel', *Sitzungsberichte der Sächsischen Akademie der Wissenschaften zu Leipzig*, Philologisch-historische Klasse, vol. 131, 3 (Berlin, 1991), pp. 6–7;

Notes

Karl Czok, 'Zur Leipziger Kulturgeschichte des 18. Jahrhunderts', in Reinhard Szekus (ed.), *Johann Sebastian Bach und die Aufklärung* (Leipzig, 1982), p. 26.

99 Estimates range from 2,000 – Reiner Gross, 'Kurfürst August I. von Sachsen – Betrachtungen über ein Fürstenleben', in *August der Starke und seine Zeit: Beiträge des Kolloquiums vom 16./17. September 1994 auf der Festung Königstein / herausgegeben vom Verein für sächsische Landesgeschichte* (Dresden, 1995), p. 18 – to 7,000 – H. B. Nisbet, *Gotthold Ephraim Lessing: His Life, Works and Thought* (Oxford, 2013), p. 22.

100 Blaschke, 'Die kursächsische Politik und Leipzig im 18. Jahrhundert', p. 29.

101 See above, p. 149, and Schnee, *Die Hoffinanz und der moderne Staat*, p. 172. The town council reimposed a ban in 1704 – Schneider (ed.), *Leipzig*, p. 163.

102 Michael Schäbitz, *Juden in Sachsen – jüdische Sachsen? Emanzipation, Akkulturation und Integration 1700–1914* (Hanover, 2006), pp. 24–5.

103 Iwan-Michelangelo d'Aprile, 'Aufklärungstransfer zwischen Sachsen und Preußen', in Göse, Müller, Winkler and Ziesak (eds), *Preussen und Sachsen*, pp. 328–9. His manifesto urging the use of the German language in academic discourse is reprinted in Schneider (ed.), *Leipzig*, p. 149.

104 Flathe, *Geschichte des Kurstaates und Königreiches Sachsen*, pp. 296–8.

105 Petra Blettermann, *Die Universitätspolitik Augusts des Starken, 1694–1733* (Cologne and Vienna, 1990), pp. 31–6.

106 Hammerstein, 'Die Universität Leipzig im Zeichen der frühen Aufklärung', in Wolfgang Martens (ed.), *Leipzig. Aufklärung und Bürgerlichkeit* (Heidelberg, 1990), p. 133.

107 Nicholas Boyle, *Goethe: The Poet and the Age*, vol. 1: *The Poetry of Desire (1749–1790)* (Oxford, 1991), pp. 61–2.

108 Czok, 'Zur Leipziger Kulturgeschichte des 18. Jahrhunderts', p. 26.

109 Wolfgang Martens, 'Zur Einführung: Das Bild Leipzigs bei Zeitgenossen', in Martens (ed.), *Leipzig. Aufklärung und Bürgerlichkeit*, pp. 13–14. Her favourable verdict had been anticipated in similar terms in 1733 by the Prussian Huguenot Charles-Étienne Jordan, *Histoire d'un voyage litteraire fait en MDCCXXXIII en France, en Angleterre, et en Hollande* (The Hague, 1735), pp. 9–18.

110 Detlef Döring, *Die Geschichte der Deutschen Gesellschaft in Leipzig von der Gründung bis in die ersten Jahre des Seniorats Johann Christoph Gottscheds* (Tübingen, 2002), pp. 149–50.

111 *Gesammlete* [sic] *Reden in dreyen Abtheilungen nochmahls von ihm selbst übersehen und verbessert* (Leipzig, 1749), pp. 129–32. On Gottsched's nationalism see Daniel Fulda, 'Die Erschaffung der Nation als Literaturgesellschaft. Zu einer meist übergangenen Leistung des Publizisten Gottsched', *Denkströme. Journal der Sächsischen Akademie der Wissenschaften*, 4 (2010), pp. 2–29 and Caspar

359

Notes

Hirschi, *The Origins of Nationalism: An Alternative History from the Roman Republic to the German Reformation* (Cambridge, 2011), p. 211.

112 Wolfgang Hardtwig, 'Wie deutsch war die deutsche Aufklärung?', in *idem, Nationalismus und Bürgerkultur in Deutschland 1500–1914. Ausgewählte Aufsätze* (Göttingen, 1994), p. 73; Wolfgang Hardtwig, *Genossenschaft, Sekte, Verein in Deutschland,* vol. 1: *Vom Spätmittelalter bis zur Französischen Revolution* (Munich, 1997), p. 237.

113 Blanning, *The Pursuit of Glory,* p. xxv.

114 Döring, *Die Geschichte der Deutschen Gesellschaft in Leipzig,* p. 177.

115 Jordan, *Histoire d'un voyage litteraire,* pp. 11, 18. His statement that the municipal library contained 30,000 volumes is surely an exaggeration.

116 James van Horn Melton, *The Rise of the Public in Enlightenment Europe* (Cambridge, 2001), p. 240; Nisbet, *Gotthold Ephraim Lessing,* p. 23.

117 Melton, *The Rise of the Public in Enlightenment Europe* , p. 243.

118 Andreas Gestrich, *Absolutismus und Öffentlichkeit. Politische Kommunikation in Deutschland zu Beginn des 18. Jahrhunderts* (Göttingen, 1994), p. 183.

119 Wolfgang Martens, *Die Botschaft Der Tugend. Die Aufklärung Im Spiegel Der Deutschen Moralischen Wochenschriften* (Stuttgart, 1968), p. 124.

120 Ibid., p. 252.

121 Rüdiger Hachtmann, 'Friedrich II. von Preussen und die Freimaurerei', *Historische Zeitschrift,* 264, 1 (1997), pp. 21–2.

122 Otto Werner Förster, 'Freimaurer in Leipzig', in *Die Verschwörung zum Guten. Freimaurerei in Sachsen, Dresdner Hefte,* 64 (2000), p. 57.

123 The best account of the *Collegia musica* is to be found in Christoph Wolff, *Johann Sebastian Bach: The Learned Musician* (Oxford, 2000), pp. 351–72.

124 Gerhard Pietzsch, *Sachsen als Musikland* (Dresden, 1938), p. 50.

125 Bouhours, *Entretiens d'Ariste et d'Eugène,* p. 38. Jonathan Swift took the view that the Germans were the most stupid people on earth – Albert Koester, *Die deutsche Literatur der Aufklärung* (Heidelberg, 1925), p. 4.

126 Florack, *Tiefsinnige Deutsche,* pp. 223–4.

127 Adrien Baillet, *Jugemens des savans sur les principaux ouvrages des auteurs,* rev. edn (Paris, 1722), pp. 146–7, https://gallica.bnf.fr/ark:/12148/bpt6k113883m. image#

128 Boyle, *Goethe,* p. 20.

129 Blaschke, 'Die kursächsische Politik und Leipzig im 18. Jahrhundert', pp. 25–6.

130 Boyle, *Goethe,* p. 22.

131 Stadtgeschichtliches Museum, *Leipzig: Historisches Kalenderblatt,* https://www.facebook.com/stadtgeschichtlichesmuseumleipzig/posts/4302459073157686/; Schneider (ed.), *Leipzig,* pp. 160–61.

Notes

132 Ulrich Siegele, 'Bach and the domestic politics of Electoral Saxony', in John Butt (ed.), *The Cambridge Companion to Bach* (Cambridge, 2012), p. 20.

133 *Leipzig Lexikon*, https://www.leipzig-lexikon.de/biogramm/Romanus_Franz_Conrad.htm

134 Ulrich Siegele, 'Bachs politisches Profil oder Wo bleibt die Musik', in Konrad Küster (ed.), *Bach Handbuch* (Stuttgart, 1999), pp. 14–18.

135 Ulrich Siegele, 'Wandlungen der Politik – Wandlungen Bachs', in Ulrich Leisinger (ed.), *Bach in Leipzig – Bach und Leipzig* (Hildesheim, 2002), p. 466.

136 Siegele, 'Bachs politisches Profil', *passim*. There is a summary in English in Siegele, 'Bach and the domestic politics of Electoral Saxony'. For criticism, see Döring, *Die Geschichte der Deutschen Gesellschaft*, pp. 13–14.

137 Frank Göse, 'Zwischen "Ständestaat" und "Absolutismus". Zur Geschichte des kursächsischen Adels im 17. Jahrhundert unter besonderer Berücksichtigung des Verhältnisses zwischen Ständetum und Landesherrschaft', in Katrin Keller and Josef Matzerath (ed.), *Geschichte des sächsischen Adels* (Cologne, Weimar and Vienna, 1997), p. 152.

138 Rudolf Endres, *Der Adel in der frühen Neuzeit* (Munich, 1993), p. 32.

139 There is a numbing account in F. L. Carsten, *Princes and Parliaments in Germany from the Fifteenth to the Eighteenth Century* (Oxford, 1959), pp. 242–56. For a more concise account see Karl Czok, 'Zur Regierungspraxis Augusts des Starken', in Günter Vogler (ed.), *Europäische Herrscher. Ihre Rolle bei der Gestaltung von Politik und Gesellschaft vom 16. Bis zum 18. Jahrhundert* (Weimar 1988), pp. 194–8.

140 Förster, *Friedrich August II. der Starke*, p. 9.

141 Czok, 'August der Starke', p. 24.

142 Czok, *August der Starke und Kursachsen*, pp. 520–23.

143 Czok, 'Zur Regierungspraxis Augusts des Starken', p. 195. Nor was all of the money actually paid – Georg Wagner, *Die Beziehungen Augusts des Starken zu seinen Ständen während der ersten Jahre seiner Regierung (1694–1700)* (Leipzig, 1903), pp. 196–8.

144 Haake, *August der Starke*, p. 42. The nobility in the Lusatias were not exempt from direct taxation – Leszczyński, 'Die Oberlausitz in den ersten Jahren des nordischen Krieges', p. 74.

145 Held, *Der Adel und August der Starke*, p. 235; Czok, 'Zur Regierungspraxis Augusts des Starken', p. 196.

146 Frank-Lothar Kroll, 'Kursachsen im Zeitalter der polnisch-sächsischen Staatenunion 1697–1763', in Kroll and Thoss (eds), *Zwei Staaten, eine Krone*, p. 14; Czok, 'August der Starke', p. 25.

147 J. Dürichen, 'Geheimes Kabinett und Geheimer Rat unter der Regierung Augusts des Starken in den Jahren 1704–1720', *Neues Archiv für sächsische Geschichte und Altertumskunde*, 51 (1930), pp. 73, 77.

148 Czok, *August der Starke und Kursachsen*, pp. 197–8; Paul Haake, 'Ein politisches Testament König Augusts des Starken', *Historische Zeitschrift*, 87 (1901), pp. 3–5. A third document dealt with the Austrian succession and will be discussed later in a different context. See below, p. 285.

149 Held, *Der Adel und August der Starke*, p. 235; Förster, *Friedrich August II. der Starke*, p. 69.

150 Ibid., p. 261.

151 Reinhard Eigenwill, 'August der Starke und der Absolutismus in Sachsen', *Dresdner Hefte*, 3 (184), p. 4. Eigenwill believes that Augustus never wished to remove the fiscal control of the Estates.

152 Reiner Gross, 'Sachsen in der sächsisch–polnischen Verbindung – Versuch eines historiographischen Überblickes', in *Sachsen und Polen zwischen 1697 und 1765*, p. 25.

Chapter 7: The Resurrection of King Augustus: The Return to Poland

1 See above, pp. 153.

2 Frost, '"Everyone understood what it meant"', p. 163; Olszewski, *Doktryny Prawno-ustrojowe Czasów Saskich*, p. 91.

3 Friedrich, *The Other Prussia*, p. 169.

4 See above, p. 126.

5 Wimmer, *Polska–Szwecja*, p. 241.

6 Regina Stuber, 'Die multiplen Strategien Zar Peters I. und seines Wiener Gesandten Johann Christoph von Urbich hinsichtlich der Krone Polen–Litauens 1707–1709', *Zeitschrift für Ostmitteleuopa-Forschung / Journal of East Central European Studies*, 69, 3 (2020), pp. 304, 308–9, 315–16.

7 This has been attributed to both Frederick the Great and Napoleon, both of whom knew what they were talking about.

8 Stephan Lehnstaedt, *Der Große Nordische Krieg 1700–1721* (Stuttgart, 2021), p. 77; Liljegren, *Karl XII*, p. 155. It has been maintained recently that 'Lewenhaupt's supply column had a theoretical length of 83 kilometres, but really was closer to 150 kilometres' – Gunnar Aselius, 'Birth of the Russian Empire. Tenacious retreat of Sweden as a great power', *Baltic Worlds* (2011), p. 30.

9 Bobylev, *Venshniaia politika Rossii epokhi Petra I*, p. 31; Lindsey Hughes, *Peter the Great: A Biography* (New Haven and London, 2004), p. 77. Shortly before he left Saxony Charles informed the Prussians that he was going to dethrone Peter – Jörg-Peter Findeisen, *Das Ringen um die Ostseeherrschaft: Schwedens*

Notes

Könige der Grossmachtzeit (Berlin, 1992), p. 233. The same message was conveyed to the French ambassador in Stockholm – Buganov, *Petr velikii i ego vremia*, p. 89.

10 This is not to say that Moscow was invulnerable, for a Swedish army had reached it in 1610 – Joachim Krüger, 'Karl XII. – Der "heroische" Militärmonarch Schwedens', in Martin Wrede (ed.), *Die Inszenierung der heroischen Monarchie: Frühneuzeitliches Königtum zwischen ritterlichem Erbe und militärischer Herausforderung, Historische Zeitschrift*, Beiheft, no. 62 (2014), p. 369 n. 49.

11 Ibid., pp. 154, 160; Sarauw, *Die Feldzüge Karl's XII*, pp. 245–7; Munthe, *Karl XII och den ryska sjömakten*, vol. 2, p. 471. Gyllenkrok wrote this account based on notes he had taken at the time. Although he was trying to disculpate himself from responsibility for the disastrous campaign, his account fits well with what others wrote – ibid., p. 395 n. 43. 'Gyllenkrok' is sometimes spelled as 'Gyllenkrook', by Ragnhild Hatton for example. I have preferred the more concise version.

12 Akunin, *Istoriia rossiiskogo gosudarstva*, p. 162.

13 Lehnstaedt, *Der Große Nordische Krieg*, p. 82.

14 On the advantages of interior lines see Clausewitz, *On War*, ed. Howard and Paret, bk 6, ch. 4.

15 For a helpful discussion of recent literature on the battle see Aselius, 'Birth of the Russian Empire', pp 29–31.

16 Wittram, *Peter I*, vol. 1, p. 299. Amazingly, the Swedes chose to regard Lesnaya as a victory and it was only towards the end of the nineteenth century that the name of the battle was removed from regimental colours – Marie-Louise Rodén, 'Försvaret av stormakten', in Nils Erik Villstrand (ed.), *Sveriges Historia* (Stockholm, 2011), p. 210.

17 Liljegren, *Karl XII*, p. 167.

18 Tarlé, *La guerre du Nord*, vol. 1, p. 122; Fuller, *Strategy and Power in Russia 1600–1914*, p. 81; Liljegren, *Karl XII*, p. 167; Hatton, *Charles XII of Sweden*, p. 280.

19 Raghnhild Hatton (ed.), *Captain James Jefferyes, Letters from the Swedish Army, 1707–1709* (Stockholm, 1954), p. 61.

20 Sarauw, *Die Feldzüge Karl's XII*, p. 244.

21 Hatton (ed.), *Captain James Jefferyes*, p. 68. His report was dated 27 June 1709, i.e. shortly before the Battle of Poltava.

22 See above, p. 151.

23 Liljegren, *Karl XII*, pp. 161–3. One of the great strengths of Liljegren's account is the amount of contemporary accounts that he has used.

24 Paul Bushkovitch, 'Peter the Great and the Northern War', in Dominic Lieven (ed.), *The Cambridge History of Russia* (Cambridge, 2006), p. 498.

25 Carol B. Stevens, *Russia's Wars of Emergence 1460–1730* (Harlow, 2007), p. 245.

26 Telpukhovski, *Severnaia voina 1700–1721*. The online edition is not paginated.

27 Andersson, *Schwedische Geschichte von den Anfängen bis zur Gegenwart*, p. 280.

28 Pavlenko, *Petr I*, p. 148.

29 Nataliia Polonska-Vasylenko, *Istoriia Ukrainy*, vol. 2 (Munich, 1976), p. 56. As the place of publication suggests, this general history of Ukraine was not published in the USSR but by the 'Ukrainische Freie Universität und Ukrainischer Verlag'.

30 Tarlé, *La guerre du Nord*, vol. 1, p. 52.

31 Konopczyński, *Dzieje polska nowożytnej*, p. 162.

32 Pavlenko, *Petr I*, p. 145.

33 Wittram, *Peter I*, vol. 1, p. 300. Almost certainly Mazepa would have been disappointed even if the Swedes had won, for Charles would have faced demands from King Stanisław that the Cossack lands be incorporated in Poland – Liljegren, *Karl XII*, p. 154.

34 Bobylev, *Venshniaia politika Rossii epokhi Petra I*, p. 34; Akunin, *Istoriia rossiiskogo gosudarstva*, p. 167.

35 Wittram, *Peter I*, vol. 1, p. 305.

36 Hatton, *Charles XII of Sweden*, p. 240.

37 Bobylev, *Venshniaia politika Rossii epokhi Petra I*, pp. 31–2.

38 Wittram, *Peter I*, vol. 1, p. 306.

39 Skworoda *Wojny Rzeczypospolitej Obojga Narodów ze Szwecją*, pp. 226–7; Wimmer, *Polska–Szwecja*, p. 242. Krassow is often spelled Krassau.

40 Lukasz Pabich, 'The Battle of Koniecpol 1708', in Kling (ed.), *Great Northern War Compendium*, vol. 1, pp. 275–86.

41 Frost, *The Northern Wars*, p. 270. 'Half-hearted' is Frost's description of Leszczyński's initiative.

42 Wittram, *Peter I*, vol. 1, p. 310. Wittram writes that the battle took place at 'Liduchovo' but I have been unable to locate it on any map. It appears to be somewhere in the region of the River San.

43 Hatton, *Charles XII of Sweden*, p. 286.

44 Wittram, *Peter I*, vol. 1, pp. 309–11.

45 There is an excellent concise account in Frost, *The Northern Wars*, pp. 289–92. The best maps – five in total, charting the stages of the battle – are to be found in Einar Lyth, 'Decision in the Ukraine: The Battle of Poltava 1709', in Kling (ed.), *Great Northern War Compendium*, vol. 2, pp. 5–11.

46 Aselius, 'Birth of the Russian Empire', p. 30.

47 Wittram, *Peter I*, p. 314.

48 Stevens, *Russia's Wars of Emergence 1460–1730*, p. 252. Figures vary: Lehnstaedt, *Der Große Nordische Krieg*, p. 100 states that 9,200 Swedes died.

49 Ibid.

Notes

50 Rodén, 'Försvaret av stormakten', p. 213.

51 Sven Grauers, 'Karl XII', *Svenskt Biografiskt Lexikon*, https://sok.riksarkivet.se/sbl/Presentation.aspx?id=12357

52 Hatton, *Charles XII of Sweden*, p. 305.

53 Ibid., pp. 305–6. Mazepa died of natural causes on 22 September.

54 Behre, Larsson and Österberg, *Sveriges Historia 1521–1809*, p. 170.

55 Haintz, *König Karl XII.*, vol. 2, p. 20.

56 Nordberg, *Leben Carls des Zwölften Königs in Schweden*, vol. 2, p. 188. Nordberg, who had been taken prisoner at Poltava, was an involuntary eyewitness. See also Voltaire, *History of Charles the Twelth King of Sweden*, trans. Winifred Todhunter (London, 1905), pp. 205–6; Akunin, *Istoriia rossiiskogo gosudarstva*, p. 178.

57 Sten Bonnesen, *Studier över August II:s utrikespolitik 1712–1715* (Lund, 1918), p. 1.

58 Czok, 'Die Personalunion als Problem des Monarchen', p. 60.

59 See below, pp. 232, 245, 281.

60 Vinzenz Czech, *Das Potsdamer Dreikönigstreffen 1709: Möglichkeiten und Grenzen höfisch-dynastischer Selbstdarstellung in Brandenburg-Preußen* (Göttingen, 2008), p. 33.

61 Bobylev, *Venshniaia politika Rossii epokhi Petra I*, p. 37. Förster, *Friedrich August II. der Starke*, p. 194.

62 Ibid., p. 192.

63 Sarauw, *Die Feldzüge Karl's XII.*, p. 274.

64 Förster, *Friedrich August II. der Starke*, pp. 191–2.

65 Olszewski, *Doktryny Prawno-ustrojowe Czasów Saskich*, p. 112; Staszewski, 'Begründung und Fortsetzung der Personalunion Sachsen-Polen 1697 und 1733', p. 45.

66 Sergei Mikhailovich Solov'ev, *Istoriia Rossii s drevneishikh vremen*, vol. (Kindle edition marked 'a public domain book'), loc. 8749.

67 Konopczyński, *Dzieje polska nowożytnej*, p. 168.

68 Jarosław Poraziński, 'Restauracja rządów Augusta II w rzeczpospolitej w 1709–1710 roku. problemy ustrojowe i prawne', in Bartkiewicz (ed.), *Polska–Saksonia w czasach Unii (1697–1763))*, pp. 108–11.

69 Markiewicz, *Historia Polski 1492–1795*, p. 608.

70 Konopczyński, *Dzieje polska nowożytnej*, p. 163.

71 Butterwick, *The Polish–Lithuanian Commonwealth*, p. 40.

72 See above, p. 295.

73 Solov'ev, *Istoriya Rossii s drevneishikh vremen*, vol. 15, loc. 8749.

74 'Княжество Лифляндское со всеми своими городами и местами его королевскому величеству польскому, как курфюрсту саксонскому, и его наследникам присвоено и уступлено быть имеет', ibid., loc. 8781.

75 Wittram, *Peter I*, vol. 1, p. 324.

76 Schuster and Francke, p. 176; Jean-Piere Bois, *Maurice de Saxe* (Paris, 1992), loc. 1629

77 Konopczyński, *Dzieje polska nowożytnej*, p. 164.

78 Gabriele Hoffmann, *Constantia von Cosel und August der Starke. Die Geschichte einer Mätresse* (Cologne, 1984), p. 390.

79 Wilfried Hansmann, *Im Glanz des Barock. Ein Begleiter zu Bauwerken Augusts des Starken und Friedrichs des Großen* (Cologne, 1992), p. 24. See also below, p. 151.

80 Bobylev, *Venshniaia politika Rossii epokhi Petra I*, p. 53.

81 Franklin Daniel Scott, *Sweden: The Nation's History* (Minneapolis, 1978), p. 233.

82 Frost, ' "Everyone understood what it meant" ', p. 42.

Chapter 8: How the Great Northern War Was Won and Lost

1 His two major works on the period are scholarly but not lively – *George I and the Northern War: A Study of British-Hanoverian Policy in the North of Europe in the Years 1709 to 1721* (London, 1909) and *The Alliance of Hanover: A Study of British Foreign Policy in the Last Years of George I* (London, 1923).

2 Frost, *The Northern Wars*, pp. 226–93 and 294–6.

3 See above, p. 104.

4 Jan Glete, *Swedish Naval Administration, 1521–1721* (Leiden, 2010), p. 123.

5 Liljegren, *Karl XII*, p. 85.

6 For example: Hughes, *Peter the Great*, pp. 24, 138; Wittram, *Peter I*, vol. 1, p. 90.

7 Alexander Brückner, *Peter der Große* (Berlin, 1870), p. 112.

8 Munthe, *Karl XII och den ryska sjömakten*, vol. 1, p. 119; B. S. Tel'pukhovskiy, *Severnaya Voyna 1700–1721 Polkovodcheskaya deyatel'nost' Petra I* (Moscow, 1946), http://militera.lib.ru/h/telpuhovsky_bs01/ The online text is not paginated.

9 Wittram, *Peter I.*, vol. 1, pp. 152–4.

10 See above, pp. 92–3.

11 Munthe, *Karl XII och den ryska sjömakten*, vol. 1, pp. 173–4. A second group added seventy officers, thirteen naval physicians and 115 petty officers.

12 https://www.openwaterpedia.com/wiki/Neva_River; Robert K. Massie, *Peter the Great* (London, 2013), p. 625.

13 See the map on p. xiii.

14 Munthe, *Karl XII och den ryska sjömakten*, vol. 2, p. 336. The pagination from vols 1 to 2 is continuous.

15 Glete, *Swedish Naval Administration*, p. 96. See also a similar verdict by Michael Roberts in *Gustavus Adolphus: A History of Sweden 1611–1632*, vol. 2: *1611–1632* (London, 1958), p. 276.

Notes

16 Roberts, *Gustavus Adolphus*, p. 277.

17 Munthe, *Karl XII och den ryska sjömakten*, vol. 1, pp. 126–31.

18 Ibid., p. 149.

19 Ibid., p. 158. It has been pointed out by Jan Kusber in 'Peter I, the Great Northern War and St. Petersburg', in Bleile and Krüger (eds), *'Princess Hedvig Sofia' and the Great Northern War*, pp. 160–61 that the notion that the mouth of the Neva was a deserted swamp was perpetrated to enhance Peter's achievement, whereas in fact the area along the lower Neva had long been cultivated and was in use as a landing place and possibly as a trading post too.

20 Cyprian A. Bridge (ed.), *History of the Russian Fleet during the reign of Peter the Great by a contemporary Englishman (1724)*, Publications of the Navy Records Society, vol. 15 (London, 1899), p. 7 n. 1.

21 Munthe, *Karl XII och den ryska sjömakten*, vol. 1, pp. 167–71. No apology is needed to justify heavy reliance on Munthe's classic account, a work of distinction but strangely neglected by most historians of the period. Honourable exceptions include Jan Glete, Bengt Liljegren and Lars Ericson Wolke. This is perhaps due to its rarity – there are only two copies in public collections in the United Kingdom.

22 Pavlenko, *Petr I*, pp. 98–100.

23 Munthe, *Karl XII och den ryska sjömakten*, vol. 1, pp. 156–7. The total seems improbable but Munthe is quite explicit: '*dessa blevo natten till 8 maj från ett bakhåll anfallna 100 ryska lodjor*' (a '*lodja*' – plural '*lodjor*' – is a rowing boat with a complement of *c*. 50). E. Arens, *Rossiyskiy flot* (St Petersburg, 1904), p. 21 stated that only eight Russian ships were involved.

24 Fryxell, *Lebensgeschichte Karl's des Zweiten*, vol. 2, pp. 2, 29.

25 John P. LeDonne, *The Grand Strategy of the Russian Empire, 1650–1831* (Oxford, 2004), p. 53.

26 See above, pp. 138–9.

27 Munthe, *Karl XII och den ryska sjömakten*, vol. 1, pp. 183–90.

28 R. C. Anderson, *Naval wars in the Baltic during the sailing-ship epoch 1522–1850* (London, 1910), pp. 137–8, 146.

29 Glete, *Swedish Naval Administration*, p. 214.

30 Jan Glete, *Navies and Nations: Warships, Navies and State Building in Europe and America, 1500–1860*, vol. 1 (Stockholm, 1993), p. 234; Fryxell, *Lebensgeschichte Karl's des Zweiten*, vol. 2, p. 29.

31 The battle is known by many different names, the most popular alternatives being Hangöudd and Rilax. There is a good contemporary illustration in Rodén, 'Försvaret av stormakten', p. 219.

32 P. A. Korotkov, *Gangutskaya bataliya 1714 goda* (St Petersburg, 1996), p. 162.

33 See above, p. 95.

34 Munthe, *Karl XII och den ryska sjömakten*, vol. 3, p. 535.

35 Ibid., vol. 2, p. 461

36 Glete, *Swedish Naval Administration*, p. 126.

37 G. A. Nekrasov, *Voyenno-morskiye sily Rossii na Baltike v pervoy chetverti XVIII v.* (Moscow, 1969), pp. 248–9.

38 Stevens, *Russia's Wars of Emergence 1460–1730*, p. 273.

39 Hughes, *Peter the Great*, p. 115.

40 Anthony Sokol, *The Imperial and Royal Austro-Hungarian Navy* (Anapolis, 1968), p. 3.

41 Plakans, *A Concise History of the Baltic States*, p. 95.

42 This barely credible statistic is conveyed by Urszula Augustyniak in her *Historia Polski 1572–1795*, p. 272 – 'budżet Gdańska w 1. pol. XVII w, 20-krotnie większy od budżetu państwa polskiego'.

43 Lukowski, *Disorderly Liberty*, p. 10.

44 Wandycz, *The Price of Freedom*, p. 61.

45 L. R. Lewitter, 'Russia, Poland and the Baltic 1697–1721', *Historical Journal*, 11, 1 (1968), p. 5.

46 Samuel Schelwigen, *Krönungs Predigt* (Danzig, 1697), p. 15. The full title is much longer, decked out with Augustus's numerous titles and a number of biblical references.

47 Jerzy Trzoska, 'Gdańsk in den baltischen Plänen Peters I. und die Versuche deren Übernahme durch August II.', in Cieślak and Olszewski (eds), *Changes in Two Baltic Countries*, pp. 149–51.

48 See above, pp. 81–2.

49 Quoted in Friedrich, *The Other Prussia*, p. 55.

50 Ibid.

51 Michael Roberts, *The Swedish Imperial Experience 1560–1718* (Cambridge, 1970), pp. 16–18.

52 Augustyniak, *Historia Polski 1572–1795*, p. 156. Another distinguished and substantial history of Poland in the same period – Markiewicz, *Historia Polski 1492–1795* – devotes just *seven lines* in a book of 759 pages to the navy, and dismisses it with the comment: 'military historians attach great importance to attempts to build the fleet of the Republic. This does not seem right, as it was of marginal importance for the defence of the country and its interests, and attempts to create it were mostly linked to dynastic plans. The country's interests, and here I mean the security of the grain trade, were assured from the mid-sixteenth to the end of the seventeenth

century by the maritime superpower that was then the Netherlands. It was able to rely on the assistance of the British fleet in case of difficulties' – p. 106. The naval history of the Commonwealth awaits its historian.

53 Gierowski, 'August II Wettyn', p. 165.

54 Jacek Staszewski, 'Polen und Sachsen im 18. Jahrhundert', *Jahrbuch für Geschichte*, 23 (1981), p. 182.

55 Czok, *August der Starke und Kursachsen*, p. 23.

56 Michael Komaszynski, 'August der Starke und seine Herrschaft an der Weichsel im Spiegel der polnischen Geschichtsschreibung', in Gross (ed.), *Sachsen und die Wettiner*, p. 135.

57 Józef Andrzej Gierowski, 'Problematyka bałtycka w polityce Augusta II Sasa', in Jerzy Trzoska (ed.), *Strefa Bałtycka w XVI–XVIII w. Polityka – Społeczeństwo – Gospodarka* (Danzig, 1993), pp. 53–5.

58 Ibid., p. 58.

59 Karl Czok, *Am Hofe Augusts des Starken* (Leipzig, 1989), p. 94.

60 Akunin, *Istoriia rossiiskogo gosudarstva*, p. 175 – 'Она не была разгромлена – она полностью исчезла'.

61 Quoted in Frost, ' "Everyone understood what it meant" ', p. 159.

62 Wittram, *Peter I*, vol. 1, p. 317.

63 Lindsey Hughes, *Russia in the Age of Peter the Great* (New Haven and London, 1998), p. 40.

64 Jörg Zapnik, *Pest und Krieg im Ostseeraum: Der 'Schwarze Tod' in Stralsund während des Großen Nordischen Krieges (1700–1721)* (Hamburg, 2007), p. 273.

65 Otto Haintz, *König Karl XII.*, vol. 2, p. 42.

66 Liljegren, *Karl XII*, p. 212.

67 Ibid., p. 215. The best account of the Battle of Helsingborg is at https://en.wikipedia.org/wiki/Battle_of_Helsingborg

68 Haintz, *König Karl XII. von Schweden*, vol. 2, p. 83.

69 Glete, *Swedish Naval Administration*, p. 127.

70 Trzoska, 'Gdańsk in den baltischen Plänen Peters I.', p. 148.

71 Ibid., p. 232.

72 LeDonne, *The Grand Strategy of the Russian Empire, 1650–1831*, pp. 40–41.

73 Quoted in Kurat, 'The retreat of the Turks, 1688–1730', p. 635.

74 Wittram, *Peter I*, vol. 1, p. 387. Ragnhild Hatton wrote that the Ottomans settled because the Grand Vizier believed the Austrians were about to mobilize – *Charles XII*, p. 335.

75 Hans Uebersberger, *Russlands Orientpolitik in den letzten zwei Jahrhunderten*, vol. 1: *Bis zum Frieden von Jassy* (Stuttgart, 1913), p. 109.

76 Kurat, 'The retreat of the Turks', p. 635.

77 V. S. Bobylev, *Vneshniaia politika Rossii epokhi Petra I* (Moscow, 1990), p. 59.

78 War was declared against Venice in December 1714, the Austrians entered the war in support of the Venetians in 1716.

79 Pavlenko, *Petr I*, p. 202.

80 P. O. Bäckström, *Svenska flottans historia* (Stockholm, 1884), p. 176.

81 Lehnstaedt, *Der Große Nordische Krieg*, p. 118.

82 Gunnar Arteus, 'Karl XII i ego armiya', p. 162.

83 Lars Ericson Wolke, *The Swedish Army in the Great Northern War 1700–21* (Warwick, 2018), p. 46.

84 Stewart P. Oakley, *War and Peace in the Baltic 1560–1790* (London, 1992), p. 113.

85 Rodén, 'Försvaret av stormakten', p. 220.

86 See above, p. 192.

87 Erdmannsdörffer, *Deutsche Geschichte vom Westälischen Frieden*, vol. 2, p. 328.

88 Oakley, *War and Peace in the Baltic 1560–1790*, p. 111; Thomas Stamm-Kühlmann, 'Prussia, neutrality and the acquisition of Stettin', in Bleile and Krüger (eds), *'Princess Hedvig Sofia' and the Great Northern War*, pp. 180–83.

89 The best accounts are in Hatton, *Charles XII*, pp. 383–96 and Liljegren, *Karl XII*, pp. 247–55.

90 I have discussed this in *George I* (London, 2017), ch. 5.

91 See above, pp. 103–4.

92 Liljegren, *Karl XII*, p. 270.

93 Oakley, *War and Peace in the Baltic 1560–1790*, p. 114; Wolfgang Michael, 'Ein schwieriger diplomatischer Fall aus dem Jahre 1719', *Historische Zeitschrift*, 88, 1 (1902), p. 61; Hatton, *Charles XII*, pp. 404–6.

94 Hatton, *Charles XII*, p. 411.

95 Lehnstaedt, *Der Große Nordische Krieg*, p. 123.

96 An example can be found in the Royal Museums collection at Greenwich and viewed online at https://www.rmg.co.uk/collections/objects/rmgc-object-37880

97 Alexander Querengässer, 'Der Traum von der Großmacht – Außenpolitik unter August dem Starken', *Blätter für deutsche Landesgeschichte*, 153 (2017), pp. 314–15.

98 Massie, *Peter the Great*, pp. 646–8.

99 Ibid., p. 650.

100 Clausewitz, *On War*, ed. and trans. Howard and Paret, p. 119.

101 See above, p. 200–1.

102 Akunin, *Istoriia rossiiskogo gosudarstva*, pp. 122, 137, 204. Jan Lindegren has speculated imaginatively that it was the memory of the mauling the Russians had received at Grodno in 1706 which prompted Peter to draw back – 'Karl XII', in Florén, Dahlgren and Lindegren, *Kungar och Krigare*, p. 194.

103 Massie, *Peter the Great*, p. 650.

104 Oakley, *War and Peace in the Baltic 1560–1790*, p. 114.

Chapter 9: Out of the Swedish Frying Pan into the Russian Fire

1 Mindaugas Šapoka, *Warfare, Loyalty and Rebellion: The Grand Duchy of Lithuania and the Great Northern War, 1709–1717* (London, 2017), p. 206.

2 The fullest account is in Wimmer, *Wojsko Rzeczpospolitej w dobie wojny północnej*, pp. 359–62.

3 Gierowski, 'The eclipse of Poland', p. 707.

4 Olszewski, *Doktryny Prawno-ustrojowe Czasów Saskich*, p. 138.

5 Andrzej K. Link-Lenczowsk, 'Adam Mikołaj Sieniawski 1666–1726', *Polski Słownik Biograficzny*, the online edition is not paginated; Wagner-Rundell, *Common Wealth, Common Good*, p. 94. On the position and powers of the hetmans see above, p. 73.

6 Gierowski, *The Polish–Lithuanian Commonwealth in the XVIIIth Century*, p. 135; Gierowski, *Rzeczpospolita w dobie złotej wolnośći*, p. 269. Šapoka, in *Warfare, Loyalty and Rebellion*, offers a more nuanced and sympathetic depiction of Pociej; see especially pp. 206–7.

7 Konopczyński, *Dzieje polska nowożytnej*, p. 170; Jacek Staszewski, *August II* (Warsaw, 1986), p. 36; Markiewicz, *Historia Polski 1492–1795*, p. 612.

8 Wimmer, *Wojsko Rzeczpospolitej w dobie wojny północnej*, p. 398.

9 Like his father, the crown prince was christened 'Frederick Augustus' but took the title 'Augustus III' when he became King of Poland in 1734. In what follows, he will be referred to as Frederick Augustus.

10 Doubek, *August der Starke*, loc. 997.

11 Augustin Theiner, *Geschichte der Zurückkehr der regierenden Häuser von Braunschweig und Sachsen in den Schoss der katholischen Kirche im XVIIIten Jahrhundert* (Einsiedeln, 1843), p. 158.

12 Jacek Staszewski, *August III. Kurfürst von Sachsen und König von Polen. Eine Biographie* (Berlin, 1996), p. 32; Paul Haake, *Christiane Eberhardine und August der Starke. Eine Ehetragödie* (Dresden, 1930), p. 134.

13 Haake, *Christiane Eberhardine und August der Starke*, p. 62.

14 Ziekursch, 'August der Starke und die katholische Kirche in den Jahren 1697–1720', p. 242.

15 See above, p. 225.

16 Mediger, *Mecklenburg, Russland und England–Hannover 1706–1721*, p. 402.

17 Gierowski, *Rzeczpospolita w dobie złotej wolnośći*, pp. 104–9.

18 Gierowski, 'The eclipse of Poland', p. 707; Wimmer, *Wojsko Rzeczpospolitej w dobie wojny północnej*, p. 362.

19 Józef Gierowski, *Między saskim absolutyzmem a złotą wolnością. Z dziejów wewnętrznych Rzeczypospolitej w latach 1712–1715* (Warsaw, 1953), pp. 178–80.

20 Józef Andrzej Gierowski, 'Ein Herrscher – zwei Staaten: die sächsisch–polnische Personalunion als Problem des Monarchen aus polnischer Sicht', *perspectivia. net*, Quellen und Studien, vol. 18 (2005), p. 140, https://perspectivia.net/receive/ploneimport_mods_00011621

21 Wojciech Kriegseisen, 'Sprawa przemykowska – przyczynek do problemu genezy konfederacji tarnogrodzkiej?', in Urszula Kosińska, Dorota Dukwicz and Adam Danilczyk (eds), *W cieniu wojen i rozbiorów* (Warsaw, 2014), p. 67.

22 Jozef Gierowski, 'Pruski projekt zamachu stanu w Polsce w 1715 r.', *Przeglad Historyczny*, 50 (1959), p. 755; Konopczyński, *Dzieje polska nowożytnej*, p. 169; Skworoda, *Wojny Rzeczypospolitej Obojga Narodów ze Szwecją*, p. 241.

23 Kriegseisen, 'Sprawa przemykowska', p. 68; Konopczyński, 'Early Saxon period 1697–1733', p. 11.

24 Frost, '"Everyone understood what it meant"', p. 171.

25 Gierowski, *Między Saskim Absolutyzmem a Złotą Wolnością*, p. 17.

26 Gierowski, *Rzeczpospolita w dobie złotej wolnośći*, p. 274.

27 Frost, 'Sächsisch–polnische Personalunion und die Katastrophe des Großen Nordischen Krieges', p. 440.

28 Gierowski, *Między Saskim Absolutyzmem a Złotą Wolnością*, pp. 10–13, 46–7.

29 Markiewicz, *Historia Polski 1492–1795*, p. 612.

30 The fullest account of this episode is to be found in Wimmer, *Wojsko Rzeczpospolitej w dobie wojny północnej*, pp. 69–74.

31 Šapoka, *Warfare, Loyalty and Rebellion*, p. 172; Jerzy Topolski, *Polska w czasach nowożytnych. Od środkowoeuropejskiej potęgi do utraty niepodległości (1501–1795)* (Poznań, 1994), p. 418; Markiewicz, *Historia Polski 1492–1795*, p. 612.

32 Gretschel, *Geschichte des sächsischen Volkes und Staates*, vol. 2, p. 570 recorded that Saxon prisoners were mutilated by the amputation of arms and legs, to which the Saxon commander Flemming retaliated by summarily hanging Polish prisoners.

33 Markiewicz, *Historia Polski 1492–1795*, p. 612.

34 Skrzypietz, *Jakub Sobieski*, loc. 4498.

35 Tomasz Ciesielski, 'Bitwa pod Kowalewem (5 X 1716) – Geneza, przebieg, konsekwencje', *Zapiski Historyczne*, 85, 3 (2019), pp. 47–8. As the author of this well-researched and written article observes, it is odd that so little attention has been paid to this important engagement.

36 Gierowski, *The Polish–Lithuanian Commonwealth in the XVIIIth Century*, p. 86; Frost, '"Everyone understood what it meant"', p. 167.

37 Gierowski, 'The eclipse of Poland', p. 713.

38 Ibid.

39 Augustyniak, *Historia Polski 1572–1795*, p. 194.

40 Gierowski, *Rzeczpospolita w dobie złotej wolności*, p. 284; L. R. Lewitter, 'Peter the Great and the Polish Dissenters', *Slavonic and East European Review*, 33, 80 (December 1954), p. 85.

41 Frost, ' "Everyone understood what it meant" ', p. 166.

42 Adam Perlakowski, 'Das Jahr 1717 oder die ungenützte Gelegenheit zur Reform der polnisch-litauischen Adelsrepublik', in Claudia Reichl-Ham (ed.), *Polen–Litauen und die Habsburgermonarchie im Zeitalter Maria Theresias* (Vienna, 2018), p. 13.

43 Skworoda, *Wojny Rzeczypospolitej Obojga Narodów ze Swecją*, p. 242; Robert Frost, 'Some hidden thunder: Hanover, Saxony, and the management of political union, 1697–1763', in Brent S. Sirota and Allan I. Macinnes, *The Hanoverian Succession in Great Britain and its Empire* (Woodbridge, 2019), p. 208.

44 Gierowski, 'The eclipse of Poland', p. 713.

45 Augustyniak, *Historia Polski 1572–1795*, p. 795.

46 See above, pp. 210, 213.

47 Gierowski, 'The eclipse of Poland', p. 714.

48 Augustyniak, *Historia Polski 1572–1795*, p. 795.

49 Urzula Kozińska, *Sejm 1719–1720 a sprawa ratyfikacji traktatu wiedeńskiego* (Warsaw, 2003), p. 28; Wittram, *Baltische Geschichte*, p. 120. Anna Ivanovna was to become Tsarina of Russia in 1730.

50 Markiewicz, *Historia Polski 1492–1795*, p. 611.

51 Jędruch, *Constitutions, Elections and Legislatures of Poland 1493–1993*, pp. 183–4

52 Antony Polonsky, 'Introduction', in Polonsky, Basista and Link-Lenczowski (eds), *The Jews in Old Poland 1000–1795*, p. 4; Davies, *God's Playground*, p. 377.

53 Heidi Hein-Kircher and Michael G. Müller, 'Souveränitätskrise', in Bömelburg (ed.), *Polen in der europäischen Geschichte*, vol. 2, p. 443.

54 Perlakowski, 'Das Jahr 1717', p. 20.

55 Šapoka, *Warfare, Loyalty and Rebellion*, p. 179; Gierowski, 'The eclipse of Poland', p. 13. Davies, *God's Playground*, p. 377, was mistaken when he wrote that 'the Tsar undertook to guarantee the agreement'.

56 Konopczyński, *Dzieje polska nowożytnej*, p. 175.

57 See above, p. 183–4.

58 Urszula Kosińska, 'Rosyjskie plany wywołania antykrólewskiej konfederacji i detronizacji Augusta II w 1719 r.', *Kwartalnik Historyczny*, 106, 3 (1999), pp. 53–4.

59 Andrzej Wyczański, *Polska Rzeczą Pospolitą Szlachecką*, 2nd edn (Warsaw, 1991), p. 349; Gierowski, *Rzeczpospolita w dobie złotej wolności*, p. 279.

Notes

60 Kosińska, *Sejm 1719–1720 a sprawa ratyfikacji traktatu wiedeńskiego*, p. 29; L. R. Lewitter, 'Poland, Russia and the Treaty of Vienna of 5 January 1719', *Historical Journal*, 13, 1 (1970), p. 12, recorded that an all-time high of 85,000 was reached in 1718, although this must surely be an exaggeration.

61 *Sbornik Imperatorskogo Russkogo Istoricheskogo Obshestva*, vol. 61 (St Petersburg, 1888), p. 478.

62 Lewitter, 'Poland under the Saxon kings', p. 373; Konopczyński, *Dzieje polska nowożytnej*, p. 177.

63 S. A. Feygina, *Alandskii kongress: vneshniaia politika Rossii v kontse Severnoy Voyny* (Moscow–Leningrad, 1959), p. 110.

64 Kosińska, *Sejm 1719–1720 a sprawa ratyfikacji traktatu wiedeńskiego*, p. 22.

65 See above, p. 208.

66 Kosińska, *Sejm 1719–1720 a sprawa ratyfikacji traktatu wiedeńskiego*, p. 50.

67 Michael, 'Ein schwieriger diplomatischer Fall aus dem Jahre 1719', p. 60; Grzegorz Chomicki, 'Dyplomacja brytyjska wobec problemów politycznych Rzeczpospolitej od wstąpienia na tron Jerzego I do zawarcia pokoju w Nystadt', in Muszyńska (ed.), *Rzeczpospolita w dobie wielkiej wojny północnej*, p. 172.

68 Konopczyński, *Dzieje polska nowożytnej*, p. 178.

69 His death has inspired speculation of Kennedy-like proportions. There seems little doubt that he was not shot by one of his own side but by one of the defenders of Fredriksten. For an excellent concise review of the evidence see Peter Englund, 'Sanningen om Karl XII:s död', *Populär Historia*, 9 (2018).

70 Kosińska, *Sejm 1719–1720 a sprawa ratyfikacji traktatu wiedeńskiego*, p. 54.

71 Behre, Larsson and Österberg, *Sveriges Historia 1521–1809*, p. 176.

72 Hatton, *Charles XII*, p. 512.

73 Konopczyński, *Dzieje polska nowożytnej*, p. 180.

74 Lewitter, 'Poland, Russia and the Treaty of Vienna of 5 January 1719', p. 23.

75 Ibid. Kozińska, *Sejm 1719–1720 a sprawa ratyfikacji traktatu wiedeńskiego*, pp. 74–6.

76 Konopczyński, *Dzieje polska nowożytnej*, p. 179.

77 Šapoka, *Warfare, Loyalty and Rebellion*, p. 209.

78 Querengässer, 'Der Traum von der Großmacht', p. 311.

79 Kosińska, *Sejm 1719–1720 a sprawa ratyfikacji traktatu wiedeńskiego*, p. 252. On the key role of the hetmans see also Zofia Zielińska, 'Poland between Prussia and Russia in the eighteenth century', in Fiszman (ed.), *Constitution and Reform in Eighteenth-century Poland*, p. 90.

80 Chomicki, 'Dyplomacja brytyjska wobec problemów politycznych rzeczpospolitej', p. 177.

81 Schilling, 'Der Wiener Hof und Sachsen–Polen (1697–1764)', p. 125.

82 Beauvois, *Histoire de la Pologne*, p. 151; Konopczyński, *Dzieje polska nowożytnej*, p. 180; Frost, *The Northern Wars*, p. 326.

83 Kosińska, *Sejm 1719–1720 a sprawa ratyfikacji traktatu wiedeńskiego*, p. 32.

84 Augustyniak, *Historia Polski 1572–1795*, p. 798.

85 Frost, *The Northern Wars*, p. 326.

86 Lewitter, 'Poland under the Saxon kings', p. 374. Lewitter (1922–2007) spent his adult life in Cambridge but had been born in Kraków, leaving for England in 1938.

87 Wandycz, *The Price of Freedom*, p. 115. Wandycz reached England via Romania and Grenoble, studying at Cambridge and the LSE before moving to the USA.

88 Konopczyński, 'Early Saxon period 1697–1733', p. 14.

Chapter 10: Augustus the Artist: The Wedding of the Century

1 See above, pp. 210–11.

2 'Ich mach mir nichts aus allen Frauen der Welt' – Staszewski, *August III*, p. 65.

3 That can be done in ibid., pp. 84–96.

4 Joachim Menzhausen, 'August III. und die Aufklärung', in *Der stille König. August III. zwischen Kunst und Politik*, Dresdner Hefte, 46 (1996), p. 29.

5 See above, p. 219.

6 *Das Königliche Denckmahl, Welches Nach geschehener Vermählung Ihro Hoheit des Königlichen und Chur-Sächsischen Cron-Printzens Herrn Friedrich Augusti, Mit der Durchlauchtigsten Fr. Maria Josepha, Ertz-Hertzogin von Oesterreich, Bey Dero Hohen Ankunfft In der Königl. und Chur-Sächs. Residentz-Stadt Dreßden, Vom ersten biß letzten Sept. 1719 gestifftet worden* (Frankfurt am Main and Leipzig, 1719).

7 Staszewski, *August III*, p. 96.

8 Watanabe-O'Kelly, 'Joseph und seine Brüder', p. 29. See also the illustrations in Julia Teresa Friehs, 'Party-time: The marriage of Leopold I and Margarita of Spain', https://www.habsburger.net/en/chapter/party-time-marriage-leopold-i-and-margarita-spain

9 'Das vielleicht größte Barockfest des. 18. Jahrhunderts' – Alexander Querengässer, *1719. Hochzeit des Jahrhunderts. Festkultur am Dresdner Hof* (Beucha, 2020), p. 7.

10 Rather than multiply the footnotes, listed here are the accounts I have used for the following paragraphs: Querengässer, *1719*, pp. 37ff.; *Das Königliche Denckmahl*, pp. 199ff.; Irmgard Becker-Glauch, *Die Bedeutung der Musik für die*

Notes

Dresdener Hoffeste bis in die Zeit Augusts des Starken (Kassel and Basle, 1951), pp. 101ff.; Bauer, *Barock*, pp. 126ff.; Claudia Schnitzer and Daniela Günther (eds), *Constellatio Felix: Die Planetenfeste Augusts des Starken anlässlich der Vermählung seines Sohnes Friedrich August mit der Kaisertochter Maria Josepha 1719 in Dresden* (Dresden, 2014) pp. 64ff.; David Charlton, *Music of the Augustan Age*, http://www.classical.net/music/comp.lst/articles/dresden/index.php; Wolfgang Braunfels, 'Der Glanz der 28 Tage. Kaiserhochzeiten in Dresden 1719 und München 1722', in Uwe Schultz (ed.), *Das Fest. Eine Kulturgeschichte von der Antike bis zur Gegenwart* (Munich, 1988) pp. 217.

11 A good illustration of a model now in the Dresden Transport Museum can be found online at https://www.facebook.com/Verkehrsmuseum.Dresden/photos/a.102590806486219/2382064905205453/?type=3&locale=ar_AR

12 According to one contemporary source, the 25 'Moors' were all of uniform height and had been bought (*sic*) by Augustus from Portugal – Schnitzer and Günther (eds), *Constellatio Felix*, p. 64.

13 Elector Frederick II married Margaret of Austria, whose father Ernst was Duke of Inner Austria. Her brother Frederick became the first Habsburg Holy Roman Emperor in 1452.

14 Norbert Oelsner and Henning Prinz, 'Das Residenzschloss zur Zeit Friedrich Augusts I. Baugeschichte und Nutzungsentwicklung', pp. 50–55 and the section 'Heimführung der Kurprinzessin Maria Josepha am 2. September 1719' in Prinz and Oelsner, 'Zeremoniell und Raum. Die Fest- und Wohnetagen im Dresdner Residenzschloss unter Friedrich August I. Lage und Funktion der herrschaftlichen Appartements und Festräume', both in André Fester (ed.), *Das Residenzschloss zu Dresden*, vol. 3 *Von barocker Prachtentfalting bis zum großen Schlossumbau im 19. Jahrhundert* (St Petersberg, 2020), pp. 77–80. This sumptuously produced volume contains many relevant illustrations. Augustus had returned to Dresden after greeting Maria Josepha on the banks of the Elbe.

15 The programme can be found in Schnitzer and Günther (eds), *Constellatio Felix*, p. 22.

16 For a remorseless account which attracts the comment 'too much information' see Becker-Glauch, *Die Bedeutung der Musik für die Dresdener Hoffeste*, pp. 101ff.

17 Walter Hentschel, *Die sächsische Baukunst des 18. Jahrhunderts in Polen*, 2 vols (Berlin, 1967), vol. 1, p. 12; Stefan Hertzig, *Das barocke Dresden. Architektur einer Metropole des 18. Jahrhunderts* (Petersberg, 2013), p. 121.

18 Monika Schlechte, 'Das barocke Architektur- und Landschaftsensemble Moritzburg (Die Umgestaltungsphase in der Regierungszeit Augusts des

Notes

Starken)', unpublished PhD dissertation of the Technical University Dresden
n.d., p. 10, http://meissenantiques.com/schlechte83dissertation.pdf

19 Hentschel, *Die sächsische Baukunst*, vol. 1, p. 91.

20 Bauer, *Barock*, p. 126. Besser was probably also the author of *Das Königliche Denckmahl*. He had been responsible for the elaborate festivities attending the coronation of Frederick III Elector of Brandenburg as Frederick I King in Prussia in 1701 but had been made redundant by Frederick William I in 1713.

21 Jean Louis Sponsel, *Der Zwinger, die Hoffeste und die Schloßbaupläne zu Dresden* (Dresden, 1924, reprint Dresden 2019), p. 96. While it has been very advantageous to have had the reprint of Sponsel's massive work, the need to reduce the size has made it difficult to view the illustrations or even to read the text. Unfortunately, there are only two copies of the full version available in public collections in the United Kingdom. I take this opportunity to record my gratitude to the Librarian of the Warburg Institute for granting me access. The other copy is in the library of the Victoria and Albert Museum.

22 Thomas Da Costa Kaufmann, *Court, Cloister and City: The Art and Culture of Central Europe 1450–1800* (London, 1995), p. 532 n. 38.

23 Hentschel, *Die sächsische Baukunst*, vol. 1, p. 12.

24 Schlechte, 'Das barocke Architektur- und Landschaftsensemble Moritzburg', p. 10. For a further authoritative judgement see Thomas W. Gaehtgens, 'Auguste le fort, patron des arts', in Béatrix Saulx (ed.), *Splendeurs de la cour de Saxe* (Paris, 2006), p. 39.

25 Reinhard Grau, 'Zur Gartenkunst unter August dem Starken', in *August der Starke und seine Zeit: Beiträge des Kolloquiums vom 16./17. September 1994 auf der Festung Königstein*, pp. 153–4; Robert Prölss, *Geschichte des Hoftheaters zu Dresden: von seinen Anfängen bis zum Jahre 1862* (Dresden, 1878), p. 120; *Herrn Johann Joachim Quantzens Lebenslauf, von ihm selbst entworfen, Historisch-Kritische Beyträge zur Aufnahme der Musik* Bd. 1, St. 3 (1755), pp. 222ff.

26 Siegfried Asche, *Balthasar Permoser und die Barockskulptur des Dresdner Zwingers* (Frankfurt am Main, 1966), p. 15.

27 Querengässer, *1719*, p. 26.

28 Dorothée Baganz, *Dresden. Architektur und Kunst* (Petersberg, 2007), p. 31.

29 Bärbel Stephan, ' "Nach Geburt ein Teutscher, im Handeln und Denken aber Franzose" 1696–1750', in *Der stille König. August III. zwischen Kunst und Politik, Dresdner Hefte*, 46 (1996), p. 21.

30 Matthäus Daniel Pöppelmann, *Vorstellung und Beschreibung des von Sr. Königl. Majestät in Pohlen, und Churfl. Durchl. Zu Sachsen erbauten so genannten Zwinger-Gartens Gebäuden oder der Königl. Orangerie zu Dresden in vier- und zwantzig Kupfer-Stichen* (Dresden, 1729), https://digitale.bibliothek.uni-halle.de/vd18/content/pageview/9794807

Notes

31 Hansmann, *Im Glanz des Barock*, p. 24. For good illustrations of medals and also a snuffbox depicting Augustus as Hercules see Łagocka and Zychowicz (eds), *Splendour of Power*, pp. 41, 50, 73–5.

32 Bärbel Stephan, *Balthasar Permoser hats gemacht. Der Hofbildhauer in Sachsen* (Dresden, 2002), pp. 56, 58, 68, with excellent illustrations.

33 Ibid., p. 5.

34 Volker Helas, 'Permoser, Balthasar', *Grove Art Online*, https://doi.org/10.1093/gao/9781884446054.article.T066487

35 Sponsel, *Der Zwinger*, pp. 152, 210, 244–5, 258. The figure of 450 is taken from *Zwinger Dresden Baumaßnahmen des Freistaates Sachsen von 1991 bis 2015* (Dresden, 2015), https://www.sib.sachsen.de/download/2016_NL_Dresden_I_Zwinger_Dresden_1.pdf

36 Wilhelm Hausenstein, *Vom Geist des Barock* (Munich, 1924), pp. 11, 46, 113.

37 Asche, *Balthasar Permoser*, p. 79.

38 Josef Matzerath, 'Die polnische Krone in Sachsen', in *Sachsen und Polen zwischen 1697 und 1765*, p. 92.

39 Hansmann, *Im Glanz des Barock*, p. 22. For a useful ground plan of the Zwinger and the surrounding buildings see Bruno Alfred Döring, *Matthes Daniel Pöppelmann. Der Meister des Dresdener Zwingers* (Dresden, 1930), p. 64.

40 Braunfels, 'Der Glanz der 28 Tage', p. 217.

41 Watanabe-O'Kelly, *Court Culture in Dresden*, p. 130.

42 Helen Watanabe-O'Kelly, 'Gabriel Tzschimmer's *Durchlauchtigste Zusammenkunft* (1680) and the German festival book tradition', *Daphnis*, 22, 1 (1993), p. 62. Tzschimmer's work is available online at https://digital.slub-dresden.de/werkansicht/dlf/32415/7

43 Hans Schnoor, *Dresden. Vierhundert Jahre Deutsche Musikkultur: Zum Jubiläum der Staatskapelle und zur Geschichte der Dresdner Oper* (Dresden, 1948), p. 65; Querengässer, *1719*, p. 47.

44 Watanabe-O'Kelly, 'Joseph und seine Brüder', p. 31.

45 Bauer, *Barock*, p. 134.

46 Horn, *Der aufgeführte Staat*, pp. 94–6.

47 Querengässer, *1719*, pp. 46–7.

48 Bauer, *Barock*, p. 127.

49 There is a good reproduction online at https://commons.wikimedia.org/wiki/File:Johann_August_Corvinus_-_Firework_display_on_the_River_Elbe_behind_the_Holl%C3%A4ndisches_Palais_on_10_September_1719_-_Google_Art_Project.jpg

50 Ortrun Landmann, 'Die Stellung Dresdens innerhalb der europäischen Musikzentren während der ersten Hälfte des 18. Jahrhunderts', *Studien zur*

Aufführungspraxis und Interpretation von Instrumentalmusik des 18. Jahrhunderts, 8 (1978), p. 50.

51 Schnitzer and Schuckelt (eds), *Im Lichte des Halbmonds*, pp. 238–9.

52 Moritz Fürstenau, *Zur Geschichte der Musik und des Theaters am Hofe zu Dresden*, vol. 2 (Dresden, 1862), p. 1; Anne Juliette Hélène Derex, *Angelo Costantini (1654–1729), Mezzetin de la Comédie Italienne. Héritier d'une tradition ou précurseur d'un nouveau modèle de comédien? Art et histoire de l'art* (Normandie Université, 2017), p. 166.

53 Leopold's court composer, Johann Joseph Fux, is reported to have flattered him by saying it was a shame that he had not been able to become a full-timer composer, to which Leopold replied: 'That may be so, but I am Holy Roman Emperor and so haven't done too badly.' I regret that I have mislaid the reference to this *mot*, but *se non e vero e ben trovato*.

54 Da Costa Kaufmann, *Court, cloister and City*, p. 325; Margit Übellacker, liner notes for La Gioia Armonica's CD entitled 'Per il Salterio' and published in 2021 on the Ramée label RAM 1906.

55 Richter is described as an oboist by Becker-Glauch, *Die Bedeutung der Musik für die Dresdener Hoffeste*, p. 23 but by *Grove* as an organist. For the names of these and many more top musicians working at Dresden see Fechner, 'Dresden 1697–1764', in Grove Music Online.

56 Manfred Fechner, 'Die Musik am Hofe zu Dresden im "Agusteischen Zeitalter" ', in *Sachsen und Polen zwischen 1697 und 1765*, p. 443.

57 Charlton, *Music of the Augustan Age*, http://www.classical.net/music/comp.lst/articles/dresden/index.php

58 Fürstenau, *Zur Geschichte der Musik und des Theaters am Hofe zu Dresden*, vol. 2, p. 129. The bill – 147,917 talers – exceeded the total (125,000) allocated by the Saxon Estates for the entire month – Michael Walter, 'L'opéra italien comme forme de représentation à Dresde aux XVIIe et XVIIIe siècles', in Damien Colas and Alessandro Di Profio, *D'une scène à l'autre. L'Opéra italien en Europe*, vol. 1: *Les prérégrinations d'un genre* (Wavre, 2009), p. 74.

59 Gurlitt, *August der Starke*, vol. 2, p. 273.

60 Prölss, *Geschichte des Hoftheaters zu Dresden*, p. 129. For a contemporary illustration of the interior in cross-section taken from the commemorative album see https://en.wikipedia.org/wiki/Opernhaus_am_Zwinger#/media/File:OpernhausAmZwinger.jpg

61 Schnoor, *Dresden. Vierhundert Jahre Deutsche Musikkultur*, p. 69.

62 Prölss, *Geschichte des Hoftheaters zu Dresden*, p. 120.

63 Michael Walter, 'Italienische Musik als Repräsentationskunst der Dresdner Fürstenhochzeit von, 1719', in Barbara Marx (ed.), *Elbflorenz. Italienische Präsenz in Dresden 16.–19. Jahrhundert* (Dresden, 2000), p. 181.

64 Fiona McLaughlan, 'Lotti's *Teofane* (1719) and Händel's *Ottone* (1723): A textual and musical study', *Music and Letters*, 78, 3 (1997), p. 351.

65 Schnoor, *Dresden. Vierhundert Jahre Deutsche Musikkultur*, p. 69.

66 Johann David Heinichen, *La Gara degli dei*, ed. Michael Walter (Madison, Wis., 2000), p. xxi. I have modified the translation slightly. There is an excellent recording available of a live performance by the Kammerorchester Carl Philipp Emanuel Bach, conducted by Hartmut Haenchen, on the Berlin Classics label 0300544BC. The accompanying booklet contains the full Italian libretto with German translation.

67 Harris S. Saunders, 'Teofane (Theophano)', Grove Music Online, https://doi.org/10.1093/gmo/9781561592630.article.O008101; Sabine Henze-Döhring, 'Höfisches Zeremoniell und italienische Oper in Deutschland am Beginn des 18. Jahrhunderts – Zu den Balletten in Antonio Lottis "Teofane" (Dresden 1719)', in Sibylle Dahms and Stephanie Schroedter (eds), *Tanz und Bewegung in der barocken Oper. Kongreßbericht Salzburg 1994* (Innsbruck and Salzburg, 1994), pp. 141–3.

68 Haake, *Christiane Eberhardine und August der Starke*, p. 153.

69 Quoted in Charlton, *Music of the Augustan Age*, http://www.classical.net/music/comp.lst/articles/dresden/index.php

70 See the liner notes by Robert King for his recording of *Ottone*, p. 9 – Hyperion CDA66751/3.

71 McLaughlan, 'Lotti's *Teofane* (1719) and Händel's *Ottone* (1723)', p. 355.

72 Walter, 'Italienische Musik als Repräsentationskunst', p. 184.

73 Henze-Döhring, 'Höfisches Zeremoniell und italienische Oper in Deutschland', p. 147.

74 Happily, there is an excellent recording of a performance of *Cleofide* by Capella Coloniensis, conducted by William Christie – Capriccio 10193/96.

75 Reinhard Strohm, 'Hasse's opera "Cleofide" and its background', in the booklet accompanying the recording referred to in the previous note.

76 I have discussed Cleofide in greater detail in *The Culture of Power and the Power of Culture*, pp. 63–9.

77 J. Falke, 'August der Starke als Jäger', *Archiv für Sächsische Geschichte*, 9 (1871), pp. 332–3.

78 It seems to have been used first by Friedrich Cramer in *Denkwürdigkeiten der Gräfin Königsmarck* (Leipzig, 1836) – Keller, 'Friedrich August von Sachsen als Herrscher', p. 94.

79 Staszewski, *August II Mocny*, p. 31. Nothing written by Pöllnitz should be accepted without good corroboration. Reports of Augustus's strength certainly enjoyed wide currency – see, for example, the letter from the Duchess

of Orléans from Fontainebleau of 16 October 1696 in Bodemann (ed.), *Aus den Briefen der Herzogin Elisabeth Charlotte von Orléans*, p. 258.
80 See above, p. 5.
81 Michael Walter, 'Introduction', in Heinichen, *Diana su l'Elba*, p. 12. The librettist is not listed but Pallavicino was on hand and so was presumably enlisted.
82 Czok, *August der Starke und Kursachsen*, p. 259. 'The ugliest princess of the century' was the verdict of Claude Rulhière, *Histoire de l'anarchie de Pologne et du démembrement de cette république*, vol. 1 (Paris, 1807), p. 204.
83 Heinichen, *Diana su l'Elba*, p. xviii.
84 Bauer, *Barock*, p. 82.
85 Ibid., p. 83.
86 See the brief but helpful article 'Eingestellte Jagd' in German Wikipedia.
87 See above, p. 278.
88 Johann Michael von Loen, 'Der Hof zu Dresden im Jahr 1718', in *Des Herrn von Loen Gesammlete kleine Schrifften*, vol. 2, pp. 56–9; Loen clearly disapproved of managed hunting; Claudia Schnitzer, 'Herrschende und dienende "Mohren" in den Festen Augusts des Starken', in Kerstin Volker-Saad and Anna Greve (eds), *Äthiopien und Deutschland: Sehnsucht nach der Ferne* (Munich, 2006), p. 95; Loen, 'Der Hof zu Dresden im Jahr 1718', pp. 56–60.
89 Ibid., p. 60.
90 Ibid.
91 Julius Bernhard von Rohr, *Einleitung zur Ceremoniel-Wissenschaft der großen Herren*, ed. Monika Schlechte (Berlin, 1733, reprint Leipzig, 1990), p. 870.
92 Sponsel, *Der Zwinger*, p. 87; Claudia Schnitzer, 'Die Festlichkeiten anlässlich des Besuchs Fredericks IV. von Dänemark 1709 in Dresden', in Jutta Kappel and Claudia Brink (eds.), *Mit Fortuna übers Meer: Sachsen und Dänemark – Ehen und Allianzen im Spiegel der Kunst (1548–1709)* (Dresden, 2009), p. 291. There is a coloured illustration in the latter which suggests that every animal did his duty before perishing. One of the 260 full-colour large-format illustrations commissioned by Augustus to commemorate the Danish king's visit, it presents an 'ideal' version of a fight-hunt.
93 Rohr, *Einleitung zur Ceremoniel-Wissenschaft der großen Herren*, p. 873.
94 Sponsel, *Der Zwinger*, p. 79.
95 Förster, *Friedrich August II. der Starke*, p. 473.
96 'An anti-intellectual, cruel waste of time, favoured only by the uncouth and spurned by such great military heroes as Gustavus Adolphus, the Duke of Marlborough and Prince Eugène', quoted in Tim Blanning, *Frederick the Great King of Prussia* (London, 2015), p. 452.
97 Schnitzer and Günther (eds), *Constellatio Felix*, pp. 34–5.

98 *Das Königliche Denckmahl*, pp. 102–3.

99 Hans Wilhelm Eckardt, *Herrschaftliche Jagd, bäuerliche Not und bürgerliche Kritik. Zur Geschichte der fürstlichen und adligen Jagdprivilegien vornehmlich im südwestdeutschen Raum* (Göttingen, 1976), pp. 80–86.

100 Hans-Günther Hartmann, *Moritzburg. Schloß und Umgebung in Geschichte und Gegenwart* (Weimar, 1989), p. 70.

101 There is a (sound only) performance available by Reinhard Goebel conducting the Musica Antiqua Köln on YouTube at https://www.youtube.com/watch?v=k-C9zIWVpZo

102 Querengässer, *1719*, pp. 33–4.

103 Fürstenau, *Zur Geschichte der Musik und des Theaters am Hofe zu Dresden*, vol. 2, p. 140; Bauer, *Barock*, p. 127; Czok, *Am Hofe Augusts des Starken*, p. 98; Monika Schlechte, '*Recueil des dessins et gravures représentant les Solemnites du Mariages*; Das Dresdner Fest von 1719 im Bild', in *Image et Spectacle. Actes du XXXIIe Colloque International d'Etudes Humanistes*, ed. Pierre Béhar, actes, Tours, Centre d'Etudes Supérieures de la Renaissance, 1989, Chloe. Beihefte zum Daphnis, 15 (Amsterdam, 1993), p. 144.

104 Loen, 'Der Hof zu Dresden im Jahr 1718', pp. 62–3.

105 *Zwey große Lichter nebst ihren Hell-leuchtenen Sternen welche bey Hoher Gegenwart Beyder Könige auch dero beyden Kron-Printzen Königlichen Hoheiten* etc. (Dresden, 1728). This is not paginated.

106 *Mémoires de Charles-Louis Baron de Pöllnitz, contenant les observations qu'il a faites dans ses voyages et le caractère des personnes qui composent les principales cours de l'Europe*, 3 vols (Liège, 1734), vol. 1, p. 178.

107 Rohr, *Einleitung zur Ceremoniel-Wissenschaft der großen Herren*, p. 734. There is general agreement that this relatively open-house policy was a conscious decision by Augustus. Katrin Keller has concluded that his festivities were distinguished by three special characteristics – the chivalric-cum-military element, his personal involvement in the planning, and the admission of the common people – 'Personalunion und Kulturkontakt. Der Hof als Schauplatz und Vermittler kultureller Wechselwirkungen: Sachsen–Polen', in Rexheuser (ed.), *Die Personalunionen von Sachsen–Polen 1697–1763*, pp. 172–3. Augustus's concern to involve the population of Dresden is stressed by Ingrid S. Weber, *Planetenfeste Augusts des Starken. Zur Hochzeit des Kronprinzen 1719. Illustriert durch die Medaillen von Oluf Wif* (Munich, 1985), p. 75. This sits uneasily with the interpretation advanced in one of the shortest but also most influential studies of European courts – Richard Alewyn's *Das grosse Welttheater. Die Epoche der höfischen Feste* (Hamburg, 1959). He argued that during the baroque period, festivities moved away from streets and squares

to the exclusive spaces of the palaces. At the same time, there was a shift from day to night, as the courtiers celebrated as the common people slept – and as the former went home in their carriages, they passed the latter on their way to work. Alewyn's views were given wide currency by Jürgen Habermas's hugely influential *Strukturwandel der Öffentlichkeit* (Neuwied, 1962), as 'in comparison to the secular festivities of the Middle Ages and even of the Renaissance the baroque festival had already lost its public character in the literal sense. Joust, dance, and theatre retreated from the public places into the enclosures of the park, from the streets into the rooms of the palace', quoted from the English translation – *The Structural Transformation of the Public Sphere* (Cambridge, 1989), p. 10.

108 There is a detailed description, well illustrated, of the Saturn Festival in Querengässer, *1719*, pp. 61–6.
109 Bauer, *Barock*, pp. 75–81
110 Helen Watanabe-O'Kelly, *Triumphall Shews: Tournaments at German-speaking Courts in Their European Context, 1560–1730* (Berlin, 1992), p. 126.
111 *Das Königliche Denckmahl*, p. 85. The author was probably Johann von Besser.
112 Ibid., p. 93.
113 Ibid., p. 85.
114 Apart from *Das Königliche Denckmahl*, there is a good account in Bauer, *Barock*, p. 133.

Chapter 11: Augustus the Artist: Refashioning the Environment

1 Dirk Syndram, 'August der Starke und seine Kunstkammer zwischen Tagespolitik und Museumsvision', in Dirk Syndram and Martina Minning (eds), *Die kurfürstlich-sächsische Kunstkammer in Dresden: Geschichte einer Sammlung* (Dresden, 2012), p. 123.
2 They can be followed in detail in Hermann Heckmann, *Matthäus Daniel Pöppelmann und die Barockbaukunst in Dresden* (Berlin, 1986), pp. 28–54. There are many helpful illustrations, although all monochrome and some are of poor quality. There is also a Technische Universität Dresden website on the project: 'Matthäus Daniel Pöppelmann (1662–1736): die Schloss- und Zwingerplanungen für Dresden. Planen und Bauen im "modus romanus"', which includes some three-dimensional projections of the various plans which show their enormous scale, https://tu-dresden.de/gsw/phil/ikm/kuge/forschung/abgeschlossene-projekte/Poeppelmann.

3 Hartmann, *Moritzburg*, p. 86. There is a good reproduction at https://www.habsburger.net/en/chapter/stately-architecture-johann-bernhard-fischer-von-erlach#o-8496

4 Syndram, 'In royal splendour', p. 26.

5 Heinrich Magirius, 'Residenztopographie unter Kurfürst Friedrich August I. (1694–1733)', in Fester (ed.), *Das Residenzschloss zu Dresden*, vol. 3, p. 45.

6 Walter May, 'Bauämter und Architektur in Dresden und Warschau zur Zeit der polnisch–sächsischen Union', in Kroll and Thoss (eds), *Zwei Staaten, eine Krone*, p. 189.

7 Hagen Bächler and Monika Schlechte, 'Komplexität und sächsischer Barock' (no editor listed), *Dresdner Hefte*, 3 (184), p. 28.

8 It can also be seen at long range in the several excellent videos produced by the palace administration and available on YouTube, especially 'Art for lunch: Live walk durch die Paraderäume Augusts des Starken im Residenzschloss Dresden', https://www.youtube.com/watch?v=AiDVtP5cepE

9 Susanne Evers, 'Textilien als Würdeformel. Die Ausstattung der Paraderäume im Schloss Charlottenburg und im Residenzschloss Dresden', in Göse, Müller, Winkler and Ziesak (eds), *Preussen und Sachsen*, p. 118.

10 Hertzig, *Das barocke Dresden*, p. 117.

11 Ibid., p. 120.

12 See above, pp. 232–5.

13 Reiner Groß, 'Vom Dreißigjährigen Krieg zum Siebenjährigen Krieg – Dresden als Zentrum kursächsischer Herrschaftsübung', in Reiner Groß and Uwe John (eds), *Geschichte der Stadt Dresden*, vol. 2: *Vom Ende des Dreißigjährigen Krieges bis zur Reichsgründung* (Stuttgart, 2006), p. 41.

14 Fürstenau, *Zur Geschichte der Musik und des Theaters am Hofe zu Dresden*, vol. 2, p. 7. On the splendour of the Flemming household see Karl Biedermann, 'Aus der Glanzzeit des sächsisch–polnischen Hofes', *Zeitschrift für Deutsche Kulturgeschichte* (1891), p. 214, which is based on a manuscript of 1722 entitled 'Kurze Relation von der Hofhaltung des hochwürdigsten, hochgeborenen Herrn, Herrn Jacob Heinrich, des heiligen Römischen Reichs Grafen von Flemming'.

15 Hagen Bächler and Monika Schlechte, *Sächsisches Barock: aus der Zeit von Matthes Daniel Pöppelmann* (Leipzig, 1986), p. 38.

16 Hertzig, *Das barocke Dresden*, pp. 99–113.

17 Bernhard Geyer, *Das Stadtbild Alt-Dresdens: Baurecht und Baugestaltung*, Abhandlungen der sächsischen Akademie der Wissenschaften zu Leipzig, Philologisch-historisch Klasse, vol. 51, Heft 2 (Berlin, 1964), p. 21.

18 Paul Schumann, *Barock und Rokoko. Studien zur Baugeschichte des 18. Jahrhunderts mit besonderem Bezug auf Dresden* (Leipzig, 1885), p. 32.

19 Bächler and Schlechte, *Sächsisches Barock*, p. 38; Geyer, *Das Stadtbild Alt-Dresdens*, p. 30.

20 Geyer, *Das Stadtbild Alt-Dresdens*, p. 36. There is an excellent illustration of the bridge, painted by Johann Alexander Thiele in 1746, in Łagocka and Zychowicz (eds), *Splendour of Power*, p. 283.

21 Magirius, 'Residenztopographie unter Kurfürst Friedrich August I.', p. 61.

22 Bächler and Schlechte, *Sächsisches Barock*, p. 36.

23 Heinrich Magirius, 'Das Reiterdenkmal für Friedrich August I., genannt "August der Starke", in Fester (ed.), *Das Residenzschloss zu Dresden*, vol. 3, pp. 223, 225.

24 I cannot be alone in thinking that Bellotto's famous view of Dresden from the Augustus bridge would have been improved if the Court Church had not been built and so did not obscure the palace.

25 Happily, its beauties can be admired in a video recording of Beethoven's *Missa solemnis* performed at the concert staged to mark the reopening of the church in 2005 following its reconstruction, available at the time of writing at https://youtu.be/S8YyogSt-JE. There is an exceptionally detailed and helpful article on the Frauenkirche (in German) on Wikipedia at https://de.wikipedia.org/wiki/Frauenkirche_(Dresden) which among other things discusses the structural problems which required later attention.

26 Manfred Fechner, 'Dresden 1697–1764', Grove Music Online, https://www.oxfordmusiconline.com/grovemusic/display/10.1093/gmo/9781561592630.001.0001/omo-9781561592630-e-0000044245?rskey=ou7njH&result=1#omo-9781561592630-e-0000044245-div1-0000044245.2

27 Bächler and Schlechte, *Sächsisches Barock*, p. 42; Stewart Pollens, 'Gottfried Silbermann's Pianos', *Organ Yearbook*, 17 (1986), p. 106.

28 Staszewski, *Die Polen in Dresden des 18. Jahrhunderts*, p. 54.

29 Heinrich Magirius, *Die Dresdner Frauenkirche von Georg Bähr: Entstehung und Bedeutung* (Berlin, 2005), p. 63. This is a huge volume with a very large number of illustrations, many of them photographs from the pre-1945 period. The point is worth making that the reconstructed church is very much more attractive than it was for much of its life when it was black with accumulated coal smoke pollution. The much-reproduced photo from 1910, for example, shows a church which is black.

30 Hans-Joachim Kuke, *Die Frauenkirche in Dresden: 'ein Sankt Peter der wahren evangelischen Religion'* (Worms, 1996), pp. 30, 33; Baganz, *Dresden*, p. 60.

31 Magirius, *Die Dresdner Frauenkirche*, p. 73.

32 Bächler and Schlechte, *Sächsisches Barock*, p. 36; Fritz Löffler, *Das alte Dresden. Geschichte seiner Bauten* (Leipzig, 1997), p. 196.

33 Ines Elsner, 'Königswege. Friedrich I. von Brandenburg-Preußen und August II. von Polen unterwegs', in Göse, Müller, Winkler and Ziesak (eds), *Preussen und Sachsen*, p. 104.

34 Good illustrations of Übigau, Großsedlitz and Pillnitz can be found in Hertzig, *Das barocke Dresden*, pp. 143–66.

35 See above, p. 9–11.

36 There is a well-illustrated history available by Hans-Günther Hartmann, *Schloss Pillnitz. Vergangenheit und Gegenwart* (Dresden, 2014).

37 Ibid., p. 23.

38 Baganz, *Dresden*, p. 72.

39 On this form of entertainment see above, p. 26.

40 Fürstenau, *Zur Geschichte der Musik und des Theaters am Hofe zu Dresden*, pp. 158–9.

41 Bächler and Schlechte, *Sächsisches Barock*, p. 33.

42 Monika Schlechte, 'Matthäus Daniel Pöppelmann und das Verhältnis von barocker Tiergartenanlage und Jagdschloß Moritzburg', in *Matthäus Daniel Pöppelmann 1662–1736 und die Architektur im Zeitalter Augusts des Starken* (Dresden, 1991), p. 240. See also her doctoral dissertation 'Das barocke Architektur- und Landschaftsensemble Moritzburg'. This distinguished work was never published and may have fallen foul of the changes brought by German reunification. However it is available online at http://meissenantiques.com/schlechte83dissertation.pdf

43 Hartmann, *Moritzburg*, p. 75.

44 See below, p. 26.

45 Emil Widemann, *Jagdschloss Moritzburg* (Dresden, 1879), pp. 7–8.

46 Hartmann, *Moritzburg*, p. 100. Some excellent illustrations can be found at https://nat.museum-digital.de/series/10790

47 Becker-Glauch, *Die Bedeutung der Musik für die Dresdener Hoffeste*, p. 92.

48 Sponsel, *Der Zwinger*, p. 263. For an exhaustive and lavishly illustrated account of Augustus's jewels see Arnold, *Die Juwelen Augusts des Starken*, *passim*.

49 Syndram, '"Shopping à Paris"', p. 268.

50 Syndram, 'In royal splendour', p. 16. This article contains much further information about Augustus's agents and purchases.

51 'Dessin d'un habit à ringrave de Louis XIV copié pour Auguste le Fort', in Saulx (ed.), *Splendeurs de la cour de Saxe*, p. 257. A 'rhinegrave' is defined by the *Oxford English Dictionary* as 'loose, wide breeches with legs resembling skirts, which had been introduced by the Rheingraf [Rhinegrave] von Salm *c.* 1640 and was in vogue at the French court until *c.* 1670 when it was replaced by *justaucorps*'. There is a good illustration of a Rhinegrave here.

52 Syndram, ' "Shopping à Paris" ', p. 277–8.

53 Schmidt, 'Das augusteische Zeitalter Sachsens', p. 309.

54 Bächler and Schlechte, *Sächsisches Barock*, p. 20.

55 Syndram, 'August der Starke und seine Kunstkammer', p. 124; Syndram, 'In royal splendour', p. 19.

56 Dirk Syndram, *Das goldene Kaffeezeug Augusts des Starken: Johann Melchior Dinglingers erstes Meisterwerk im Grünen Gewölbe* (Leipzig, 1997), p. 8.

57 Anyone with access to an internet browser need only type in 'Dresden Green Vault' to be overwhelmed with illustrations of high quality as the result of the Dinglinger–Augustus collaboration.

58 Erna von Watzdorf, *Johann Melchior Dinglinger: Der Goldschmied des Deutschen Barock*, 2 vols (Berlin, 1962), vol. 1, p. 131; Syndram, 'In royal splendour', p. 23.

59 Herbert Pönicke, *August der Starke. Ein Fürst des Barock* (Göttingen, 1972), p. 71.

60 Hoffmann, *Constantia von Cosel und August der Starke*, p. 163.

61 Dirk Syndram, 'Peter und August – eine "Entente cordiale" zwischen Russland und Sachsen', *Dresdner Hefte*, 21, 74 (2003), pp. 9–19.

62 Watzdorf, *Johann Melchior Dinglinger*, vol. 1, p. 28. The portrait is now in the Hermitage in St Petersburg.

63 Suzanne L. Marchand, *Porcelain: A History from the Heart of Europe* (Princeton, 2020), p. 30. Debate continues as to whether Tschirnhaus or Böttger has the best claim to be the inventor, but need not concern us here.

64 Ulrich Pietsch, ' "Mehr zur Pracht als zur Notwendigkeit". Die Gründung der königlichen Porzellan-Manufaktur Meissen vor dem Hintergrund der Sammlung Augusts des Starken und der merkantilistischen Wirtschaftspolitik', in Ulrich Pietsch and Cordula Bischoff (eds), *Japanisches Palais zu Dresden. Die Königliche Porzellansammlung Augusts des Starken* (Munich, 2015), p. 31; Klaus Hoffmann, *Johann Friedrich Böttger. Vom Alchemisten zum weißen Porzellan* (Berlin, 1985), p. 431, stated that the 'eureka' moment did not occur until October but Pietsch's dating must be regarded as authoritative.

65 Hoffmann, *Johann Friedrich Böttger*, pp. 241, 446.

66 Karl Berling, *Das Meissner Porzellan und seine Geschichte* (Leipzig, 1900), p. 12.

67 W. von Seidlitz, 'Die Meissner Porzellanmanufaktur unter Böttger', *Neues Archiv für sächsische Geschichte* 9 (1888), pp. 119, 130.

68 Friedrich August Freiherr von O'Byrn, *Die Hof-Silberkammer und die Hof-Kellerei zu Dresden* (Dresden, 1880), p. 94.

69 Quoted in Pietsch and Bischoff (eds.), *Japanisches Palais zu Dresden*, p. 19 n. 7.

70 Czok, *August der Starke und Kursachsen*, p. 62.

71 Hoffmann, *Johann Friedrich Böttger*, pp. 448–9, 453–4.

72 Marchand, *Porcelain*, p. 37.

73 Berling, *Das Meissner Porzellan*, p. 39.
74 Hoffmann, *Johann Friedrich Böttger*, p. 488.
75 Bächler and Schlechte, *Sächsisches Barock*, pp. 22–3; Berling, *Das Meissner Porzellan*, p. 17.
76 Ibid., p. 46.
77 Ibid., pp. 54–5.
78 https://collections.vam.ac.uk/item/O70991/figure-kandler-johann-joachim/figure-k%C3%A4ndler-johann-joachim/
79 Jean Louis Sponsel, *Kabinettstücke der Meissner Porzellan-Manufaktur von Johann Joachim Kändler* (Leipzig, 1900), p. 45.
80 https://www.antiquetrader.com/auctions/meissen-porcelain-collection-shatters-auction-estimates#:~:text=The%20pieces%20were%20expected%20to,was%20meticulously%20assembled%20by%20Dr
81 Bächler and Schlechte, *Sächsisches Barock*, p. 45. See, for example, the illustration on p. 39 of Pietsch and Bischoff (eds), *Japanisches Palais zu Dresden* of two 'Chinese lanterns', the one Chinese and the other made in Meissen.
82 Julia Weber, 'Auguste le Fort et la manufacture de porcelaine de Meissen', in Mathieu Deldicque (ed.), *La Fabrique de l'extravagance: Porcelaines de Meissen et de Chantilly* (Château de Saint-Rémy-en-l'Eau, 2020), p. 37; Janet Gleeson, *The Arcanum: The Extraordinary True Story of the Invention of European Porcelain* (London, 1998), chs 12–14.
83 John George Keyssler, *Travels through Germany, Hungary, Bohemia, Switzerland, Italy and Lorrain*, vol. 4 (London, 1758), p. 264. The original German edition was published in 1741.
84 Dirk Syndram and Martina Minning (eds), *Die kurfürstlich-sächsische Kunstkammer in Dresden: Geschichte einer Sammlung* (Dresden, 2012). There is a helpful review by Jeremy Warren in *Journal of the History of Collections*, 29, 2 (2017), pp. 366–9.
85 Syndram, 'August der Starke und seine Kunstkammer', pp. 126–7; Gerald Heres, 'Die Museumsprojekte Augusts des Starken', *Jahrbuch für Regionalgeschichte*, 16, 1 (1989), pp. 102–15.
86 Werner Schmidt, 'Das Kupferstich-Kabinett', in Arnold and Schmidt (eds), *Barock in Dresden*, p. 277.
87 Ibid.
88 Syndram, '"Shopping à Paris"', p. 269; Virginie Spenlé, 'Les acquisitions de Raymond Leplat à Paris', in Saulx (ed.), *Splendeurs de la cour de Saxe*, pp. 71–6.
89 Czok, *August der Starke und Kursachsen*, p. 216.
90 Syndram, '"Shopping à Paris"', p. 271, where it is referred to as *Le Triomphe de Flore*, but Poussin's painting with that title is in the Louvre – Thomas

Worthen, 'Poussin's paintings of Flora', *The Art Bulletin*, 61, 4 (1979), pp. 575–88.

91 Hildegard Gabriele Boller, 'Die Dresdner Antikensammlung', in Bénédicte Savoy (ed.), *Tempel der Kunst: die Geburt des öffentlichen Museums in Deutschland 1701–1815* (Mainz, 2006), p. 125.

92 Leplat knew what he had bought, but over time the identity of the sculptor was forgotten and it sank to being catalogued as 'Italian, around 1700'. Only recently has the Dresden curator Claudia Kryza-Gersch reattributed it to Bernini – Cheyenne Wehren, 'How this masterful marble skull became attributed to the great Baroque artist Bernini', https://www.tefaf.com/stories/how-this-masterful-marble-skull-became-attributed-to-the-great-baroque-artist-bernini

93 *Recueil des marbres antiques qui se trouvent dans la galerie du Roy de Pologne à Dresden* [*sic*] (Dresden, 1733), https://babel.hathitrust.org/cgi/pt?id=gri.ark:/13960/t1dk04967&view=1up&seq=7. Leplat did not list the draughtsmen and engravers but they are listed on a (London) Royal Academy website at https://www.royalacademy.org.uk/art-artists/book/recueil-des-marbres-antiques-qui-se-trouvent-dans-la-galerie-du-roy-de

94 Syndram, 'In royal splendour', p. 20.

95 Harald Marx, *Gemäldegalerie Alte Meister. Sammlung, Bau, Geschichte* (Leipzig, 2008), pp. 171–2; Werner Schmidt, 'Kunstsammeln im augusteischen Dresden', in Arnold and Schmidt (eds), *Barock in Dresden*, p. 193; Carl Niedner, 'Der sächsische Kabinettsminister Graf August Christoph von Wackerbarth und die königliche Gemäldegalerie in Dresden', *Neues Archiv für sächsische Geschichte*, 31 (1910), pp. 94–5.

96 Katharina Pilz, 'Die Gemäldegalerie in Dresden unter Berücksichtigung der Mengschen Abgusssammlung', in Savoy (ed.), *Tempel der Kunst*, p. 151.

97 Oelsner and Prinz, 'Das Residenzschloss zur Zeit Friedrich Augusts I.', p. 47.

98 Pönicke, *August der Starke*, p. 62.

99 Jacek Staszewski, *August II* (Warsaw, 1986), p. 37.

100 Ulrich Pietsch, 'Porzellangeschenke in augusteischer Zeit, 1697–1763', in Pietsch and Bischoff (eds), *Japanisches Palais zu Dresden*, pp. 43–5.

101 Elisabeth Schwarm, 'Die erste Ausstattung des Holländischen Palais', in Pietsch and Bischoff (eds), *Japanisches Palais zu Dresden*, p. 96.

102 Hansmann, *Im Glanz des Barock*, p. 57.

103 Pietsch and Bischoff (eds), *Japanisches Palais zu Dresden*, p. 16.

104 Pietsch, ' "Mehr zur Pracht als zur Notwendigkeit" ', p. 37.

105 Baganz, *Dresden*, p. 42.

106 Pietsch, 'Porzellangeschenke in augusteischer Zeit, 1697–1763', pp. 46–8.

107 Cordula Bischoff, 'Die Bedeutung des Japanischen Palais', in Pietsch and Bischoff (eds.), *Japanisches Palais zu Dresden*, p. 295.

108 Dirk Syndram, *Prunkstücke des Grünen Gewölbes zu Dresden* (Munich, 1994), p. 6.

109 Joachim Menzhausen, 'Das Grüne Gewölbe', in Arnold and Schmidt (eds), *Barock in Dresden*, p. 369. Also involved was Zacharias Longuelune – Baganz, *Dresden*, p. 48.

110 Dirk Syndram, 'Le Monument d'un roi collectionneur. La voûte verte d'Auguste le Fort', in Saulx (ed.), *Splendeurs de la cour de Saxe*, p. 57; Dirk Syndram, *Der Traum des Königs. Die Schätze des Grünen Gewölbes* (Dresden, 2021), pp. 11–25.

111 Keyssler, *Travels through Germany*, vol. 4, p. 103.

112 Gaehtgens, 'Auguste le fort, patron des arts', p. 42.

113 Joachim Menzhausen, 'Das Grüne Gewölbe', p. 369.

114 This improbable name is also paradoxical, for it dates from 1411 when the synagogue was confiscated. The Jewish community was expelled from the city in 1430 – Thomas Kantschew, 'Der Jüdenhof als Teil der Dresdner und jüdischen Stadtgeschichte', http://archiv.neumarkt-dresden.de/juedenhofgeschichte.html

115 Syndram, 'August der Starke und seine Kunstkammer', p. 136. Trying to translate Augustus's tortuous prose, with its endless sentences, is a nightmare, but I am confident this captures the gist.

116 Peter Plassmeyer, ' "Liegen hir und da in der grösten confusion herum". Die Verwahrung der Dresdener Kunstkammer im Zwinger bis zu ihrer Auflösung im 19. Jahrhundert', in Syndram and Minning (eds), *Die kurfürstlich-sächsische Kunstkammer in Dresden*, p. 143.

117 Heres, 'Die Museumsprojekte Augusts des Starken', p. 110.

118 See above, pp. 242–7.

119 Karl von Weber, 'Eine sächsische Expedition nach Afrika', *Archiv für die sächsische Geschichte*, 3 (1865), p. 9.

120 Dr Koepert, 'Zur Geschichte des Jägerhofes zu Dresden', *Landesverein Sächsischer Heimatschutz – Mitteilungen*, 11, 10–12, *Monatsschrift für Heimatschutz und Denkmalpflege* (Dresden, 1922), p. 223.

121 von Weber, 'Eine sächsische Expedition nach Afrika', p. 4.

122 Martin Grosse, 'Die beiden Afrika-Forscher Ernst Hebenstreit und Christian Gotttlieb Ludwig. Ihr Leben und ihre Reise', *Mitteilungen des Vereins für Erdkunde zu Leipzig* (1901), pp. 5–7.

123 The fullest account is in ibid., pp. 27–54, although it should be recorded that Grosse took much of his material from von Weber. There are excellent maps

printed as the inside front and back covers of Peter Pretsch and Volker Steck (eds), *Eine Afrikareise im Auftrag des Stadtgründers. Das Tagebuch des Karlsruher Hofgärtners Christian Thran 1731–1733* (Karlsruhe, 2008).

124 Grosse, 'Die beiden Afrika-Forscher', p. 56. A rather different but similar list is to be found in Koepert, 'Zur Geschichte des Jägerhofes zu Dresden', p. 224.

125 Grosse, 'Die beiden Afrika-Forscher', pp. 73–7.

126 Detlef Döring, 'Die sächsische Afrikaexpedition von 1731 bis 1733', in Pretsch and Steck (eds), *Eine Afrikareise im Auftrag des Stadtgründers*, p. 47. Alas, almost all the specimens and documentation housed in the Zwinger were destroyed by fire during the insurrection of May 1849.

127 *Memoiren der Markgräfin Wilhelmine von Bayreuth*, p. 81. Mercifully, I have decided to spare the blushes of those numerous historians who continue to repeat this old canard. Even Homer nods.

128 Keller, 'Friedrich August von Sachsen als Herrscher', p. 86.

129 See above, p. 18.

130 Sharp, *Pleasure and Ambition*, pp. xiv, 84, 87.

131 Manners Sutton (ed.), *The Lexington Papers*, p. 85.

132 There is a good illustration of a portrait of Aurora (and also of several other mistresses) in Łagocka and Zychowicz (eds), *Splendour of Power*, pp. 304–21.

133 Tim Blanning, *George I: The Lucky King* (London, 2017), pp. 9–10.

134 Ralf Giermann, 'Maria Aurora von Königsmarck am Dresdner Hof', in Rieke Buning, Beate-Christine Fiedler and Bettina Roggmann (eds), *Maria Aurora von Königsmarck: Ein adeliges Frauenleben im Europa der Barockzeit* (Cologne and Vienna, 2014), p. 184.

135 Staszewski, *August II Mocny*, p. 38.

136 Jean-Piere Bois, *Maurice de Saxe* (Paris, 1992), loc. 781.

137 See above, p. 116.

138 Sylvia Krauss-Mely, 'Maria Aurora von Königsmarck – Überblick über das Leben der "berühmtesten Frau zweier Jahrhunderte"', in Buning, Fiedler and Roggmann (eds), *Maria Aurora von Königsmarck*, pp. 40–41. The sobriquet 'the most famous woman of two centuries' was one of Voltaire's sillier remarks.

139 See above, p. 59.

140 Schuckelt, 'Die Rolle Sachsens in den Türkenkriegen', p. 177.

141 Staszewski, *August II Mocny*, p. 45.

142 Doubek, *August der Starke*, loc. 816.

143 O'Byrn, *Die Hof-Silberkammer*, p. 110 n. 4.

144 Jacek Staszewski, *August II* (Warsaw, 1986), p. 16.

145 Förster, *Friedrich August II. der Starke*, p. 440. For the cardinal's relentless conspiring against Augustus see above, pp. 56–7.

146 Doubek, *August der Starke*, loc. 602; Anna Eunike Röhrig, *Mätressen und Favoriten. Ein biographisches handbuch* (Göttingen, 2010), pp. 252–3.

147 Quoted in Sharp, *Pleasure and Ambition*, p. 84.

148 Hoffmann, *Constantia von Cosel und August der Starke*, pp. 31, 96. This is an important book but flawed. The author does herself no favours by inserting wholly imagined episodes, as at the very beginning: 'On 23 July 1727, the King awoke. He had had a dream', nor by waiting until the very end before revealing that there are sources for all the various quotations in the text.

149 Ibid., pp. 153, 169; Weber, 'Anna Constance Gräfin von Cossell', p. 13.

150 Hoffmann, *Constantia von Cosel*, p. 256. On Pillnitz see above, p. 257–9.

151 Later attempts to obtain promotion to princely status were evaded by the emperor – Weber, 'Anna Constance Gräfin von Cossell', pp. 31–2.

152 Hoffmann, *Constantia von Cosel*, pp. 177–8. As Gabriella Hoffmann acknowledges, this must be taken with a large handful of salt, as the ultimate source is Pöllnitz's *La Saxe galante*.

153 Ibid., p. 409.

154 Loen, 'Der Hof zu Dresden im Jahr 1718', p. 194.

155 Weber, 'Anna Constance Gräfin von Cossell', p. 52.

156 Ibid., pp. 126–7.

157 See for example the portrait of her in riding habit by Louis Silvestre, https://upload.wikimedia.org/wikipedia/commons/7/78/Painting_of_Silvestre_Anna_Orzelska_in_riding_habit.jpg

158 Maria Czaplińska, 'Anna Katarzyna Orzelska (po mężu Holstein-Beck)', *Polskiego Słownik Biograficzny*, vol. 24 (Warsaw, 1979), p. 273.

159 Kenneth Rose, *King George V* (London, 1983), p. 303.

160 Otto Eduard Schmidt, 'Zur Charakteristik Augusts des Starken', in Johannes Ziekursch, Otto Eduard Schmidta and Paul Haake, 'Zur Geschichte Augusts des Starken', *Neues Archiv für sächsische Geschichte* (26) (1905), p. 125.

161 Hartmann, *Moritzburg*, pp. 55–6.

162 Claudia Schnitzer, 'Die Festlichkeiten anlässlich des Besuchs Fredericks IV. von Dänemark 1709 in Dresden', in Jutta Kappel and Claudia Brink (eds), *Mit Fortuna übers Meer: Sachsen und Dänemark – Ehen und Allianzen im Spiegel der Kunst (1548–1709)* (Dresden, 2009), p. 201. There is a good illustration in *Constellatio Felix*, p. 19.

163 Sponsel, *Der Zwinger*, p. 88.

164 See above, p. 244.

165 Elsner, 'Königswege', p. 103.

166 Hentschel, *Die sächsische Baukunst*, vol. 1, p. 91.

167 Ibid., p. 160.

168 May, 'Bauämter und Architektur in Dresden und Warschau', p. 210.

169 Lukowski, 'Poland–Lithuania', p. 246. For all their faults, the two Augustuses presided over a marked increase, reaching 25,000 by 1750 – Butterwick, *The Polish–Lithuanian Commonwealth*, p. 69.

170 Staszewski, *August II*, p. 16.

171 Keller, 'Personalunion und Kulturkontakt', pp. 173–4. For a revealing account of the modest musical life of Warsaw during the period see Alina Zórawska-Witlowska, 'The Saxon court of the kingdom of Poland', in Samantha Owens, Barbara M. Reul and Janice B. Stockigt (eds), *Music at German Courts, 1715–1760: Changing Artistic Priorities* (Woodbridge, 2011), pp. 51–63. Even the Polish magnates saw Warsaw as a place to pursue political interests, not as a cultural centre – Jacob Nuhn, 'Aktuelle polnischsprachige Perspektiven auf die polnisch–sächsische Union', *Neues Archiv für sächsische Geschichte*, 86 (2015), p. 217.

172 This position is argued at a level of sophistication to which I cannot aspire by Hans Ulrich Gumbrecht, especially in *Production of Presence* (Stanford, 2004).

173 A prime example of this kind of approach is Peter Burke's *The Fabrication of Louis XIV*.

174 Watzdorf, *Johann Melchior Dinglinger*, vol. 1, p. 25.

Epilogue: The Posthumous Triumph

1 The best account of the extremely confusing and inconsequential diplomacy of these years is to be found in McKay and Scott, *The Rise of the Great Powers 1648–1815*, pp. 118–34.

2 One for which he was not responsible was the scheme for the partition of Poland which surfaced in 1721, which was either a personal initiative on the part of the banker Berend Lehmann or was floated by the Prussians – Urszula Kosińska, *Sondaż czy prowokacja? Sprawa Lehmanna z 1721 r., czyli o rzekomych planach rozbiorowych Augusta II* (Warsaw, 2009), pp. 85–6.

3 See above, p. 226.

4 Schilling, 'Der Wiener Hof und Sachsen–Polen (1697–1764)', p. 126.

5 Ziekursch, *Sachsen und Preußen*, p. 6.

6 Józef Andrzej Gierowski, *Rzeczpospolita w dobie złotej wolności (1648–1763)* (Krakow, 2001), p. 336.

7 Paul Haake, 'La société des antisobres', in *Neues Archiv für sächsische Geschichte*, 21 (1900), pp. 242–3.

8 Urszula Kosińska, 'Z dziejów stosunków polsko – pruskich w ostatnich latach panowania Augusta II: Misja Franza Moritza von Viebahna w Saksonii i

Notes

Polsce w latach 1727–29', in Ryszard Skowron (ed.), *Polska wobec wielkich kon-fliktów w Europie nowożytnej. Z dziejów dyplomacji i stosunków międzynarodowych w XV–XVIII wieku* (Kraków, 2009), pp. 484–5.

9   I have discussed this natural hostility in *Frederick the Great, King of Prussia*, pp. 85–6, 191.

10 See above, pp. 218–20.

11 Leopold von Ranke, *Zwölf Bücher preußischer Geschichte*, Sämtliche Werke, vols 27–28 (Leipzig, 1874), pp. 191–3.

12 See above, pp. 134–5.

13 Gierowski, *Rzeczpospolita w dobie złotej wolności*, pp. 337–8.

14 Jan Kusber, 'Vorfeldkontrolle durch militärische Intervention: Russland und der polnische Thronfolgekrieg 1733–1736', in *Sachsen und Polen zwischen 1697 und 1765*, pp. 148–9.

15 Andrzej Link-Lenczowski, 'Teodor Potocki', *Internetowy Polski Słownik Bio-graficzny*, https://www.ipsb.nina.gov.pl/a/biografia/teodor-andrzej-potocki-h-pilawa-1664-1738-prymas-polski.

16 Ibid. Linck-Lenczowski's entry in the *Dictionary of Polish Biography* is both detailed and archivally based.

17 Richard Butterwick, *The Polish–Lithuanian Commonwealth*, p. 46.

18 Lewitter, 'Poland under the Saxon kings', p. 225.

19 Rulhière, *Histoire de l'anarchie de Pologne*, p. 230.

20 Gierowski, *Rzeczpospolita w dobie złotej wolności*, p. 333; Butterwick, *The Polish–Lithuanian Commonwealth*, p. 51.

21 Martina Thomsen, 'Der Thorner Tumult 1724 als Gegenstand des deutsch–polnischen Nationalitätenkonflikts', *Zeitschrift für Geschichtswissenschaft*, 57, 4 (2009), p. 294.

22 Stanisław Kujot, *Sprawa Toruńska z 1724* (Poznan, 1893), p. 3.

23 Augustyniak, *Historia Polski 1572–1795*, p. 801. There is an odd slip in this passage when there is a reference to 'Frederick II' as King of Prussia when Frederick William I must be meant.

24 Friedrich, *The Other Prussia*, p. 186; Konopczyński, *Dzieje polska nowożytnej*, p. 188.

25 Jacek Burdowicz-Nowicki, 'Polityka Piotra I w związku ze sprawą toruńską 1724 r.', in Kosińska, Dukwicz and Danilczyk (eds), *W cieniu wojen i rozbiorów*, pp. 91–2; Oscar Halecki, *Istorija tsentral'noy Evropy s drevnikh vremeni do XX veka* (Moscow, 1952), p. 444.

26 Patrick Milton, 'Debates on intervention against religious persecution in the Polish–Lithuanian Commonwealth: European reactions to the Tumult of Thorn, 1724–1726', *European History Quarterly*, 47, 3 (2017), p. 424.

27 Ibid., p. 425. See also Friedrich, *The Other Prussia*, p. 189. Indeed, plans for partition were in circulation during the episode itself, although they were of uncertain provenance and came to nothing – Urszula Kosińsa, 'L'affaire secrete, czyli nieznany plan rozbioru Polski z lat 1724–1726', in Kosińska, Dukwicz and Danilczyk (eds), *W cieniu wojen i rozbiorów*, pp. 105–35.

28 Czok, 'August der Starke', p. 9.

29 Kroll, 'Kursachsen im Zeitalter der polnisch–sächsischen Staatenunion 1697–1763', p. 20.

30 Czok, *August der Starke und Kursachsen*, p. 260.

31 Ibid., p. 262. See also the extensive collection of engravings and plans made available by the Marburg Digital Archive at https://www.digam.net/index.php?page=10&lput=887&id=0

32 Hans Beschorner, 'Das Zeithainer Lager von 1730 (Mit Karte)', in *Neues Archiv für sächsische Geschichte*, 28 (1907), pp. 50–54. See also Renate Schönfuß-Krause, *Das "Zeithayner Lustlager" Augusts des Starken – kein Lustlager für Lotzdorfer und sächsische Bauern*, which draws attention to the burdens placed on the local population, https://slub.qucosa.de/api/qucosa%3A78600/attachment/ATT-0/

33 Elisabeth Mikosch and Holger Schuckelt, 'Das sächsische Janitscharenbataillon beim Zeithainer Lager 1730', in Claudia Schnitzer and Holger Schuckelt (eds), *Im Lichte des Halbmonds: das Abendland und der türkische Orient* (Dresden, 1995).

34 Beschorner, 'Das Zeithainer Lager von 1730', pp. 74–5, 78–9; Kroll, 'Kursachsen im Zeitalter der polnisch–sächsischen Staatenunion 1697–1763', p. 20.

35 Staszewski, *Die Polen in Dresden des 18. Jahrhunderts*, p. 171; Jutta Charlotte von Bloh, 'Ritterorden im Dienst der neuen Königswürde', in Göse, Müller, Winkler and Ziesak (eds), *Preussen und Sachsen*, p. 123.

36 Peter Langen, 'Eine Armee für den König in Preußen. Das Zeithainer Lager 1730', in Göse, Müller, Winkler and Ziesak (eds), *Preussen und Sachsen*, p. 222.

37 Karl Czok, *August der Starke und Kursachsen* (Leipzig, 1987), p. 261; von O'Byrn, *Die Hof-Silberkammer und die Hof-Kellerei zu Dresden*, p. 107.

38 There is an excellent illustration of a painting by Johann Samuel Mock of the Czerniaków camp in Maja Łagocka and Izabella Zychowicz (eds), *Splendour of Power: The Wettins on the Throne of the Polish–Lithuanian Commonwealth* (Warsaw, 2023), pp. 202–3.

39 See above, p. 217–18.

40 Jacek Staszewski, *August II* (Warsaw, 1986), p. 47.

41 Wyczański, *Polska Rzeczą Pospolitą Szlachecką*, p. 353.

42 Gretschel, *Geschichte des sächsischen Volkes und Staates*, vol. 2, p. 573. Maurice's adventures, which also involved his mother, Aurora von Königsmarck, and his lover, the famous French actress Adrienne Lecouvreur, are best followed in Jean-Piere Bois, *Maurice de Saxe* (Paris, 1992), ch. 4, 'Entre la France et la Courlande'.

43 Ines Elsner, 'Königswege. Friedrich I. von Brandenburg-Preußen und August II. von Polen unterwegs', in Göse, Müller, Winkler and Ziesak (eds), *Preussen und Sachsen*, p. 103.

44 As early as 1722 the Russian envoy Sergei Dolgoruki reported that Augustus's frequent illnesses suggested that his demise was imminent – Kosińska, *August II w poszukiwaniu sojusznika*, p. 59.

45 Hans Beschorner, 'Augusts des Starken Leiden und Sterben', *Neues Archiv für Sächsische Geschichte*, 58 (1937), pp. 57–8. The doctor, Johann Friedrich Weiss, was rewarded with a supplementary payment of 12,000 talers. The French specialist, Jean Louis Petit, summoned from Paris, arrived too late to be of assistance but was also royally rewarded for his post-operative care.

46 This account of Augustus's last illness and death is based on Beschorner's substantial article cited in the previous footnote and on the detailed account in Staszewski, *August II Mocny*, pp. 275–8. They disagree on certain particulars, not the least being the actual date of his death. Staszewski's appears to be the more authoritative, although Beschorner's is also based on archival sources.

47 Staszewski, *August III*, pp. 153–4.

48 Augustyniak, *Historia Polski 1572–1795*, p. 806.

49 Gierowski, *Rzeczpospolita w dobie złotej wolności*, p. 339.

50 In her scholarly article on the episode, drawing on all appropriate archival sources, Urszula Kosinska makes it clear that the Portuguese prince was unable to muster the necessary support from the Polish szlachta – 'Could a Portuguese prince become King of Poland? The candidacy of Don Manuel de Bragança for the Polish throne in the years 1729–1733', *Slavonic and East European Review*, 94 (2016), p. 506.

51 Helmut Neuhaus, 'Die polnisch–sächsische Union, Habsburg und das Reich', in Kroll and Thoss (eds), *Zwei Staaten, eine Krone*, p. 38; Leopold von Ranke, *Zwölf Bücher preußischer Geschichte*, Sämtliche Werke, vols 27–28 (Leipzig, 1874), p. 196.

52 Kusber, 'Vorfeldkontrolle durch militärische Intervention', p. 150.

53 Augustyniak, *Historia Polski 1572–1795*, p. 808.

54 Ibid., p. 810. However, he was allowed to continue using his royal title.

Conclusion

1 This was set out in a manifesto composed in February 1697 but not discovered until the early twentieth century – Komaszynski, 'August der Starke und seine Herrschaft', p. 135.

2 Jacek Kurek, *U schyłku panowania Augusta II Sasa: z dziejów wewnętrznych Rzeczypospolitej, 1729–1733* (Katowice, 2003), pp. 25–7.

3 Robert Frost, ' "Initium Calamitatis Regni"? John Casimir and Monarchical Power in Poland–Lithuania, 1648–68', *European History Quarterly* 16 (1986), p. 184.

4 Jarochowski, *Dzieje panowania Augusta II*, p. iii.

5 Konopczyński, *Polska a Szwecja*, p. 42; idem, *Dzieje polska nowożytnej*, pp. 182–3.

6 F. C. Schlosser, *Geschichte des achtzehnten Jahrhunderts und des neunzehnten bis zum Sturz des französischen Kaiserreichs*, vol. 1 (Heidelberg, 1836), p. 12. An English translation was published in eight volumes between 1843 and 1852.

7 Flathe, *Geschichte des Kurstaates und Königreiches Sachsen*, pp. 232–3.

8 Stefan Stenius, 'Sachsen och Preussen i den nordiska krisen 1709', *Karolinska Förbundets Årsbok* (1949), p. 41.

9 Paul Haake, *August der Starke*, p. 7. See also his article 'Polen am Ausgang des XVII. Jahrhunderts', *Neue Jahrbücher für das klassische Altertum Geschichte und deutsche Literatur*, 15 (1905), p. 41. He was following in a long tradition of Saxono-phobe German historians, beginning with Barthold Georg Niebuhr in 1813/14 – Detlef Döring, 'Brandenburg-Preußen in der Frühen Neuzeit im Vergleich', *Neues Archiv für sächsische Geschichte*, 85 (2014), pp. 155–83. Haake was a menace, without the wit to make effective use of his labours in the Saxon and Prussian archives. Commissioned to produce an edition of Augustus's correspondence, he failed to deliver. What looks like a biography – *August der Starke* – is a strange mixture of detailed examinations of relative trivia interspersed with brief summaries of important episodes and issues. In the view of Stefan Stenius it was rushed out to counterbalance what he regarded as the unsatisfactory work of Cornelius Gurlitt (*August der Starke*).

10 For example, Paul Haake, 'Polen am Ausgang des XVII. Jahrhunderts', *Neue Jahrbücher für das klassische Altertum Geschichte und deutsche Literatur*, 15 (1905), pp. 723–36 or Helbig, 'Polnische Wirtschaft und französische Diplomatie', p. 380. None, however, could match Thomas Carlyle's contemptuous dismissal: 'To this condition of beautifully phosphorescent rot-heap has Poland ripened, in the helpless reigns of those poor Augusts;—the fulness of time not now far off, one would say?' – *History of Friedrich II of Prussia*, bk 21, ch. 3.

11 Leopold von Ranke, *Zwölf Bücher preußischer Geschichte*, Sämtliche Werke, vols 27–28 (Leipzig, 1874), p. 187.

12 Józef Gierowski, 'Polska, Saksonia i plany absolutystyczne Augusta II', in Bogusław Leśnodorski (ed.), *Polska, w epoce oświecenia; państwo, społeczeństwo, kultura* (Warsaw, 1971), p. 60.

13 Komaszyński, 'August der Starke und seine Herrschaft', p. 136.

14 Olszewski, *Doktryny Prawno-ustrojowe Czasów Saskich*, p. 5; see also Adam Krzemiński, 'Sachsen und Polen – eine gescheiterte Union?', in 'Polen und Sachsen. Zwischen Nähe und Distanz', *Dresdner Hefte*, 50, 2 (1997), p. 6.

15 Kosińska, *August II w poszukiwaniu sojusznika*, p. 56.

16 Gierowski, *The Polish–Lithuanian Commonwealth in the XVIIIth Century*, p. 62.

17 Frost, *After the Deluge*, pp. 13–14.

18 Frost, 'Sächsisch–polnische Personalunion und die Katastrophe des Großen Nordischen Krieges', p. 425. Augustus was the only Polish king since Stephan Bathory (1576–86) not to speak Polish. As a result, he was unable to communicate with the numerous Polish ministers who did not speak French – Frost, 'Some hidden thunder', p. 198.

19 See above, pp. 205–7.

20 Blanning, *Frederick the Great King of Prussia*, pp. 282–96. Dorota Dukwicz, in her short article 'The internal situation in the Polish–Lithuanian Commonwealth (1769–1771) and the origins of the First Partition (in the light of Russian sources)', *Acta Poloniae Historica*, 103, (2011), pp. 69–84, shows that the part played by the Confederation of Bar in deciding Russian policy has been exaggerated. Her further assertion that 'it is beyond any doubt whatsoever [that] Prussian inspirations for partition are overestimated in the scholarly literature' is not supported adequately.

21 John Brewer, *The Sinews of Power: War, Money and the English State 1688–1783* (New York, 1989), p. 137.

22 Gierowski, *Rzeczpospolita w dobie złotej wolnośći*, p. 320.

23 Fassmann, *Des glorwürdigsten Fürsten und Herrn*, pp. 1–13.

24 Komaszynski, 'August der Starke und seine Herrschaft', p. 133. For other examples see Karl Czok, 'Aufgeklärter Absolutismus und kirchlich-religiöse Toleranzpolitik bei August dem Starken', in ibid., p. 161, and Förster, *Friedrich August II. der Starke*, p. 284.

25 'A za Króla Sasa/ Jedz, pij i popuszczaj pasa' – quoted by Michael G Müller and Misloš Reznik in 'Jacek Staszewski und sein Werk "Die Polen im Dresden des 18. Jahrhunderts"', the Introduction to Staszewski, *Die Polen in Dresden des 18. Jahrhunderts*, p. 8.

26 https://en.wikisource.org/wiki/Constitution_of_3_May_1791#VII._The_King,_the_Executive_Authority

Index

Index

Bouhours, Dominique, 6, 163
Boyle, Nicholas, 164
Brandenburg, battle of Fehrbellin
    (1675), 95
Braubach, Max, 36–7
Braudel, Fernand, 83
Brewer, John, 300–1
British Royal Navy, 205
Brockdorff, Countess Marie Elisabeth,
    18, 273
Bulavin, Kondraty, 176
Burensköld, General Jacob, 151
Butterwick, Richard, 68, 183, 315n5,
    342n103

Caldara, Antonio, *Sirita* (opera), 227
Cambrai, Congress of (1724), 285
Caprara, Count Enea Silvio, 32, 35–6
Carlowitz, Georg Karl von, 93, 102
Carlson, Ernst, 152
Carreño de Miranda, Juan, 15–16
Castagnères, François, Abbé de
    Chateauneuf, 48
Catherine Ivanova of Russia, 217
Catherine the Great, Empress of
    Russia, 286
Catholicism, in Poland, 61, 76–82
Cederhielm, Josias, 118
ceramics *see* porcelain
Chance, James Frederick, 186
Charles II, King of Spain, 15–16, 43, 89
Charles IX, King of France, 65
Charles of Neuburg, 45
Charles Philip, Elector of the
    Palatinate, 39
Charles VI, Holy Roman Emperor, 6,
    222, 285, 294; Pragmatic Sanction,
    225–6
Charles XI, King of Sweden, 95–6
Charles XII, King of Sweden: youth

and immaturity, 97–101;
    successful defence of Travendal
    (1700), 103–4; siege of Narva
    (1700), 106–8; crosses the Düna
    river, 110; determination to
    dethrone Augustus, 111–12,
    114–18; enters Lithuania and
    Poland, 113–14, 117–18; victory at
    the battle of Kliszów, 123–5;
    attempts to conquer Poland,
    127–30; places Stanisław
    Leszczyński on Polish throne,
    130–5; victory at battle of
    Fraustadt (1706), 140–2; marches
    on Saxony, 143; and the Treaty of
    Altranstädt, 145–7; sadistic
    execution of Patkul, 147–9;
    ambition to depose the Tsar,
    149–50; marches on Russia, 171–5;
    underestimation of the Russian
    army, 173–5; defeat at the battle
    of Poltava, 178–80; in exile in
    Bender, 179–80; neglect of
    defence of the Baltic, 191; takes
    command in Stralsund, 205;
    death, 220, 388n69; harsh
    character, 114–15, 352n24;
    religiosity, 350n84
Charlton, David, 237
Chełstowski, Dionizy, 77
Chiaveri, Gaetano, 256
chinoiserie, in Dresden, 258
Chrisian August of Saxony-Zeitz,
    Bishop of Raab, 47–8
Christian V, King of Denmark, 96–7, 99
Christiane Eberhardine, Queen of
    Poland, Electress of Saxony,
    250, 273–4
Cicero, 60, 71
Clausewitz, Carl von, 105, 117, 207

Index

Index